Small Business Clustering Technologies:
Applications in Marketing, Management, IT and Economics

Robert C. MacGregor
University of Wollongong, Australia

Ann T. Hodgkinson
University of Wollongong, Australia

IDEA GROUP PUBLISHING

Hershey • London • Melbourne • Singapore

Acquisition Editor:	Michelle Potter
Senior Managing Editor:	Jennifer Neidig
Managing Editor:	Sara Reed
Development Editor:	Kristin Roth
Copy Editor:	Sue VanderHook
Typesetter:	Marko Primorac
Cover Design:	Lisa Tosheff
Printed at:	Integrated Book Technology

Published in the United States of America by
Idea Group Publishing (an imprint of Idea Group Inc.)
701 E. Chocolate Avenue
Hershey PA 17033
Tel: 717-533-8845
Fax: 717-533-8661
E-mail: cust@idea-group.com
Web site: http://www.idea-group.com

and in the United Kingdom by
Idea Group Publishing (an imprint of Idea Group Inc.)
3 Henrietta Street
Covent Garden
London WC2E 8LU
Tel: 44 20 7240 0856
Fax: 44 20 7379 3313
Web site: http://www.eurospan.co.uk

Library of Congress Cataloging-in-Publication Data

Small business clustering technology : applications in marketing, management, IT and economics / Robert C. MacGregor and Ann Hodgkinson, editors.
    p. cm.
  Summary: "This book examines the development and role of small business clusters from a variety of disciplines : economics, marketing, management and information systems. It gathers perspectives from varied disciplines and countries, extending current knowledge by emphasizing the pressure that international competition and IT have on the geographic structure of clusters, possibly leading to a new 'a-spatial' option developing"--Provided by publisher.
  ISBN 1-59904-126-X (hardcover) -- ISBN 1-59904-127-8 (softcover) -- ISBN 1-59904-128-6 (ebook)
  1. Small business--Management. 2. Strategic alliances (Business)--Management. 3. Business networks--Management. 4. Cluster analysis. I. MacGregor, Robert C., 1951- II. Hodgkinson, Ann.
  HD2341.S5685 2007
  658'.044--dc22
                                    2006019159
British Cataloguing in Publication Data
A Cataloguing in Publication record for this book is available from the British Library.

All work contributed to this book is new, previously-unpublished material. The views expressed in this book are those of the authors, but not necessarily of the publisher.

Small Business Clustering Technologies:
Applications in Marketing, Management, IT and Economics

Table of Contents

Section VI: Information Technology

Preface

This book brings together a collection of applied studies covering attempts to develop clusters in a range of industry sectors in a number of different countries. Despite the variety of examples presented, strong common themes are found across these papers. There is common agreement as to what constitutes a cluster, what the benefits expected from cooperation are, what the objectives of intervention are, and even of the type of barriers encountered by cluster programs. The objective of this book was to counter-position studies of cluster formation from authors with various discipline backgrounds in order to observe the different approaches used. This has been achieved, with economists taking a more theoretical, conceptual approach which provides the basis on which other disciplines have developed. Management studies focus more on how clusters can be encouraged and made to function effectively, the governance issue. Marketing studies emphasise 'branding', or how each cluster can achieve a distinct identity among its competitors based on what it does most effectively. Information technology studies, on the other hand, return to basic concepts of cost efficiency, and unlike the other three disciplines represented here, use an a-spatial concept of networks rather than the spatial concept of clusters.

Within this common framework, the studies presented here address a number of specific themes common to cluster analysis.

- The role of government in the promotion of clusters (Efendioglu; Perry) or
- The role of government-business partnerships (Nasir, Bulu and Eraslan, Teigland, Hallencreutz and Lundequist) or
- The role of business led standardisation programs (Gerst and Jakobs).

- The function of innovation systems (Teigland, Hallencreutz and Lundequist; Rosson and McLarney, Efendioglu).

- Problems of industry definition to facilitate data collection and analysis (McRae-Williams; Rosson and McLarney), which results in

- The widespread use of Case Study methodologies in cluster analyses (Efendioglu; Brown; Teigland, Hallencreutz and Lundequist; Nasir, Bulu and Eraslan; Rosson and McLarney).

- The differences between clusters (collaborations of firms in geographical space) versus groups (Perry), or

- The differences between clusters and networks, which do not require geographic proximity (Rowe and Burn), or

- The evolution of clusters over time (Falcone 1)

- The differences between clusters (informal) versus alliances, which involve tight pro-active interaction (MacGregor and Vrazalic).

- The importance of distinctiveness and reputation of each cluster particularly in heavily populated industries such as biotechnology and software development (Rosson and McLarney, Merrilees, Miller and Herington, Falcone 2).

Contrary to the expectation that clusters are most relevant to 'high technology' sectors, the studies included this book covered a range of different sectors.

- Biotechnology (Efendioglu; Teigland, Hallencreutz and Lundequist; Rosson and McLarney);

- High Technology (Merrilees, Miller and Herington)

- Tourism (McRae-Williams, Nasir, Bulu and Eraslan);

- Engineering and Manufacturing (Perry, Gerst and Jakobs, Falcone 1);

- General spread (Rowe and Burn, MacGregor and Vrazalic, Falcone 2).

Clusters have often been proposed as a means of encouraging economic development in developing countries, which lack to presence of large companies able to establish an international presence in their own right. It is argued that a cluster of small businesses cooperating together in different parts of the value-chain could duplicate the internal economies of scale available to large firms and so become internationally competitive on a collective basis. This was how Italian industrial districts, the forerunner of cluster analysis, functioned. However, the range of studies presented in this book suggests that clusters are still found mostly in the advanced, industrialised world. Only two case studies came from middle-income economies, and none from developing countries. Thus clusters appear to be following the example previously established with networks and alliances and, despite their obvious applications in developing economies, are very much a mechanism used in the developed world and which helps those economies to remain at the forefront of economic development.

The geographical spread of the studies in this book is as follows:

- USA (Efendioglu)
- European Union (Gerst and Jakobs)
- Sweden (Teigland, Hallencreutz and Lundequist; MacGregor and Vrazalic)
- Italy (Falcone)
- Canada (Rosson and McLarney)
- Australia (McRae-Williams; Rowe and Burn; Merrilees, Miller and Herington)
- New Zealand (Perry)
- Turkey (Nasir, Bulu and Eraslan)
- Taiwan (Efendioglu).

In Chapter II, a framework synthesised from the literature on applied cluster analysis is provided. Using that framework, it is clear from the studies provided in this book that clusters arise in response to two main sets of conditions: psychological and cultural conditions and market-orientated conditions. To a large extent this reflects the dominance of management orientated research in applied cluster analysis derived particularly from the seminal works by Porter (1990) and Saxenian (1996) as discussed in that chapter.

The importance of psychological and cultural conditions to the development of clusters is demonstrated in many of the studies in this book. The role of entrepreneurship is particularly highlighted by Efendioglu, who discusses it in terms of the culture in western California which encourages risk-taking and independence, creating an environment encouraging new firm start-ups. McRae-Williams, Falcone and Nasir, Bulu and Eraslan highlight the importance of developing trust between members before cooperation can occur. The movement of labour between firms implies that the tacit knowledge of firms, often a major source of the competitive advantage of small firms, is also shared and only firms that are prepared to trust each other would take this risk. Rowe and Burn also focus on the importance of relationships between firms, arguing that while trust and commitment were important, geographical proximity was not if appropriate ICT were used. Merrilees, Miller and Herington emphasise the importance of relationship management in cluster development, arguing that high levels of interaction are necessary to develop the culture and identity of the cluster and thus conditions need to be established where firms believe they can safely cooperate for a cluster to function successfully. Falcone argues that the social and cultural relationships associated with trust form the basis of the transaction cost savings that result in the efficiency benefits enjoyed by firms in clusters.

Thus an essential lesson from the studies in this book is that clusters can only be effective and contribute to improved industrial and regional economic development if the pre-condition of a 'safe' environment is established where business owners and managers feel they can freely communicate and discuss their 'trade secrets' relating to production technologies, marketing strategies, etc., without risk of 'moral hazard'. It is seen to be the role of the government agency, as a third party, to develop this environment in which trust, the essential cultural element, can develop among members. It takes time to do this, five years was mentioned in Nasir, Bulu and Eraslan, and it is difficult to have small business owner/manages commit to such a program without any early outcomes, when they have many immediate demands on their time. Nevertheless, our studies indicated that if sufficient commitment could be maintained over this time, positive outcomes for the businesses involved could be achieved.

The second major focus in these studies was on the importance of establishing essential business relationships between firms if successful outcomes from clusters were to be achieved. Many of the authors highlighted the particular importance of the relationship between producer firms and local suppliers to the success of a cluster. Thus the 'value chain' or supply relationship within the local regional economy was considered an essential element to successful cluster performance. Where producer firms had access to a strong range of local suppliers which could respond to their needs for specialised inputs and services in a quick, efficient and technologically proficient manner, clusters enhanced the international competitiveness of local firms. This component of cluster performance was emphasised in the studies by Efendioglu, Perry, MacGregor and Vrazalic, and Rosson and McLarney, and essentially reflects the diamond model from Porter. Falcone discusses how cluster branding brings collective benefits to firms in a particular geographical area.

The importance of this client-supplier relationship to successful cluster functions highlights the dilemma facing proponents of cluster development programs. A strong, specialised and diversified supplier base is only available in highly developed advanced industrial regions, to be found in the initial countries from which cluster analysis originated – Western Europe, USA Japan. Smaller economies cannot duplicate the mass of suppliers available in large industrial regions, and this becomes an essential constraint on cluster development in the rest of the world, particularly the developing world. Firms supplying international markets need to be able to respond quickly to any technological innovations by their competitors, and need suppliers who have the technical capacity to help them in this response. Firms embedded in clusters which have only a thin spread of suppliers are disadvantaged in this competitive process. Information technology relationships offer a means of overcoming this problem by allowing regional firms to establish supply and other relationships with firms from a broader geographical network. However, in doing so they break down the essential nature of clusters, which requires geographical proximity to facilitate personal communication and the transfer of tacit knowledge, and gives rise to the regional development benefits which lie at the heart of many cluster development initiatives.

More recently, analysts have used the concept of a 'creative milieu' as discussed in Chapter II, to describe the conditions necessary for successful cluster activity, especially in technologically advanced industries. The essential additional feature of creative milieu clusters is the role of educational and research institutions as a means of providing a 'safe' mechanism to disseminate new knowledge to member firms. Educational and research institutions can also act as a mechanism to facilitate the spin-off of innovation into new business start-ups by providing business planning and venture capital support. The role of educational institutions in providing this function is particularly discussed in Efendioglu who gives the example of a university sponsoring an international business planning competition, which encourages start-up firms to locate in its area. Teigland, Hallencreutz and Lundequist discuss the role of an institution combining university, business and government partners as a mechanism for developing innovations and value-chain suppliers for the biotechnology industry. While the creative milieu concept has been subjected to much analysis, the number of regions which host appropriate educational and research institutions is much more limited and again, most are found in western Europe, the USA and Japan again ensuring that the benefits from cluster development are mainly to be found in the advanced industrialised countries.

The final condition for cluster development which was addressed by studies in this book was the role of large organisations as an initiator and means of spreading technological improvement to the smaller firms which form part of that cluster. This issue was particularly addressed by Gerst and Jakobs, who from an IT perspective, discussed the role of large automobile companies in enforcing standardisation of information and technical systems on their smaller suppliers. Stardardisation brings efficiency benefits and potentially widens the market by allowing one supplier to service a number of clients. However, it is costly for small firms to implement these systems and they have little input into their design. Cluster organisations provide one means for smaller firms to participate in such decision-making processes.

Summary of Chapters

Chapter I: *Small Business Clustering Across Disciplines*, Ann Hodgkinson. This chapter provides a summary of the main concepts and relationships used in applied cluster analysis from a predominantly theoretical and economic perspective. It develops the theoretical concepts from regional economics in the form of three models: pure agglomeration (internal returns to scale, localization and urbanisation economies), industrial complex (input-output and supply-chain), and social networks (transaction costs, trust and entrepreneurship). It then discusses the relevant technological change concepts in terms of various types of innovation systems. Finally it develops a framework of 10 conditions considered to result in cluster formation grouped as market conditions, psychological and cultural conditions, role of large organisations, creative milieu conditions and innovation processes. The concepts developed in this chapter are now widely used across all disciplines and form the theoretical basis of the applied studies which follow.

Chapter II: *Leveraging the Benefits of Small Business Clusters: A Branding and Stakeholder Management Framework*, Bill Merrilees, Dale Miller and Carmel Herington. This chapter begins with a short summary of the status of cluster development in Australia. It then builds a conceptual framework based on branding and stakeholder management principles in which clusters can be assessed from a marketing perspective. It then moves into the key problem associated with marketing clusters, which is their lack of distinctiveness. This makes it difficult to determine their particular competitive advantage, particularly for smaller clusters in industries where numerous well know clusters already exist. The question of how such as cluster can be branded is addressed. It is argued that effective branding can improve the governance of the cluster and help develop trust among members. It is further argued that information technology platforms can be well utilized in this process through the internet and ideas such as specialist e-malls.

Chapter III: *Small and Medium Enterprise Clusters: Marketing and Communication Management*, Paola Falcone. This chapter provides an overview of Italian industrial districts, the specific collective structure which was the forerunner of the more general concept of clusters. It discusses the factors resulting in the evolution of these structures over time in response to exogenous (e.g. demand, competition, technology) and endogenous (adaptability, organizational and innovation capability) factors. Industrial districts go through a four stage life-cycle. Firstly, district initiation due to a spontaneous convergence of pioneer firms attracted by some particular attraction in an area. Secondly, district growth as suppliers of specialized goods and services move into the area. Consequently a specific labour market develops and knowledge and information circulate among firms. Growth continues with new start-ups and spin-off firms, attracting more investors into the area. Thirdly, at district maturity, non-market advantages are most important arising from the presence of layers of sub-contractors, dense circulation of knowledge, large numbers of suppliers and customers in the district. However, at this stage the danger of crystallization occurs which may create rigities blocking innovation. The final stage is decline as the district becomes static and looses competitiveness. It is argued that many Italian industrial districts are now facing this threat of decline. Pressures arise from demand contraction for many manufactured goods, aggressive global price competition and non-spatial means of knowledge diffusion utilizing ICT. Industrial districts have to adapt to these pressures if they are to survive.

Chapter IV: *Italian Industrial Districts: Nature, Structure, and Value Creation*, Paola Falcone. This chapter discusses how small and medium enterprises within a geographical cluster, when faced with substantial international price competition, can use marketing strategies, and in particular, cluster branding to preserve their competitive position. By using a collective local brand they create a common image and gain benefits from joint marketing activities. The cluster brand reflects a combination of the region's imagery, culture and history and the productive image and resources of the firms comprising the cluster. The cluster's image, reflected in its brand, can be stimulated through a variety of strategies. These include initiatives to regenerate the dynamics of the region by encouraging young entrepreneurs and students and by organizing specialized training courses, while also conserving the district's historical memory and identity with museums, databases, etc. The cluster can also build its own collective Internet portal and undertake national and international advertising campaigns and produce information materials such as samples, CD-roms, videos or souvenirs. Further, it can promote the district through delegations, competitions, special events, organize and participate in industry fairs, etc. The collective brand helps smaller firms to compete in non-price terms, reduces marketing and transaction costs and because it works as a guarantee, helps build trust between the firms and their customers.

Chapter V: *Industry Clusters in Peripheral Regions: A Biotechnology Case Study*, Philip Rosson and Carolan McLarney. This chapter addresses the question of whether cluster development can occur in more distant, peripheral regions using a case study of the biotechnology industry in Halifax, Canada. The study focuses on the relationship between the industry firms and local suppliers of support services. The most commonly used services were finance, human capital (attraction and retention of technically skilled employees) and research infrastructure (research space, technology networks). The main barriers encountered were access to start-up capital, lack of experienced technical workers, and lack of government leadership and assistance. They also identified a poor commercialization culture, inadequate research facilities and the inadequacy of the R&D tax credit system as problems. The biotechnology grouping in Halifax was considered to be a nascent cluster but one suffering from organizational 'thinness'. It is argued that initiatives such as developing an industry — research centre of excellence to promote joint research, linkages between players, training and technology transfer programs would help. Improvements in infrastructure, promotion of spin-offs and expansion of existing firms and provision of venture capital were also suggested.

Chapter VI: *Cluster Development: Issues, Progress and Key Success Factors*, Alev M. Efendioglu. This chapter provides a comparison of two biotechnology clusters, one well developed in California, USA and the other less developed in Taiwan. It compares the economics driven development path of the Californian cluster with the government driven path in Taiwan. The Californian cluster developed from 1976 in conditions similar to a creative milieu with a concentration of research centres, financial sources, pharmaceutical customers, contracting and outsourcing opportunities and workforce training and educational institutions. The Taiwanese cluster began in 1980 but in 2003 the government deliberately established a science park in the area with a range of research and networking centres. A number of biotechnology firms are establishing in the park and growth rates are now increasing. Comparisons of the growth paths of the two clusters show that the Californian cluster has been considerably more successful. The main factors contributing to this better performance were considered to be: the focus of educational institutions which encourage business planning and new firm spin-offs, the availability of venture capital, the entrepreneurial culture in the area, the infrastructure and supporting activities available and the range of design and service firms in the area.

Chapter VII: *Regional Clusters: Classification and Overlap of Wine and Tourism Micro-Clusters*, Pam McRae-Williams. This chapter uses the concept of micro-clusters to analyse wine and tourism enterprises in regional Victoria, Australia. It provides a brief review of the development of tourism and wine clusters in Australia. It then examines how co-location has led to the development of wine tourism enterprises in smaller boutique producers. Comparison is made with similar developments in the Napa Valley in California. Clusters were generally found to be under-developed in Victoria relative to potential. However, they were considerably more developed in the wine industry than in tourism. It was felt that cluster-related benefits could be enhanced in wine-tourism establishments by linking into wine cluster activity already established in the region.

Chapter VIII: *From Networks to Clusters and Back Again: A Decade of Unsatisfied Policy Aspiration in New Zealand*, Martin Perry. This chapter provides a thorough critique of Government programs aimed at encouraging cluster development in New Zealand since the 1990s. Several of these programs were inspired by the work of Michael Porter. The first involved joint action groups of larger firms working together to develop export markets. The second involved formal alliances between small firms, and was inspired by Danish experiences. The third, The Cluster Development Program, provides support to groups of businesses located in the same region. He queries whether there is any justification for policy intervention in this area, arguing that we have jumped too quickly from a few particular experiences to a universal belief in the capacity for concentration to generate growth, and that we have moved too quickly from claims of business advantage to calls for cluster promotion. The current program has been implemented through a series of 'cluster musters' where businesses in local regions are encouraged to search out their own specializations to promote local growth. It is argued that the limits to achieving benefits from cluster developments in New Zealand arise from the lack of suppliers in the country due to small size, constraints on which organizations can be members, dependence on publicly funded facilitators, lack of leading firms, absence of clusters in areas with concentrations of economic activity, and the need for national rather than regional links between firms in small economies.

Chapter IX: *The Analysis of Tourism Cluster Development in Istanbul: A Longitudinal Study in Sultanahmet District (Old Town)*, Aslihan Nasir, Melih Bulu and Hakki Eraslan. This chapter provides a detailed discussion of an attempt to establish a cluster by improving linkages between firms in the tourism sector in the 'old town' historical tourism precinct in Istanbul, Turkey. It provides an overview of the tourism industry in Turkey, with visitor numbers now recovering after the effects of the Iraq war. This cluster promotion attempt was also inspired by the work of Michael Porter and implemented by a non-governmental organisation of private business leaders. It identified this sector as being one where Turkey had an international competitive advantage. Data was initially collected in 2001, with the firms again interviewed in 2005, and linkages mapped in both time periods. In between the two surveys, a local development committee was established to encourage cluster relationships, which initiated new products, undertook common marketing activities, provided training and education to employees and established IT services. Revenue and employment in the firms increased as did the intensity of the relationships between members as trust improved.

Chapter X: *Uppsala BIO – The Life Science Initiative: Experiences of and Reflections on Starting a Regional Competitiveness Initiative*, Robin Teigland, Daniel Hallencreutz and Per Lundequist. This Chapter provides a detailed discussion of an attempt to establish a collaborative institution involving academia, industry and government to encourage growth and employment in the biotechnology industry in the Uppsala region of Sweden. The project is relatively new, but is being evaluated by the local university, which collected baseline data in 2004. The objectives of the institution were to encourage more innovation to be commercialized within the local area and to improve the supply of investment funds and specialized, skilled labour for local firms. Its main strategies were to promote product-orientated biotech research, to strengthen the regional innovation system, to ensure a supply of relevant skills in the region, and to improve the region's image in order to attract investment. The barriers affecting biotechnology development in Uppsala were felt to come from the maturity of the local environment, which was already characterised by strong networks and interaction among actors. It was felt this could be leading to rigidity and thus one of the objectives was to open up these networks to new actors. While there was significant innovation occurring, the extent of local commercialization was low. Thus a strategy to ensure this intellectual property was commercialized locally was needed. A follow-up study is scheduled for 2006 to assess how effective the institution has been in achieving its goals.

Chapter XI: *Clustering, Collaborative Networks and Collaborative Commerce in Small and Medium Enterprises*, Michelle Rowe and Janice Burn. The benefits which smaller firms obtain from collaboration are impacted by c-commerce, which can reduce the significance of geography, globalises the labour market, increase connections between enterprises and lead to the establishment of virtual companies. Clustering can benefit users of ICT by reducing the amount of investment and other resources needed to implement the new technologies. However, they also reduce the significance of geography and fosters inter-regional collaborations, which significantly impacts on the traditional concept of clusters as involving geographic proximity as the means of achieving relationships and trust between firms. Collaborative or c-commerce relationships involve a soft network of firms pursuing joint benefits which would not accrue if they operated alone. They still require trust and commitment, but not necessarily proximity, and a willingness to share information without acting opportunistically. This chapter reports the results of a study of drivers/enablers and inhibitors to the adoption of c-commerce by small and medium enterprises in Australia. A number of factors associated with the adoption of c-commerce were identified. It was felt that the lack of these characteristics in SME entrepreneurs and a low level of awareness of its benefits explained the low rate of adoption in Australia.

Chapter XII: *The Role of Small Business Strategic Alliances in Small/Medium Enterprises (SMEs)*, Robert MacGregor and Lejla Vrazalic. This chapter provides a summary of the benefits and disadvantages to SMEs in adopting E-commerce, as well as identifying the criteria for adoption and its barriers based on a review of the literature, incorporating both adopting and non-adopting firms. It reviews the literature on strategic alliances and SMEs, which involve both financial and social relationships. This study looks at the role of strategic alliances in adopting E-commerce by SMEs in Sweden using factor analysis to compare the behaviour of firms in alliances versus those who are not. It was found that all firms predominantly adopted E-commerce for marketing and internal business objectives. The main barriers against adoption were organisational if firms were not in alliances, while members of alliances mainly identified technical barriers. The main benefits for all firms from adoption were increased efficiency, reduced costs and improved inventory control. The disadvantages of adoption were predominantly organizational, increased day-to-day demands on workload, and also for alliance members, technical issues. The results from this study do not support the hypothesis that small business strategic alliances reduce technological concerns due to sharing skills and experience.

Chapter XIII: *E-Business Standardization in the Automotive Sector: Role and Situation of SMEs*, Martina Gerst and Kai Jakobs. This chapter extends the argument that using ICT, particularly e-business systems, facilitates the creation of network relationships in a supply chain by looking at the significance of agreed standards as part of the functioning of those supply relationships. It looks at the situation within the automotive supply chain where large OEMs create networks of suppliers which are typically SMEs. Standards are usually set by the OEM and without them collaboration is not possible. However, if the SME supplies a number of OEMs, each with different standards, the process becomes very inefficient. Standards are usually enforced through inter-organisational systems, which reduce coordination and transaction costs, but also improve communication and information flows. Standards can be based on international agreements among stakeholders or by establishing a sector specific electronic marketplace. The paper provides a number of examples of these two approaches applied in the European automotive industry. To date, SMEs have had little involvement in the process and it is suggested that setting up SME regional user groups may improve their participation by informing and educating them as to the process through websites, etc. and that they might ultimately represent the interests of small firms in negotiations over standards and other business issues.

Conclusion

This book contains applied studies of clusters across a range of industries that operate in a number of countries and written by analysts from a variety of disciplines such as economics, marketing, management, and information systems. The first aspect that strikes the reader is the commonality of approaches across these disciplines, drawing on a standard knowledge base of concepts, analytical frameworks, and methodologies. Cluster analysis at both the theoretical and applied levels is truly interdisciplinary and lacks the ideological barriers often found in other areas of business studies, which prevents analysts from different disciplines working together on common problems. This finding is positive for the future development of this area of study and indicates that our understanding of clusters will continue to develop rapidly in both conceptual and applied terms.

In applied studies, there is a particular interest in the questions of what type of intervention can or should be used to promote clusters and how it can be implemented most effectively. The argument that clusters contribute to industrial and regional development is well established at the conceptual level and has been demonstrated in a number of well-known cases such as Silicon Valley in the U.S., Toyota City in Japan, and the industrial districts in northeastern Italy. In this book, Efendioglu provides another example of the biotechnology sector in California. The current question addressed by several chapters in this book is whether these success stories can be duplicated elsewhere, and, if so, how.

Our authors look at interventions in terms of government programs, government-business partnerships, private sector association programs, and big-business initiatives. Overall, they conclude that clusters appear to arise in response to special economic environments and have developed spontaneously through natural, organic economic forces. The authors in this book conclude that it is extremely difficult to artificially recreate such conditions in order to induce the formation of clusters as a tool for regional development. This is demonstrated by the case studies presented by Efendioglu for Taiwan, McRae-Williams for Australia, Perry for New Zealand, and Rosson and McLarney for Canada.

Conceptually, it is argued that clusters provide a useful development tool for smaller economies. However, the case studies presented in this book question their relevance for small, open economies such as Australia, New Zealand, and Canada. The concept of clusters developed in large, industrialized countries with specific cultural preconditions that facilitated cooperation (Italian industrial districts) and in industries in which rapid technological change necessitated cooperation (biotechnology, information technologies). Such countries also had the advantage of a large domestic market in which new products could be developed in conjunction with customers and quick sales achieved before commencing international exports. Smaller economies do not have these preconditions, and there are only a limited number of partners available for joint production or specialist supply. They suffer from the problem of organizational thinness, as demonstrated by Rosson and McLarney and Perry, which makes it difficult to establish the client-supplier linkages identified as essential in order to achieve the business relationship model of clusters. They also need to export in order to gain economies of scale, which immediately exposes them to the full strength of international competition before having the time to develop their products, customer relationships, joint production, and trust within a domestic market first. In smaller, open economies, competition tends to dominate cooperation, limiting the natural development of clusters.

A number of authors discussed the appropriate nature of intervention to assist cluster formation. Effective intervention is not about reducing business costs via cheap loans or provision of subsidized buildings and land, even though businesses often initially expected this. It is not even essentially about the provision of technological or export support programs. Effective intervention is more about encouraging a supportive environment and building trust among local firms in order to overcome their natural tendency toward local competition. The role of government or other support agencies is to act as an honest broker where competitors safely can meet, communicate, and demonstrate their capacities. Then, opportunities for joint activities—production, marketing, sharing of labor, and so forth—can be recognized and acted upon. Trust takes time to develop, and cluster promotion programs do not show quick results. The importance of trust as a component in cluster development programs is demonstrated clearly in the project developed for the Sultanahmet region of Istanbul in Turkey. It also was highlighted in the chapter by Merrilees, Miller, and Herington. As trust developed, interfirm cooperation increased, resulting in strong improvements in revenue and employment.

The importance of regional innovation networks was another common theme in these studies, particularly those in high-technology sectors, which are represented by three studies of the biotechnology sector included in this book. Cluster relationships generally were considered less relevant to the function of generating new products but more concerned with the process of encouraging entrepreneurship and commercialization of that research. The chapter by

Teigland, Hallencreutz, and Lundequist provides an example of establishing a new institution in order to encourage closer links between business/researchers in an attempt to encourage more commercialization of innovations developed in that region within its own boundaries. This demonstrates that the innovation issue still can be a problem even in well-established regions such as Uppsala in Sweden. That study illustrates the problem of rigidities that can arise in mature regions, as discussed in Falcone (Chapter III), and provides one means of rejuvenating such districts.

Rosson and McLarney, on the other hand, address the problems of trying to establish a new cluster in the biotechnology industry in a peripheral region. They also identified a poor commercialization culture as a barrier in Halifax, Canada, and suggested developing an industry—a research center as a solution. The Uppsala BIO Institute provides an example that they could consider. Efendioglu provides a study of the successful biotechnology cluster in San Francisco, California. This study emphasizes the role of the University of San Francisco's international business-planning competition, which attracts innovators into the region to help sustain that region as well as a natural entrepreneurial culture and also generates startup firms. This has ensured that cluster, despite being in existence since 1979, has remained in its growth phase. All of these studies emphasize the importance of research institutions and of establishing effective business/research relationships to cluster development in high-technology sectors.

Some insights into methodological issues also can be obtained from a review of the chapters in this book. The widespread use of case studies is demonstrated clearly. As clusters now are a well-established area of research, it might be expected that analytical studies would move into more rigorous statistical investigations based on broad databases. Yet, only one chapter, the one by MacGregor and Vrazalic, based on a sample of more than 300 Swedish SMEs, ventures into this methodology in a sustained manner. The other chapters provide an explanation of why case studies are still dominant.

First, it can be explained by definitional issues, as discussed by McRae-Williams. Clusters normally do not contain one simple industry sector as defined by statistical authorities. Their very nature involves synergies and interactions among firms from a variety of different sectors through joint production and in supply relationships as well as complementarities in research among organizations in different sectors, which is the keystone of innovation. Further, many clustered sectors, such as tourism, biotechnology, and information technologies, are not readily classified into standard industry codes. Thus, large secondary databases that provide the resource for most econometric analyses cannot be utilized readily in cluster analyses.

MacGregor and Vrazalic demonstrate that important issues in cluster research can be analyzed by using common statistical techniques; in this case, whether firms in clusters or alliances behave differently from those that are not. However, it also demonstrates that in order to undertake this type of analysis, researchers have to undertake original data collection involving surveys of relevant firms. This is time-consuming and expensive. Thus, statistical analyses often are restricted to instances in which such databases, generated for other purposes, fall into the hands of cluster analysts. In such cases, the data may not be collected on the definitions or coded in a way that is most appropriate to apply to cluster analysis questions.

Third, of course, many of the questions asked by cluster analysts are inherently qualitative, particularly those around the important issue of trust, and are not readily analyzed in quantitative terms. Nevertheless, it may be time for cluster analysts to venture beyond specific case studies and to attempt to establish some of their elemental propositions on a more rigorous basis. One way in which this is occurring is by using a panel approach in which baseline data are collected at the beginning of the cluster process and then repeated after a period of time, often five years. If these data collections are undertaken rigorously, the observed changes can be traced to elements in that cluster.

As argued earlier, there is common acceptance across disciplines of the definition of clusters as a group of firms that are both located in close geographical proximity to each other and that have some forms of interaction with each other, either as customers/suppliers undertaking joint activities (production, marketing, research), exchanging information either formally in established institutions or tacitly through informal personal relationships, and/or sharing a common resource pool, including labor. However, not all studies examined relationships purely within this definition of clusters. Some used the more nebulous term *groups*, which simply required firms in a sector to be collocated. Groups of firms in one or similar sectors frequently are located in the same region but may not have any active interrelationships. They do, however, form the basis on which it is believed that clusters can be developed using government-sponsored intervention programs in order to facilitate relationships among these firms or by providing encouragement through financial incentives, as discussed by Perry for New Zealand. Industrial districts is an earlier term derived from the work of Alfred Marshall in England and Piore and Sabel in Italy. They are a forerunner of clusters but are more limited in that they emphasize mainly business relationships among constituent firms. The cluster concept places more explicit focus on psychological and cultural factors that are always inherent in the Italian industrial district concept and on applications to higher technology rather than traditional manufacturing industries. Thus, research, innovation, and technology transfer become more important in cluster analysis, evolving into the latter concept of an innovative or creative milieu. The final terms used in these studies are networks and strategic alliances, which are most common in the information systems studies. This is not a coincidence. These terms are well-established in the business literature on collaboration. However, unlike groups, industrial districts, clusters, and innovative milieu, they are not innately spatial. Networks and strategic alliances involve productive relationships among firms but do not require these firms to be collocated. Often, these relationships are international in scope. The development of long-distance, interfirm collaborations was facilitated by developments in information and communication technologies. Thus, the range of terms used in cluster analysis reflects an evolution of the concept over time.

Information technology strategies—e-commerce, e-business, c-commerce, as discussed in this book—challenge the specific geographical component that is essential to the economic and managerial analyses of clusters. Collocation is no longer necessary to establish relationships among firms, although trust is still essential for successful collaborations, whether virtual or personal. Whereas other disciplines make clear distinctions between clusters and other forms of collaboration such as groups or strategic alliances, arguing that clusters provide the most substantial and enduring economic development potential, IT studies return to the earlier concepts of networks and alliances. They argue that electronic communication systems allow the development of relationships with suppliers, customers, and partners that provide the same business and efficiency benefits as geographically constrained clusters but allow these to occur in an unconstrained aspatial or international context. It is argued here that IT strategies to date have not been heavily adopted by small businesses. As they become more common, it raises the question of whether they may cause an end to clusters as an economic development tool.

The second factor that is contributing to the decline of clusters is the growing significance of international competition as product and service markets inextricably become global. With markets throughout the world rapidly opening to foreign imports due to reduced tariffs and other forms of trade protection and the movement into market economics by previously centrally controlled countries, few firms, no matter how small, now are not exposed to some level of external competition, if only through the Internet. Conversely, this process is opening up new export market opportunities to firms throughout the world. International competition is having a profound effect on the industrial districts of Italy, as discussed in Falcone (chapter three). Previously stable, dense, supply-chain relationships are breaking down in the face of cheaper imports and as leading firms relocate many of their activities to low-wage foreign regions. High-technology clusters have been better able to survive under this pressure. Cluster analysts have to confront the impact of this realignment of world production systems with the technology-intensive, design-intensive, and corporate activities that remain in the industrialized world, while production moves into cheaper labor regions. Clusterlike relationships still may continue to exist among firms but at an international level facilitated by information technology. Further, the imperative of needing to be internationally competitive in terms of cost, quality, design, and customer service may be making it extremely difficult to establish new clusters outside the industrialized countries. Firms no longer may have the time to establish local interfirm and personal relationships, the essence of cluster advantages, before confronting the pressures of international competition. These items form the next agenda for cluster analysts both in theoretical and applied studies.

The question of how clusters establish, grow, and survive in competitive environments particularly has been the focus of marketing analysts. They universally look to the concept of branding as a means of differentiating clusters in different regions and those operating in particular sectors. Branding is not just image projection. It requires firms in a cluster to analyze their strengths and to identify what particular unique attributes they can offer members. Further, it requires members to accept a common framework of values, which forms the basis of developing trust among themselves, leading to the density of relationships that generate the advantages that being a member of a cluster generates. Once this branding process is established, the cluster organization then can undertake the activities that are needed in order to position its member firms in the global market and to ensure its continuing growth and regeneration within this new global market environment.

Finally, the preeminence of the work of Michael Porter in applied cluster analysis must be acknowledged. Reading these chapters, his name appears repeatedly in the literature reviews, regardless of the discipline of the author. His contribution occurs at the conceptual level with the Porter diamond and supply-chain analysis taking over from input-output analysis as the essence of the industrial complex approach to analyzing regional industrial development. The economic antecedents of this model now have been overshadowed almost completely outside that discipline. Second, his contribution has been paramount at the applied level. It has been the inspiration for numerous government and other programs aimed at encouraging clusters as the major means of regional development. The prevalence of this ideology is now so great that it is very difficult to argue, as several authors in this book do, that outside the established industrial regions, existence of groupings of firms in a sector in a region will not necessarily mean that a cluster can be developed as the basis of regional development. Perhaps this book will help to encourage a more critical evaluation of the value of clusters as a regional development policy. It highlights both the practical difficulties of this approach and the need to rethink the position of clusters as they are increasingly exposed to international competition.

Acknowledgments

The editors would like to acknowledge the help of all those involved in the collation and review process of the book, without whose support the project could not have been satisfactorily completed. A further special note goes to all the staff at Idea Group, Inc., whose contributions throughout the whole process from inception of the initial idea to final publication have been invaluable.

All of the authors of chapters included in this also served as referees for articles written by other authors. Thanks go to all those who provided constructive and comprehensive reviews. A special thanks goes to Associate Professor Charles Harvie, University of Wollongong and Dr Jean Pratt, Utah State University, who agreed to act as reviewers for certain chapters of the book.

Special thanks also go to the publishing team at Idea Group Inc. In particular to Jan Travers and Kristin Roth who continuously prodded via email for keeping on schedule, to Megan Kurtz who assisted in the marketing of the book and to Medhi Khosrow-Pour, whose enthusiasm motivated us to initially accept his invitation for taking on this project.

In closing, the editors wish to thank all authors for their insights and excellent contributions to this book. We also want to thank all those involved in the reviewing process. Finally the editors wish to thank their families for their support throughout this project.

Associate Professor Rob MacGregor
Associate Professor Ann Hodgkinson

Section I

Introduction to Clustering

Chapter I

Small Business Clustering Across Disciplines

Ann Hodgkinson, University of Wollongong, Australia

Abstract

The literature on clusters is vast and growing rapidly. Moreover, it is truly multidisciplinary with researchers from all perspectives borrowing heavily from each other's works. This chapter summarizes the theoretical approaches that have defined the concepts and relationships used in the applied cluster analyses that follow. The perceived benefits from participating in clusters are now well established at a theoretical level. It is argued that this theoretical basis was developed within regional economics by using the concepts of agglomeration economies, which originated with Marshall (1890); industrial input-output analysis, since developed by Porter (1990), and social networks based on the works of Williamson (1985) and Saxenian (1994). As technological change has become more important, ideas related to regional innovation systems also have been incorporated into cluster analysis. Now the challenge is to put these ideas into practice.

Introduction

The concept of clusters has been adopted with great enthusiasm by analysts from a range of different disciplines and with interests in a variety of issues. Clusters have been used in studies of industrial development, regional development, and entrepreneurship in both developed and developing countries. Despite these different foci, most of these studies have common elements in terms of definitions, concepts, perceived interactions and processes, and expected outcomes. While perceptions may vary with the discipline of the researcher, similar interrelationships are identified and evaluated in most of these studies. This commonality of approaches means that there is a large multidisciplinary literature on the topic that borrows heavily from each other. This chapter examines the essential concepts used in cluster analysis and analyzes how they are used in the different disciplines covered in this book.

It can be argued that the earliest analyses of cluster activity are based on economic concepts such as agglomeration economies, input-output relationships, and transaction costs. Nevertheless, all these concepts have been developed in a multidisciplinary environment so that it is now extremely difficult and rather pointless to present analyses of clusters from a purely economic perspective. In particular, the importance of geographic proximity in firm location decisions to the whole analysis of clusters prevents a pure economic analysis, which is innately spaceless, from being presented. Further, the importance of entrepreneurship in explaining small business behavior cannot be ignored, considering that clusters often are comprised of small and medium-sized enterprises. While entrepreneurship originally was an economic concept, management discipline analysts substantially have developed this element of cluster study.

As demonstrated in this book, the literature on clusters is vast and growing rapidly. These studies have a strong conceptual element. The theory of clustering, although developed in the 1980s, has gone through a continuous process of refinement. Theoretical interest in clustering of firms stems from the inherent logic of this approach, which, if applied in practice, offers substantial rewards to policymakers pursuing national, industrial, and regional development objectives. Interfirm cooperation provides the means to overcome a range of barriers that have been identified as inhibiting growth at all levels. Most studies attempt to support their theoretical framework with empirical research, either as original case studies or based on databases of secondary material. In this chapter, a review of theoretical material is presented. We then will review how these concepts have been used by the authors of this book.

The term *cluster* has been defined in various ways. Some analysts use a simple definition such as sectoral and spatial concentrations of firms (Schmitz & Nadvi, 1999). However, the collocation of a number of firms in the same industry in one region will not generate in itself the external benefits that form the basis of a cluster's contribution to economic growth. Most definitions require spatially concentrated firms in order to interact with each other in a range of ways that generate these external benefits or economies. One documentation of the relationships that can be expected in a cluster includes the following:

- Positive external effects emanating from the existence of a local pool of skilled labor, which can move among the member firms.
- Forward and backward linkages among firms within the cluster.

- Intensive information exchange among firms, institutions, and individuals in the cluster, which gives rise to a creative or innovative milieu.
- Joint action geared to create locational advantages.
- Existence of a diversified institutional infrastructure supporting the specific activities in the cluster.
- A sociocultural identity made up of common values and the embeddedness of local actors in a local milieu, which facilitates trust (Altenburg & Meyer-Stamer, 1999).

While cluster relationships involve a range of transactions, recent analyses have focused particularly on the role that they can play in facilitating technological change in constituent firms. In economies increasingly exposed to international competition, local firms can survive only if they achieve and maintain levels of technological competence at least equivalent to world standards. The external benefits generated by cooperative action in clusters offers one way to achieve this objective. Thus, in this chapter, the focus is particularly on how clusters can support industrial technological change at both theoretical and empirical levels.

Theoretical Concepts

Regional Economic Concepts

As already indicated, much of the theoretical basis of clustering is derived from the argument that cooperation among firms gives rise to external benefits or economies. The concept of external economies is used widely in social economic analysis in order to explain the existence of benefits (or costs) that arise from economic transactions that fall upon third parties not directly involved in the original transaction. The concept of external costs is most developed in environmental economics. Regional economics uses the concept of external benefits, also known as agglomeration economies, to explain how advantages accrue to firms that are located close together and was first documented as localization and urbanization economies. These ideas can be traced to the work of Alfred Marshall's *Principles of Economics* (1890). In modern regional economics, the external benefits that arise from clustering have been analyzed within three models: pure agglomeration, industrial complex, and social network.

The model of pure agglomeration is based on economies related to the existence of a local pool of specialized labor, the provision of nontraded specific inputs such as specialized infrastructure, and the informal flow of industry-useful information and ideas among neighbors, which explains why firms locate in the same area (sometimes called Marshallian externalities). The impact of these external benefits on local firms is to reduce search costs for labor; to provide economies of scale in nontraded inputs, which allow higher quantities and qualities to be provided beyond what the firm could afford; and to increase the rate of research and development (R&D). These benefits are external to all firms in that location and accrue purely because of geographic proximity.

They can be broken down further into the following categories:

- **Internal returns of scale:** Accruing to a single firm due to production cost efficiencies realized by serving a large local market.

- **Localization economies:** External economies that arise due to a high level of local factor employment within a group of local firms and tend to occur when firms from the same sector are located together.

- **Urbanization economies:** Economies that accrue to all local firms, irrespective of sector, such as, for example, from the provision of higher quality infrastructure, universities and training facilities, airports, specialized labor, venture capital, quality of life factors, and so forth, due to large urban size. This aspect has been associated with the higher level of innovation typically found in larger metropolitan regions (Markusen, Hall, & Glasmeier, 1986; Malecki, 1997; Davelaar, 1991).

This version of clustering does not assume any explicit cooperation among actors beyond their individual interests in a competitive environment. They are considered to be particularly important to smaller firms that are unable to exploit internal economies of scale. Continuing on from this perspective, cluster studies thus have emphasized frequently their impact on small and medium enterprises (Gordon & McCann, 2000; Schmitz & Nadvi, 1999; Baptista & Swann, 1998).

The industrial complex model emphasizes relationships among firms primarily in terms of transactions between buyers and sellers or patterns of intermediate purchases that provide cost savings or other benefits in production. This approach has spawned a vast economic literature on regional input-output studies. More recently, these studies have been adapted to include information as well as trading flows. Noneconomists have added to this approach through an alternative but highly related analysis of value chains. This is not unlike the well-known diamond analysis of Michael Porter (1990) in *The Competitive Advantage of Nations*. Consequently, concepts associated with factor conditions, demand conditions, links to related and supportive industries, and firm strategies have been incorporated into cluster analyses. Firms make physical and research capital expenditures in order to set up these regional trading relationships that return monopoly profits that are relatively evenly distributed among the member firms of the cluster (Gordon & McCann, 2000).

The social network model emphasizes interpersonal relationships that transcend firm boundaries and result in strong interfirm interactions. While network analyses of clusters are common across all disciplines, the particularly economic contribution is derived from transaction cost analysis, as developed by Williamson (1985). Clusters allow firms to minimize transaction costs and to maximize the benefits of agglomeration economies (Scott, 1992). Thus, these interactions are considered to depend crucially on trust, are relatively informal, and reflect incomplete contracts. Consequently, firms in these relationships are willing to take risky cooperation and joint ventures, to have the flexibility to reorganize their relationships as conditions change, and to act as a group in order to support common mutually beneficial goals. The strength of these relationships is measured by the level of embeddedness of this social network within the local economic structure (Granovetter, 1985). By reducing uncertainty and instability, networks encourage both specialization and the flow of information supporting innovation (Loveman & Sengenberger, 1991; Chesnais, 1988; Porter & Fuller, 1986; Dosi, 1988).

While social networks are spatial, they are not necessarily local. The incentives for investing heavily in purely local networks may be limited in a world in which competitiveness in international markets requires a high degree of flexibility in business strategies and the cultivation of suppliers or partners with very specialized capabilities (Gordon & McCann, 2000). The social network model originally was developed from studies of the Italian industrial districts, which saw it as a specifically regional institution based on horizontal collaboration among local firms (Piore & Sabel, 1984; Becattini, 1990). However, Suarez-Villa and Walrod (1997), Echeverri-Carroll, Hunnicutt, and Hansen (1998), and Zucker, Darby, and Armstrong (1998) suggest that innovation also is related to information obtained from outside the local region. More recent work has focused on investigating how these networks have responded to international competition, a phenomenon that frequently has led to the breakdown of regional clusters and the reassertion of the importance of leading multinational firms as the center and driving force in networks (Tiberi Vipario, 1996).

The focus on small and medium enterprises has led to the incorporation of the concept of entrepreneurship into cluster analysis. The significance of entrepreneurship as a driving force in economic growth and particularly in innovation stems from the ideas developed by Joseph Schumpeter in *The Theory of Economic Development* (1934). While the need for entrepreneurship in order to foster regional economic development is well acknowledged, mechanisms for encouraging this are scarce. Clusters are identified as one means of mobilizing entrepreneurial talent as a means to increase regional industrialization. Clusters provide a means to draw out the less exceptional and more common ordinary entrepreneurs by allowing them to take smaller and more calculable risks through joint action. Thus, potential entrepreneurs who may not have the resources or the psychology to make large risky investments in isolation will be more willing to do so within the supportive and cooperative framework of the cluster. This process also provides small firms with technical, financial, and market support, which allows them to take the additional investments necessary in order to grow into medium-scale enterprises (Schmitz & Nadvi, 1999).

The cluster literature emphasizes the importance of local-level governance and the role of incremental upgrading through interactions among firms and between these firms and their local institutions. More recently, analysts have focused on how these regional clusters respond to the pressures of international competition. Clusters may allow firms to respond to the challenges from trade liberalization and globalization by helping them to meet world standards in cost, quality, speed of response, and flexibility through joint action, thus converting local firms into exporters. Many studies focus on the role of clusters in helping local firms to make the transition to global competitors.

As already indicated, within the context of the global market, there has been a renewed interest in the role of leading firms and, particularly, transnational corporations (TNCs) (Amin & Robins, 1991). The extent to which TNCs are embedded in regional networks influences their capacity to act as disseminators of new knowledge, information, and innovation from abroad into the region, thus improving the standards and productivity of host country suppliers. In addition, this relationship may enhance the technological competence of the TNC (van der Berg, Braun & van Winden, 2001; Ivarsson, 2002). It has been suggested that clustering that involves the geographical proximity of firms and institutions engaged in technology development makes a region more attractive for asset-seeking foreign direct investment (FDI), as TNCs attempt to tap foreign centers of innovation excellence in order to augment their own firm-specific competencies. The acquisition of existing companies has been used increasingly to obtain these competencies. In doing so, they acquire the competencies that are generated through the linkages between the target firm and its cluster partners (Ivarsson, 2002). Thus, TNCs provide a dilemma for clustered firms. On the one hand, they may provide opportunities for upgrading by local producers. Alternatively, they provide a threat to clusters either by breaking up cooperative arrangements among small local firms or by inhibiting upgrading and knowledge flows by isolating innovation processes to internally controlled entities (Humphrey & Schmitz, 2002; Morris & Ferguson, 1993).

Technological Change Concepts

Parallel to the growth of the theory of regional clusters as a mechanism for economic development has been the development of a new range of concepts related to industrial technological change. These two theoretical developments come together in the concept of the local knowledge base or regional innovation systems. It is not appropriate to trace all elements of the evolution of the economic theory of knowledge here (see Freeman & Soete, 1997, for a comprehensive review) but only to acknowledge those elements relevant to develop the importance of clusters in facilitating technology transfer.

Within that context, technology is defined as a complex bundle of knowledge that incorporates product specifications and design; materials and components specifications and properties; machinery and its operating characteristics; and the various kinds of know how, operating procedures, and organizational arrangements needed to integrate technology into a range of different production systems. Thus, it involves not just the machinery-embodied technologies but also the creative problem solving and innovative processes needed to adapt these technologies to a series of new situations, particularly as conditions change over time. Technology-related investments involve not just R&D and investment in new facilities but also improvements in existing production systems and reassessment of the existing knowledge base in order to meet new situations (Bell & Albu, 1999).

Institutional economics focus on the set of factors that mold and define human interaction both within and among organizations. Modern evolutionary economics focus predominantly on the processes of technological advance. A country's level of technological competence is seen as the basic factor constraining its productivity, and technological advance is the driving force behind economic growth. Institutions mold the technologies used by that society and, hence, the rate of technological change (Nelson & Nelson, 2002). Institutions have been described by Veblen as general habits of action and thought. Embedded social technologies provide low transaction cost ways of getting something done. Clusters thus support innovation by providing collaborative communication among customers, suppliers, and competitors (Stiglitz, 1987; Lundvall, 1988; Saxenian, 1994).

Within this perspective, economic actors are considered to be constrained by the limited range of routines that they have mastered. Technological progress is thus both path-dependent and irreversible, locking firms into technological specializations (Henderson, 1997). Learning new routines is time-consuming, costly, and risky. Economic growth is the result of progressive introduction of new technologies into these established routines, which results in higher levels of worker productivity and the ability to produce new or improved goods and services. Institutional structures that support technological innovation include universities, government funding programs, and corporate R&D laboratories. These are known generally in the literature as innovation systems (Nelson & Nelson, 2002). Regions in which strong learning and information transfer occurs among local firms are referred to as innovative milieu. Such regions not only circulate knowledge within their cluster but also collect information from external sources and then use it to develop successful new export products (Tiberi Vipraio & Hodgkinson, 2000; Maillat & Perrin, 1992).

The concept of national systems of innovation has been defined narrowly by Lundvall (1992) as organizations and institutions such as R&D departments, technological institutions, and universities, and broadly as all parts of the economic structure and institutional set-up affecting learning and exploration involved in the production, diffusion, and use of new and economically useful knowledge, including the production system, the marketing system, and the system of finance. A system's innovative capacity is related to the extensiveness and efficiency with which it distributes and absorbs knowledge (Mytelka & Smith, 2002). National innovation systems explain the differing degrees of competitiveness of economies, especially their technological competitiveness and ability to innovate (Kuhlmann, 2001).

This concept of national innovation systems has been extended into the concept of local industrial systems in which the system is geographically based and focuses on the interdependence of the innovation process within clusters of firms. A further development involves sectoral innovation systems that are based on the idea that different industries operate under different technological regimes based on a specific industry knowledge base. That concept can be related to the idea of technological systems. Many such systems will operate in each country, each based on a generic technology that is applicable over a set of industries. Technological systems involve three types of networks: buyer/supplier relationships, problem-solving networks, and informal networks (Kuhlmann, 2001; Carlsson, Jacobsson, Holmen, & Richne, 2002).

Each industry will have its own technology regime or base set of knowledge from which innovations are developed. However, technology regimes also have a spatial dimension. If industry knowledge is primarily tacit in nature and cannot be easily codified, innovators will tend to concentrate geographically as new knowledge is learned through everyday practice and generally transmitted through informal personnel contact or the movement of skilled staff among firms. The more this knowledge base involves simple generic information that is well codified, the less important it is for related firms to be geographically concentrated (Saviotti, 1988; Suarez-Villa & Walrod, 1997). Thus, cluster relationships are much more likely to influence the rate of innovation in the first situation relative to the second. However, innovation also may be concentrated geographically in situations in which the knowledge base is simple and codified, if those industries operate in clusters dominated by large technological leaders, as most innovation logically will occur in those regions in which these leading firms are located, particularly in the earlier stages of the product cycle (Baptista & Swann, 1998; Glaesser, Kallal, Scheinkman & Shleifer, 1992; Audretsch, 1998).

By merging the concepts of local industrial systems and sectoral innovation systems or technology regimes, the idea of regional innovation systems is developed. These systems now consist of the knowledge bases of all industries located in a particular region; the institutions available to support their technological innovations; and the institutional context of laws, regulations, political cultures, and acknowledged rules of the game that operate in that region (Mytelka & Smith, 2002). Thus, the process of innovation is path-dependent, location-specific, and institutionally shaped. This means that clusters provide a relevant framework in which to analyze the process of innovation in particular industries.

Framework of Analysis

The concepts discussed previously are used by all disciplines when studying cluster behavior. There is increasing acceptance that economic growth emerges from fruitful cooperation among economic actors that form innovative complexes of firms and organizations, generally referred to as clusters. Actors engage in these clusters in order to survive in volatile international markets and in situations of rapid technological change. It provides them with flexibility or the ability to react quickly in partnership with complementary organizations and to increase their rate of innovation by concentrating on core capabilities while accessing other resources from the network. While networks can extend worldwide, clusters normally are referred to as being the local or regional dimensions of these networks. Clusters unite suppliers and customers with service units, government agencies, research institutions, and so forth within a specific geographical area and cultural milieu. Despite advances in information technologies, face-to-face contact is important in establishing the preconditions of trust among actors and thus enabling the exchange of information and, particularly, tacit knowledge (van der Berg et al., 2001; Ivarsson, 2002).

Research now is focused on applying these concepts to real-world examples of cluster activity. In such studies, the relationships among spatial economic conditions, cluster functioning, and technological change are considered to be influenced by the following conditions.

Market Conditions

1. Local demand conditions, including the extent to which they limit further growth opportunities, forcing regional firms to seek wider national and international markets. The formation of clusters is enhanced when markets are not local, as this reduces the level of competition among local firms and, hence, increases the opportunities for cooperation. It is also beneficial when cooperation is not seen as a disadvantage to competition (van der Berg et al., 2001; Gordon & McCann, 2000).

2. The extent of local supply or purchases from other firms in the local region, as cluster activity is enhanced if these firms sell directly to other firms rather than to the public or government. Cluster activity is enhanced if the links with customers and/or suppliers have a significant impact on firms' operations, particularly if referrals or personal contacts are important in developing the business. The existence of joint ventures with other local firms and the use of local private consultants or professionals for external advice encourage cluster activity (Gordon & McCann, 2000).

3. The size of the cluster in terms of number of firms, value added, and employment. This will be affected by the level of new firm creation. The size of firms in itself does not affect the probability of clusters forming, although the existence of large firms can

provide benefits, as discussed later. Firms located in clusters that are also strong within their own industry and have significant market share were more likely to innovate (van der Berg et al., 2001; Gordon & McCann, 2000; Baptista & Swann, 1998).

Psychological and Cultural Conditions

1. The ease with which actors can form strategic cooperations determined by the level of trust in that community, the extent and nature of psychological and business cultural barriers to cooperation, and so forth. Cooperation is enhanced by cultural values such as the willingness to adopt new products, the value placed on entrepreneurship, and the willingness to engage in strategic alliances with other firms. Cooperation is enhanced if actors see proximity as an advantage in providing opportunities to interact or in developing a shared labor pool (van der Berg et al., 2001; Gordon & McCann, 2000).

2. The history and culture of the sector in that region, which determines the sociocultural and physical infrastructure available to support its future development (van der Berg et al., 2001).

Role of Large Organizations and Foreign Investment

1. The presence of institutions or large organizations in a dominant position in the sector or regions that can act as cluster engines to drive future development. A transnational corporation located as part of a cluster can enhance regional innovation, depending on the extent it procures inputs and transmits new knowledge to local suppliers, provides additional market outlets for local firms and encourages them to invest in more advanced technologies and distributional systems, uses local professional service firms, transfers tacit knowledge that can be passed to other local clients, and becomes involved in local technological collaborations. Transnational corporations generally will have a positive impact on local cluster activity in regions that already have a high level of indigenous technological capacity and where local firms have competencies to offer the larger firms in return for transfers of capital, knowledge, know-how, skills, brand names, and organizational and managerial practices from outside sources (van der Berg et al., 2001; Ivarsson, 2002; Ernst & Kim, 2002).

Creative Milieu Conditions

1. The extent of linkages among firms and educational and research institutions and among these institutions themselves. Transnational corporations can enhance this process by establishing linkages with local standards and quality-control agencies, research institutions, universities, and vocational training organizations in order to

increase the transfer of knowledge and education into the local region (van der Berg et al., 2001; Ivarsson, 2002; Ernst & Kim, 2002).

2.   The organizing capacity of the local area management and its vision and strategy to develop the cluster, including the involvement of cluster actors in relevant policy making (van der Berg et al., 2001).

3.   The functions undertaken by firms in the region, particularly the extent to which they undertake not only production but also logistics, administration, sales, and service to customers (Gordon & McCann, 2000).

Innovation Processes

1.   The extent of product or process innovation occurring within the region and the existence of products in the earlier stages of their product cycles. Cluster activity is enhanced if innovation is associated with observation or shared intelligence. Technological change occurs within cluster systems through two different processes: diffusion and replication of knowledge within clusters; acquisition and generation of knowledge that is new to the cluster. Knowledge diffusion within a cluster can occur either passively as a largely unintended by-product of other firm relationships or actively involving deliberately constructed structures to transfer knowledge within and among firms. New knowledge can be introduced into a cluster either as a by-product of other transactions or actively by developing learning processes in specifically designated functions within the firm (Bell & Albu, 1999; Gordon & McCann, 2000).

Application Across Disciplines

It has been argued here that the essential concepts used in cluster studies were developed from economics and, particularly, from regional economic theory. However, other disciplines have been more involved in developing the application of these ideas to real-world development problems. Management analysts have focused on issues related to how clusters can be initiated and facilitated to bring these theoretical benefits forward. In particular, the question of whether such an important development tool can be left to natural economic forces driven by self-interest and the pursuit of profits or whether some form of benign government or other agency intervention is required has been a focal point in recent analyses and lies behind many applied cluster studies. This approach is traced back to the seminal work by Porter (1990) and involves a development of the industrial complex model discussed previously.

The basic elements of Porter's (1990) diamond model and its argument that local conditions determine international competitive advantage, thus forming the basis of regional industrial development, do not need repeating here. A good summary of this argument is provided by Perry in chapter eight of this book. Porter's (1990) book and subsequent papers are fundamental to defining the management approach to cluster analysis and the heightened interest by government agencies, particularly in smaller countries that promote clusters as a means of economic development.

A second major influence on the development of applied management cluster analyses was Saxenian's (1994) study of Silicon Valley, California. This study emphasized the importance of informal relationships among co-located firms, particularly in newer IT industries. Here, knowledge was shared through social relationships among highly skilled technical workers in which the imperative to solve new problems quickly in a rapidly developing technological environment transcended traditional fears of competitors. The mutual advantages arising from open communication were recognized, with trust resulting in cooperation, which facilitated technological development to the growing competitive advantage of the region as a whole.

Clusters are analyzed by the marketing discipline from a similar conceptual base as management. Porter (1990) is again the seminal work, which focuses the analysis on the relationships among producer firms and suppliers within a geographically constrained industry. Marketing studies, however, place stronger emphasis on branding the cluster. Thus, they ask how one particular cluster (e.g., one specific national cluster in the biotechnology industry) can distinguish itself from its many international competitors. This, then, leads to a focus on the uniqueness and quality of the product and services produced in that cluster. The more intensive the relationships within the cluster, the stronger will be its business culture, and hence, more members will be willing to adhere to that culture, which will give the cluster a unique image or brand within the international community. A secondary conceptual approach used in marketing is derived from the stakeholder theory, which emphasizes the importance of primary vs. secondary members of the cluster. The nature and needs of primary members determine the boundaries of the cluster, its culture, its most effective management and communication procedures, and the values and ethics that determine its brand.

Information technology analyses of clusters (or networks, as tends to be used in studies in this discipline) are less explicit in identifying their theoretical and conceptual basis than are studies from other disciplines. A key element in these studies is the importance of developing trust among collaborators before effective IT communication systems can be implemented. There is also considerable emphasis on the importance of business efficiency and cost savings to adopters of e-commerce type business systems. These factors indicate that the theoretical basis of IT cluster analysis is based on concepts from the social network model described previously and derived from the institutional framework developed by Williamson (1985).

The development of e-commerce applications facilitates the breakdown of social relationships within regionally based clusters in response to the pressures from growing international competition. It allows particularly large firms to gain the cost minimization benefits from overseas locations while retaining the relationship benefits from their established networks of small specialized suppliers. Thus, while this field of cluster analysis to a large extent has developed separately from initially a largely technical perspective focused on cost and efficiency benefits, a consistency with the more traditional commerce approach is evident.

Conclusion

This chapter summarizes the theoretical approaches that have defined the concepts and relationships used in applied cluster analysis. The following chapters illustrate how these ideas are used repeatedly by analysts from a variety of disciplines in their studies regarding the implementation, governance, and promotion of clusters. The perceived benefits from participation in clusters have been well established at the theoretical level. The real challenge is to develop an understanding of how to facilitate these relationships in those regions and industries when they do not emerge naturally. These questions are addressed in the following chapters.

References

Altenburg, T., & Meyer-Stamer, J. (1999). How to promote clusters: Policy experiences in Latin America. *World Development, 27*(9), 1693-1713.

Amin, A., & Robins, K. (1991). These are not Marshallian times. In R. Camagni (Ed.), *Innovation networks: Spatial perspectives* (pp. 105-118). London: Belhaven Press-GREMI.

Audretsch, D.B. (1998). Agglomeration and the location of innovative activity. *Oxford Review of Economic Policy, 14*(2), 18-29.

Baptista, R., & Swann, P. (1998). Do firms in clusters innovate more? *Research Policy, 27*(5), 525-540.

Becattini, G. (1990). The Marsahallian industrial district as a socio-economic notion. In F. Pyke, G. Becattini, & W. Sengenberger (Eds.), *Industrial districts and inter-firm cooperation in Italy* (pp. 37-51). Geneva: Bureau International du Travail.

Bell, M., & Albu, M. (1999). Knowledge systems and technological dynamism in industrial clusters in developing countries. *World Development, 27*(9), 1715-1734.

Carlsson, B., Jacobsson, S., Holmen, M., & Richne, A. (2002). Innovation systems: Analytical and methodological issues. *Research Policy, 31*, 233-245.

Chesnais, F. (1988). Technical co-operation agreements between firms. *STI Review, 4*. Paris: OECD.

Davelaar, E.J. (1991). *Regional economic analysis of innovation and incubation.* Aldershot: Avebury.

Dosi, G. (1988). Sources, procedures and microeconomic effects of innovation. *Journal of Economic Literature, 26*, 139-144.

Echeverri-Carroll, E.L., Hunnicutt, L., & Hansen, N. (1998). Do asymmetric networks help or hinder small firms' ability to export? *Regional Studies, 32*(8), 721-733.

Ernst, D., & Kim, L. (2002). Global production networks, knowledge diffusion, and local capacity formation. *Research Policy, 31*, 1417-1429.

Freeman, C., & Soete, L. (1997). *The economics of industrial innovation.* London: Pinter.

Glaesser, E.L., Kallal, H.D., Scheinkman, J.A., & Shleifer, A. (1992). Growth in cities. *Journal of Political Economy, 100,* 1126-1152.

Gordon, I.R., & McCann, P. (2000). Industrial clusters complexes. Agglomeration and/or social networks? *Urban Studies, 37*(3), 513-533.

Granovetter, M. (1985). Economic action and social structure: The problem of embeddedness. *American Journal of Sociology, 91*(3), 481-510.

Henderson, V. (1997). Externalities and industrial development. *Journal of Urban Economics, 42,* 449-470.

Humphrey, J., & Schmitz, H. (2002). How does insertion of global value chains affect upgrading in industrial clusters? *Regional Studies, 36*(9), 1017-1028.

Ivarsson, I. (2002). Collective technology learning between transnational corporations and local business partners: The case of West Sweden. *Environment and Planning A., 34,* 1877-1897.

Kuhlmann, S. (2001). Future governance of innovation policy in Europe—Three scenarios. *Research Policy, 30,* 953-976.

Loveman, G., & Sengenberger, W. (1991). The re-emergence of small-scale production: An international perspective. *Small Business Economics, 3,* 1-38.

Lundvall, B.A. (1988). Innovation as an interactive process: From user-producer interaction to the national system of innovation. In G. Dosi, C. Freeman, R. Nelson, G. Silverberg, & L. Soete (Eds.), *Technical change and economic theory* (pp. 349-369). London: Pinter.

Lundvall, B.A. (Ed.). (1992). *National systems of innovation, towards a theory of innovation and interactive learning.* London: Pinter.

Maillat, D., & Perrin, J.C. (1992). *Innovative enterprises and territorial development.* GREMI: University of Neuchatel.

Malecki, E.J. (1997). *Technology and economic development* (2nd ed.). Essex: Longman.

Markusen, A., Hall, P., & Glasmeier, A. (1986). *High tech America: The what, how, where and why of the sunrise industries.* Boston: Allan and Unwin.

Marshall, A. (1890). *Principles of Economics* (8th ed. 1925). London: Macmillan.

Morris, C.R., & Ferguson, C.H. (1993, March-April). How architecture wins technology wars. *Harvard Business Review,* 86-96.

Mytelka, L.K., & Smith, K. (2002). Policy learning and innovation theory: An interactive and co-evolving process. *Research Policy, 31,* 1467-1479.

Nelson, R.R., & Nelson, K. (2002). Technology, institutions and innovation systems. *Research Policy, 31,* 265-272.

Piore, M., & Sabel, C. (1984). *The second industrial divide: Possibilities for prosperity.* New York: Basic Books.

Porter, M.E., & Fuller, M.B. (1986). Coalitions and global strategy. In M.E. Porter (Ed.), *Competition in global industries* (pp. 315-343). Boston: Harvard Business School Press.

Saviotti, P.P. (1988). On the dynamics of appropriability of tacit and codified knowledge. *Research Policy, 26*, 843-856.

Saxenian, A. (1994). *Regional advantage—Culture and competition in Silicon Valley and Route 128.* Cambridge, MA: Harvard University Press.

Schmitz, H., & Nadvi, K. (1999). Clustering and industrialization: Introduction. *World Development, 27*(9), 1503-1514.

Scott, M. (1992). A new theory of endogenous economic growth. *Oxford Review of Economic Policy, 8*(4), 29-42.

Stiglitz, J. E. (1987). Learning to learn: Localised learning and technological progress. In P. Dasgupta, & P. Stoneman (Eds.), *Economic Policy and technological performance* (pp. 125-153). New York: Cambridge University Press.

Suarez-Villa, L., & Walrod, W. (1997). Operational strategy, R&D and intra-metropolitan clustering in a polycentric structure: The advanced electronics industries of the Los Angeles basin. *Urban Studies, 34*(9), 1343-1380.

Tiberi Vipraio, P. (1996). From local to global networking: The restructuring of Italian industrial districts. *Journal of Industry Studies, 3*(2), 135-171.

Tiberi Vipraio, P., & Hodgkinson, A. (2000). Globalisation within a local context: Methodology and pilot study. *Journal of International Marketing and Exporting, 5*(1), 25-43.

van der Berg, L., Braun, E., & van Winden, W. (2001). Growth clusters in European cities: An integral approach. *Urban Studies, 38*(1), 185-205.

Williamson, O.E. (1985). *The economic institutions of capitalism: Firms, markets and relational contracting.* New York: Free Press.

Zucker, L., Darby, M., & Armstrong, J. (1998). Geographically localized knowledge spillovers or markets? *Economic Inquiry, 36*, 65-86.

Section II

Marketing

Chapter II

Leveraging the Benefits of Business Clusters:
A Branding and Stakeholder Management Framework

Bill Merrilees, Griffith University, Australia

Dale Miller, Griffith University, Australia

Carmel Herington, Griffith University, Australia

Abstract

In terms of managing the cluster, emphasis is given to how the diverging and converging interests of members can be managed. A stakeholder framework is used as a means of theoretically unifying the common interests of group members, which at the same time recognizes that they are independent entities. In terms of marketing the cluster, a key issue addressed in this chapter is branding. Many clusters are obscure with limited awareness. We take the view that precincts of small business clusters need to be branded properly, and we develop a framework in order for this to be done. Branding principles guide this work. The chapter also explores how multiple clusters can be comarketed in one region, generally through e-commerce and specifically through e-malls.

Introduction

Clusters have been defined as "localized accretions of people, infrastructure and finance that, in sum, can develop a world-leading industry capability, not necessarily in the high tech area" (James & Thomson, 2003, p. 44).

Although clusters tend to be industry-based, they are not restricted to industry and can incorporate a range of supporting institutions, including universities, technical colleges, and governments.

An increasing number of authors spell out the importance of clusters. The World Bank, the OECD, and many multilateral organizations are developing cluster-related policies. The following indicates the best-known clusters: "Biela in Italy has a cluster of 200 companies that leads the world in textile weaving. Another cluster of 700 companies in northern Italy makes half of Europe's socks. Medina, also in Italy, has a high-level sports car cluster that makes all the Ferraris, Lamborghinis and Maseratis. Doltan, a town of 45,000 people near Atlanta, Georgia, makes a fairly high percentage of the world's carpets. Even Hollywood, which occupies only a small section of Los Angeles, is a movie-making cluster. And Silicon Valley, of course, is a software cluster" (James & Thomson, 2003, p. 44).

Other examples can be added to this list. For example, Eng (2004) notes that Cambridge City in England is a British example of Silicon Valley with the largest concentration of high-tech firms in Europe. Although the importance of clusters, especially reflected through the previous well-known international examples, seems evident, the corresponding academic research seems underdeveloped. The research seems to be very fragmented with few seminal studies.

This chapter directly addresses the research gap by analyzing the following two major problems that face clusters: (1) managing the loose alliances in order to maximize synergies across the disparate businesses and (2) marketing/projecting the collective/combined business solutions emanating from different businesses. This chapter develops a conceptual/theoretical framework that addresses these two major issues, thereby contributing to the greater potential success of clusters. We begin with the Australian context followed by an outline of the benefits of clusters.

Australian Context

A useful summary of what is happening in clusters throughout Australia is given by James and Thomson (2003). Examples of the identified industries include aluminium and ferro-manganese (Tasmania), water management, defense and advanced electronics, multimedia (South Australia), thoroughbred racehorse breeding (NSW), defense (ACT), oil and defense as the cornerstones of the Australian Marine Complex (Western Australia), Australian Tropical Foods (Queensland), surfing (Victoria) and marine services, mineral processing, and NT Food Group (Northern Territory).

Enright and Roberts (2001) also provide a useful perspective of clustering in Australia. In the early 1990s, various government reports began to highlight the importance of networking and regional industry partnerships (Bureau of Industry Economics, 1991; Kelty, 1993; Pappas, Carter, Evans, Koop, & Telesis, 1990). The McKinsey report, *Lead Local, Compete Global*, apparently was the first report to explicitly suggest clustering as a basis of industry development (McKinsey & Company 1994). More recent policies include Cooperative Research Centres (CRCs) and the Regional Assistance Program. It would seem that policies and programs ebb and flow without an ongoing consistent framework other than some sort of regional cluster support. One also can question the detail of some of these policies. For example, CRCs were conceived as groupings of centers of excellence, but the method of government implementation has lowered potential outcomes by encouraging the involvement of elements that were of a lower standing.

Most of the research of Australian clusters seems to suggest that they are not well developed when compared to counterparts in other countries (Enright & Roberts, 2001; Marceau, 1999; National Economics, 2000). Even the three case studies of successful clusters given in Enright and Roberts (2001) indicate a struggle to cope with changing financial and other support. Indeed, an open question is whether these types of private government partnerships in general or specifically are flexible enough to cope with the dynamic changes that beset any industry. Purely private industries have a better track record of handling fluctuating external environments. The particular critique of clusters given by Brown (2000) is instructive for our research. He has identified three common problems with cluster development in Australia: failure to reach a critical scale, lack of distinctiveness, and administrative difficulties. This chapter addresses the last two factors by proposing potential solutions or at least partial solutions to the achievement of distinctiveness (through branding) and a more efficient administration or management system (through stakeholder management) for clusters.

Benefits of Clusters

Much of the cluster literature has been incorporated into the relevant section of this chapter. However, just as it is important to portray the broad Australian context of clusters, it is also useful to summarize the broader, more macro research that outlines and analyzes the benefits of clusters, especially in relation to regional development and innovation.

One of the key benefits of clusters is that they foster regional development, a phenomenon that explains why government policies have been introduced in this area, as discussed in the Australian context section. The work by Porter (1998) highlights the global economic context of clusters. He argues that paradoxically, the sustainable competitive advantages in a global economy more likely are found in local elements such as knowledge and relationships that distant rivals are unable to match. Part of his case is that many such clusters exist and in places that are not immediately obvious. Porter (1998) sees clusters as a new spatial organizational form that is between arm's-length markets on the one hand and hierarchies or vertical integration on the other. It thus is more exposed to the market and has less organizational inflexibilities than vertically integrated firms. Put simply, there are some advantages to clusters, which explains their existence. We now turn to these advantages, starting with productivity.

In effect, productivity is a benefit that reflects a new organizational form. Porter (1998) suggests that clusters allow firms to operate more productively in sourcing inputs, accessing information technology and institutions, coordinating with related companies, and monitoring performances of suppliers. Elaborating on these points, sourcing specialized employees is easier, because the cluster acts as a beacon and magnet, attracting workers (and suppliers). Linkages among the cluster members can generate synergies. Porter (1998) gives a tourism example in which the quality of the visitor's experience depends not only on the appeal of the main attraction but also on the quality of the complementary businesses such as hotels, restaurants, shops, and transportation.

A second benefit of clusters is that they foster innovation. Enright and Roberts (2001) summarize a number of studies that connect innovation with innovation and argue that clusters provide a supportive framework for innovation in terms of the collection of workers, researchers, managers, information, suppliers, customers, and finance. Additionally, they argue that clusters are associated with informal, unplanned, face-to-face oral communication that is conducive to the innovation process. Porter (1998) adds that firms in a cluster can experiment at lower costs and can delay large commitments until they are more confident that the innovation will work. Baptista (1996), drawing on a range of theories, suggests that a localized pattern of development facilitates a collective learning process and increases the speed of diffusion of new innovations by reducing uncertainty. However, he notes that there is limited empirical research on the matter. One of the few empirical research papers is somewhat negative about narrowly defined clusters alone being able to generate higher levels of innovation. Romijn and Albaladejo (2002) place more emphasis on connections to the scientific community and to local-global interfaces. Some clusters have an explicit innovation objective, including collaborative research centers (Liyanage 1995) and incubators with respect to new businesses (Colombo & Delmastro, 2003). In such cases, innovation is the main intended benefit of the cluster. The detailed micromechanism by which the cluster facilitates innovation has not received much attention in the literature, but Caniels and Romijn (2003) emphasize dynamic collaboration and lead firms.

Clusters are with us as a market reality. Although we have briefly outlined some Australian programs and policies in the previous section and noted the potential regional development benefits in this section, we have not attempted to argue fully the need for government intervention in this domain. Indeed, the ideas in this chapter are directed at the cluster stakeholders and not necessarily the government. In broad terms, we are content with some government role in clusters but do not elaborate here on the nature or extent of that role. This section has not tried to justify the government role in clusters, although it could relate to externalities and spillovers. Notwithstanding, it is important to note that some of the literature does oppose a major and even a minor role of government in cluster development or facilitation. Desrochers and Sautet (2004) argue that there is a risk of governments trying to pick winners, focusing on narrowly defined industries, neglecting market forces in innovation, being out of tune with tacit knowledge flows, and focusing on specialization to the neglect of diversity in city development. Further research is needed to address the concerns of the authors.

Gap in the Literature

The main gap that we have identified through the literature is the lack of many cases of successful clustering. Further, we argue that there may be a lack of an appropriate conceptual framework in order to assess clusters. As we noted, there is the potential to use branding and stakeholder management principles in order to assess clusters. As a point of departure, the chapter is dedicated to building such a conceptual framework.

All Types of Clusters Can Benefit from Marketing, Branding, and Stakeholder Management

Before getting into details about the how clusters can benefit from marketing, stakeholder management, and branding, we should address the issue that all types of clusters can benefit from these principles, not just formally organized clusters that have a legal identity. There are three main types or groups of clusters:

1.   A geographic cluster of firms often within a particular industry and with fairly loose connections to each other; for example, a wine district.

2.   A geographic cluster of like-minded firms in an industry that have formalized in some way their association; for example, HunterNet.

3.   An electronic grouping of firms not necessarily in the same geographic location; for example, an online club (note that the second group potentially could have an electronic interface, as well).

With respect to the second and third types of clusters, marketing and branding are inevitable, whether recognized or not. Groups like HunterNet or furniture exporters in South Australia enter formal contracts to do some of their business. Implicit branding is present, so we argue that it is better to do the branding properly and cost-effectively rather than to muddle through it. Similar stakeholders need to be managed in some way, so again, the cluster can benefit from stakeholder management.

The first group might seem to have less need for marketing and branding and, indeed, might have minimal contact with each other. This could be true of wineries in the Hunter Valley or South-East Queensland or tropical food suppliers and manufacturers in North Queensland. However, there are benefits (externalities) to these groups in promoting brand awareness of the clusters. For example, the more well known a wine district is, the greater the number of visitors, from which all wineries can benefit. It therefore pays the wineries to get together to jointly and cooperatively promote the cluster as a whole. Similarly, it would pay such a group to keep some rogue wineries in train (through stakeholder management); otherwise, all wineries might be worse off if bad behavior occurs.

Managing the Cluster: The Challenge

In terms of managing the cluster, emphasis needs to be given to how the diverging and converging interests of members can be managed. Clusters represent a difficult governance challenge, because members tend to be independent business entities with each pursuing its own objectives. The alliances across firms sometimes can be very loose, especially when the common ground might be no more than cooperative promotion. The alliance may be stronger when there are customer and supply interdependencies; for example, when one member supplies to another member. In such a case, the commonality is the normal business contract, and the cluster does not necessarily add additional governance issues. Other clusters might be linked through complementarities in joint tendering, such as the engineering consortium HunterNet in Newcastle, NSW, Australia. In this case, cluster alliances tend to be of a hard-soft character. The alliance is hard (close) through tendering toward a particular contract. Not all of the members would be part of the tender in a contract (if successful). Outside the specific contract, the alliance reverts to a loose or soft nature, lacking any legalistic teeth.

So the problem of a loose contractual alliance is the norm, with a handful of special-purpose exceptions. How can such an alliance be managed? By necessity, the alliance is primarily a voluntary one without power to enforce breeches of the common agreement or goal or even to prevent free riders from benefiting when they don't contribute. The relative benefits and costs of joining the alliance need to be appropriate. A further problem that represents the cost side of the equation is that independent businesses often have independent minds and enjoy their freedoms. That is the nature of small businesses and, indeed, all businesses. Thus, small businesses will be reluctant to give up some of their autonomy to a third party, which adds to the challenge of management.

A counter to the cost side is the benefit side. If a cluster is able to demonstrate success in creating heightened awareness or is able to generate new business or new contracts, then voluntary participation in the alliance is likely to continue. This approach guides the actions of the cluster. For example, HunterNet, the engineering cluster, decided that it was important to invest in an efficient, fast tendering system. An efficient tendering system necessitates good databases that include the capabilities of member firms and histories of previous tenders. A fast tendering system is also important, because a late tender is next to useless. One might see an efficient, fast tendering system as a key success factor for this type of cluster. The cluster arrived at this approach through a strategic planning workshop facilitated by one of the authors of this chapter. The workshop also helped to articulate exactly what the core capabilities of the cluster members were and how they complement each other.

Managing the Cluster: A Stakeholder Approach

Notwithstanding the foregoing, the challenge of designing an appropriate governance system for the majority of clusters remains. A stakeholder framework will be used as a means of theoretically unifying the common interests of group members.

Stakeholder theory has been applied mainly to situations in which an outside, disconnected group has been affected adversely by mainstream business operations. For example, stakeholder analysis has been applied to how the interests of, say, the green, environmental movement is affected by the petroleum industry. Surprisingly, much stakeholder research has been concerned with identifying and prioritizing who the stakeholders are (Mitchell, Agle & Wood, 1997; Nasi, Nasi, Phillips & Zyglidopoulos, 1997; Polonsky, 1995). The same literature emphasizes secondary stakeholders that are not germane to the lead firm's main business. Secondary stakeholders have a limited connection to the business, and thus, it is optional for the lead firm to decide whether the interests of the secondary stakeholders is acknowledged or factored in. Notwithstanding, secondary stakeholders are more likely to be factored in when the lead firm takes a strategic approach to stakeholder management. Research has shown that strategic alliance building between a lead firm and secondary parties (e.g., green lobby groups) can benefit from the strategic objectives of both parties (Mendleson & Polonsky, 1995; Polonsky, 2001).

A major limitation of existing explicit stakeholder theory and research is the neglect of primary stakeholders, especially primary marketing stakeholders. A key exception is the research by Merrilees, Getz, and O'Brien (2005). Primary marketing stakeholders are those entities that are actively and vitally engaged in value creation. Merrilees, Getz, and O'Brien (2005) used the marketing unit of the Goodwill Games organization as the lead entity and mapped out the relations with other stakeholders such as the public relations unit, television media, newspapers, ticket selling companies, and retail merchandisers. The relevance for clusters is obvious, because most of the industry partners in a cluster are likely to be primary stakeholders. This is not to say that all members have the same priority, but it is unlikely they would be secondary (and hence, incidental, optional) stakeholders, although some clusters may choose to have such members. Institutional members to a cluster (e.g., a university) also are more likely to be primary rather than secondary members through a training, advisory, or research and development role.

Although the Merrilees, Getz, and O'Brien (2005) study was not about a cluster, per se, nonetheless there are three lessons or principles that might be useful for cluster stakeholder management. First, as a principle, stakeholder management requires a "tolerant organizational culture that understands the importance of stakeholder roles and treats all stakeholder groups with fairness and respect" (Merrilees et al., 2005, p. 1074). In the case of the Goodwill Games, the sponsorship background of the managers was felt to be conducive to developing this cultural mindset. Sponsorship agreements and implementation require diverse parties to work together toward a common and sometimes intangible end. In the cluster context, there are several things a cluster can do to move in this direction. Learning by doing is the best way that culture can be developed. Collaboration on developing strategic direction via workshops would be helpful. Similarly, trialing a number of joint ventures (either marketing or production), even on a modest scale, also would help. The more interaction the better will be the ongoing development of the culture.

The second principle for stakeholder management refers to the operational competencies of flexible management that integrates the interests of different stakeholders. In the Goodwill Games case study, flexible management competencies were learned through negotiation skills that related to sponsorship deals. In the cluster context, the governance of the cluster needs to be managed in a facilitating rather than a top-down manner. Agility vs. rigidity is the key. Regular meetings might be one way to achieve flexibility, although too many meetings might worsen the situation. Meetings, per se, would be insufficient. Agility requires not just better communication, which could be achieved through a combination of meetings and the Internet, but also rapid problem solving that leads to quick reaction and sometimes pro-activity. Thus, the cluster executive team needs to ensure that regular effective communication, rapid problem solving, and rapid decision making are built into the business model.

The third principle is the use of branding concepts as a tool to unify stakeholders. This could include the use of strong values that are shared across stakeholders so that everyone pulls in one direction. The values might pertain to business ethics or a can-do attitude as examples. Essentially, such shared values strengthen the interdependency across businesses. In the context of clusters, there would be a benefit to identifying and articulating common values. Ideally, this would be done early in the formation of the cluster but could be reassessed and reimplemented at any time. A strategic planning workshop could be the vehicle to ascertain common values and would help to deepen the understanding and trust across members.

Marketing the Cluster: The Challenge

One of the key problems of clusters identified by Brown (2000) is the lack of distinctiveness, which also can be interpreted as a problem in marketing the cluster. A standard marketing solution might be to develop a market-positioning plan, one that appropriately reflects the competitive advantages of the cluster. Getting agreement on exactly what is a competitive advantage of the cluster might be a difficult process, because firms could emphasize their own self-interests rather than the collective interests of the cluster. Nonetheless, a strategic planning exercise could facilitate the articulation of a market position for the cluster. The authors believe that the achievement of distinctiveness can be extended beyond market positioning through the use of more modern marketing tools such as branding, to which we now turn.

Marketing the Cluster: A Branding Approach

The marketing challenge that faces clusters is considerable. Numerous cities are striving for IT and biotech clusters. Markets leading new technology clusters such Silicon Valley or Cambridge City are well known, have achieved on a large scale, and have made their marks. What can smaller high-tech clusters do to avoid oblivion? Part of the answer may be specialization, which reflects a narrow breadth but deep coverage. In other words, what are the distinctive competencies of a cluster, and how can they be projected to the market?

The branding approach begins by asking what the core essence of an entity is; that is, a need to build the brand platform. What is the purpose of the brand? What needs does it meet, and what benefits does it provide? What are the core values of the brand? For example, does it have a reputation for solving complex problems quickly? What is the look and feel of the brand? Exactly how is the brand different from what is offered by competitors? Can the promises be backed up? These are complex questions, and the cluster might need a consultant in order to address them appropriately.

After the brand is designed, it needs to be implemented through product and service delivery, in particular. A key requirement of any brand is consistent delivery of product and service, which is a considerable challenge to service industry entities. Brands need to be monitored closely in order to achieve this. The challenge is especially great when the entity (the cluster) is an alliance of otherwise independent firms. How can consistency be achieved with such an entity? Clusters need to be closely managed so that good relationships are developed, which will help to build trust in the system. Apart from consistent delivery of products, there is a need to ensure that communication to external parties reflects the brand rather than generates conflicting messages.

Branding offers very high benefits in terms of achieving distinctiveness relative to the competition and can be designed and managed to achieve an optimal level of distinctiveness. However, branding comes at a cost; it takes a high level of investment to build the brand in terms of design, operations, consistent delivery, and monitoring.

Enhancing the Management and Marketing of Clusters Through the Internet: A Study by Eng (2004)

The study by Eng (2004) explicitly examines the implications of the Internet for knowledge creation and dissemination in clusters of hi-tech firms. Case research was used to discern four Internet drivers; namely, open systems, virtual channels, multi-user engagement, and extended customisability. The cases were located in the Cambridge City technology precinct in England.

The emergent theory emanating from Eng (2004) places open systems as a major driver for knowledge creation and dissemination. Essentially, open systems facilitate communication and the exchange and sharing of information. The Internet increased transparency of business processes. Virtual channels also acted as a facilitator. Virtual channels included information systems, business processes, logistic processes, and supply chains that were mobilized to deliver products and services electronically to markets. A significant benefit of the Internet was the speeding up of information flows and greater sensitivity to changing needs in the market. The Internet opened up new ways of doing business with other entities on both a domestic and global scale. Multi-user engagement was a third way in which the Internet helped clusters. Users included both suppliers and customers within and outside the cluster. One interesting finding of the case research was that the local firms in the cluster seemed to gain relatively more benefits than external firms outside the cluster. This reflected the extra benefit of face-to-face exchanges within the cluster, adding to trust and reducing risks. The literature referred to previously mentioned this point with respect to the cluster-innovation link. Finally, the Internet enabled greater customization and differentiation of products and services. This benefit flowed from the greater presence of specialized firms, collaboration on supply chains, and joint product development and harnessing of complementary strengths and innovations. In a nutshell, relationship management is enhanced through the Internet.

In conclusion, we need to be mindful that the research conducted by Eng (2004) was intended to be emergent. It clearly applies to a fairly large concentration of firms in a high-tech industry. What is not known is whether the same drivers and factors (e.g., open systems) would work in smaller clusters and in less technologically intensive industries. Thus, although the findings may be tentative, Eng (2004) does support a very positive role for the Internet to improve the performance of clusters. Further, Eng (2004) reinforces the extra benefits of firms that belong to localized clusters rather than simply accessing remotely an Internet site. Based on this research, all clusters should consider the relevance of the Internet as a unique cluster for them, not simply as a communication device but as a tool to actively develop products and services and to manage supply chain processes better.

Before leaving this section, it can be noted that further research (possibly independent) reinforces the contribution of IT to clusters. In a study of Italian industrial districts, Carbonara (2005) found that information technology helped the cluster in the following ways:

- Improved communication with external parties and open networks that interconnect cluster firms with the global market

- Increased interaction, including information exchange among firms within the cluster

- Enhanced production and supply chain processes

Enhancing the Marketing Approach Through an E-Mall Solution

Eng's (2004) approach is not very specific about the exact nature or configuration of the Internet in facilitating the cluster. Our work proposes a specific Internet mechanism to contribute to the marketing role: an e-mall.

E-malls are not well researched, with a few exceptions: Dennis, Fenech, and Merrilees (2004), Hill (2000), and O'Hara (2001). As one would expect, e-malls usually cater to final consumers; for example, the British e-mall www.indigosquare.com and the American fashion e-mall www.fashion-world.com. There were some Australian examples (www.sofcom.au and www.ozeshopping.com.au), but they are now defunct. Nonetheless, there are cases of more industrial-based e-malls, such as one geared to American defense procurement (O'Hara, 2001). So anything is possible, which is the approach taken in this chapter.

The common feature of e-malls is that a common cyber site brings together a number of independently owned firms and other parties (e.g., universities). A single entity owns the e-mall, which, in our case, could be a cluster. Some form of central management is needed in order to manage the site in terms of developing the overall interface design and controlling the entry and exit of internal parties on the site and access by external parties. An e-mall could be an attractive way to bring together cluster members in particular industries such as wine or tourism, but there is also potential for any type of cluster, including IT firms.

If a cluster wishes to explore this option, it is referred to the work by Dennis, Fenech, and Merrilees (2004, chapter 9), which outlines a number of conditions for enhancing the performance of e-malls, including control of member mix quality, navigability, interactivity, and trust.

Conclusion

The context of this chapter is the somewhat mixed history of clusters in Australia. At any point in time, there seems to be enthusiastic support for clusters by industry and state or local governments. However, sustaining this enthusiasm has been a problem. We argue that the key to sustainability of clusters is the development of higher-level marketing and management capabilities and appropriate harnessing of information technology. Our attention to these priorities is consistent with Brown (2000), who suggests that failure to achieve distinctiveness and administrative difficulties are two of the three biggest challenges to clusters in Australia (and other countries, no doubt). We analyzed four major areas and concluded as follows.

First, stakeholder management has great potential to make clusters more cohesive. To this end, several stakeholder management propositions were put forward, including the need to develop supportive and tolerant cultures capable of integrating diverse members. Note that the stakeholder contribution is much more than simply having good communication.

Second, branding also has potential as an effective and powerful way to make the cluster distinctive in the market. Various branding propositions were put forward, including the need to build a brand platform. Developing a relevant and consistent brand to represent the diverse members of a cluster is a major challenge.

Third, the Internet can help to facilitate both marketing and management in the cluster. The Internet can increase effective communication among members, stimulate innovation, help to jointly develop products (services) and to streamline supply chain flows.

Fourth, a special application of the Internet is the e-mall. The cluster literature has not discussed this option. However, e-mall research by Dennis, Fenech, and Merrilees (2004) offers great potential to clusters. E-malls enable individual, independent parties to come together in a combined presence on a single site. Specialist e-malls, such as wine, fashion, or IT, are one option. Alternatively, multicategory malls also could be an option.

Implications for Cluster Stakeholders

The chapter reminds cluster stakeholders (e.g., firms or governments) that it is not easy to manage clusters effectively. Initial enthusiasm quickly can turn into conflict, confusion, and poor performance. Enthusiasm is needed, but sustainability of cluster development requires high levels of marketing and management capabilities. Some positive, proactive ideas were put forward to enhance the benefits of clusters, including:

- Using stakeholder management principles
- Using branding/marketing principles
- Using the Internet to facilitate marketing and management of the cluster
- Using e-malls, either single (specialist) or multiple categories, to enhance the branding and marketing of the cluster

Future Research

Although we have pursued new cluster governance structures in terms of stakeholder theory, other approaches are possible. For example, it would be useful to compare the different management and organizational approaches of successful vs. other clusters. The different management approaches unearthed from this comparison might have contributed to the success of clusters and, therefore, might guide the design of either new or weakly performing clusters.

To a large extent, we have focused on developing a conceptual framework that helps to integrate several aspects of designing, marketing, branding, and managing clusters. Key principles have been articulated in order to guide cluster development. Current and new clusters can use these principles to give themselves more insight into redesigning the cluster. In other words, the conceptual model can facilitate executive action with respect to improving cluster performance. Conversely, these principles can be used as propositions to guide future empirical research by academics in pursuing more empirical, quantitative research. This would enable the proposed conceptual framework to be tested in the field.

References

Baptista, R. (1996). Industrial clusters and technological innovation. *Business Strategy Review*, 7(2), 59–64.

Brown, R. (2000). *Clusters, innovation and investment: Building global supply chains in the new economy*. Canberra: Australian Project Developments Pty Ltd.

Bureau of Industry Economics. (1991). *Networks: A third form of organization*. Canberra: Australian Government Printing Service.

Caniels, M., & Romijn, H. (2003). SME clusters, acquisition of technological capabilities and development: Concepts, practice and policy lessons. *Journal of Industry, Competition and Trade*, 3(3), 187–210.

Carbonara, N. (2005). Information and communication technology and geographic clusters: Opportunities and spread. *Technovation, 25*, 213–222.

Colombo, M., & Delmastro, M. (2002). How effective are technological incubators? Evidence from Italy. *Research Policy, 31*, 1103–1122.

Dennis, C., Fenech, T., & Merrilees, B. (2004). *E-retailing*. London: Routledge.

Desrochers, P., & Sautet, F. (2004). Cluster-based economic strategy, facilitation policy and the market process. *The Review of Austrian Economics, 17*(2, 3), 235–245.

Eng, T. (2004). Implications of the Internet for knowledge creation and dissemination in clusters of hi-tech firms. *European Management Journal, 22*(1), 87–98.

Enright, M., & Roberts, B. (2001, August). Regional clustering in Australia. *Australian Journal of Management, 26*, 66–85.

Hill, S. (2000). To de-mall or e-mall? Shaping Web shopping. *Apparel Industry Magazine*, 36–37.

James, D., & Thomson, J. (2003, July 31-August 6). Why togetherness works. *Business Review Weekly*, 2003, 42–47.

Kelty, B. (1993). *Developing Australia: A regional perspective* [Report to the Federal Government by the Taskforce on Regional Development]. Canberra: National Capital Printing.

Liyanage, S. (1995). Breeding innovation clusters through collaborative research networks. *Technovation*, *15*(9), 553–567.

Marceau, J. (1999). The disappearing trick: Clusters in the Australian economy. In J. Guinet (Ed.), *Boosting innovation: The cluster approach* (pp. 155–176). Paris: OECD.

McKinsey & Company. (1994). *Lead local compete global: Unlocking the growth potential of Australia's regions*. Sydney: McKinsey & Company.

Mendleson, N., & Polonsky, M. (1995). Using strategic alliances to develop credible green marketing. *Journal of Consumer Marketing*, *12*(2), 4–18.

Merrilees, B., Getz, D., & O'Brien, D. (2005). Marketing stakeholder analysis: Branding the Brisbane goodwill games. *European Journal of Marketing*, *39*(3), 1060-1077.

Mitchell, R., Agle, B., & Wood, D. (1997). Toward a theory of stakeholder identification and salience: Defining the principle of who and what really counts. *Academy of Management Review*, *22*(4), 853–886.

Nasi, J., Nasi, S., Phillips, N., & Zyglidopoulos, S. (1997). The evolution of corporate social responsiveness. *Business Society*, *36*(3), 296–321.

National Economics. (2000). *State of the regions report*. Canberra: Australian Local Government Association.

O'Hara, C. (2001). Defense e-mall changes hands. *Federal Computer Week*, *19*(4), 1.

Pappas, Carter, Evans, Koop, & Telesis. (1990). *The global challenge—Australian manufacturing in the 1990s*. Melbourne: Australian Manufacturing Council.

Polonsky, M. (1995). A stakeholder theory approach to designing environmental marketing strategy. *Journal of Business & Industrial Marketing*, *5*(3), 29–46.

Polonsky, M. (2001). Strategic bridging within firm-environmental group alliances: Opportunities and pitfalls. *Academy of Management Executive*, *5*(2), 51–75.

Porter, M. (1998, November/December). Clusters and the new economics of competition. *Harvard Business Review*, 77–90.

Romijn, H., & Albaladejo, M. (2002). Determinants of innovation capability in small electronics and software firms in southeast England. *Research Policy*, *31*, 1053–1067.

Chapter III

Small and Medium Enterprise Clusters:
Marketing and Communication Management

Paola Falcone, University of Rome "La Sapienza," Italy

Abstract

Small and medium enterprise clusters can get consistent benefits from a specific joint marketing and communication strategy. This chapter intends to identify, describe, and interpret motivations and factors that influence a cluster-collective promotion strategy. It also identifies and describes possible operational tools that can be adopted by cluster metamanagement organizations with a specific focus on collective brands introduction and management.

Introduction

International economic environment has been living a constant economic, social, political, technical, and technological evolution. Apart from country-specific factors, global competition rules and dynamics have become harder and particularly selective for small and medium enterprises. Global hypercompetition has brought upon the business arena a massive group of new competitors from countries (e.g., the Asiatic ones) that exploit their social, economic, and regulatory differences and, thus, lower wages and the cost of labor, social costs, and the like, and impose price-competition dynamics that are difficult for firms in other countries to compete with.

This becomes particularly evident in traditional labor-intensive manufacturing sectors such as textiles, garments, and footwear, which suffer particularly from enlarged competition. In these sectors, product imitation (e.g., product and packaging counterfeiting) is easier. This kind of unfair competition, made through an illegal appropriation of the firms' brand names, extensively damages them.

Markets also have changed. Consumers change, and their desires and behaviors evolve, which changes their buying patterns. They have easier access to goods produced in other countries, and production places become far from the consumption ones. The growing amount of information and selection alternatives, always more accessible (often directly from producers through the Internet) and tailor-made, have made consumers more and more proactive, informed, and demanding.

Firms have to live in this environment and must adapt to it. They have to respond to these changes by revisiting their value chains and the sources of their specific competitive advantages. This means that they have to check and critically analyze processes, logics, and places of implementation for each operation in a metanational perspective (Doz, Santos & Williamson, 2001). Firms have to decide which role to play in their international game—leader, partner, satellite firm, or independent marginal player—and make their corporate and product strategies fit this role. For those who aim to become or confirm themselves as leaders or partners and also for those who want to survive in a more competitive scenario as satellite firms or independent marginal players, the word is the same: innovation.

The need for innovation requires firms to operate mainly upon two areas (Zanni & Labory, 2002):

1. Productive technologies and products by investing in R&D, new cost reducing or quality improving technologies, design, materials, lines, and processes.

2. Internal and international marketing strategies, specifically:

    •   Their communication strategy, choosing a distinctive strategic positioning and building a strong, recognizable brand and corporate image;

    •   Their distribution strategy through better control of networks and channels.

Investments in order to get improvements in these fields are not sustainable for small and medium-sized enterprises, mostly those regarding marketing strategies, because of commercial barriers that are difficult to overcome. Specific resources and competences are needed. Big firms already have them, or, if not, they can acquire them. The situation is different for small and medium-sized firms.

This chapter intends to analyze the benefits that small and medium-sized firms can find by belonging to a local, geographically defined cluster in order to be more effective in their marketing and communication strategies. It also aims at identifying and describing the advantages for the system, and for final consumers too.

After this explication, it identifies structural and firm-specific factors to be taken into consideration in order to craft an effective marketing and communication collective strategy.

The second part of the chapter is dedicated to the identification of the factors that influence cluster products image, the role of brands, and how products are perceived in regional and extra-regional markets.

The third part of the chapter analyzes operational tools that are useful in a marketing and communication collective strategy, with specific attention to the role of collective brands, and some related management issues.

Marketing and Communicating Cluster Firms Products

How Firms Can Take Advantage of Their Cluster Belongingness

As Pyke and Sengenberger (1992) pointed out, the real problem for many firms is not their dimension but their isolation. The cluster solution overcomes this unfavourable condition, because a firm inserted in a cluster is not alone.

An industrial cluster can be defined as "a geographically bounded concentration of similar, related or complementary businesses, with active channels for business transactions, communications and dialogue, that share specialized infrastructure, labour markets and services, and that are faced with common opportunities and threats" (Rosenfeld, 1997, p.10).

Inside a cluster, firms can find and develop forms of horizontal cooperation with other firms, share with them environmental threats, and get opportunities. They also can get the support of specific scaffolds (Lane, 2003) that are implemented by policymakers or other metamanagement players such as consortia, associations, and export consulting and trading companies. This is specifically interesting when it is applied to marketing and communication. An example is the California wine cluster, an effective system that counts several wine producers and wineries and that has the support of universities, research centers, and players that are dedicated to three levels of promotion activity: California wine country (the cluster), Californian wines (the local product), and specific wine brands (single firms' brands and products).

Firms that belong to clusters can share marketing and communication resources and competences such as a collective local brand (infra), an area image, and a collective management and/or consultancy. They also can plan and promote joint activities that concern analytical marketing, strategic marketing, and, above all, operational marketing such as collective promotional initiatives that are carried on both by private and public metamanagement organizations.

The possibility to share both marketing and communication resources and competences as well as joined activities realization in the field allows firms to have the following specific benefits:[1]

- They enrich their own resources and competences set.
- They become more efficient for costs reduction.
- They become more effective in their marketing activities in both domestic and international markets, since they can obtain better results than those obtainable by using their own resources, specifically getting:
  - More visibility
  - A better image
  - Better market penetration and a connected increased number of clients and revenues
  - Better products distribution
  - A better selling proposition definition
  - An enriched service package (Normann, 1984), thanks to the possibility of introducing new coproduced services as well as an enriched supplying system through higher quality standards.[2]

On these basis, small cluster manufacturing firms, as the ones in the Italian industrial districts, can concentrate better on their resources, as well as on organizational and productive quality issues, taking advantage of initiatives carried on with more qualified resources and superior investments.

Firms vertically connected in the cluster-productive value chain can find specific market advantages. In fact, providers find a privileged market within the cluster. Geographic proximity and regular interactions with their clients make their marketing a relationship-based one. This close interaction with manufacturing client firms enables providers to more easily develop contacts and contracts, better relationships, better order execution, and a better capability to meet customers' needs by tailor-made products and solutions. Providers, in fact, can take ideas for new products or services from their clients in order to offer improvements and upgrades. Both formal and informal multiple occasions to talk and easier and continued productive observations clearly allow needs and related solutions to emerge in a knowledge coproduction.[3]

Systemic Advantages

Besides advantages for firms, the entire local system can benefit by sharing marketing and communication resources and competences as well as copromoting activities. In fact, this can induce a higher efficiency, due to the absence of expensive and useless duplications of functions. The result, to which both firms and metamanagerial organizations contribute, is an increased local systemic competitiveness.

The system gets more specialized, gets specific target marketing knowledge, obtains scale and scope economies that are common resource for all cluster firms, and inherits new spin-off firms. Thanks to productive firms, the local system gets visibility for its distinctive competences.

The enriched systemic territorial competitiveness generates several benefits as higher levels of local employment, revenues, and specific image benefits, which are sometimes useful to other more or less related industries.

Local cluster competitiveness attracts external attention to the local system by media, investors, community, and opinion leaders, thus reinforcing the local system image. This can attract new capital and investments inside the area, not just for the presence of possible incentives such as tax reduction but for the virtues of the system.

In the case of typical products, the improved systemic territorial competitiveness and connected better reputation of the area at home and abroad also can sustain the promotion of incoming tourism.[4]

For the exposed reasons, it can be very dangerous for local institutions, as other metamanagerial organizations, neglect marketing development strategies and activities to area firms.

Clusters do not work automatically but need a specific management and support. This is evident in the case of the development policy of Indonesian districts, which did not get the best possible results (Tambunan, 2005), for some lacks and factors not properly driven, as an unsupported link with growing markets, national and international.

Advantages for Customers

The belongingness to a cluster enriches firms' resources and competences set and can modify their marketing mixes with specific consequences on customer value. In fact, customers also benefit from buying from a firm in a cluster. This is both indirect and direct.

Anything that enriches a firm's resources and competences indirectly benefits the customers, that buy, through firms' products, a bundle of symbolic, aesthetic, and functional values. A firm in a cluster allows customers to access a wider set of resources and competences. Many homogeneously specialized clusters, in fact, share their knowledge and often promote observatories to analyze qualitative trend consumptions in the field, which provides a cognitive resource for all the cluster firms in order to know their markets better. This generates a firm's capacity to adhere better to customers' demands.

But for customers, there are also direct advantages obtainable by buying from cluster firms who share their marketing and communication activities. In fact, this is accomplished through better product communication and distribution as well as specific projects of joint initiatives, common standards (as a guarantee quality label), joined services, and anything else that enriches a firm's selling proposition.

A more extended and better distribution makes it easier for customers to find other countries' goods;[5] better communication makes information about products and service more accessible to them, thanks to Internet sites and information portals. In addition, the spatial concentration of the cluster, often considered only from a productive point of view for its ability to generate localization economies and to reduce transaction costs, also provides several benefits to customers as they carry out their buying processes. This is specifically relevant in the phases of information search, definition of the set of alternatives, and products evaluation. As Marshall (1919) points out, "[T]here is also the convenience of the customer to be considered. He will go to the nearest shop for a trifling purchase; but for an important purchase he will take the trouble of visiting any part of the town where he knows that there are specialty good shops for his purpose. Consequently shops which deal in expensive and choice objects tend to congregate together; and those which supply ordinary domestic needs do not" (p. 273). Spatial proximity among firms gives the customer the chance to make an easier matching among different offerings, which creates comparison-shopping clusters (Mills, 1992). This is a specific benefit for industrial buyers.

An example is the high-fashion garment district, where national and international buyers arrive to see new models and fashion trends and have the opportunity to negotiate face-to-face regarding all contractual aspects. In the Internet era, some operations and transactions are still better if done in person.

Thus, clusters become like big shopping centers with many aggregated shop windows. Strictly proximal competition among cluster firms also can affect product pricing. Two solutions are possible:

- Cluster firms decide to make an arrangement (cartel) to keep prices to some medium-high level, which induces a reduction of consumer rent.
- Producers do not respect the arrangement or simply decide to keep prices free; this keeps prices lower than in case of arrangement, as in the typical competition model.

All these aspects (quality, communication, distribution, and pricing decisions) directly and specifically affect customers' value equations.

Structural and Firm-Specific Factors That Influence a Cluster Marketing and Communication Management

Supportive players within a cluster can promote, as said, coordination in cluster marketing and communication activities, planning, and managing joint initiatives. In order to be effective, a marketing and communication collective strategy at a cluster level has to be oriented by both cluster characteristics and marketing-specific needs of the firms within the cluster.

The following are the main cluster factors that affect marketing needs of cluster firms:

1. **Cluster-productive specialization:** A typical products cluster (e.g., the textile cluster) requires strategies and promotional tools that are different from a technology-based

cluster (e.g., electrobiomedical products); different are products, buying motivations, and buying behaviors use occasion and target and, finally, technology.

2. **Cluster relevance in the national and international competitive arena:** The more relevant the cluster, the stronger are its firms' marketing needs.

3. **Sector life cycle:** Clusters in the growth stage require different strategies and tools than mature ones do.

4. **Density of the cluster:** The cluster can be more or less concentrated and, thus, count a different number of small-medium-large firms.

5. **Presence of scaffolds and previous supportive actions toward cluster firms:** This directly influences firms' expectations of support.

Besides cluster factors, a marketing and communication collective strategy is influenced by firm-specific factors that determine firms' demands, expectations, and commitment to the actions by both policy makers and meta-management organizations.

The following are firm-specific factors that affect marketing needs of cluster firms:

1. **Company size:** In a resource-based perspective, small and medium-sized enterprises specifically need supportive scaffolds in order to develop their marketing strategies; they are conscious of the advantages of cluster membership, so they usually are co-operative, motivated, and active players in the cluster.

2. **Degree of openness to both national and international markets:** Through cluster initiatives, small firms can get a major international openness. An example is Italian industrial district firms, typically small and medium-sized, which, thanks to the district's joint activities, adopted an international marketing perspective. For firms operating only on the regional market, marketing needs are more reduced. These players do not take full short-time benefits from the cluster activity, but by the effect of being inserted into an internationally open system, they can get competences, relations, and stimuli necessary to cultivate the ambition to get an ampler market perspective.

3. **Role in the cluster productive chain:** Providing firms such as subcontractors find their market within the cluster; so they get their marketing advantages simply by their strategic locations inside the cluster close to their clients through the intrinsic social and relational value of the cluster, apart from its management. On the contrary, manufacturing firms that are usually open to an extra-cluster market specifically find in the metamanagement initiatives an important support for their activities.

4. **A firm's reputation in the cluster and, in general, in the sector:** This parameter, which is connected to the previously identified ones, can be combined usefully with cluster relevance in the national and international competitive arena (see Figure 1). A firm can be the following:

    a. **An international leader:** The firm is a leader in its cluster, and the cluster has an international leadership.

    b. **A courtisan:** The firm is a small player in a cluster that has an international leadership in its sector.

Figure 1. Firm's competitive position within the cluster, compared to the importance of the cluster in international competition

		INTERNATIONAL ROLE OF THE CLUSTER	
FIRM'S COMPETITIVE POSITION INSIDE THE DISTRICT	LEADER	INTERNATIONAL LEADERSHIP	LOW RELEVANCE
		TOP LEADER	NEIGHBOR BOSS
	SMALL PLAYER	COURTISAN	ANT

c. **A neighbor boss:** The firm is a leader in its cluster, but the cluster has a low relevance in international competition.

d. **An ant:** The firm is a small player in a cluster that has a low relevance in international competition.

Leaders in a cluster that is relevant in the international arena are top leaders and global players, so they probably can be self-sufficient in their marketing and communication activities, having less interest to carry along small district enterprises. The interest they can have is to preserve their local image within the local system, which confirms their leadership role and avoids possible sanctions that a closed small group can direct in response to opportunistic behaviors, as in the clan mechanism (Ouchi, 1980). The firm can feel the responsibility to act as an older brother to small local firms, sharing in the territory some of what it has been able to gain in the international competitive dynamic. This is not a strategic firm need for its intrinsic strength upon the national or even international markets but an entrepreneurship's personal need to preserve his or her social image in the local environment in which he or she and the firm have to live. This strictly depends on the social economy embeddedness in clusters (Granovetter, 1985).[6]

On the contrary, the leader in a cluster that is not specifically relevant in the international dynamic is similar to a neighbor boss and surely will have a higher degree of local involvement in order to preserve its consensus. If the firm is aspiring to entering international markets, it can try to use the cluster membership to get the necessary strength and resources.

In the case of a small firm operating in an internationally relevant cluster as a courtisan, it can desire to try to consolidate its international leadership or possibly to improve its position. If the cluster is relevant and the firm is a follower, it can be moved to act autonomously with a less cooperative behavior in order to get some points of market share and thus emerge.

The last case is the one of a small player inserted in a cluster with no international relevance. As an ant, its behavior is supposed to be highly cooperative, because its chances to survive depend on the group.

Clusters, Brands, and Products Image

Cluster Identity and Image

Cluster metamanagement organizations work to get consolidation and improvement of the cluster role and image on the national and international competitive arena.

Not rarely clusters have a very strong identity. Especially those that specialize in handi-craft-typical products date back several centuries,[7] and thus, they have a valuable historical heritage that consists of productive and cultural traditional local roots connected to the territory, which has been preserved through the years by families. This strong identity that is based on territorial roots is also present in products that use place-specific natural resources (agro-food-typical products) and may be present even in modern design products in which the product is an expression of local taste and productive tendency. Such a strong identity is a strategic asset for the cluster as well as for its enterprises, because it is absorbed by products and comes to consumers wherever they live.

Thus, cluster identity has to be valorized by local cluster coordinators and managers in terms of its image, because a favorable brand concept through mental associations connected to it is functional for market success (Keller, 1993). A good definition of firm reputation—"if consumers believe its products to be of high quality" (Shapiro, 1983, p. 659)—can be applied to clusters, too.

So the development of cluster image helps to promote the products of firms that operate under its umbrella.

The Image of Cluster Products on the Extra-Cluster Market

How product image influences consumers' choice processes is a long-time studied mechanism (see, among others, Firat & Schultz, 1997; Keller, 2002): customers buy a product to get the perceived value in its image. Firms invest in corporate and product image in order to build their reputations in markets by sending consumers different but connected messages through time. Different messages are interpreted and composed socially and thus form a puzzle in the consumer's mind and, as a result, generate his or her attitude toward the product.

A good image through a high reputation stimulates a firm's demand, attracting and fidelizing clients, and allows firms to do the following:

- Increase production and sales.
- In the presence of capacity constraints (Segre, 2003) raise prices and improve profits by asking a premium price and operating as a quality signal and element of differentiation from competitor's offers.

As Stigler (1961) remarked, "'Reputation' is a word which denotes the persistence of quality, and reputation commands a price (or exacts a penalty) because it economizes on search" (p. 79).

A positive image of the provenience place in the case of a cluster with a specific productive specialization can become a source of competitive advantage for firms operating in it. In fact, this positive cluster image can support its firms' products with a regional made-in effect (Johansson, Douglas & Nonaka, 1985; Han & Terpstra, 1988; Roth & Romeo, 1992), a place-based reputation effect (Molotch, 1996; Scott, 1999, 2001; Henchion & McIntyre, 2000) occurring if the location where the firm operates and where products are supposed to be made[8] influences their properties and characteristics in a relevant way.

A rich literature (see, among others, Levy, 1959; Hirschmann & Holbrook, 1982; Khan, Dhar & Wertenbroch, 2005) has described that consumption is not limited to functional values but, according to the kind of product, also considers aesthetic and symbolic values; both utilitarian and hedonistic motivations take part in consumers' buyer behaviors, which is specifically true for experience goods (Nelson, 1970, 1974) such as typical products that have a specific experiential value. For their strong link to the territory, they satisfy a need of roots for those people not living in their region and mostly for those not living in their home country.[9] Rather, in the case of country estimators, these products can satisfy the desire even for a moment to feel like they belong to or just "meet" places and communities.

The territory also can be a specific reason to buy credence goods[10] (Darby & Karny, 1973). Also by consumption acts, people define themselves and build their self identity (McCracken, 1993; Ouwersloot & Tudorica, 2001). The desire to know and live new experiences moves consumers toward what is new, far, and exotic. In times of globalization, after the big flow of general, global product offers of the 1980s, differences are appreciated by customers (Storper, 1997) that feed their natural need of novel stimuli and connected variety-seeking behaviors (Vankatesan, 1973; Kahn & Ratner, 2005). In fact, a product coming from a different region or a different country carries with it the values of the territory from which it comes and of which it is an expression, or maybe it just carries with it those values that consumers attribute to the territory on the basis of a specific mental association. Thus, an area-specific mix of natural, social, productive, and cultural characteristics influence products realization and differentiate their essence (Molotch, 2003). This differentiation can be:

- Resource-based, as in the case of Sicilian wines produced by a mix of atmospheric conditions, specific soil conditions, and local productive knowledge, which guarantees a certain quality of product, gives it distinctive characteristics, and thus makes it unique.

- Competence-based, as in the case of Paris, Roman, or Milan haute couture, whose products can benefit from the set of subcontractors and special materials to make their suits and dresses but also from specific competences, manufacturing techniques, and learning.

- Internal-market-demand-based, as in the case of the Californian Big Style interior design and furniture products, such as sofas, made on the basis of apartments that are usually ampler than UE ones and, thus, larger and more comfortable, which have been appreciated and recognized as specific by foreign markets (Street-Porter, 1986; Molotch, 2003).

In all cases, markets attribute an added value to products origin; the indication of the cluster of origin becomes a sort of trademark that goes beyond the value of the company brand.

This recognizable and distinctive element influences product image and its strategic positioning toward competitors, as some research works have shown (Han, 1989; Tse & Gorn, 1993).

The value of country-of-origin label is described by Clemens and Babcock (2004) regarding the New Zealand lamb mark: "As a country, New Zealand cultivates a 'clean green' image and the perceptions about lifestyle and values implied by this image, especially in marketing the country as a tourist destination. These promotional efforts have had a strong, positive carry-over effect for New Zealand's agricultural products, and the New Zealand meat industry has adopted the image in promotional campaigns in international markets" (p.9). As the authors show, the strong mental association is products coming from New Zealand = healthy and high quality products. In some cases, the country of origin acts as a product quality guarantee (Henchion & McIntyre, 2000). For example, Biørn (1982, cited by Andersen, 1994), in trying to explain why Danish butter became a leader in the British market, attributes it to the presence of "the uniform good quality, the even supply during the twelve months of the year, and the unqualified trust in the genuineness of the butter" (p. 33). Customers simply trusted Danish producers and considered them able to produce a good, genuine butter.

The role of the country-of-origin label also clearly emerges from an opposite example. In the 19th century, U.S. firms producing marmalades, gelatines, and pickles (Goody, 1982), in consideration of the negative attitude toward these kinds of products made in the U.S., sold them abroad with a made-in-England label. With that label, products were accepted more by extra-U.S. markets, because England's reputation in the field was better. But in addition to this functional value, those products keep inside the characteristics of their origin country and promise the customer a mostly cognitive and somehow sensorial[11] experience; through product buying, consuming and/or using, just for a moment customers can get a piece of local atmosphere in a cheaper and easier way than visiting the region or country (Molotch, 2003).

The experience can be reinforced by a visual communication support for those elements the firms can decide to use upon the packaging of the product. The more detailed and evocative the firm's communication is, the richer is the customer experience. The narration of cluster identity transforms and enriches customers' product buying and consuming behavior, making it a cultural, living experience that helps to develop a trust-based relationship with the cluster and the firm.

Products, as said, create sorts of access relationship networks (Rifkin, 2000), and customers pay to enter them, even for just a short time. In this perspective, price is a sort of pay per use. In the case of a cluster that already has worked on its own image promotion, has created sense, and has given meaning to its name, firms belonging to it usefully can leverage the cluster-made-in effect merely by citing places and concepts that will evoke in the consumer's mind the specific atmosphere and associated image. This also can be in the case of unknown producers. In other terms, the market cannot know the single manufacturer, but the fact that it and its products come from that specific location makes the product appealing.[12]

Therefore, a local cluster's good image gives a common reputation advantage to each member firm and can be used by exploitation of its rent (Scott, 2000). This leverage effect gives the following two advantages to firms in communicating their products:

- The gain of better results with fewer investments in communication, and so communication costs reduction

- A major strength in their own communication, because customers give the cluster of origin sense and significances, which enriches the buying and fruition and generates customer value.

The Product and Internal Market: Externalities for Extra-Cluster Markets

The same examined for extra-cluster markets variables affect internal markets' perceptions of internal products. Obviously, the place effect (i.e., country of origin image, regional imagery, and cluster productive image) is less relevant, because consumers live in the region.

Evaluation for internal brands are supposed to be more brand- or firm-related. Internal customers also should know more about products and firms than do extra-cluster customers; this information can concern the types of input quality, transformation processes, quality tests, hygiene measures, and so forth, and can be more diffused by workers by word of mouth.

Besides, internal markets are the first to test products and generally are supposed to be a more selective and demanding target than foreign ones are (Storper, 1997; Molotch, 2005). This is especially true for those cases of productive specialization connected to a specific local consumption of a product, and related preference and knowledge. An example is South American markets of coffee; a brand that imposes itself on these markets has more credits abroad, because it has passed a hard selection. On the contrary, brands that are not strong enough to compete on a more selective domestic market decide to offer their products to an extra-cluster target market. Several are the cases, in fact, of brands that reach popularity abroad, where product standards and expectations are lower or where they can exploit a foreign country-of-origin positive effect, remaining quite unknown in their country of provenience.[13]

Even though domestic markets are supposed to be more selective than foreign ones and the mentioned place effect variables are scarcely relevant, there is an exception in the case of consumer ethnocentrism that is "a consumer preference for domestically produced products or, conversely, a bias against imported products" (Huddlestone, Good & Stoel, 2001, p. 238).

In this case, consumers prefer their regional products for more or less rational[14] reasons. It is interesting to note, as some research has shown (Sharma, Schimp & Shin, 1995), that in the case of need of a product, this effect on consumer behavior appears to be moderated.

A Cluster Firm's Image and Branding Policy

Brands have both identification and qualification functions (Aaker, 1991; Keller, 2002) and become a powerful factor in buying decisions. For example, in cases of nonobservable quality (both experience and credence goods) (Rao, Qu, & Ruekert, 1997; Shapiro, 1983) by customers, brands can make credible the firm's offer.

Referring to the buyer behavior model, the brand influences the process from the first stage of information search (Ouwersloot & Tudorica, 2001; Bristow, Schneider & Schuler, 2002). If a firm's product is well-known and has a good reputation, it will be inserted in the evaluation set. In the following alternatives evaluation phase, products with a strong brand can get a competitive plus, and even in customers' post-buying stages, brands reveal their importance, because they are able to influence expected quality and so condition customers' perceptions about products. The brand mediates the relationship between the firm and its markets.

Consumers establish relationships with chosen brands; social relationships among people are usually functional, emotional, or sociocultural (Ouwersloot & Tudorica, 2001), and something not so dissimilar happens for brands in consideration of the kind of product. Functional relationships are essentially rational and affect the cognitive area; sociocultural relationships (Holt, 2005) are mediated by cultural and subcultural received inputs, while emotional relationships are elective for noncognitive reasons.

Clearly, a product brand can propose functional more than emotional or sociocultural benefits if it is a technology-intensive product; on the contrary, a manufacturing product can have stronger emotional and sociocultural values by using its contest of origin. This happens if a brand image has been built properly through time by a codefinition process made by both firms through the branding strategy[15] and the markets, positively perceiving, interpreting, and accepting brand associations in their associative network memory model (Poiesz, 1989).

These associations are not abstract, as cultural research regarding symbolism has shown (Mick & Buhl, 1992; Holt, 2005) that brand symbolism is the result of a market recognition and a sense-shared interpretation "in terms of concrete stories and images" (Holt, 2005, p. 276). "Every good brand has a story behind it" (Martin, p.7, cited in Clemens and Babcock, 2004), which is especially true for those iconic brands that become myths,[16] so it is really important for firms or their communication agencies to be able to narrate this story.

An effective brand image building is a prerequirement in order to develop a customer-based brand equity, a familiarity with the brand (i.e., a favorable mental association and connected differentiation) (Keller, 1993), which originates a market response that can be both of the following:

- Attitudinal (e.g., the develop of a positive attitude toward the brand)
- Behavioral (e.g., a shopping action).

Both responses are useful for firms, as the former is relevant to induce the latter. Brand equity development is also important for firms for its consequences on product distribution; in fact, a product with a strong brand has better distribution chances (Aaker, 1991) in domestic as well as international markets.

In the case of a cluster firm, the set of variables that influence its products brand image is a bit more complex than in case of a single firm. A model to analyze how cluster products brand image results and what its main determinants are is illustrated in Figure 2. The resulting brand image of a product made in a cluster is the result of several factors, some fully controlled by the firm, some not, some others just in part, but all influencing brand image and each other. The firm can directly control its products with its attributes and brand artifacts.

A firm's image and brand personality are codefined with markets. Brand personality is enriched by brand associations, which can be the following (Holden & Lutz, 1992; Krishnan, 1996):

- Product-related in terms of functional concrete associations (Keller, 1998)
- Nonproduct-related, image-based associations (Biel, 1993), and brand artifacts (Ouwersloot & Tudorica, 2001), specific users' stories, testimonials for advertising campaigns, symbols, logos, and so forth

A firm's image is influenced by and can be sustained by some not directly controllable factors such as the country of origin image, the regional imagery and culture, and the cluster—productive image. These variables can be influenced positively by cluster metamarketing and communication activities.

The country of origin generates, as said, a made-in effect, which appears to influence consumer behavior more in those cases in which customers are "unfamiliar with the product or the manufacturing company" (Niss, 1995, p.10).

This country-of-origin effect can be combined positively or negatively with the following:

- The regional imagery and culture; that is, the set of "an individual's beliefs, impressions, ideas and evaluations of different parts of the country" (Burgess, 1982); this imagery results from eventual personal traveling experiences, readings, or other

Figure 2. Brand image of a cluster firm's products (Source: Author's modification and enrichment from Ouwersloot & Tudorica, 2001)

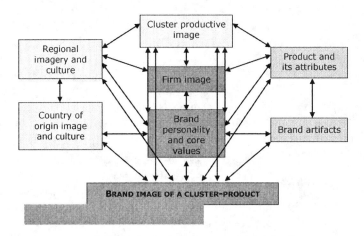

Note:

☐ Factors not controlled by the firm

▨ Factors controlled by the firm

▨ Factors co-defined by firm and markets

people's narrations. But above all, regional imagery is mediated by a social and cultural representation (Holt, 2005) of those places, highly influenced by specific factors such as media, advertising, and even movies (Henchion & McIntyre, 2000).

• The cluster productive image made up of a set of resources and, most of all, competences that are recognized as a cluster's specific assets.[17]

A positive loop is made up of a reciprocal validation; for example, a cluster that specializes in dairy products can better reach markets in which both the region and the country have a positive green image, as the previously cited New Zealand case, and/or a generally favorable image in the food industry. There also can be reciprocal validation in the case of complementary sectors in which the symbolic regional imagery (Holt, 2005) is the common link. An example is a Hollywood movie production cluster, a symbol of star system and beauty, which is validated as a country of origin and use also for some cosmetic producers. This is a case of demand based place influence upon products image.

More difficult is the case of a technological district inserted into a country with different diverging values and symbols; in this case, the cluster has to develop a specific communication in order to build a reliable image.[18] This also can happen in a case of a multi-specialization region in which images can interfere with each other and not give a coherent, compact image.

Thus, the definition of cluster firms products image is the result of all the previously cited factors, which are all connected so that one validates (Niss, 1995) or invalidates the other on consumers' maps. Each factor and the resulting cluster firms product image is the consequence of a sense cocreating process made by multiple interpretive communities (see, among others, Kates, 2001) (e.g., other firms, forces, and mostly internal and extra-cluster consumers).

Cluster firms can have a specific advantage by the cluster complex structure made of interconnected variables and players by reducing their single investments and relying upon the collective cluster marketing and communication strategy. Obviously, this kind of strategy is not able to build strong brands, and none of the firms will emerge from its cluster. But it is a cost-saving strategy and can support a small regional producer that arrives on the national or international market.

Cluster Marketing and Communication

Management of Coordinated Promotional Activities at a Cluster Level

Clusters need to be promoted systemically. In fact, single promotion initiatives carried on individually by firms cannot be as systemic, coordinated, or balanced in tone, message, regularity, or coverage. In addition, their promotion is self-oriented, not cluster-oriented.

Thus, metamanagement supportive institutions (i.e., export consortia, local chambers of commerce, local policymakers) are called to promote the cluster and thus its firms and products (Powell & Smith-Doerr, 1994) by valorization of the cluster image on national and international markets. Sometimes they use national support that comes from national institutions devoted to give financial and consulting/training support.

Some initiatives are aimed at getting a better knowledge and, thus, a better marketing plan, such as the production of market analysis and research reports, seminars with experts and specific meetings, and consultant and technical assistance in approaching a specific country market and the related distribution system.

Some initiatives work directly on customer value equations through an intervention upon firms' marketing mixes and, thus, concern the following:

- Products, as they are aimed at giving homogeneity to the regional offer of different producers through the definition of standards regarding both the input and the transformation process.[19]
- Branding, by choosing to get a collective brand for local manufacturers (infra).
- Pricing by defining a standard, collective price (cartel) for the goods that are sold in foreign markets.
- Distribution by drawing up contracts with foreign countries' trading companies or distribution chains in order to place cluster products on their shelves, or by directly contacting big clients in order to arrange for a continuous supply of local products.
- Promotion, such as the organization and connected joint participation in promotional exhibitions or sectoral fairs, by drawing up contracts with foreign countries' trading companies or distribution chains, and so forth. Through these interventions, firms benefit from a collective regional promotion, which can be a good basis on which to build their own images in national as well as international markets.

Sometimes collective support of promotion activities involves different districts with the same productive specialization, as in debates, discussions, and sometimes the same collective brand.

Operational Promotional Tools

Metamanagement organizations have a wide range of operational promotion tools in order to implement their marketing and communication collective strategy. Briefly described here are some of the most used and effective ones, with some examples of application taken from recent Italian industrial districts' marketing experiences.[20] The following are complementary and versatile tools, because each of them helps more or less to obtain diverse benefits: promote district identity-image, communicate activities, and directly promote initiatives and products.

Initiatives Targeted for Internal Markets

Cluster identity has to be strengthened first from the inside. This is important for local customers but more so for district firms' workers and citizens. Sometimes districts lose their attractiveness; small countries see their populations getting old and unable to retain young people.[21] If a district declines socially and culturally, it is difficult to build any kind of external image; so a strategic positioning strategy has to start from the inside. It can be useful, for example, to stimulate meetings and debates with entrepreneurs and students, which helps to generate commitment around the district project, thanks to the association of young entrepreneurs, which gives a more dynamic image to the status and makes it more attractive to new generations.

Conservation and Exhibition of Materials That Are Part of the District Historical Evolution

District memory is a fundamental value in the typical mix of the social and economic base inside the district. No image can be built or be believable and appreciated by markets if the district's identity roots have been neglected. District management has to work to preserve identity, which thus needs to be protected and made accessible through time. This goal can be obtained by both museums and data banks. Fitting out production museums is a fascinating project. Some firms have their own museums, but a district museum has a higher local identity sense due to its collective social and cultural imaginary. The museum keeps and preserves traces of the past, catalogues and organizes them, and reconstructs the district historical memory made up of cultural and productive local traditions. Visitors who enter a cluster museum meet this memory through the collection of working clothes, old manual machines, and rusted tools.

External visitors can learn a lot about a district from its museum, but citizens, entrepreneurs, and workers also know that traditions and past are the roots of the district image and its product image. They are aware of the fact that any search for productive or technological innovation must begin there.

Training Specialization Courses

Usually, the organization of training courses is considered a human resource management tool. In the case of the district, these kinds of initiatives also have image-positive consequences, because they show a cluster knowledge-related image. The cluster is perceived as a production as well as a learning and training context for specialized workers. This lets the cluster attract people who are motivated to learn productive traditional or rather the most modern productive techniques. This competence-based mental association, a synonym for higher products quality, reinforces cluster products image. An example is the prestigious gold manufacturing schools located in the districts in Arezzo and Valenza Po, where young scholars learn how to craft handmade jewels.

Building a Cluster Internet Portal

In addition to firms' Internet sites, districts usefully can build collective portals. The creation of a common portal can give firms and the cluster itself several advantages, such as the following:

- Presenting the district and its firms to customers, providers, and interested people with a coordinated image, a synonym of district organization and compactness
- Producing information centralization
- Giving complete and updated information regarding district initiatives

In addition to these advantages, a cluster portal also makes firms aware of the importance of an effective Internet strategy, which induces them to think about the quality of their actual Internet presence. Besides, a cluster portal also can be used as an internal communication tool that creates an intranet for all district firms.

Launching Collective Advertising Campaigns (National and International)

Advertising campaigns are important in order to communicate about the district, its identity, its image, and its activities to potential and effective customers, providers, opinion leaders, and the public. Mature manufacturing districts will create a sort of ideal cognitive and emotional continuity between the past (e.g., tradition, culture, etc.) and the present of the district, addressing them to national and international markets. Communication also will remark the cluster distinctive cases, as the use of specific materials and/or manufacturing techniques, product uniqueness, and related prestige. On the other hand, hi-tech districts will point out their investments in R&D activities, the degree of technological innovation their productions have reached, and the modernity of chosen materials.

Production of Information Materials for Trade and Opinion Leaders

For the district, it is also important to prepare some informative materials such as newsletters, brochures, electronic materials, CD-ROMs, and videos. Clearly, the quality of the presented material (i.e., content and aesthetics of presentation) is fundamental in order to give a positive image of the district.

Samples and Gadgets Production

Samples and gadgets are useful for district image. People usually like them and use them, thus diffusing the district logo. Sometimes, district gadgets are high quality and specifically creative.[22]

External Relations

High-level public relations are relevant to district promotion in both formal and informal interpersonal meetings. One possibility is to invite political and/or economic delegations of foreign countries that are potentially growing markets.

Competitions and Prize Organization

This kind of initiative is specifically creative. Ideas and project competitions and prizes are one way to raise people's interest in the cluster. In fact, they get people (e.g., customers, providers, general public) closer to the district, make them observe and analyze it, and then create something concerning the activity done inside of it.

There is only one winner, but all participants come into cognitive and sometimes geographical contact with the district. Besides, the media will be interested in talking about it. Private buyer-seller contracts are not interesting, but a competition is, which is one reason district metamanagement institutions for example willing to design or restyle a cluster logo sometimes decide to launch a competition. Ceremonies to award the winner are also public relations occasions. An example is GoldSign, the international competition launched in the Arezzo district in 2005 for golden jewels young designers.

In other cases, the competition does not ask for a project effort. A very original case is the case of Textile Olimpic Games promoted in the Prato textile district in 2005, a real competition among teams made up of workers in all textile national districts that compete in some ability, strength, and creativity competitions[23]. This sportive initiative has both internal and external communication goals. First of all, it is an occasion to stimulate motivation and firm belongingness. It is also an occasion to let the most relevant industrial players meet during scheduled roundtable sessions parallel to competitions to talk about industry trends and to launch new proposals. In addition, its originality is a way to attract public and media interest in the sector and, specifically, the district.

Events and Special Evening Organization

Special events such as concerts, fashion shows, gala dinners, and art exhibitions (organized as sponsored) can be ways to attract target and media interest in the district and its activity.

Participation in International Industry Fairs

Metamanagement institutions participate in organizing the most attractive international sectoral fairs on the basis of the expected target audience. They support firms in stand design and equipment, in brochures and other document preparation, and in event and meeting planning with emergent key market interlocutors (e.g., distributors, importers, local authorities). Entrepreneurs are accompanied by trade analysts who are experts in their fields.

Organization of Industry Fairs and Ad Hoc Promotional Initiatives

Sometimes clusters decide to organize and promote fairs by themselves in order to attract a certain number of qualified and potentially interested buyers. Usually, costs are shared by organizing institutions and participating firms. In other cases, district metamanagement institutions in their trade assistance programs organize missions, workshops, and business-to-business meetings with selected country buyers in order to show the firm's new collections.

During these ad hoc initiatives abroad, typical local food products are offered to foreign interlocutors. In this way, they try to reinforce through taste sensation the experience of the territory. In order to establish a more effective mental association with the territory and to let interlocutors get a better feeling of it, visual communication can be helpful; thus, stands often reproduce peculiar regional landscapes or diffuse country music.

Creating a Collective Brand for the Cluster Firms

Collective Brands for Cluster Firms

A very relevant marketing and communication tool for clusters is the adoption of a collective brand. A collective brand establishes a diffused property right (Segre, 2003) as the origin denomination that can be used by more than one firm. It can be created and registered by any private or public actor such as cooperatives, associations, consortia, district committees, and service centers. Firms that are willing to use the collective brand have to respect some predefined standards and are subjected to periodic controls. A collective brand is a marketing and communication resource shared among cluster firms. Sometimes the use of the collective brand is subjected to the payment of an annual fee.

In Box 1, three collective brands taken from different Italian industrial districts' experiences are described. Obviously, a collective brand has the same necessities as individual brands and thus needs to be communicated and promoted (officially launched through a conference with the press and then sustained) in order to be alive and recognizable and to make sense to consumers. Otherwise, despite its design efforts, it is just a visual sign on the product, a label attached to it or more frequently on its packaging, with no specific meaning to customers (Henchion & McIntyre, 2000). A similar situation is also less motivating for adopting firms.

On the contrary, if the collective brand is well-promoted, its use can provide several advantages to the adopters.

A collective brand has a guarantee function: it guarantees the product's origin, nature, and quality (Alberti & Sciascia, 2004). In the case of clusters[24], it often contains the country of origin denomination. In this case, it reinforces the value of the product's origin and helps to promote the territory and its image. At the basis is a problem of reputation. As Tirole (1996) shows, collective reputation affects and, in turn, is affected by the conduct and

Box 1. Three examples of collective brands for different kind of products

---

Case A: A brand for typical food products of Lodi

www.provinciadilodi.it

source:

The brand Lodigiano Terra Buona (the Lodi area is a good land) is a brand made and promoted by local institutions for the development and control of products supply chain and the agricultural services operating in the territory.

The brand is colorful with naïve drawings of different subjects that evoke elements of local productions. The collective marketing action intends to valorize production activities and typical products of the territory regarding quality, integrity, and hygiene standards through a system of tracking.

It also aims to valorize environmental protection through a set of product standards to be respected by firms. An independent controlling organism periodically controls firms' behaviors.

Case B: A collective brand for the sportswear district in Montebelluna

The district located in the Montebelluna area is specialized in the production of high-quality sports footwear (e.g., ski boots, ice skates, motorbike boots).

source: www.museoscarpone.it

---

reputation of each cluster member. A collective brand can act as a quality signal with an image advantage for all firms that are allowed to use it (Choi, Lee & Oh, 1995; Gergaud & Livat, 2004). If all cluster members respect a specific set of standards[25], a collective brand reputation is supported and all members benefit from it. Standards pose firms' offers within a quality min-max range.

Thus, a collective brand stimulates market expectations of almost equivalent quality for the products labeled with it, which produces a reputation linkage, although unknown, for all firms adopting it (Erdem, 1998; Landon & Smith, 1998). As Marshall (1919) already recognized, standards are to facilitate consumers' buying processes, especially for difficulties in the evaluation of product quality. This is specifically true for both experience and credence goods, which have a specific need for reputation and are sometimes characterized by information asymmetries between producers and consumers.

Box 1. continued

The district decided to get a new collective brand that had to be coherent with the productive image of the cluster and its export vocation. The brand name Montebelluna Sportsystem directly links it to the local productive specialization. The brand mark is consistent with sectoral firms' logos that often show geometrical abstract elements. The sign, similar to an arrow, should give the idea of dynamism, which is typical of sports, and be valid for different kinds of sports for which district firms design their products. The sign is inspired by 1930s futurist paintings that were Italian typical works that had sports and sportsmen as subjects.

Case C: The Brand Seri.co for Silk Textile Producers

The brand Seri.co, launched in 2001, is a quality brand that carries in its brand name the kind of product and place of realisation. The brand acts as a guarantee about the high quality of the silk textile, and productive system. It certifies the quality of both products and firms.

source: www.seri.co.it

The brand is strictly territorially connected, as it displays a blue sign that has the shape of Como Lake (Alberti & Sciascia, 2004) but does not have strict territorial belonging conditions in order to be used. In fact, the committee left its use open to other Italian districts' silk producers, as long as they respect the given production standards in terms of quality and safeness for consumers. In addition, the mark asks adopting firms to respect deontological codes, environmental protection, and workers' safe conditions, and to guarantee the condition that at least two phases of the production process are made in Italy.

The presence of a standards-related common reputation makes each player aware of the fact that the single member's success depends on but also contributes to the whole cluster's success. Conversely, errors made by single members have their consequences on the collective brand image and the reputation of all the firms using it. This should make firms control each other in a state of reciprocal strict correlation.

The existence of a quality standards range can pose two main problems. The first is the risk to inibit innovation in adopting firms; customers get a standardized product from cluster firms, which exposes cluster firms to the competition of other noncluster innovating firms. The second problem is related to internal cluster dynamics. The presence of standards can induce opportunistic firms to try to put in action free-rider behaviors. In fact, aware of the shirking possible effect, a firm can offer products with a slightly inferior quality than average but within the range, saving costs and making profits. So, the risk is that standards flatten quality toward the inferior limit, penalizing firms that are oriented to a better quality. This orientation, if general, reduces quality, exposing even more cluster firms to extra-cluster competition. These are the most recurrent problems appearing to be connected to a collective brand adoption.

On the contrary, collective brands do not seem to create economic convenience problems to adopting firms, as operators sometimes think. In fact, as Andersson (2002) shows (see also Gergaud & Livat, 2004), profits obtained by a firm that produces two high-quality products under a collective brand are not inferior to the sum of the profits obtained by two firms making high-quality products with their own brands.

Collective Brands and Firms' Brands

Collective brands can have problems of coexistence with individual firms' brands. As long as a firm's brand is not particularly affirmed, the problem is not relevant; on the contrary, in the case of a leading firm's brand, the relationship between the two can be at risk.

The collective brand image strength also is due sometimes to the image of its top leading manufacturer. According to Gergaud and Livat (2004), "The group's reputation is a simple computation of its most famous members' reputation" (pp. 24–25). A collective brand reduces marketing costs (Segre, 2003) and, specifically, transactional costs, because it works as a guarantee that helps to build a trust relationship between the enterprise and its markets. As observed by Tirole (1996), those lesser known smaller firms (i.e., those players whose actions previously have not been observable), not the leaders, benefit most from collective reputation resources. That is to say that a leader known by the market for its long-lasting successful presence does not specifically need a collective brand and, thus, probably will have a weaker commitment to its introduction.

The problem is in the specific dynamic of a collective brand. At the very beginning stage of its introduction (Segre, 2003), firms act cooperatively, because their interests coincide and the new initiative gains some enthusiasm in the business community. Later, firms' commitment risks go down, and some firms compete with their own brands. This happens because in the group everyone is responsible for the group's value and take the risk of becoming less visible as part of the whole.

Besides, if a producer offers a quality product that is superior to the standard quality offered by other firms in the cluster under the same collective brand, then it will have to evaluate the alternative to exit the collective brand and to just compete with its own brand. This problem is connected directly to the described problems related to standards adoption. In these cases, the problem is solved by a previous analysis of the structure of the district and subsequent negotiation with leading firms.

If the cluster is fragmented and made up of several small players, and if the product can almost be standardized, then the collective brand can be dominant. This was the case in the introduction of the collective Danish butter brand, also cited by Marshall (1919). Dairy cooperatives that up until then sold their butter abroad through export associations, adopted by governmental indication a collective national mark, the Lurmark (then turned into Lurpak). The collective mark is central on the packaging with a big font. Individual company trademarks still appear on the packaging but in a secondary position and dimension.

In other cases, in the presence of a leading brand and a various product differentiation, the collective brand usually is conceived as an integration of and not overlapping each firm's product and brand characteristics. This is a way to reassure the leading regional producers (i.e., a top leader or neighbor boss) of the nature of the new brand. Firms go on with their own brand identity, and the collective brand is just a plus quality guarantee that sometimes reinforces the cluster of origin perception linkage. This has been the adopted solution in both wool and silk districts located in Biella and Como, respectively (Alberti & Sciascia, 2004). In both cases, regional brands reinforce the cluster productive identity but do not cast a shadow on firms' brands. This is also supported by visual communication, because the collective cluster brand and connected label are smaller than those of the producers.

Territorial Brands

Most of the described brands are local and production-specific, as they are related to the district specialization in their symbols and graphic expressions. Although the territory is not circumscribed to follow a single productive vocation but may integrate more than one, its local institutions can decide to launch a collective brand that is not production-specific but rather place-specific. This brand aims to reinforce regional imagery, despite single productions.

As in any case of brand extension, a territorial generic brand has to be kept ample in order to be able to cover all these diversified productions. For its nature, a territorial brand should not cause problems of coexistence with individual firms' brands. It is just a sign of belonging-ness for firms that display it. The risk is a limited brand efficacy, which concerns people's perceptions and attribution of distinctive significance. In fact, in a territory specialization perspective, a similar brand lacks competitive strength.

An Example of Effective Strategic Orientation to Cluster Marketing and Communication

An interesting case study of metamanagement-effective strategic orientation to build a cluster image, to communicate and promote it, and to support local specialized firms, is the district in Biella. Located in Northern Italy, this district specializes in the production of top-quality yarns. It is one of the most ancient business in which traces of pre-Roman wool working have been found. Today, the production is still completely made in the area with no productive delocalization (Alberti & Sciascia, 2004).

The district has 1,350 firms that use technologies at the vanguard and hires 25,000 workers; annual financial turnover is 4 mld and 300 million euros; the export share is 40% of the total annual production (www.theartofexcellence.com, 2005). In 2002 in the district, a marketing and communication project has been planned and implemented in order to reinforce cluster image, and in doing so, firms' competitiveness and reputations (Alberti & Sciascia, 2004). This was done thanks to a coordinated effort of a network of players and sponsors, including institutional players, local authorities, the Chamber of Commerce, two foundations (one pre-existent and one expressly created), and private firms that included most of the leading local firms. The name of the project, The Art of Excellence, expresses the concept idea. Biella produces top-quality yarns based on the experience of many years, which gave firms special competences similar to an art. The project expressly aims to valorize this experience and the related know-how.

Most of the promotional tools presented previously have been used by district metamanagement organizations in the district. The first step was to preserve the district identity, so two different initiatives were launched in order to save its historical memory. The first initiative was the creation and equipping of a museum for historical objects, hosting old memories and old evidences, such as 19th-century looms. The second initiative was the project Constructing Memory, which was the construction of a databank accessible by several players; it contained publications such as old historical paper documents, digitalized images, bibliographies, and other references. The project also was created in order to have material to use in any initiative of district communication (www.theartofexcellence.com, 2005).

The second step was creating a logo: Biella, the Art of Excellence. Launched in 2003 and shown in Figure 3, the logo aims to create a sort of "made in Biella" for wool textiles, offering a guarantee of superior quality to customers who buy products labeled with it. As the choice of the English language shows, it is an internationally oriented brand. The brand mark shows a spool and some yarn, recalling the cluster productive specialization.

Graphic materials such as books and brochures were made with a high quality graphic and used paper. A Web portal was created (www.theartofexcellence.com), which uses the same elegant graphic of the paper materials. Pages flow smoothly, suggesting the softness of the yarns.

The portal gives information about the district and its activities and is strictly related to the local museum site. An international magazine advertising campaign was launched in 2003 and 2004. It uses the same kind of elegant graphic design to transmit the product's prestige over time, and in both campaigns, there were people touching yarns or labels. In Figure 4 is a 2003 subject, maybe the most effective one of the six subjects produced in the two campaigns, that shows a man playing a cello, whose chords are made of yarn. Yarn is the only colored element on a black and white image. The subject created a correlation between the art of music and the art of top-quality yarnmaking[26]. The claim is "get in touch with fabrics and yarns excellence".

The district organized promotional initiatives, such as the participation in sectoral fairs and the direct organization of meetings and products presentations. External relations and special events also were used, always with careful media diffusion.

One of the most interesting initiatives was the design, organization, and promotion of an international arts exhibition in 2005 titled "Biella, on the wool tread. Myth and rites of wool in the arts." The exhibition, with its high-quality curators, was the first world art exhibition on the theme of wool art[27]. The exhibition's goal was to expose local wool handicraft manu-

Figure 3. The brand "The Art of Excellence" on a label (Source: www.theartofexcellence. com)

Figure 4. A subject taken from the international district advertising campaign in 2003 (Source: www.theartofexcellence.com)

Figure 5. The poster (a) and the card (b) related to the exhibition (Source: www.museodel-territorio.biella.it)

(b)

(a)

facturers' abilities, which is a relevant part of territorial identity. Communication materials such as the poster in Figure 5a focused on wool production by showing a ball and a lamb.

Many collateral initiatives were launched during the exhibition as an information service by SMS, a free bus that took visitors to the exhibition, and a card (Figure 5b). Visitors were given prizes such as discounts for hotels, restaurants, yarns, and knitting wear outlets in the area. A toll-free number provided information about local tourism, cultural activities, shopping, services, and so forth. As a result, the exhibition project and the local commercial supportive network converged.

Conclusion

Clusters can have a significant benefit from a collective marketing and communication strategy. This benefit operates at both the cluster level as well as at the single firm level. Through an effective collective marketing and communication strategy, small and medium-sized firms get resources and competences to exit their regional market dimension and move toward national and sometimes international markets.

This can be done through operational communication and promotional tools that are selected, applied, and organically combined in a coherent mix. In order to be successful, cluster marketing and communication plans need specific skills, both managerial and relational, and need to be tailor-made; that is, designed considering the cluster's structural, productive, social, and cultural peculiarities.

Acknowledgments

The author thanks the editors and especially Robert MacGregor for the support in writing this chapter, and gratefully acknowledges the anonymous reviewer's thoughtful comments. Special thanks to Eva Cutolo, for her helpful support and comments.

References

Aaker, D. A. (1991). *Managing brand equity*. New York: The Free Press.

Alberti, F., & Sciascia, S. (2004). *Le politiche di marchio per i distretti industriali. i casi di Como e Biella*. University of Castellanza

Andersen, A. S. (1994). *The evolution of credence goods: A transaction approach to product specification and quality control* (MAPP Working Paper No. 21).

Andersson, P. (2002). Connected internationalisation processes: The case of internationalising channel intermediaries. *International Business Review, 11*, 365–383.

Becattini, G., & Menghinello, S. (1998). Contributo e ruolo del made in Italy distrettuale nelle esportazioni nazionali di manufatti. *Sviluppo Locale, 9*, 5–41.

Biel, A. (1993). Converting image into equity. In D. Aaker, & A. Biel (Eds.), *Brand equity and advertising: Advertising's role in building strong brands*. Hillsdale: Lawrence Erlbaum Associates Press

Biørn, C. (Ed.). (1982). *Dansk mejeribrug 1882-2000*. Danske Mejeriers Faellesorganisation.

Bristow, D. N., Schneider, K. C., & Schuler, D. K. (2002). The brand dependence scale: Measuring consumers' use of brand name to differentiate among product alternatives. *Journal of Product and Brand Management, 11*(6), 343–356.

Burgess, J. (1982). Selling places: Environmental images for the executive. *Regional Studies, 16*(1), 1–17.

Choi, C. J., Lee, S. H., & Oh, D. (1995). The strategy of grouping and reputation linkage in clubs and multi-products firms. *European Journal of Political Economy, 11*, 521–533.

Clemens, R., & Babcock, B. A. (2004). *Country of origin as a brand: The case of New Zealand lamb*. Iowa State University.

Darby, M. R., & Karny, E. (1973). Free competition and the optimal amount of fraud. *Journal of Law and Economics, 16*, 67–88.

David, P. A. (1987). Some new standards for the economics of standardization in the information age. In P. Dasgupta, & P. L. Stoneman (Eds.), *Economic policy and technology performance*. London: Cambridge University Press.

Doz, Y., Santos, J., & Williamson, P., (2001). *From global to metanational*. Boston: Harvard Business School Press.

Erdem, T. (1998, August). An empirical analysis of umbrella branding. *Journal of Marketing Research*, 339–351.

Firat, A. F., & Schultz II, C. J. (1997). From segmentation to fragmentation: Markets and marketing strategy in the postmodern era. *European Journal of Marketing, 31*(3/4), 183–207.

Franz, P., Heimpold, G., & Rosenfeld, M. T. W. (2005). The pattern of spatially concentrated industries in East Germany: A contribution to the discussion of economic "clusters." In *Proceedings of the International Conference on Regional Growth Agendas*, Aalborg, Denmark.

Gergaud, O., & Livat, F. (2004). *Team versus individual reputations: A model of interaction and some empirical evidence*. Sorbonne, Paris: Universitè Paris Panthèon-Sorbonne.

Goody, J. (1982). *Cooking, cuisine, and class*. Cambridge: Cambridge University Press.

Granovetter, M. (1985). Economic action and social structure: The problem of "embeddedness." *American Journal of Sociology, 91*(3), 481–510.

Han, M.C. (1989). Country image: Halo or summary construct?. *Journal of Marketing Research, 26*(2), 222–229.

Han, M. C., & Terpstra, V. (1988). Country of origin effects for uni-national and bi-national products. *Journal of International Business Studies, 48*, 235–255.

Henchion, M., & McIntyre, B. (2000). Regional imagery and quality products: The Irish experience. *British Food Journal, 102*(8), 630–644.

Hirschmann, E. C., & Holbrook, M. B. (1982). The esperiential aspects of consumptions: Consumer fantasies, feelings and fun. *Journal of Consumer Research, 9*, 132–40.

Holden, S. J. S., & Lutz, R. J. (1992). Ask not what the brand can evoke; ask what can evoke the brand? *Advances in Consumer Research, 19.*

Holt, D. B. (2005). How societies desire brands. Using cultural theory to explain brand symbolism. In S. Ratneshwar, & D. G. Mick (Eds.), *Inside consumption. Consumer motives, goals, and desires.* New York: Routledge.

Huddlestone, P., Good, L. K., & Stoel, L. (2001). Polish consumers' perceptions of quality. *International Journal of Retail and Distribution Management, 29*(5), 236–246.

Johansson, J. K., Douglas, S. P., & Nonaka, I. (1985, November). Assessing the impact of country of origin on product evaluations: A new methodological perspective. *Journal of Marketing Research, 22*, 388–396.

Kahn, B. E., & Ratner, R. K. (2005). Variety for the sake of variety? Diversification motives in consumer choice. In S. Ratneshwar, & D. G.Mick (Eds.), *Inside consumption. Consumer motives, goals, and desires.* New York: Routledge.

Kahn, U., Dahr, R., & Wertenbroch, K. (2005). A behavioral decision theory perspective on hedonic and utilitarian choice. In S. Ratneshwar & D.G.Mick (Eds.), *Inside consumption. Consumer motives, goals, and desires.* New York: Routledge.

Kates, S. M. (2001). Marketing's interpretive communities: A new form of sociocultural segmentation? In *Proceedings of the Australia New Zealand Marketing Academy Conference,* Auckland, New Zealand.

Keller, K. L. (1993). Conceptualizing, measuring and managing brand equity. *Journal of Marketing, 57.*

Keller, K. L. (1998). *Strategic brand management: Building, measuring and managing brand equity.* Englewood Cliffs, NJ: Prentice Hall.

Keller, K. L. (2002). *Branding and brand equity.* Cambridge, MA: Marketing Science Institute Relevant Knowledge Series.

Krishnan, H. S. (1996). Characteristics of memory associations: A consumer-based brand equity perspective. *International Journal of Research in Marketing, 13.*

Landon, S., & Smith, C. E. (1998). Quality expectations, reputation and price. *Southern Economic Journal, 64*, 628–647.

Lane, D. (2003). Complexity and local interactions: Toward a theory of industrial districts. Retrieved November, 2005, from www.iscom.unimo.it

Levy, S. J. (1959). Symbols for sale. *Harvard Business Review, 37*(4), 117–214.

Marshall, A. (1919). *Industry and trade: A study of industrial technique and business organization and their influences on the conditions of various classes and nations* (2nd ed.). London: MacMillan.

McCracken, G. (1993). The value of the brand: An anthropological perspective. In D. Aaker & A. Biel (Eds.), *Brand equity and advertising: Advertising's role in building strong brands*. Hillsdale: Lawrence Erlbaum Associates Press.

Mick, D. G., & Buhl, C. (1992). A meaning-based model of advertising experiences. *Journal of Consumer Research, 19*.

Mills, E. S. (1992). Sectoral clustering and metropolitan development. In E. S. Mills, & J. F. McDonald (Eds.), *Sources of metropolitan growth* (pp. 3–18). New Brunswick: Center for Urban Policy Research.

Molotch, H. (1996). L.A. as product: How design works in a regional economy. In A. J. Scott & E. Soja (Eds.), *The city: Los Angeles and urban theory at the end of the twentieth century* (pp. 225–725). Berkeley: University of California Press.

Molotch, H. (2003). *Where stuff comes from. How toasters, toilets, cars, computers, and many other things come to be as they are*. New York: Routledge.

Nelson, P. (1970). Information and consumer behavior. *Journal of Political Economy, 78*.

Nelson, P. (1974). Advertising as information. *The Journal of Political Economy, 82*, 4.

Niss, H. (1995). Country of origin marketing over the product life cycle: A Danish case study. *European Journal of Marketing, 30*(3), 6–22.

Normann, R. (1984). *Service management: Strategy and leadership*. Baffins Lane: John Wiley & Sons.

Ouchi, W. G. (1980). Markets, bureaucracies and clans. *Administrative Quarterly, 25*, 129–141.

Ouwersloot, H., & Tudorica, A. (2001). *Brand personality creation through advertising* [working paper]. Maastricht Academic Center for Research in Services.

Poiesz, T. (1989). The image concept: Its place in consumer psychology. *Journal of Economic Psychology, 10*.

Powell, W. W., & Smith-Doerr, L. (1994). Networks and economic life. In N. Smelser & R. Swedberg (Eds.), *Handbook of economic sociology*. Princeton University Press

Pyke, F., & Sengenberger, W. (Eds.). (1992). *Industrial districts and local economic regeneration*. Geneva: ILO-International Institute for Labour Studies.

Rao, A., Qu, L., & Ruekert, R. W. (1997, March). *Brand alliances as information about unobservable product quality* (Rep. No. n.97-100). Marketing Science Institute.

Rifkin, J. (2000). *The age of access: How the shift from ownership to access is transforming modern life*. London: Penguin.

Rosenfeld, S. (1997). Bringing business clusters into the mainstream of economic development. *European Planning Studies, 5*, 3–23.

Roth, M. S., & Romeo, J. B. (1992). Matching product category and country image perceptions: A framework for managing country of origin effects. *Journal of International Business Studies, 23*(3), 477–497.

Scott, A. J. (1999). The cultural economy: Geography and the creative field. *Media, Culture, Society, 21*, 807–815.

Scott, A. J. (2000). *The cultural economy of cities: Essays on the geography of image-producing industries.* London: Sage.

Scott, A. J. (2001). Industrial revitalization in the ABC municipalities, Sào Paulo: Diagnostic analysis and strategic recommendations for a new economy and a new regionalism. *Regional Development Studies, 7*, 1–32.

Segre, G. (2003). *D.O.C., exit e innovazione. Property rights nel distretto culturale del vino nelle Langhe* [working paper no. 04/2003]. Università di Torino.

Shapiro, C. (1983). Premiums for high quality products as returns to reputation. *The Quarterly Journal of Economics, 98*, 659–680.

Sharma, S., Schimp, T.A., & Shin, J. (1995). Consumer ethnocentrism: A test of antecedents and moderators. *Journal of the Academy of Marketing Science, 23*(1), 26–37.

Stigler, G. J. (1961). The economics of information. In D.M. Lamberton (Ed.), *Economics of information and knowledge: Selected readings.* Harmondsworth: Penguin.

Storper, M. (1997). The regional world. New York: Guilford.

Street-Porter, T. (1986). *Freestyle: The new architecture and interior design from Los Angeles.* New York: Stewart, Tabori and Chang.

Tambunan, T. (2005). Promoting small and medium enterprises with a clustering approach: A Policy experience from Indonesia. *Journal of Small Business Management, 43*(2).

Tirole, J. (1996). A theory of collective reputations (with applications to the persistence of corruption and to firm quality). *Review of Economic Studies,* 1–22.

Tse, D. K., & Gorn, G. J. (1993). An experiment on the salience of country-of-origin in the era of global brands. *Journal of International Marketing, 1*(1).

Vankatesan, M. (1973). Cognitive consistency and novelty seeking. In S. Ward, & T.S. Robertson (Eds.), *Consumer behavior: Theoretical sources.* Englewood Cliffs, NJ: Prentice Hall.

Zanni, L., & Labory, S. (2002). Le formule imprenditoriali nel settore moda: Caratteri strutturali e strategie competitive delle imprese protagoniste. In L. Bacci (Ed.), *Distretti e imprese leader nel sistema moda della Toscana.* Milano: Franco Angeli.

Endnotes

[1]   It is not by chance that in the Italian experience of industrial districts, mainly made up of small enterprises, district firms have developed through the years a higher degree of commercial orientation and, most of all, a specific export vocation superior to nondistrict firms.

[2]   Together, firms can commit to a packaging firm the development of a specific packaging structure with specific functional benefits in conservation or storage, put together a better contract (pool buying), and differentiate it in a second stage of labeling.

[3] An example is given by software created in 2005 by a Florence service provider in order to calculate working times and determine real costs of leather manufacturers, reducing possible errors in price determination. This product, which gives a CAD integration with related firms, is the result of an emerged need from the dissastifcation of leather cluster entrepreneurs about how product prices were determined.

[4] In fact, typical products, such as experience goods (Nelson, 1970, 1974), are an attractive factor which joins natural and cultural factors for people who are willing to live an experience of local tastes and smells.

[5] This is specifically true for typical products made by small and medium local firms, which can take benefit from a joined marketing and communication promotion activity in order to penetrate foreign markets and overcome commercial barriers too high for single firms.

[6] This dynamic in the case of Italian industrial districts is even more accentuated.

[7] Some European clusters date back to 1300 and some even before that.

[8] In times of delocalization, firms indicate homemade products even though one or more productive stages have been done in other countries.

[9] In a global world with a high mobility from countries and even continents, many people live in foreign countries. One of the first and very rapidly diffused typologies of products moving together with communities is local typical food. Small markets start selling in neighborhoods with a specific ethnic or cultural homogeneity the food from the community's country of origin. In some cases, there are specific cultural and religious patterns to be respected in individual alimentation. In other cases, consuming one's own country's food is a matter of affective consumption, which makes people feel comforted.

[10] Also, for some single aspects, credence goods are more diffused than it was thought, especially for actual consumers who demand information about a wide-range production cycle, including a legal and fair human resources management. Aspects such as equal commerce and real working conditions and salary for workers cannot be checked personally by consumers, who have to trust the firm's communication, unless some different news shows an eventual gap between what has been said and what has been done.

[11] In the case of food-typical products, the experience is taste- and smell-based; in the case of a country music CD, it is a listening experience; in the case of a special textile, it is a touch-based experience; in any case, the experience can be supported by visual communication.

[12] A consumer may have never heard of a single Napa Valley winemaker but may have a mental and sensorial image of what a Napa Valley wine is like.

[13] This is the case of some Italian tomato or pasta producers.

[14] Evidently, in the case of far-from-home produced goods, customers can have access to a more reduced information about how they have been made. But sometimes, these attitudes are just ideological and not based on an effective products comparison.

[15] As Holt (2005) defines it, "the goal of branding is to claim virgin cognitive associations in a product category, and consistently communicate these associations in everything

the brand does over time to sustain the brand's hold on this cognitive territory" (p. 275).

[16]   One of the factors at the basis of iconic brands creation, according to Holt (2005), is a national ideology: people search for successful individual and valid-for-mankind stories, cases and connected ideals.

[17]   Leading firms can positively influence their cluster's productive image.

[18]   For example, the Italian industrial biomedical district located in Mirandola has approached markets and built its image without a country-of-origin supportive image, as more competitive Italian industries are mature and traditional. The same is for Indian biotechnological district firms or the movie production industry in Bombay, known as Bollywood, which have built their own reliability in the absence of a related country-of-origin positive effect.

[19]   These regional cluster standards can be addressed in order to give customers a guarantee that their products have the same high quality. In other cases, productive standards introduced at a cluster level for belonging firms are aimed at introducing measures that are able to preserve the environment and thus to try to give their products a "green" image.

[20]   The choice to give examples taken from the Italian experience is due to the author's familiarity with them but also due to the interest of the cases. The typical size of firms in Italian districts is small, and thus, the analysis of their promoting strategies can be interesting in order to see how collective marketing and communication activities can be effective and creative.

[21]   The crisis of technical high schools related to local productions occurred in several manufacturing districts in terms of sensible decreasing of the number of new students, which is something to worry about. For the strict linkage between a social and economic basis inside industrial districts, this fact has several consequences upon image and district capability to develop its specialized workers, and can be a first sign for a lack of interest in the field by new generations.

[22]   An example of a product that is a mix of sample and gadget is the Francobusta® a specific product made in the silk textile district in Como (Alberti & Sciascia, 2004) and consisting of an envelope with a stamp on it, all made of silk.

[23]   Some contests include throwing textile-related objects, the race with a trolley containing cotton skeins, a multiple relay race whose participants run and give each other a roll of fabric, and so forth. There is also a creative competition that requires participants to prepare a piece of cloth in a given time.

[24]   This chapter concerns clusters for the ample range of marketing and communication-specific aspects they have, but also in the case of networks, collective brands act as a guarantee. An example is consortia that work to promote a fair commerce; products coming from third-world countries and showing this collective label are supposed by consumers to be more ethically produced and distributed than those that do not have it.

[25]   Standards can concern (David, 1987) technical or behavioral aspects and can consist of specific measures and references, minimal attribute levels, and compatibility.

26   The expression on the face of the player shows concentration and pleasure, which can come both from the music he is playing and from touching the soft chords made of precious soft yarn.

27   The exhibition has proposed a multisensorial travel following the wool thread through different times; 100 works coming from international museums let the visitor follow a path going from prehistorical times to the present, from the thread of Arianna's legend to a red thread in the hands of a Russian Madonna of the 16th century and to Warhol's ball of wool (www.theartofexcellence.com, 2005).

Chapter IV

Italian Industrial Districts:
Nature, Structure,
and Value Creation

Paola Falcone, University of Rome "La Sapienza," Italy

Abstract

The high performance levels gained by firms of Italian industrial districts raised both the international economic and managerial scientific communities' interest and stimulated the production of a series of research studies concerning the micro as well as the macro level of analysis. This chapter aims to identify, describe, and interpret the phenomenon of Italian industrial districts with a specific focus on the analysis of the sources and the forms of value creation in light of the last 30 years of scientific research.

Introduction

During the last 30 years, Italian districts have raised a growing international interest supported by publications and study tours; they have been proposed as a model of industrial organization, an alternative to those that are dominant in mainstream managerial theory. The main reason for interest was the analysis of economic results gained by district firms, higher than the ones obtained by similar nondistrict firms. By a more detailed analysis, theorists discovered that the most interesting thing was in the way these results were obtained.

Many authors (e.g., Piore & Sabel, 1984), following Marshall's analysis (1919), were specifically fascinated by the flexible specialization implemented within districts as well as by the way buyer-seller relationships and even those among competing firms were managed. Italian industrial districts proposed a new spatial organization and a new type of value creation (Porter, 1984; 1998) that was different from both vertical integration (Chandler, 1977) and markets (Williamson, 1979).

Small firms that are disadvantaged by the small size in the competition in the district become competitive for the exploitation of external economies that are obtained through a work division (Berger & Locke, 2000; Marshall, 1919; Rullani, 2003) and connected specialization. The value created inside Italian districts appeared interesting both by a single-firm point of view (competitive advantage and value created) and by a systemic one (revenues, employment).

For these reasons, the chapter intends to analyze models and history in Italian industrial districts in light of more than 30 years of research and meanwhile produced upon them. It specifically focuses on the identification, description, and interpretation of value creation forms within districts and their sustainability throughout time.

The first part of the chapter aims to analyze the basic elements of districts, such as their main characteristics, their players, different types of districts, and the steps of their life cycle. After this introduction to districts, the chapter deals with the value creation, commenting on some data and analyzing the drivers of their growth and how district firms have been able to exploit these factors. The third part describes the changes that have occurred during the last 10 years and the consequences they have had on district developments in terms of competitiveness. At the end of the chapter, some possible future actions in order to face these changes are traced.

Italian Industrial Districts: An Overview

Defining the Italian Industrial District Through Its Components and Main Characteristics

Becattini (1991) describes the Italian industrial district as a socioterritorial entity "characterized by an active compresence of a community of people and firms population[1], within a naturally and historically specific area" (author's translation). Pyke and Sengenberger (1992) define Italian industrial districts as "composed of geographically concentrated small and medium sized firms targeting their products at the upper market segment where they possess a competitive advantage regarding their flexibility and specialisation. This advantage is obtained through decentralised production in specialist firms with vertical cooperation and horizontal competition. A supportive social environment enables this mode of production and sustains it against economic crisis" (pp. 2-3).

According to Rosenfeld's (1995) definition, a district is a group of geographically concentrated firms that "either work directly or indirectly for the same end market, share values and knowledge so important that they define a cultural environment, and are specifically linked to one another in a complex mix of competition and cooperation" (p. 13).

The three selected definitions clearly identify the main characteristic of districts: they are socioeconomic systems. In addition, they give a first trace of the following specific traits that are identified by the literature (Alberti, 2001; Franz, Heimpold & Rosenfeld, 2005; Rosenfeld, 1995b):

- The presence of a high geographical concentration of mostly small and medium sized industrial firms that are highly specialized and concentrated in specific market niches with a strong productive tradition.
- The lack of a formal property of the district.
- Stakeholder heterogeneity.
- The territory meant as place but also as cultural environment, where firms operate and where both entrepreneurs and workers live, which gives common culture, history, and traditions.
- The presence of industry-specific competences as traditional or modern productive techniques.
- High interaction intensity.
- Social and economic interconnection of the players and related easiness of information transmission based on reciprocal trust.
- Simultaneous presence of both cooperative and competitive behaviors among firms.
- Horizontally diffused productive system.
- Common share of homogeneous resources as capital, education, services, and workforce.
- The combination of both formal and informal communication channels.
- Workforce mobility.
- Entrepreneurial spirit.
- General compactness toward the protection of the district and the development of all of its local stakeholders, both private and public.

Clearly, each Italian industrial district has its own characteristics, giving specific emphasis to some of the previous points, which is why most researchers decided to describe and interpret single cases[2]. What appears to be true is that districts present the previous and numerous characteristics (variety), which can evolve (variability) through time, and so surely can be classified as complex systems.

Some Data Regarding Industrial Districts Diffusion in Italy

The use of different parameters has produced different esteems about the number of industrial districts in Italy. According to the ISTAT (Italian Central Institute for Statistics) esteem[3] (2002), Italian districts are 199, distributed as described in Table 1.

Table 1 indicates a strong presence of districts in northeast Italy (32%) followed by central Italy and northwest. A reduced diffusion of districts, in line with an inferior industrial development, is in the South. The number of district manufacturing units is 239.000 (Istat, 2002). Fourteen million people (25% of the total Italian population) live in district areas, and 2.2 million people are employed in local firms (Istat, 2002). The average number of employees for a single manufacturing unit is 9 (Istat, 2002). These firms operate mainly in mature sectors.

As shown in Figure 1, district principal productive specialization is in the textiles and clothes industry (70 districts) followed by house goods (this category is very heterogeneous, because it consists of things such as furnishings, electrical appliances, and tiles) (37 districts); mechanical tools and components (33 districts); leather, skin, and related products, such as bags and footwear (28 districts); food products (17 districts); paper and prints (six districts); others (eight districts).

Table 1- Districts spatial distribution

Area	Number of Districts
Northwest	59
Northeast	65
Central Italy	60
South and Islands	15
Total	199

Figure 1. Districts' productive specialization (Source: ISTAT, 2002)

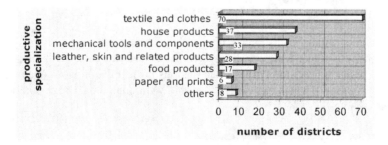

The Players

In the industrial district, some of the following players live, operate, and interact (Rosenfeld, 1997):

- Manufacturing firms
- Related firms, providers of complementary products (e.g., inputs, machinery) and services (e.g., transportation, consulting, technical support)
- Banks and financial institutions
- Research centers and universities
- Social infrastructures such as schools, kindergartens, and so forth
- Metamanagement organizations that are responsible for district orientation and its develop (e.g., entrepreneur associations, consortia)
- Local policymakers

Manufacturing district firms are, as said, mainly small and medium enterprises. Among them there can be one or more leading firms[4]. In the district, it is possible to find two kinds of leading district firms (Zanni & Labory, 2002):

- Global leaders that compete on the global market
- Local small and medium enterprises that are brand leaders able to develop specific resources and competences

These players are important, since they act as district locomotives that make the district move toward innovation, exploration, international openness, technology progress, and so forth. The leading firm generates demand for local subcontractors.

Sometimes, leading firms are global players, with brands very popular also out of the district, which can generate some attention and a sort of positive halo effect toward other less-known local productions. Leading firms' knowledge is often spread around them by the effect of a spin-off generation. Least but not last, leading firms' successful images also are encouraging for younger generations and give a local example of a possible successful industrial model.

District observation has shown how the presence of one or more leading firms does not inhibit the growth of the districts themselves, because the success of leading firms is not made at the expense of smaller players (Berger & Locke, 2000), for they do not play in a zero-sum system.

Related firms, district providers of goods or services to manufacturers, can be classified (Zanni & Lavory, 2002) as the following:

- **Pure providers** sometimes but not necessarily working exclusively for a single leading firm (satellites). They do simple activities in the productive chain; they do not have any codesign activity with the manufacturing firm. The buyer imposes on them models, inputs, and other partners.

- **Phase providers** that work for one or more firms; they are technologically more specialized and, thus, do more complex activities or even make complete products for their clients, who can decide their production processes.

- **Partner providers** that often supply complete products, codesign products with their clients, and have both technical and managerial higher competences .

- **Mixed providers** that are similar to partner-providers but offer their products on the market.

The role of supporting firms offering goods or services is important for both the district and the leading firm's development. A high degree of district internal commercial interaction between district manufacturers and district providers is shown by a national research (Omiccioli, 2000):

- 61% of the value of goods and services is bought by district providers.

- 27% by national non-district providers.

- 12% by international providers.

The less district-dependent appear to be local providers; in fact, the research has shown that they distribute their sales as follows (Omiccioli, 2000):

- 23% of the value of sold goods and services derives from district firms.

- 49% of it derives from national non-district clients.

- 28% of it derives from international clients.

Local banks are another important part of district infrastructure (Becattini, 1991). As statistics prove (Signorini, 1994), district firms tend to get in debt more than the nondistrict ones, which perhaps can be explained by an easier access to loans. Trust in local relationships and an easier control over firms make local banks less selective in giving loans. This is a resource for local firms but can be a risk for local banks that may be financially overexposed; in fact, their main debtors are local and all operate in the same industry in which the district is productively specialized.

Another important role is played by university and research centers that provide knowledge development and sharing[5].

Social infrastructures are also important, because they guarantee a good quality of life for the community and, most of all, for workers.

Metamanagerial institutions and local policymakers, which are responsible for district development, are described later in the chapter.

The number of players for each described group and their degree of interactions are district-specific and feed the district growth.

Districts Typologies

Different parameters can be used to define an industrial district. The most relevant are the following:

- Structural parameters
- Strategic importance of the district
- Degree of productive specialization
- Type of productive specialization
- Width of operating markets
- Structure of the district
- Entity and kind of relationships among its firms (Jacobs & De Man, 1996)
- The way the district works
- Use of common resources (Rosenfeld, 1997) among its firms

Structural parameters can be the territorial or population dimension, the number of employees, the size of the firm, entrepreneurial density, production and sales dimensions, and so forth, and can identify small, medium, or large districts[6]. The strategic relevance of industrial districts can be identified according to parameters such as employment rate, value produced, relevance of the sector (e.g., biotechnologies), international market share, and so forth. Another distinction can be operated in consideration of the degree of product specialization, which determines the difference between the following:

- Mono-type districts specialized in a single production
- Multi-type aggregated districts—territories specialized in different productions that are more or less correlated with each other.[7] Their development is facilitated by the presence of an economic base that is able to induce productive diversification (Harrison & Glasmeier, 1997).

The former evidently are more exposed to demand and conjuncture fluctuations than the latter.

Industrial districts can have the following types of productive specialization:

1. Traditional, labor-intensive manufacturer. These districts operate in mature sectors and have a specific export vocation, such as textiles, garment, wood and furniture, food-typical products. Their main competitive advantage source is design and manufacturing techniques.

2. Products related to traditional productions, such as machines. Some districts produce and export machineries used by local firms. They sell machines that are able to create products similar to made-in-Italy ones, and often, their business is an evolution of traditional manufacturers (type 1) described previously (Signorini & Omiccioli, 2005). Their main competitive advantage source is an experience-based knowledge.[8]

3. High-technology productions (science-based districts) (UE Commission, 2002), such as biomedicine, which have technological innovation and R&D as their main competitive advantage source and can be strategically very relevant.

According to their operating markets width, districts can be classified in the following categories:

*   Prevalent domestic market districts, whose firms sell less than 40% abroad
*   Balanced portfolio mixed districts, whose firms sell from 40% to 50% abroad
*   High export vocation districts, in which more than 50% of the output is sold to foreign markets

The structure of the district, its entity, and type of relationships among its firms, such as the use of common resources and the way districts work, are all interconnected parameters and depend upon both district structure and the presence or absence of a central focal player, which is typically a leading firm[9] or a strong metamanagement organization.

District as an Evolving System: Different Stages of Its Life Cycle

The district is a complex, dynamic, adapting system, evolving and changing its shape through time on the basis of several factors:

*   Exogenous factors that generate pressure upon its firms such as demand, competition, technology, and so forth, or helping district firms such as in public (state or regional), financial, or operational support.
*   Endogenous factors, such as its evolving interactions (internal and external), its adaptability, its organizational capability, and its innovation capability.

District evolution occurs by a deep settlement of single firms with the territory and with the local social and industrial tissue. This kind of relationship firm-territory is not a predatory one; neither is it a simple co-existence one. Rather, it is ample, deep, and co-evolving (Bellandi, 2001); each firm gives and takes in a perfect complementary relationship.

The district grows by propagation (Rullani, 2003) and by spin-offs that are encouraged by the industrial atmosphere[10].

Factors that promote district development are several. First of all is the demand for nonstandardized goods (Sforzi & Lorenzini, 2002), to which the firm can answer through a flexible horizontal organization. This demand is both internal and external, national or international. Besides the demand, the district grows for technology development, knowledge transfer, development of a specialized workforce, and economies of agglomeration.

As the empirical observation has shown, the district evolves toward different paths (Berger & Locke, 2000; Biggiero, 1999); sometimes it comes to an end, sometimes it moves spatially in search of a better location, and sometimes it modifies its productive specialization[11]. Other times, it chooses the path of diversification, mixing existing productions with new ones.

With respect to different evolutionary paths, it is possible to recognize some evidences regarding district life cycle. The district life cycle, similar to a single firm's, can be divided into four stages (GTZ, 2005; UE Commission, 2002):

1. First settlement
2. Growth stage
3. Maturity stage
4. Decline stage

First Settlement

A spontaneous unplanned start is the usual characteristic of a district's birth (Rosenfeld, 2002). Districts are different from industrial poles (Perroux, 1955), because they typically are not born by a top-down process guided by a strategic mind (Rullani, 1998). On the contrary, they are the result of a spontaneous and multiple convergence of players producing a clotting of forces and resources that modify the territory, starting just from its characteristics and resources. Usually, some pioneer firms in the presence of specific local conditions settle in an area, followed by new startup or spin-off firms that establish a first geographical concentration of players that share the same production o productive phase.

District settlement in a certain place can be explained by a cross of several theoretical approaches in which both path dependence and resource-based perspectives have their part. According to Arthur (1990) (see also Britton, 2004), the agglomeration of firms in a cluster is a sort of stochastic process and "settlement patterns are path-dependent" (p. 249). Historical events can determine the concentration of specific industry firms in a certain location[12].

"Even accidental origins can lead to spatial concentrations of industrial activity" (Britton, 2004, p. 2). In these cases, a historical accident (Krugman, 1993) may generate a subsequent positive feedback. As Martin (1998) shows, "places produce path dependence" (p. 80), and here, the path dependency theory meets the resource-based perspectives. Specific resources needed by a certain industry are available in a certain location[13] with certain transaction costs.

For example, "new, dynamic industries are likely to locate in large urban centers, where they can benefit from the cross-fertilization provided by diverse actors[14]. Older, mature industries concentrate in smaller, more specialized cities, where congestion costs are low and localization economies can be high[15]" (World Bank 2000, p. 117.). So, a local attraction is generated by specific cost advantages obtainable in the area (Doeringer & Terkla, 1995) or by the valorization of available natural resources[16]. It is possible to distinguish (Krugman, 1993) so-called first nature advantages (e.g., natural resources, climate, geographical position, closeness to transportation) and second-nature advantages, such as the presence of several facilities encouraging industrial settlements in the area.

Places with a specific attractiveness have a sort of "selectional advantage" (Arthur, 1990, p. 249) in a firm's decision-making process. This advantage is even higher in Italian industrial districts, because they are an expression of local socioeconomic environment.

Different motivations can bring different location choices, but every district settlement is based on a diffused entrepreneurial spirit.

Growth Stage

The growth of firms generates demand for goods and services in the area for all local firms. For this reason, in this phase, providers of specialized goods and services, such as training, consulting, research and development, and assistance, emerge in the district. Knowledge and information circulate within it. The district becomes a specialized labor market, attracting workers from the outside, which improves efficiency in the use of factors, often producing cost reduction and making the district gain in competitiveness. The district shows the proper conditions to new firm startups, encourages spin-offs[17], and increases its attractiveness toward firms and investors.

Interaction and cohesion among participants have grown during previous stages, as well as their collective identity (Rehfeld, 2005) of being part of a system, which means reciprocity and goal sharing. Structures are light, roles and relationships between producers and providers are clear, and the value chain is short and not very articulated. Providers are small firms, strictly dependent from ordering firms; district firms are more self-contained, and relationships are stable. The district growth and the attraction of workers from the outside increases the need of social infrastructures, such as apartments for rent, and so forth. In case of foreign countries employment, as many Italian districts have been experiencing in recent years, a multicultural perpective is needed, involving many more socio-cultural aspects.

Maturity Stage

As the district enters its maturity stage, it gives added advantages to firms and local communities. They are nonmarket advantages, institutional ones promoting the exchange of information and knowledge. Organizational routines are a fundamental part of production processes. The structure of the districts, typical of central-north Italy (Signorini, 2002), becomes more structured in this stage, with different levels of subcontractors and related players and a high number of customers and firm providers.

In this stage, the district has gained an almost stable shape. New settledowns are not so easy as in the growth stage (Porter, 2000) for a matter of firms' adaptabilities to the new environment and for the way the environment will let them insert inside its consolidated dynamics. The risk in this stage is a sort of district crystallization. As Porter (2000) remarks, "When a cluster shares a uniform approach to competing, a sort of groupthink often reinforces old behaviors, suppresses new ideas, and creates rigidities that prevent adoption of improvements. Clusters also might not support truly radical innovation, which tends to invalidate the existing pools of talent, information, suppliers, and infrastructure. In these circumstances, a cluster participant ... might suffer from greater barriers to perceiving the need to change" (24).

Decline Stage

This stage is a reorganization phase. The district loses its attractiveness toward external investors, workers, and internal population. The district gets static. Young people lose interest in traditional productive techniques and sometimes leave the district. The not occurred generation change is a risk for the system, which has to attract human resources from the outside. This makes the district lose some of its competitiveness. The district image needs a restyling and needs effective investments in communication activities.

The Competitiveness of Italian Industrial District Firms

District Export Vocation

A first emerging characteristic of Italian industrial district firms is their specific export vocation, which makes them give an important contribution to national exportations (see Table 2). The presented data regarding main Italian productive sectors show the variety of district productions but, most of all, their very high contribution to total national export. Specifically interesting is the datum regarding the most relevant production (i.e., tiles and slabs mainly concentred in the Sassuolo district), which contributes 84.4% to the total national production, having a market share of 54.8%.

Export vocation of district firms can be explained considering some factors. On the supply side, selling abroad implicates for firms the availability of specific skills, competences, and

Table 2. Italian market share on global export flows and the contribution of district manufacturing SMEs (Source: Istat, 2002)

Categories	Italian Market Share of Total World Export	% Contribution of Local Manufacturing SME Systems to National Export
Ceramic tiles and slabs for floors and coverings	54.8	84.4
Cut or construction stones modeled and refined	34.7	46.9

Table 2. Continued

Leather	19.2	85.4
Footwear (mostly leather shoes)	17.1	67.6
Furniture	15	68.2
Domestic electronic machines for domestic use (electrical appliances included)	15	42.8
Tanks and metal containers, radiators, and boilers for central heating	14.8	67.9
Textiles and clothing industry	14.4	74.3
Cycles and motorcycles	12.7	34.5
Travel articles, bags and such, saddles, and articles for horseback riders	12.5	25.9
Agriculture machines	11.5	84.8
Knitting (textile)	10.9	71.0
Furs and fur articles	10.8	50.3
Tubes	10.7	63.3
Jewels	10.4	72
Other general use machines	9.6	48.1
Weapons and ammunition	9.6	63
Beverages	9.5	39.9
Average Italian data	4.4	46.1

resources (e.g., active distribution channels, specific information, consulting services, etc.). These resources and capabilities may be absent in small firms, which are traditionally the natural dimension of Italian firms.

District metamanagement (infra) helps small firms to get this strategic guide, which allows them to develop a strategic export vocation. District collective dimension also helps sharing among firms and sometimes, with the contribution of an external financial support, some sunk costs connected to exportations, making them affordable to district firms. Besides these aspects, there is a strategic market positioning that is directly connected to the specific kind of production of district firms. They often address their offer to an upper-level target, which can appreciate the plus in terms of quality and is willing to pay for this plus. This strategic choice requires that, in order to expand their sales and growth, firms that have saturated domestic markets need to search for that niche (both industrial and consumer) abroad. So, it has been natural for district management to develop a real export vocation that also is supported by demand acceptance.

As known, a main competitive factor for products offered by district firms has been a set of intangible resources, such as traditions, culture, and specific competences. The result is a highly accurate manufacture enriched by a superior design and positive territorial image (Rullani & Bonomi, 2001). To these factors should be added a general made-in-Italy favorable image, which determines a general international positive attitude toward these products.

District Economic Performance

Italian industrial districts have specifically fascinated researchers for gained economic performance above the one attained by similar nondistrict firms as well as for the way it has been obtained.

It is useful to analyze district competitiveness also in terms of profitability.

An interesting quantitative study has been addressed to test districts' economic performances in order to show their specific competitiveness (Fabiani, Pellegrini, Romagnano & Signorini, 2000a, 2000b). The study compared (see Figure 2) the aggregated performance of district firms with the one nondistrict firm used as a control group; the elements of both groups were comparable by dimension and productive specialization. Results show that district firms' performances estimated over a long period of time (1982-1995) have been superior to the ones obtained by correspondent (i.e., same size and productive specialization) nondistrict ones[18], both in terms of ROI and ROE. As the analysis has shown, a higher profitability for district firms in the considered period of time is not the result of specific, occasional conjunctures, but a persistent evidence.

The results induce one to think that belonging to a district may be a discriminative factor for small and medium-sized firms, as mainly Italian firms are. The analysis of the causes is strictly related to the way value is created inside districts.

Figure 2. A comparison between district and nondistrict firms' profitabilities (Source: Fabiani, Pellegrini, Romagnano, and Signorini, 2000b)

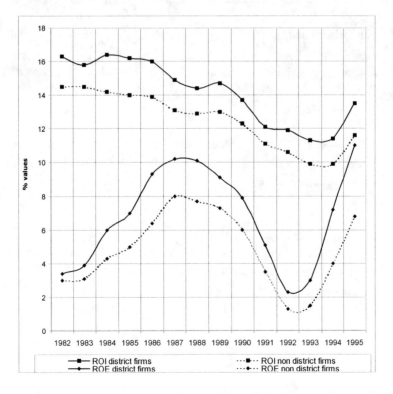

The Italian District:
Multidimensional Roots of Value Creation

How Value is Created in Districts: A Brief Introduction

Statistical data quoted previously (see Table 2 and Figure 2) stimulate an inquiry into the nature of this superior performance for district firms compared to nondistrict firms. As remarked by several authors (see, among others, Markusen, 1996), Italian industrial districts have proposed in a revised version the model of districts described by Marshall[19] (1919). As in the case of Marshallian districts, the Italian ones have obtained benefits by agglomeration economies, which are external to single firms but internal to the district and differ from typical scale economies. They offer both production and transaction cost advantages, which are induced by a resource leverage but mostly by the development of a dynamic capability to create and maintain a systematic internal equilibrium made of a high interaction intensity among the players—interdependency-productive specialization and organizational flexibility.

Resource Leveraging and District Firms' Competitive Advantage

Tangible Resources

District firms have exploited both natural and human-made resources.

Natural resources as described previously have been sometimes relevant in districts' historical settle down, as they acted as an aggregative force to develop similar productions by different players in the same place. District firms have leveraged natural resources, as in the case of the following:

- Location-specific productions, whereas productive inputs are given by specific territory conditions (climate, soil, animal species, etc.)
- Closeness, easy access to input markets, or to end markets

In other cases, district firms have exploited technical, human-made resources, such as in the case of some machineries that incorporate specific local know-how. Examples of these resources go from simple tools (e.g., iron knitting needles) up to highly technological machineries that are necessary to create made-in-Italy style products.

Tangible resources in some cases have been a specific resource but are not the most relevant asset to get their competitive position. In fact, the best-leveraged resources by districts have been intangible.

The Relational Resource: The Basis for Interaction

One of the most relevant resources that can explain district firms' performances is a special mix of local social and economic dimensions. Technically productive and sociocultural relationships are simultaneously present in the district and recomposed by the territory (Becattini, 2000), so they establish a double tie between local community and local firms (Becattini, 1987) in line with a perfect economy-social embeddedness (Granovetter, 1985).

In fact, districts have generated a specific commitment of local people in firms and district future, because of economic and social value creation, in terms of employment increase or, in time of negative conjuncture, employment guarantee; self-employment.

District territory is meant as a social construction that is a social infrastructure made of the interdependence and dynamic relations of its players (Doeringer & Terkla, 1995; Rosenfeld, 1997). Social networks (Nohria & Eccles, 1992) are essential in each economic organization (Powell & Smith-Doerr, 1994) and, most of all, in districts[21]. Interactive forms, mostly informal, such as those in districts, are reinforced through time by developed trust mechanisms. Face-to-face interaction for a long time has been an important factor (Doeringer & Terkla, 1995; Rosenfeld, 1997) in districts for strategic orientation, commercial exchange, codesign, and recruiting processes and labor markets (Granovetter, 2005). Stable and reliable relationships plus connected trust and social reputation are parts of social capital (Lin, 2001), a specific district asset able to reduce firms' transaction costs. Uncertainty and perceived risk are reduced[22] by limited opportunistic behaviors and reduced control costs[23], which has made district firms more competitive on the local market. Besides, this kind of social capital encourages firms to give in outsourcing phases of their production process, stimulating labor division, flexible specialization (infra) and the creation of new small firms.

Relationships among firms can increase their efficiency (Williamson, 1989), but above all, they create proper conditions necessary to transfer intangibles (Lipparini & Sobrero, 1994), which is specifically true for stable relations such as those in districts. From a systemic point of view, the Italian industrial district finds its equilibrium (Sforzi, 1987) between competition and cooperation. Vertical cooperation occurs in buyer-seller relationships; horizontal competition among firms on the same level of the supply chain is not disruptive nor exasperated in the awareness of the width of the market and of their small dimension. For Porter (1990), local competition is the first source of advantage for clusters[24]; on the contrary, most district researchers (see, among others, Becattini, 1987; Bergman & Feser, 1999; Rosenfeld, 1997) address historical district success to trust-based and cooperative relationships[25]. In fact, district firms take benefit from "active channels for business transactions, communications and dialogue" and sharing "specialized infrastructure, labour markets and services" (Rosenfeld, 1997). Bergman and Feser (1999) remark the peculiarity and rareness of having trust-based relationships among competitors (among buyer-seller is less surprising) and indicate it as a peculiarity of Italian industrial districts.

The result has been the creation of a sort of competitive mutually reinforcing system further supported by community participation.[26] In fact, districts have generated a specific commitment of local people in firms and district future, because the district generates economic and social value in terms of employment increase or, in times of negative conjuncture, employment guarantee;, self-employment development by the effect of spin-offs generation; and so forth[27]. Local identification is with the district and the territory and not with the single leading firm, as occurs on the contrary in big industrial poles[28] (Sforzi & Lorenzini, 2002).

Information and Knowledge Exchange

In the district, knowledge is created, managed, and shared among its players. It is prevalently a tacit knowledge (Nonaka, 1994) that is localized, experience-related, application-specific (Becattini & Rullani, 1993), and both refined and stratified through time for the daily replication of productive processes in the district. At the basis of district knowledge creation is easy information circulation. Thanks to the social infrastructure, information is shared, analyzed, and collectively evaluated. Costs of coordination and information are low, and information asymmetries among local players are reduced spontaneously by informal mechanisms.[29] That is what Marshall (1919) calls the buzz, giving a continuous information flow to local players. The mechanism of knowledge propagation within the district is clearly described by Rullani (2003), who puts in evidence how, through multiple passages within the district, the same knowledge is co-used and co-exploited more than one time. This is, the author explains, a natural mechanism based upon the awareness of each district member, of the impossibility to retain its knowledge, and of the willingness to compensate this loss somehow. The result (Rullani, 2003) is a knowledge multiplicative process.

The district has information networks (Lane, 2003) that help players to know news about other players, products, processes, and solutions in order to be aligned with others and to decide their own future conduct. Information circulation is mostly informal, but somehow, it also is given by planned mechanisms in order to promote social interaction[30]. District meta-managerial organizations plan regular meetings specifically aimed at knowledge exchange. These players, as local CNA (national handicraft confederation) in Emilia Romagna, become a sort of information broker (Lane, 2003). They select and put together those entrepreneurs whose competences can be combined to create new products that fill a market potential niche; these opportunities may be identified by some other local entrepreneurs' indications during their travels abroad. Other ways to promote knowledge exchange is through services provided by metamanagerial organizations to all district members.

A facilitative process has been given by the investment in ICT technologies, by the integration of project CAD, production systems, and some modules that facilitate the interaction between the firm and its products and services providers as well as their customers. These systems provide the possibility to get a data interexchange through the Internet.[31]

District firms have leveraged their stratified knowledge and have built specific competences (Hamel & Prahalad, 1990) upon a know-how diffused on the territory and transmitted and improved from generation to generation, as in many manufacturers. In the district grow communities of practice and systems sharing ways of doing things learned by experience with no negotiation (Lane, 2003). Their learning is a learning by doing, by using, and by interacting[32] (Franz, Heimpold & Rosenfeld, 2005). It is a reciprocal mechanism (Polanyi, 1966) that has worked, thanks to an absorptive capability of single firms. This learning has made firms develop through time specific competences, generating organizational routines (Cyert & March, 1963; Nelson & Winter, 1982) that are able to improve their product offering. So, firms have leveraged their knowledge, creating the basis for value creation.

Reputation

Image and reputation have been essential resources for Italian industrial districts. They typically have been the result of a codefinition process made by both producers and markets. The development of technical competences in mature markets that distinguish firms' productive processes and output has made firms able to keep themselves close to the technological frontier in their fields.

Through product consumption or use, the buyer keeps in contact with the district firms' set of knowledge, competences, and experiences directly absorbed by products. As said, a district firm's offering always has been addressed naturally toward a specific target market, asking for high-quality products and willing to pay a premium price for that plus. So, firms have been able to create brands synonym of design, tradition in innovation, reliability, and quality. This specific reputation plus a general positive concept of the country by its cultural as well as natural resources have met in a general positive attitude toward products with a made-in-Italy label.

The Role of an Effective District Metamanagement

Belonging to a district for small firms also has meant the possibility of getting benefits from upper-level management. In fact, even though a district evolves by effect of firms' strategies, especially leading firms, it needs a general coordination and management, which can be done by metamanagement institutions both private and public. This allows district firms to count on a "a supportive tissue of local institutions" (Powell & Smith-Doerr, 1994, p. 370), which can positively drive and support district growth.

It is preferable that this player is a territorial expression. The district lead is often up to a board, the district committee, composed of all main local stakeholders interested in its development (e.g., local institutions' top representatives, chamber of commerce, category representatives, and trade unions). Metamanagement institutions operate directly or use other organizations (public, private, or with a mixed participation) to deliver services. A coordination and address role also is given by firms' consortia, which often also attract leading local firms.

An effective district metamanagement consists of the following (Alberti, 2001; Lane, 2003; Normann, 1979; Visconti, 2002):

- Defining a strategic orientation of the district and local development strategies; creating synergies with regional policy
- Supporting local structure and creating social and economic infrastructures in order to increase district competitiveness
- Supporting and assisting existing firms in their needs (e.g., how to access regional/national/UE financing programs, how to sell abroad)
- Promoting and supporting new startups promotions and support
- Protecting district identity and its intangibles

- Promoting district image by marketing and communication activities on both national as international markets

- Managing player relationships in order to get an internal equilibrium, to conciliate different firms' interests[33], and to valorize possible synergies with research institutions

- Helping firms to overcome difficulties (Rehfeld, 2005) such as lack of commitment, collaboration, and initiative, by promoting communication and alliances and by promoting the support of initiatives and cooperation

- Promoting human resources training activities

- Promoting initiatives that can improve product quality (i.e., standards, parameters, certifications) and new technology adoption

- Promoting environmental protection initiatives, especially in the case of productions that generate negative externalities on the environment in which they are located (e.g., chemical productions), such as eco-labels and adoption of green technologies.

- Promoting social accountability tools such as social balance sheets

- Attracting financial resources for the district and managing their local distribution

- Managing relationships with regional and nationally relevant institutions

- Representing local interests by a lobbying activity

District metamanagement is articulated and requires specific managerial skills in planning, organizing, and networking players. Small firms usually do not have these competences and skills inside and lack network resources[34]. So, during these years, for Italian small and medium-sized firms, belonging to a district also has meant benefiting from this district metamanagement as a specific added resource.

Public Support

Even though districts are born as spontaneous processes, above all, they can benefit from policymakers' interventions by a bottom-up process (Rosenfeld, 2002)[35]. Policymakers are responsible for the area development and attractiveness, especially for new capital, in order to "add to and sustain the Marshallian 'atmosphere' and 'buzz' of an economically successful place" (Taylor, 2005).

Supporting local strategies and connected scaffolds carried on by these players has to be done in consideration of specific local conditions. Public intervention more or less can impact district structure and strategy. In the case of a supportive and confirmative intervention, it is possible to identify (Rehfeld, quoted in Bruch-Krumbein & Hochmuth, 2000, p. 87) the following four main situations and corresponding best strategies:

- **Regions with existing productive districts:** Public support consists of strengthening localization factors (e.g., infrastructures, technology advisors, financing facilities).

- **Regions with emergent productive clusters:** Complementary institutions, such as R&D or research centers, specifically need to be supported, because they can sustain firms and district development.

- **Regions with structural economic prerequisites for district growth:** Policymakers encourage information and communication flows, and create opportunities and incentives for both existing and new firms.

- **Regions with declining or atrophic districts:** Dialogue and change have to be promoted by public support through new initiatives and development of joint promotional and revitalising programs.

Local policymakers can effectively valorize district resources, improving their competitiveness, by a financial and consulting contribution. Public sector financial support is in addition to the local bank's. It can be:

- Direct, if the public institution gives its own funds to district firms

- Indirect, if the public institution supports district firms to get access to both national and international (e.g., UE) funds

Policymakers also have an important role in district coordination (i.e., their representatives are members, as said, of the district committee) for their possibility to produce norms and standards to respect (Rullani & Bonomi, 2001). In some cases, standards can concern social issues such as workers' security and/or protection of environment and citizens (e.g., to prevent and reduce environmental damages, to establish incentives to use green technologies, to invest in toxic wastes treatment). Standards creation can facilitate district firms' interactions on the basis of defined norms, which can operate as a deterrent for eventual opportunistic behaviors. This action is necessary for external firms (e.g., international) that later come into the district more than for local firms that have their social norms.

Public support also can consist of promoting new spin-offs by incentives (e.g., as low-interest loans or sunk capitals) to the creation of new firms by women, young people, or disadvantaged people. In other cases, public support can facilitate employment through local incentives. Finally, policymakers can simplify administrative procedures (i.e., contracts, inspections).

In the described cases, district public support aims to reinforce the existing structure. In other cases, public intervention changes the district shape. There are two possibilities of change:

- A geographical reshaping (Taylor, 2005) through incentives to firms' locations in certain areas of the district

- An economic reshaping by promoting new industrial productive diversifications

Lighter or heavier, policymaker support is crucial, especially during the intermediate growth and maturity stages (Rehfeld, 2005). This has been and is still true for Italian districts' growth more than in other countries' cluster experiences.[36]

Dynamic Capabilities: Combining Specialization, Flexibility, and Integration

Leveraging resources and transforming knowledge into competences is a first key of inter-pretation of why belonging to a district may be a discriminative factor for firms. But district researchers went further.

One of the first factors to be analyzed by regional studies, industrial organizations, and strategic management theorists naturally has been firms' proximities and connected spatial externalities. Firms' proximities reduces transactional costs (Coase, 1937; Williamson, 1975, 1981, 1991), generates external localized economies, and makes the productive chain more efficient, not just for obvious reasons of physical distance. As said before, the advantage is in terms of reducing costs for the search and selection of partners and providers in negotia-tion and the coordination and control of contracts. This occurs for the described buyer-seller relationships that are trust-based and long-lasting in districts and able to minimize information asymmetries, moral hazard, and perceived risk of transaction[37]. This also means:

- For manufacturing firms, the immediate availability of specific goods and supportive services, sometimes co-designed
- For providers, the availability of a captive market with which they have a business preference lane

Transactional cost reduction also affects the market labor, allowing firms to get a trustworthy specialized workforce.

Thus, improved input-output relationships are one of spatial externalities (Mills, 1992); to these, it is possible to add shopping comparison reasons (i.e., in the district, buyers can find and evaluate a wide multiform offering and then negotiate face-to-face) and information reasons (i.e., a higher, more rapid diffusion of detailed information).

Thus, firms' proximities is the first, more evident source of competitive advantage of district firms (Doeringer & Terkla, 1995), but it is not the only source. The agglomeration explanation cannot be sufficient to explain value creation and the performance of district firms. So, the reason can be in the district dynamic capability to find an internal organization and to carry it on through further adjustments; specifically, the model proposed by districts[38] has been a model of flexible specialization, resulting from the work division and the combination of fragmented specialized activities made by different players. The competitiveness of a single district firm is up to the quality of local organization and its interaction with the environment.

Districts reproduce the condition of a geographically concentrated value constellation (Nor-mann & Ramirez, 1994). In fact, all the different players collaborating to the realization of a product do not simply add value, but they cocreate it in simultaneous ways (Normann & Ramirez, 1994) through a stable and territorially defined set of coproduction relationships. This is true for both effectiveness and efficiency considerations.

Regarding efficiency, the research results shown in Figure 2 (Fabiani, Pellegrini, Romag-nano & Signorini, 2000a, 2000b) give interesting evidence about the connection among the performance made by district firms (superior to the one by non-district firms in the period 1982-1995), work division, and a systemic flexibility. Relevant differences between district and non-district firms, configuring specific sources of a better performance for the former, were specifically recognized in a lower total cost of labor and capital and in a superior productivity per worker. The lower cost of labor was not due to lower salaries; on the contrary, sometimes salaries paid by district firms were even a bit higher than those paid by non-district firms (Casavola, Pellegrini & Romagnano, 2000). In comparing solutions adopted in order to face temporary production increases or decreases between the two groups, researchers found that a sensible difference of management conduct was in the kind of contracts stipulated and the kind of workers hired (see Table 2). In fact, district firms, in order to overcome temporary production increases, used various flexibility tools more than non-district ones did. District firms:

- Mostly used the tools to adopt outsourcing more than other firms and to employ home workers (especially women) and apprentices (usually paid less than full-time specialized workers)[39]; this is the biggest difference in use by the two groups (40.9% vs. 27.4%)
- Adopt overtime work (59.5% vs. 50.8%)
- Add other shifts over the weekend or at night (7.8% vs. 6.6%)

On the contrary, in case of temporary production reduction, district firms show they make (see Table 3) a smaller use than nondistrict firms of no renewal

Table 3. Flexibility tools and related use by firms in case of temporary production increase/ reduction (% values) (Source: Omiccioli and Quintilliani, 2000)

Flexibility Forms	District Firms	Non-District Firms
In case of temporary production increase		
Hours flexibility with equal total annual amount	34.8	36
Overtime work	59.5	50.8
Research of limited-time personnel	30.8	30.5
Introduction of added weekly shifts	8.1	8.6
Introduction of added weekend or night shifts	7.8	6.6
Higher outsourcing or home work	40.9	27.4
In case of temporary production reduction		
Hours flexibility with equal total annual amount	48.7	50.5
Ordinary social security program	26.8	25.3
No renewal of limited time contracts	22.5	28.9
Dismissals	4.2	4.7
Local social shock absorbers programs	3.9	5.8
Lower outsourcing or home work	43.6	26.8

As the research shows, flexibility is not specifically a contractually based one, but rather a flexibility in firms' relationships, which has its roots in the district social-economic embeddedness. According to data in Table 3, the system shows a systemic flexibility as a local productive system and not a firm-specific characteristic made up of high internal mobility. This makes the district a tank of slack resources (Bourgeois, 1981; Bourgeois & Singh, 1983; Cheng & Kesner, 1997; Cyert & March, 1963), a cushion of addable productive resources that are available to firms' management, if they occur[40]. The result is a sort of self-containment of the district, which becomes a source of better efficiency; fixed costs go down, and thus, the break-even and equilibrium revenues are also lower.

Italian Districts' Crisis Stage: Mining the Drivers to Competitiveness

The start of the new millennium was not favorable to Italian industrial districts that have been suffering specific conjuncture effects, some continental and some global. Euro introduction, the lack of control on prices, the new coin appreciation in foreign markets, which made national exports more expensive, have been the main UE internal factors. To them, other global factors already present in the 1990s have dramatically increased their negative pressure on industrial district firms. Among the latter, it is possible to identify a demand contraction for many manufacturing industries and a more aggressive global competition with new players (especially China) that are able to produce lower-quality goods, often by imitation,[41] at lower prices, most of all thanks to a much lower labor cost.

The presence on the market of these producers that offer products similar to Italian ones, but with a lower quality and at a lower price, have modified world demand patterns and have become very dangerous competitors in many segments of both industrial and consumer demands. Price-based competition moved some demand segments from traditional and personalized high-quality goods from Italian districts (Signorini & Omiccioli, 2005) to the new comers.

In recent years, demand and competitive conditions have changed, and district manufacturing firms are now specifically suffering these factors, because they see a slow erosion of their competitive position. Italian district firms' competition historically has been a non-price competition, but it has been based upon design and product quality. Natural resources exploited by the location of specific productions (e.g., some food products) are less replicable by competitors, as previously stated, and thus may have guaranteed district firms a specific sustainable competitive advantage. But, as said, they are not so relevant, and the Italian system is a manufacturing system.

Products imitation also has been made easier by the previously described business diversification inside districts in which application-specific machineries are produced and sold; this, in fact, has obtained two opposite results:

- Reinforced competitive position of machinery producers (operating on a business-to-business market) that are recognized as specialists in their field.

• It has also made accessible to foreign country competitors those machineries, and thus has created the condition of an easier imitation/replication of their output. This has weakened the competitive position of final made-in-Italy producers (operating on a business-to-consumer market).

Just high technological productions seem to be protected by high levels of entry barriers in terms of capital and competencies required. But, as shown by Figure 1, also high technology districts are a minority, since the Italian manufacturing system is mainly concentrated on traditional mature industries.

Another problem still present in the 1990s and rapidly grown through the years was the ICT world diffusion. Modern ICTs created a favorable knowledge diffusion (Malone & Rockart, 1991) by the reduction of information costs and helped firms to manage their international virtually integrated value chains. Italian district firms have a slowly reducing gap in ICT adoption, but this is not the focal point. Global scale relationships can do without constant face-to-face interactions, and so it is easy to notice how district firms can see the value of their proximity and the agglomeration economies decrease (Rullani, 1997).

Besides, ICT diffusion makes it easier for single firms to autonomously access external resources; district firms could be attracted in order to be more competitive and to join international value chains (Humphrey & Schmitz, 2001), which can represent a potential risk of reducing district internal cohesion.

ICT development plus globalization have changed the rules of competition and have been a dangerous mix for a system such as the district one. A district is characterized by flexibility and high relationship intensity in its internal organization, but districts historically have been rigid in a worldwide competition and sometimes have tended to be closed system (e.g., internal providers and internal production chains). Many districts have relied too long on their own resources, remaining not perfectly permeable by the external environment, which has limited the kind of acquirable knowledge in times of rapid change, blocking innovation.

It is clear that the described occurred changes are asking Italian industrial districts for both a technological (Signorini & Omiccioli, 2005) and an organizational adaptation.

Districts' Ongoing Evolution and Future Perspectives

Clearly, districts are living a transition stage in their development path (Corò & Grandinetti, 1999) and need an upgrading strategy. The challenge is mainly strategic and has consequences regarding production, finance, organization, and marketing. Some authors already have criticized district metamanagement organizations as well as policymakers' strategies for having sustained small firms instead of medium and large ones that are more able to contrast multinational competition, and for having specialized the district in not so competitive industries, leaving them exposed to negative demand fluctuations (see Rosenfeld, 1997, for an analysis of these critics). But it is clear that districts' changes cannot be a sort of distortion of their nature.[42] It is also clear that Italian districts cannot run for a price competition but have to valorize their own strengths and be coherent with their strategic positioning choices made of high-quality, reliable products.

District firms have to reinforce and consolidate their own market shares upon their world target markets by reinforcing their product offerings through process innovation and marketing. The search for competitiveness has to start from there.

A point with which most industrial districts researchers agree (see, among others, Becattini, 1990; Bellandi, 1996; Berger & Locke, 2000; Guerrieri & Pietrobelli, 2000; Rullani, 2003) is the necessity for districts to leave a too much closed and self-referential approach to business, passing to a major international openness and adopting a metanational perspective (Doz, Santos & Williamson, 2001).

During past years, districts gradually have started to modify their value chains, which have been opened up not just at the end phases (i.e., selling abroad) but also in the upper and intermediate productive ones. This has been done through the development of extensive partnerships with extra-district, mostly international players.

Through this process, district firms have started to realize the following three principle benefits:

- New knowledge acquisition
- New financial resources acquisition
- Cost advantages and, thus, a competitive improvement

About the first issue of knowledge, as said, a system that learns to protect itself by closing itself to the external environment and whose knowledge is a self-generated and internally propagated one is not sustainable anymore, at least not after the Internet revolution[43]. What districts are called to do is to amplify their cognitive openness (Grandinetti & Rullani, 1996). A new knowledge fertilization is required as well as a comparison with different ways of doing things.[44]

Joining an international value constellation can mean that firms must revise internal knowledge. But a dominant tacit and experience-based knowledge, such as the typical district one, is less easily imitated and does not help firms in case of knowledge sharing. In fact, it is neither easily analyzed nor exportable to new non-district value coproducers and needs to be codified. Codified knowledge, making tacit knowledge explicit (Nonaka, 1994; Polanyi, 1966), easily can be exchanged with both providers and clients, internal as well as external to the district (Rullani & Bonomi, 2001). Joining an international value system also can mean that firms must be more selective toward themselves and their internal providers; in fact, opening up the system to extra-district subcontractors can help local providers to consider their market a noncaptive one and, thus, improve their quality.

The second point concerns new capital acquisition. Fresh financial resources are needed to make new investments for firms' competitiveness, and foreign capital incoming mobility toward districts can be a solution, and in a short-time perspective, it is.[45] Thus, opening the district to one or more consistent foreign industrial players, component can be useful in order to strengthen the district. But it is a practice that requires a gradual selection of possible players, because as some authors specify (Bergman & Locke, 2000), this also can be perceived by actual players as a threat, as an altering factor for local equilibrium able to dilute local culture and values and to modify community practices.

The last benefit of the district's possible evolution through a major international openness is cost-related and the most critical point; in fact, it implies consideration about localization. Globalization has shown (Berger & Locke, 2000) the cost gaps obtainable by delocalizing productive phases in lower-wage countries (Bartlett & Ghoshal, 1989; Berger & Locke, 2000; Dunning, 1981) and has reshaped the industrial international map by overdividing firms' managements from productive locations.[46]

Research of 182 leading firms of a sample of Italian districts (Micelli, Chiarvesio & Di Maria, 2003) has shown that 90% of the interviewed firms has outsourced at least one productive phase, and 41% of the sample has opened the value chain to foreign suppliers and subcontractors. Among these firms (41% of the sample), 34.7% has made direct investments abroad (e.g., plants building) in order to exploit lower wage advantages and to keep themselves closer to emerging, attractive final markets[47], and 61.3% has chosen leaner solutions, such as foreign suppliers and subcontractors.

Direct investments have been made especially toward Eastern UE followed by Western UE and South America. Strategic suppliers mainly are chosen in the UE and Far East; subcontractors mainly are chosen in Eastern UE followed by the Far East (e.g., China, Taiwan) and other UE countries plus emerging Tunisia. The study (Micelli, Chiarvesio & Di Maria, 2003) also has revealed some differences in consideration of different districts' productive specializations; for example, fashion and mechanical industry districts have opened up their frontiers to foreign suppliers and subcontractors; home productions have done it less, preferring local partners.

In case of massive adoption by districts' firms of both production delocalization and foreign suppliers and/or subcontractors choosing, it is possible to imagine consequences on the social and economic local systems. The extreme of this delocalization process with its consequences is given by the fascinating solution of district structure replication in low-wage countries[48]. From a strategic point of view, in this way, firms and districts can perceive new locations as a sort of international subsidiary and can build the benefit of long-term trusty relationships at lower costs. But the solution emphasizes the threats about general massive delocalization districts' policies. The first regards districts impoverishment (Alberti & Sciascia, 2004); the district loses value, resources, employees, subcontracting, and supply contracts, which has social and economic consequences and can be evaluated in a long-term systemic analysis. The other problem consists of knowledge systemic transfer toward another area, which has different cost structures, and in this way gets specialized knowledge. These problems have to be carefully analyzed by metamanagement organizations.

Thus, delocalization should be gradual and should concern some low added value phases. Within, the district firms have to maintain their management activities and their R&D functions and keep investments in technology and design in order to get higher value-added products (Istat, 2002) and make a parallel specialization—upgrade of local workforce.

In this way, competitive advantage can be defended by intangibles that are less mobile factors and, thus, more competitive in the international context (Becattini & Rullani, 1993, Istat, 2002). But clearly, districts are moving from their original shape and concept.

The strategic and organizational adaptation has to be carried on together with a parallel technological adaptation (Belussi, Gottardi & Rullani, 2003) that mainly is focused on ICT evolutions.

Districts have to launch programs aimed at a renewal of available information and communication technology by the adoption of tools such as intranets, vertical and horizontal portals, virtual marketplaces,[49] videoconferencing, CAD shared use, groupware solutions, and EDI integrations. The use of these tools actually needs to be improved, specifically with subcontractors and extra-district suppliers[50] (Micelli, Chiarvesio, & Di Maria, 2003).

In order to achieve a technological improvement, it will be necessary to invest in universities and research centers (see, among others, Viljamaa & Martinez Vela, 2003; Wolter, 2003); districts' productive sides coevolve with their scientific sides. So, technological innovation can be made sustainable through time by:

- Giving firms and their personnel a continuous learning upgrade stimulation through research projects and training programs.
- Being a regular tank of young skilled technicians, the owner of a formalized knowledge.

Both strategic and technological adaptations are necessary; the first, as said, requires much time and care of social and cultural issues. Technological adaptation can and has to be more rapid. It must be seen by district entrepreneurs, metamanagement, and public supporting institutions as a necessary investment.

Conclusion

Districts have proposed a different model of growth. Recent global challenges ask them to revises that patterns in order to remain competitive. Different solutions as ICTs development, joining global value chains, and so forth, can be proposed.

Districts are complex systems, and in complex systems, modifying a single element implies the need for the system to find a new balance.

The most important challenge for the districts will be to identify an evolving path, considering all social, cultural, and economic short- and medium-term consequences. This path will have to be designed without letting districts lose their main resources; that is, their own identity, respecting their complex, fascinating natures.

Acknowledgments

The author thanks the editors and especially Robert MacGregor for the support in writing this chapter, and gratefully acknowledges the two anonymous reviewers' thoughful comments. Special thanks to Eva Cutolo, for her helpful support and comments.

References

Alberti, F. (2001). *The governance of industrial districts: A theoretical footing proposal* (LIUC Paper No. 82). University of Castellanza.

Alberti, F., & Sciascia, S. (2004). *Le politiche di marchio per i distretti industriali. i casi di Como e Biella* (LIUC Paper No.147). University of Castellanza.

Arthur, W. B. (1990). Silicon Valley locational clusters: When do increasing returns imply monopoly? *Mathematical Social Sciences, 19*, 235-251.

Barney, B., & Ouchi, W. G. (1984). Information cost and organizational governance. *Management Science, 10*.

Bartlett, C. A., & Ghoshal, S. (1989). *Managing across borders: The transnational solution.* Boston: Harvard Business School Press.

Becattini, G. (1987). *Mercato e forze locali—Il distretto industriale.* Bologna: Il Mulino.

Becattini, G. (1991). Il distretto industriale marshalliano come concetto socioeconomico. In F. Pyke, G.Becattini, & W.Sengenberger (Eds.), Distretti industriali e cooperazione fra imprese in Italia. Studi & Informazioni. *Quaderni, 34*. Banca Toscana: Firenze.

Becattini, G. (2000). *Il distretto industriale.* Torino: Rosemberg & Sellier.

Becattini, G., & Rullani, E. (1993). Sistema locale e mercato globale. *Economia e Politica Industriale, 80*.

Bellandi, M. (1996). Innovation and change in the marshallian industrial district. *European Planning Studies, 4*(3), 353-364.

Bellandi, M. (2001). Local development and embedded large firms. *Entrepreneurship and Regional Development, 13*(3), 189-210.

Belussi, F., Gottardi, G., & Rullani E. (Eds.). (2003). *The technological evolution of industrial districts.* Boston: Kluwer.

Berger, S., & Locke, R.M. (2000). *Il caso italiano and globalization.* MIT IPC Globalisation Working Paper 00.008.

Bergman, E. M., & Feser, E. J. (1999). Industrial and regional clusters: Concepts and comparative applications. In *The Web book of regional science.* WVU Regional Research Institute. Retrieved November, 2005, from http://www.wvu.edu

Biggiero, L. (1999). Markets, hierarchies, networks, districts: A cybernetic approach. *Human Systems Management, 18*(2).

Bourgeois, L. J. (1981). On the measurement of organizational slack. *Academy of Management Review, 6*(1), 29-39.

Bourgeois, L. J., & Singh, J. V. (1983). Organizational slack and political behaviour within top management teams. *Academy of Management Proceedings, 43-47.*

Britton, J. N. H. (2004). The path dependence of multimedia: Explaining Toronto's cluster. In *Proceedings of the 6th Annual ISRN National Meeting*, Vancouver.

Bruch-Krumbein, W., & Hochmuth, E. (2000). *Cluster und clusterpolitik. Begriffliche grundlagen und empirische falldeispiele aus ostdeutschland.* Marburg: Schueren.

Casavola, P., Pellegrini, G., & Romagnano, E. (2000). Imprese e mercato del lavoro nei distretti industriali. In L. F. Signorini (Ed.), *Lo sviluppo locale*. Roma: Donzelli.

Castilla, E. J., Hwang, H., Granovetter, H., & Granovetter, M. (2000). Social networks in Silicon Valley. In C. M. Lee, C. F. Miller, M. C. Hancock, & H. R. Rowen (Eds.), *The Silicon Valley edge: A habitat for innovation and entrepreneurship* (pp. 218-247). Stanford, CA: Stanford University Press.

Chandler, A. D. (1977). *The visible hand*. Cambridge, MA: Harvard University Press.

Cheng, J. L. C., & Kesner, I. F. (1997). Organizational slack and response to environmental shifts: The impact of resource allocation patterns. *Journal of Management*.

Coase, R. (1937). The nature of the firm. *Economica, 4*(16), 386-405.

Corò, G., & Grandinetti, R. (1999). Evolutionary patterns of Italian industrial districts. *Human Systems Management, 18*(2).

Cyert, R. M., & March, J. G. (1963). *A behavioural theory of the firm*. Englewood Cliffs, NJ: Prentice-Hall.

Doeringer, P. B., & Terkla, D. G. (1995). Business strategy and cross-industry clusters. *Economic Development Quarterly, 9*, 225-237.

Doz, Y., Santos, J., & Williamson, P. (2001). *From global to metanational*. Boston: Harvard Business School Press.

Dunning, J. H. (1981). *International production and the multinational enterprise*. London: Allen & Unwin.

Fabiani, S., Pellegrini, G., Romagnano, E., & Signorini, L. F. (2000a). Efficiency and localisation: The case of Italian districts. In M. Bagella & L. Becchetti (Eds.), *The competitive advantage of Italian districts: Theoretical and empirical analysis*. Heidelberg: Physica Verlag.

Fabiani, S., Pellegrini, G., Romagnano, E., & Signorini, L. F. (2000b). L'efficienza delle imprese nei distretti industriali italiani. In L.F. Signorini (Ed.), *Lo sviluppo locale. Un'indagine della banca d'Italia sui distretti industriali*. Roma: Donzelli-Meridiana.

Franz, P., Heimpold, G., & Rosenfeld, M. T. W. (2005). The pattern of spatially concentrated industries in East Germany: A contribution to the discussion of economic "clusters." In *Proceedings of the International Conference on Regional Growth Agendas*, Aalborg, Denmark.

Grandinetti, R., & Rullani, E. (1996). *Impresa transnazionale ed economia globale*. Roma: NIS.

Granovetter, M. (1985). Economic action and social structure: The problem of "embeddedness." *American Journal of Sociology, 91*(3), 481-510.

Granovetter, M. (2005). The impact of social structures on economic outcomes. *The Journal of Economic Perspectives, 19*(1), 33-50.

Hamel, G., & Prahalad, C. K. (1990, May-June). *The core competence of the corporation. Harvard Business Review*, 79-91.

Harrison, B., & Glasmeier, A. K. (1997). Response: Why business alone won't redevelop the inner city: A friendly critique of Michael Porter's approach to urban revitalization. *Economic Development Quarterly, 11*(1), 28-38.

Humphrey, J., & Schmitz, H. (2001). *Developing country firms in the world economy: Governance and upgrading in global value chains* (INEF Report no.61). Duisburg: Institut fur Entwicklung und Frieden der Gerhard-Mercator-Universitat.

Jacobs, D., & De Man, A.P. (1996). Clusters, industrial policy and firm strategy: A menu approach. *Technology Analysis and Strategic Management, 8*(4), 425-437.

Krugman, P. (1993). First nature, second nature and metropolitan location. *Regional Science, 33.*

Lane, D.A. (2003). Distretti industriali come sistemi complessi. *Impresa e stato*, 63-64.

Lin, N. (2001). *Social capital. A theory of social structure and action.* Cambridge: Cambridge University Press.

Lipparini, A., & Sobrero, M. (1994). The glue and the pieces: Entrepreneurship and innovation in small-firms networks. *Journal of Business Venturing, 2.*

Malone, T. W., & Rockart, J.F. (1991). Computers, networks and the corporation. *Scientific American, 265*(3), 128.

Markusen, A. (1996). Sticky places in slippery space: A typology of industrial districts. *Economic Geography, 72*(2), 294-314.

Marshall, A. (1919). *Principles of economics* (8th ed.). London: Macmillan.

Martin, R. (1998). The new "geographical turn" in economics: Some critical reflections. *Cambridge Journal of Economics, 23*, 65-91.

Micelli, S., Chiarvesio, M., & Di Maria, E. (2003). *Processi di internazionalizzazione e strategie delle imprese distrettuali tra delocalizzazione e innovazione.* Proceedings of the Conference of the Istituto Nazionale per il Commercio Estero: Internazionalizzazione e frammentazione della produzione nei distretti industriali, Roma.

Mills, E. S. (1992). Sectoral clustering and metropolitan development. In E.S. Mills, & J.F. McDonald (Eds.), *Sources of metropolitan growth* (pp. 3-18). New Brunswick: Center for Urban Policy Research.

Mohr, L. B. (1969). Determinants of innovation in organizations. *The American Political Review, 63*, 111-126.

Nelson, R.R., & Winter, S.G. (1982). *An evolutionary theory of economic change.* Cambridge, MA: Harvard University Press.

Nohria, N., & Eccles, R. G. (Eds.). (1992). *Networks and organizations. Structure, form and action.* Boston: Harvard Business School Press.

Nonaka, I. (1994). A dynamic theory of organisational knowledge creation. *Organisation Science, 5*, 1.

Normann, R. (1977). *Management of growth.* Baffins Lane: John Wiley & Sons.

Normann, R., & Ramirez, R. (1994). *Designing Interactive strategy. From value chain, to value constellation.* Baffins Lane: John Wiley & Sons.

Omiccioli, M. (2000). L'organizzazione dell'attività produttiva nei distretti industriali. In L. F. Signorini (Ed.), *Lo sviluppo locale. Un'indagine della banca d'Italia sui distretti industriali.* Roma: Donzelli-Meridiana.

Omiccioli, M., & Quintiliani, F. (2000). Assetti imprenditoriali, organizzazione del lavoro e mobilità nei distretti industriali. In L.F. Signorini (Ed.), *Lo sviluppo locale. Un'indagine della banca d'Italia sui distretti industriali*. Roma: Donzelli-Meridiana.

Ouchi, W.G. (1979). A conceptual framework for the design of organisational control mechanisms. *Management Science, 25*, 838-848.

Ouchi, W.G. (1980). Markets, bureaucracies and clans. *Administrative Quarterly, 25*, 129-141.

Perroux, F. (1955). La notion de pole de croissance. *Economie Appliquèe*, 1-2.

Piore, M., & Sabel, C. (1984). *The second industrial divide: Possibilities for prosperity*. New York: Basic Books.

Polanyi, M. (1966). *The tacit dimension*. New York: Doubleday.

Porter, M. (1998). *On competition*. Boston: Harvard Business School Press.

Porter, M.E. (1990). *The competitive advantage of nations*. New York: The Free Press.

Porter, M.E. (2000). Location, competition and economic development. Local clusters in the global economy. *Economic Development Quarterly, 14*(1), 15-31.

Powell, W.W., & Smith-Doerr, L. (1994). Networks and economic life. In N. Smelser, & R. Swedberg (Eds.), *Handbook of Economic Sociology*. Princeton, NJ: Princeton University Press.

Pyke, F., & Sengenberger, W. (Eds.). (1992). *Industrial districts and local economic regeneration*. Geneva: ILO - International Institute for Labour Studies.

Rehfeld, D. (2005). *Cluster management, sectoral change and the context of structural policy*. Proceedings of the Regional Studies Association Conference, Aalborg, Denmark.

Rosenfeld, S.A. (1995). *Industrial strength strategies: Regional business clusters and public policy*. Washington, DC: The Aspen Institute.

Rosenfeld, S. A. (1997). Bringing business clusters into the mainstream of economic development. *European Planning Studies, 5*(1), 3-23.

Rosenfeld, S.A. (2002). *Creating smart systems: A guide to cluster strategies in less favoured regions*. Brussels: European Union Regional Policy.

Rullani, E. (1997). L'evoluzione dei distretti industriali: Un percorso tra decostruzione e internazionalizzazione. In R. Varaldo & F. Ferrucci (Eds.), *Il distretto industriale tra logiche di impresa e logiche di sistema* (pp. 54-85). Milano: Franco Angeli.

Rullani, E. (1998). Internazionalizzazione e nuovi sistemi di governance nei sistemi produttivi locali. In G. Corò & E. Rullani (Eds.). (1998). *Percorsi locali di internazionalizzazione. Competenze e auto-organizzazione nei distretti industriali del Nord Est*. Milano: FrancoAngeli.

Rullani, E. (2003). I distretti industriali al tempo dell'economia globale. *Impresa e stato, 63-64*.

Rullani, E., & Bonomi, A. (2001). *Rapporto sui distretti industriali italiani. Introduzione. Quaderni di impresa artigiana*. Milano: Aaster-confartigianato.

Sforzi, F. (1987). *L'identificazione spaziale*. In G. Becattini (Ed.), *Mercato e forze locali. il distretto industriale* (pp. 143-167). Bologna: Il Mulino.

Sforzi, F., & Lorenzini, F. (2002). *I distretti industriali.* In IPI, *L'esperienza italiana dei distretti industriali.* Roma: IPI—Istituto per la Promozione Industriale.

Signorini, L.F., & Omiccioli, M. (2002). *L'indagine della banca d'Italia sui distretti industriali.* In IPI, *L'esperienza italiana dei distretti industriali.* Roma: IPI—Istituto per la Promozione Industriale.

Simmie, J., & Sennett, J. (1999). Innovative clusters: Global or local linkages? *National Institute Economic Review, 170.*

Taylor, M. (2005). "Clusters": The mesmerising mantra. In *Proceedings of the Regional Studies Association Conference,* Aalborg, Denmark.

Taylor, M. (2005). Embedded local growth: A theory taken too far? In R.A. Boschma, & R.C. Kloosterman (Eds.), *Learning from clusters. A critical assessment from an economic-geographical perspective* (pp. 69-88). Dordrecht: Springer.

Thorelli, H. (1986). Networks: Between markets and hierarchies. *Strategic Management Journal, 7.*

Viljamaa, K., & Martinez Vela, C. (2003). Regional competence building as a coevolution of industry and university. The case of mobile machines industry in Tampere region. In *Proceedings of the Regional Studies Association International Conference,* Pisa, Italy.

Visconti, F. (2002). *Il governo dei distretti industriali. Strategie, strutture e ruoli.* Milano: Egea.

Williamson, O. E. (1975). *Markets and hierarchies.* New York: Free Press.

Williamson, O. E. (1979). Transaction-cost economics: The governance of contractual relations. *Journal of Law and Economics, 22,* 233-261.

Williamson, O. E. (1981). The economics of organization: The transaction cost approach. *American Journal of Sociology, 87,* 548-577.

Williamson, O. E. (1991). Comparative economic organization: The analysis of discrete structural alternatives. *Administrative Science Quarterly, 36,* 269-296.

Williamson, P. J. (1989). *Corporatism in perspective: An introductory guide to corporatist theory.* London: Sage Publications.

Wolter, K. (2003). Knowledge, industrial organisation and spatial distribution of firms: Some lessons from the German biotechnology industry. In *Proceedings of the Regional Studies Association's International Conference on Reinventing Regions in a Global Economy,* Pisa, Italy.

Zanni, L., & Labory, S.(2002). Le formule imprenditoriali nel settore moda: Caratteri strutturali e strategie competitive delle imprese protagoniste. In L. Bacci (Ed.), *Distretti e imprese leader nel sistema moda della Toscana.* Milano: Franco Angeli.

Endnotes

[1] Different from networks (Rosenfeld, 1997), districts have specific characteristics (described later) such as open participation, both cooperative and competing dynamics, a collective and not just a business vision, respect of social norms, trust, and reciprocal mechanisms. Districts stimulate the generation of new spin-off firms with similar and linked capacities, that makes them grow by propagation.

[2] This choice, induced by district specificities, has attracted for a long time some critics of literature fragmentation.

[3] Istat (2002) analysis considered different parameters that were able to identify a district; among these parameters are industrialization ratio (i.e., number of employees in the area/number of employees in the manufacturing industry) and the productive specialization ratio (i.e., number of employees in the specific sector/number of employees in the area). Researchers considered district indicators, whereas both ratios were superior to 30% of the national data.

[4] Good examples of leading Italian firms that operate as global players are Ferragamo and Gucci (global players in the fashion industry), Luxottica (leader in the production of glasses and sunglasses labeled with the most known global brands), and Natuzzi (producer of sofas and armchairs).

[5] Universities and research centers play a key role in knowledge sharing. Universities, for example, introduce specific courses in order to prepare human resources to be employed in district firms, activate exchange programs, organize seminars, provide post-graduate training to managers, send their students to local firms for internships, generate papers and dissertation writing, and so forth.

[6] See, for example, the Istat ratios in endnote no. 3.

[7] For example, the territory of Como has two important districts relevant for export: textiles and garment industry (correlated), and knives and metal utensils (uncorrelated to the previous two), both in the first 20 districts by contribution to national export. Besides the two, there are other secondary productions. Similarly, Lucca is within the first 20 districts for the footwear district but also has developed a paper production district and marble production district.

[8] An example of this kind of vertical productive integration and connected business diversification is given by Biella yarns district, which evolved also to make the related machineries.

[9] In this case, the district can show some similarities with the hub-and-spoke industrial cluster described by Markusen (1997) and centered on one or more externally oriented leading firms (supra) with other smaller firms revolving around them.

[10] After several years of hired work in a district firm, workers leave and create their own firms; this happens within districts more than outside (Omiccioli & Quintiliani, 2000).

[11] An example of district evolution is given by the Cusio-Valsesia district, which produces taps and valves. The first activity in the area, which goes back to 1500, is regarded as bronze fusion for producing bells. The specific competence is tacit and rare. Masters

have been transmitting it from generation to generation. As this demand went down, in 1890, a family spin-off started, diversifying their production and using the same technology to produce valves and taps for the hydro-thermo-sanitary industry.

[12] An interesting example is given by the paper district in Lucca. Paper production was introduced locally at the beginning of 14th century. In 1307, local manufacturers who specialized in high-quality paper production gathered in a specialized productive association. The diffusion of a substitutive product (a paper obtained by rags and, thus, cheaper) stopped their production. In 1700, some miles away, local paper traditional production was diffused again for the growth of local editorial productions, demanding good quality paper. In the area close to Fermo, the location of the footwear district, this production started because local agriculture gave good results—enough to live. This fact, combined with an entrepreneurial spirit, induced the idea of productive diversification. The agricultural good performance had the role of an insurance for the risk of a new industrial activity; without it, the industrial production perhaps would have not had the chance to develop.

[13] In the first industrial stage, water was a crucial factor as a source of energy. For this reason, many manufacturers, such as textiles and leather products, were strategically located close to lakes and rivers. For similar reasons, in Belluno, the glass district settled down and grew thanks to the local availability of important natural resources in the area. Crystal came from local mountains, and water came from the Venice lagoon. So, the presence of natural resources created the favorable conditions to let glass production grow.

[14] This explains the generation and growth of multitype aggregated districts, a sort of multiclusters related to urban centers (Simmie & Sennett, 1999), which are relevant trading nodes. In this case, the agglomerative factor is the city and its logistic.

[15] District localization is critical for its development. Porter (1990) says that "successful firms are frequently concentrated in particular cities or states within a nation" (p. 29). Not by chance, goes on Porter, main industrial pharmaceutical firms are located in Basel, and many advertising agencies are concentrated on Madison Avenue in New York City.

[16] For example, the hills close to Biella gave local farmworkers a scarce quantity of agricultural resources; the most valuable resource was sheep. Since 1400, shepherds have treated their wool and sold it to merchants.

[17] Spin-offs are encouraged by a virtuous system. An example is the couch district in Matera. The biggest firm, Natuzzi, was a spin-off that was created by a worker of another local firm. On the same token, the actual second and third firm in the district (Nicoletti and Calia) both were created by two of Natuzzi's employees.

[18] This means, for example, that a firm producing tiles in the Sassuolo district (specialized in tile production) gets an economic performance superior to the one gotten by a same-sized firm producing tiles located outside a tile specialized district.

[19] Marshall (1919) dedicates an entire chapter to economies derived by spatial proximity and compares the district to the big firm. He recognizes that a big firm is more competitive in the long run but, on the other hand, sees that the same economic benefits obtainable through wide-scale production by some big firms can be obtained by a group of small or medium enterprises that are spatially concentrated and interconnected.

Marshall (1919) identifies three kinds of agglomeration economies: input or infra-structures sharing; a more qualified labor demand and better interaction among firms; and a greater accumulation and sharing of information. This is possible, as Marshall (1919) points out, thanks to the work division and connected specialization gained by single units that are part of the system and are reorganized into smaller productive subsystems. So, district firms become more specialized and complementary.

20   District firms (in the persons of their entrepreneurs, managers, and workers) share a common cultural identity, values, codes and references, uses, and common knowledge, which make sense to them.

21   Granovetter (1973) identifies and describes "the role of weak ties" and points out their utility in order for individuals to integrate themselves in the community. A strong tie occurs through a longlasting relationship, an emotional intensity, intimacy, and recip-rocal services. As Lohr (1982) describes it, "Friendships and longstanding personal connections affect business connections" (cited in Granovetter, 1985). In both formal and informal districts, strong and weak ties are present; regarding the Silicon Valley experience, Castilla, et al. (2003) remark how they have been a crucial aspect in the history of the district.

22   Common language and culture, common unwritten codes of conduct, peer pressure, and information circulation make entering and observing contracts easier (Signorini & Omiccioli, 2002).

23   The social linkage within the district establishes a mechanism that shows some simi-larities with the clan (Ouchi, 1979, 1980) in terms of high levels of solidarity, interde-pendency, identification with the group, trust, and discipline. Information circulation is high, and high is the coordination. Common goals commitment and reciprocity avoid that members search for an immediate advantage. They know that in a medium-long term what they have given is balanced by what they have taken (Butler, 1982; Barney and Ouchi, 1984).

24   "Geographic concentration of rivals, customers, and suppliers in a region will promote innovation and competitiveness in a cluster" (Porter, 1990).

25   Also Chandler (1990) views cooperation as one of the most crucial factors in modern capitalism.

26   The specialization degree is a useful ratio calculated as workforce employed in district firms/total workforce in the area. For example, this ratio in the case of the silk textile production district in Como is 55.2%, which means that one out of every two local workers is employed in a district firm (Alberti & Sciascia, 2004).

27   If a small village offers work opportunities, thanks to district firms, young people have one more reason to stay.

28   An example of industrial Italian pole is the Turin pole, rotating around the Fiat car manufacturing company.

29   Local media, universities, banks, and even bars and restaurants promote intradistrict communication.

30   These are mechanisms similar to those introduced in the Silicon Valley (Castilla, Hwang, Granovetter & Granovetter, 2000; Lane, 2003) that stimulate interaction among

similar professional figures working for different companies and produce situations that can generate multiplicative effects. Some of these initiatives are cognitive scaffolds (Lane, 2003) such as, for example, the lack of sanctions for workers leaving a firm for another in the cluster. Some others are concrete scaffolds to promote information exchange, such as the introduction of a happy hour by pubs or research seminars and meetings. In some cases, the architectural structure of industrial areas also is built to preserve some open-air meeting space, which enables talks.

[31]   One of these projects has been developed by Firenze Tecnologia, a special firm of the local Chamber of Commerce, in order to support local prestige designed handicraft productions, especially leather productions, and to integrate the players (www. firenzetecnologia.it). Another integrated data exchange system through the Internet (Opto-idx) has been made in the glasses industry of Belluno, which was created by input of some leading firms of the district. The project includes price lists, orders, their confirmations, factures, and other kinds of administrative document exchange. Both projects give specific guarantees for data and information security.

[32]   Within the district, people naturally learn by observing people doing things. Still today, in some districts' small firms, especially easy operations in the productive process are done by workers at home. This lack of physical separation between working and living places has its value in knowledge transfer by socialization (Nonaka, 1994). This is a characteristic also present in the Marshallian district in the so-called industrial atmosphere described by the author as an unique set of competences accumulated over time in the district: "The mysteries of the trade become no mysteries; but are as it were in the air, and children learn many of them unconsciously. Good work is rightly appreciated, inventions and improvements … have their merits promptly discussed: if one man starts a new idea, it is taken up by others and combined with suggestions of their own; and thus it becomes the source of further new ideas" (Marshall, 1920, p. 271).

[33]   The district metamanagement has to prevent and cure possible temporary power inequalities such as in the case of a too powerful leading firm. This fact may produce (Taylor, 2005) negative effetcs in the district, such as refusals of coordination, generation of subordination mechanisms in buyer-seller relationships, closeness and exchange crystalization, and reduction of information flow.

[34]   The value of metamanagement resources is lower in case of firms that are global players, who can perceive it as a managerial freedom limitation. But in that case, a smart guide has to involve them into the district strategic orientation and is useful to global firms for aspects such as the network and lobbying activity.

[35]   The law concerning Italian industrial districts requires them to be recognized formally by regional governments in terms of definition and localization in order to access public support and financing tools.

[36]   This did not happen in other countries. For example, in California, collective services first were organized and provided by private self-support: the Santa Clara Manufacturing Group created by local senior entrepreneurs (Lane, 2003).

[37]   If transactional costs were equal to zero, the most efficient organizational form would be the market. But when transactional costs exist, firms opt for hierarchy and activities internalization (Williamson, 1975, 1981, 1991). But also, this solution has its costs

(i.e., costs of coordination and control). The intermediate solution of firms' networks produces a higher single and systemic performance (Thorelli, 1986), which is also true for the district.

[38]   As Porter (1998) summarizes, areas' productivity and wealth are not due to the chosen sector but to the way in which areas and their firms compete.

[39]   Homeworkers and apprentices can appear less qualified, and thus, the quality of their work can be supposed to be lower, but this is not so. In fact, they are employed for specific easy-to-do activities, and besides, the kind of knowledge in the district (i.e., tacit, experience-based, etc.) is easier to socialize.

[40]   According to some authors (Cheng & Kesner, 1997; Cyert & March, 1963; Mohr, 1969), slack resources help firms in innovation and change management. They can help find solutions in a dynamic, evolving environment, a tool that enables a firm's adaptation. Bourgeois (1981) defines slack resources as "shock absorbers," and they prevent "a tightly wound organization from rupturing in the face of a surge in activity" (p. 30).

[41]   Sometimes the problem goes beyond imitation and is in products replication and counterfeiting. The number of discovered frauds in products replication is very high. In many cases, brand marks, packaging, and identification labels also are falsified.

[42]   The creation of industrial poles through incentives toward high-tech productions can be possible in other forms apart from districts' futures.

[43]   As Norton points out, uniquely relying on Marshall's (1919) "something in the air" can become a unique reliance and an obstacle to change.

[44]   Global knowledge can be different and somehow contrast with the local one.

[45]   For example, Nike presence in Montebelluna, the sportswear district, can be considered a discreet presence (Bergman & Locke, 2000).

[46]   This separation, evident and normal to be accepted by U.S. corporation, is not so in small and medium Italian firms, where the concept has been traditionally more "compact."

[47]   Delocalization policy is also useful to know emerging markets better and to develop a proactive marketing strategy. Metanational perspective just implies the chance to learn globally and to compete by an advantage made of interconnected territorial systems.

[48]   Each district, for its social strong component (i.e., core values, culture, entrepreneurial characteristics), has its own characters and is not perfectly replicable somewhere else. But its formula can be replicated in other places, and new subsidiary districts can take advantage from an original imprinting feature (Biggiero, 1999). An interesting example is given by the textile and fashion pole Chartage Fashion City in Tunisia, a project for area development and qualification of local workers. Several Italian textile firms settled in the area, attracted by lower wage costs and production costs, and have transferred technical know-how to local workers. Another interesting case of districts abroad creation is the Timisoara district in Romania. Here, too, better economic conditions attracted investments and created the opportunity of a brand new district system.

[49]   An example of district virtual marketplace is given by Tilesquare.com, a marketplace launched in 2001 by the tile district in Sassuolo to let demand and supply meet.

[50]   Here, again, is the matter of trustful relationships; with local suppliers it is a bit easier to share applications.

Chapter V

Industry Clusters in Peripheral Regions:
A Biotechnology Case Sudy

Philip Rosson, Dalhousie University, Canada

Carolan McLarney, Dalhousie University, Canada

Abstract

This chapter examines a nascent biotechnology cluster in a city that lies outside Canada's industrial heartland. The purpose of the study was to focus attention on the nature of cluster development in peripheral regions. The research findings reveal that many support services are provided to Halifax-based biotechnology companies and made use of by companies. However, barriers to development still exist, and support organizations and companies are not certain that a cluster truly exists in Halifax at this time. What results is a case study of a cluster at an early stage in its development cycle and in a peripheral region. The authors encourage other researchers to examine cluster development outside of major industrial centers.

Introduction

The view is widely held that industry clustering and regional economic development go hand-in-hand. Over the years, studies have linked the collocation of companies to industry growth and success. This has led many governments and other organizations to develop programs to encourage and support companies in cluster development. This chapter represents one more study of cluster development. It has three distinguishing features: (1) its emphasis is not on clusters in major centers but rather on those located in peripheral regions; (2) the analysis focuses on support service provision and use in an early stage cluster; and (3) an attempt is made to identify the factors that influence cluster development.

The setting for the research reported here is the biotechnology industry in Halifax, Nova Scotia, Canada. Given projections of its impact in fields such as agriculture, energy, and human health, most developed nations have targeted biotechnology as an industry for development. In fact, many regions within countries emphasize biotechnology. In Canada, for example, biotechnology companies are primarily concentrated in Montreal, Toronto, and Vancouver, but other cities and regions have ambitions in this regard. Halifax is one such city with plans to grow its biotechnology industry.

The chapter begins by examining the literature on innovation and clustering, particularly as these apply in peripheral regions (i.e., those located beyond industrial centers). The development of biotechnology in the region is traced, and the scale of activity is compared to that in other Canadian centers. The chapter then presents analysis from a study conducted among 38 biotechnology companies and support organizations. A number of questions are examined, including the services that are provided to companies and the extent to which these are used, the barriers identified as impeding further development of the industry locally, and the degree to which companies and organizations regard a cluster to exist. These data and the resulting discussion provide insights into the characteristics of a nascent cluster in a peripheral region as well as the challenges facing the industry in getting to the next stage of development.

Literature Review

In this section, we briefly review work on innovation and industry clustering before turning to contributions that have addressed these questions from the standpoint of peripheral or less favored regions.

Innovation is crucial to development, and progress and has attracted considerable research attention. Whereas the traditional literature viewed innovation to proceed in a simple linear fashion within the confines of the firm, this has changed, and innovation is now seen as having a complex and systemic nature. The latter viewpoint argues that innovation occurs in an evolutionary, non-linear, and interactive fashion that involves communications between numerous participants, some of whom are employees of the innovating company, while others may reside in research institutes, financial organizations, regulatory bodies, government agencies, and elsewhere. This conception of innovation is reflected in studies that show that the number of research linkages between companies is accelerating (Hotz-Hart, 2000) and that firms that cooperate intensely are more innovative than those that do not (Smith, 1995). The impetus to collaborate is stronger among smaller firms, because they need to produce breakthrough innovations in order to survive and grow and, at the same time, are constrained in terms of resources (Lorenzoni & Baden-Fuller, 1995).

The newer approach to studying innovation has led to research on the related topics of regional innovation systems (de la Mothe & Paquet, 1998) and industrial clustering. Both approaches recognize that interaction among organizations, knowledge spillovers from firm to firm (or from research institute to firm), and mobile workforces all spur innovation, and that these effects are stronger when organizations are in close proximity (Longhi, 1999; Audretsch, 2003)

Industry clustering has spawned a huge amount of literature that crosses many disciplinary boundaries. The literature is also one of long standing with some tracing the lineage of clustering back to the early 20th century and writers such as Weber, Marshall, and Schumpeter. But it was Porter's (1990, 1998a, 1998b) work on the competitive advantage of countries, regions, and cities that produced a broader interest in the topic and gained the attention of governments and policymakers around the world. In the past 20 years, there has been an explosion of research on clusters, and studies in various countries have pointed to a link between the clustering of firms and supporting infrastructure in a region and its economic performance. Industry clusters have been defined simply as "groups of firms within one industry based in one geographical area" (Swann & Prevezer, 1996, p. 139) to the more embracing "geographic concentrations of interconnected companies, specialized suppliers, service providers, firms in related industries, and associated institutions (for example, universities, standards agencies, and trade associations) in particular fields that compete but also cooperate" (Porter, 1998a, p. 197).

Colocation, the argument goes, produces a critical mass and dynamism that accounts for the success of regions such as the Third Italy (Brusco, 1990), Baden-Wurttenberg (Cooke and Morgan, 1990), and Silicon Valley (Saxenian, 1994). When they are located in close proximity, firms benefit from shared costs for infrastructure, the development of a skilled workforce, transaction efficiency, and knowledge spillovers that produce learning and innovation (Malmberg & Maskell, 2002). Proximity is especially important for face-to-face dealings and the conveying of tacit (as opposed to codified) information.

Although the literature on clusters is substantial, it has been criticized in some quarters. The objections raised concern definitions, methods, and causality. Contrasting and/or imprecise definitions have been employed by cluster researchers for important variables such as geographical and industrial boundaries, proximity measures, and linkage-density and contact-intensity metrics. Much of the literature on industry clusters either relies on a case study approach or offers anecdotal evidence rather than employing larger-scale samples that lend themselves to more robust analysis. Finally, some resarchers are not convinced that the link between cluster membership and superior performance has been demonstrated (Staber, 2001; Martin & Sunley, 2003).

The best-known and most intensely researched clusters are those in major centers. In biotechnology, for example, attention has been focused on Boston in the United States and Cambridge in the UK. These and other large cities have all the necessary ingredients for the establishment of a cluster in this industry, including large, research-intensive universities and hospitals, a supply of well-trained professionals, anchor firms that have deep pockets and global interests, and the availability of venture capital. But what about locations that do not have these characteristics? What does the literature have to say about biotechnology and other clusters in peripheral regions? There is a relatively small number of contributions in this area, but it provides useful perspectives. Two are discussed below.

Rosenfeld (2002a) identifies three types of less advantaged regions that are relevant here: (1) older industrialized regions that have lost their cost advantage to others; (2) semi-industrialized regions with small craft-based firms with low technology levels; and (3) less-populated regions that have been dependent on resource-intensive industries and need to create more jobs because of rising productivity levels and out-migration.[1] These regions face a variety of barriers to cluster development, including the following:

- Weak infrastructure (e.g., lack of broadband availability, poor transportation)
- Lack of access to capital (e.g., distance from venture capital firms and bank decision-makers)
- Weak technology institutions (e.g., research institutes either not connected to marketplace or not aligned with economic development plans)
- Regional insularity and lock-in (e.g., lack of connection to outside ideas and best practices)
- Low educational/skill levels (e.g., region exhibits thin labor market).

Similar observations are made by Tödtling and Trippl (2004), who cite research showing that peripheral and old industrial regions exhibit lower levels of R&D intensity, lower shares of patenting and product innovation, and a greater focus on incremental and process innovations. Drawing on the work of Isaksen (2001) and Nauwelaers and Wintjes (2003), three significant barriers to innovation are posited—organizational thinness, lock-in, and fragmentation. Organizational thinness is the barrier most closely associated with peripheral regions and produces the following problems:

- Missing or weakly developed clusters. SMEs with low absorptive capacity dominate
- Low level of R&D and product innovation. Emphasis on incremental and process innovation
- Few or low profile research institutes
- Emphasis on low- to medium-level qualifications
- Some knowledge transfer services but generally thin and not specialized. Too little orientation to marketplace demand
- Few networks in the region due to weak clustering and thin institutional structure

Policy measures for mitigating these problems are suggested by the researchers in question and are discussed in the final part of the chapter. We now turn to the context for the present study. First, we discuss biotechnology; then we move on to consider Canadian biotechnology and then focus explicitly on activities in Halifax.

The Context: Biotechnology in Canada

Biotechnology[2] is a scientific knowledge base that is transforming industries such as agriculture, the environment, medical devices, and pharmaceuticals. It is estimated that biotechnology firms alone generated global revenues of $50 billion in 2002–2003, while those affected by biotechnology innovations such as pharmaceuticals and medical devices were much more substantial.[3] Biotechnology companies also are poised for strong growth; about half of the respondents in a recent survey expected revenues to increase by 15% a year over the next decade (Deloitte Touche Tomatsu, 2005). As a result, many governments have identified biotechnology as an engine of growth and are making substantial investments in science and technology, anticipating that these will produce significant economic returns. Many different types of investments have been made, including funding for research institutions and programs, attracting inward investment, supporting technology-based entrepreneurship, and collaborating with local groups to nurture industry clusters.

Studies demonstrate that biotechnology activity, as is the case in other industries, is concentrated in space. For example, a Brookings Institution (Cortright & Meyer, 2002) report revealed that biotechnology activities in the U.S. are found where there is a confluence of research-oriented universities and hospitals, venture capital, and supporting financial and management structures. These conditions usually are found in major cities such as San Diego. However, other studies show that small cities and regions also feature in biotechnology activity. In France, for example, Paris accounts for half of all biotechnology companies, but five regions on the periphery of the country have developed vibrant clusters (Mytelka, 2001). The same is true in Canada, where the three largest cities dominate biotechnology activity, but smaller cities such as Edmonton and Saskatoon have biotechnology agglomerations (Niosi & Bas, 1999).

Biotechnology in Canada

Tracking biotechnology is more difficult than other economic activities because it is not an industry with its own SIC codes. However, it is estimated that there were more than 400 biotechnology innovator companies[4] in Canada in 2002, second only to the US in global terms. Most companies are small (82% have fewer than 50 employees) and focus on human health applications (84%). These firms are located in large urban areas with about 60% found in Montreal, Toronto, and Vancouver. A minority of companies (19%) are publicly traded.

Griller and Viger (2004) show that the distribution of biotechnology firms in Canadian cities is related to a number of factors, including population, venture capital investments, Canadian Institute of Health Research grants, research publications, academic research collaborations, and industrial alliances. Halifax scores at the level that might be expected: it is Canada's 10th largest city, ranks between ninth and 12th on the other listed measures, and is ninth in terms of the number of biotechnology companies. These rankings make it clear that Halifax is likely, at best, to play a secondary role in Canadian biotechnology.

Nontheless, biotechnology is significant at the local level. In 2000, for example, biotechnology research in the Halifax Regional Municipality alone was estimated to involve spending of more than $86 million, employment of 2,340 researchers and technicians, annual salaries of $124 million, and provincial tax revenues of $25 million (Life Sciences Development Association, 2002). At the corporate level, the compound annual growth rate for sales (10.3%), profit (7.7%), and employment (9.0%) was strong for private-sector life sciences firms in Nova Scotia between 1999 and 2002. Combining both private and public sector activities, it is estimated that life sciences contributed at least 1.1% to Nova Scotia's GDP in 2001 (The Conference Board of Canada, 2004). Biotechnology is seen to be an industry with considerable potential for development in Halifax, Nova Scotia, and is targeted in the economic development plans of federal, provincial and municipal agencies.

All of the participants normally found in a cluster (see Figure 1) are present in Halifax, and some were established many years ago. However, participants were brought together, and a discussion took place about clustering through an industry roundtable in 2000. There is a core group of companies that are working in a variety of scientific and application areas and that are at different stages in their corporate development. A sizable number of support organizations is also present. Governments at three levels (federal, provincial, and municipal) are involved in biotechnology cluster development. Two venture capital firms exist locally and serve high-growth, technology-based firms. Several research institutions have a long history in the region. These include universities as well as federal and provincial laboratories.

Figure 1. Cluster participants

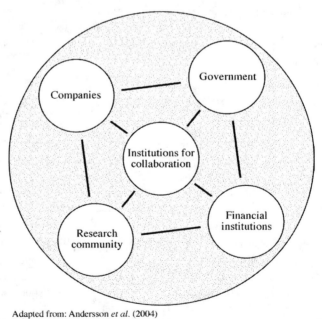

Adapted from: Andersson *et al.* (2004)

Finally, industry associations are also present, providing a vehicle for interaction. These are the most obvious institutions for collaboration (IFCs)—"formal or informal actors, which promote interest in the cluster initiative among the actors involved" (Andersson, Serger, Sörvik & Hansson, 2004, p. 24). The Halifax companies and support organizations are described in more detail next.

Study Methods and Organizations

The cluster study reported here is one of 26 that are being carried out in a program of research funded by the Social Sciences and Humanities Research Council of Canada (SSHRC). Further information can be found in the latest volume based on the research (Wolfe & Lucas, 2005) and at the program Web site (www.utoronto.ca/isrn). Despite examining clusters at different stages of development in various industries and in regions across the country, a common approach was used by all investigators. This employed on-site meetings that were guided by the same interview protocol. As a result, both quantitative and qualitative data were collected, permitting analytical rigor in some areas and rich commentary on particular issues. Because a combination of methods was employed, some of the pitfalls associated with single methods could be avoided. We now describe the approach taken in the Halifax study.

Fieldwork

A database of biotechnology companies and support organizations in Nova Scotia was constructed using lists from government and industry associations as well as entries in business directories. The database then was restricted to include only biotechnology activity within 100 kilometers (62.5 miles) of Halifax.[5] We contacted the organizations by mail and followed up with a phone call within one week. Of the 28 biotechnology companies that were identified, 17 were interviewed, eight did not reply or refused to participate, two had ceased operations or moved back into a university laboratory, and one had moved out of the province. All 21 of the support organizations that were identified (including research institutes, government agencies, industry associations and venture capitalists) agreed to be interviewed.

Interviews followed a semi-structured approach. An interview guide was used to collect the required information, but when it seemed important, additional questions were asked, or probing took place. Five interview guides were employed (company, research institute, government agency, industry association, and venture capitalist); they included both common and more particular questions. Interviews usually were conducted on-site although in a few cases, upon request, the meeting was held at the university. Interviews ranged in duration from one hour to two hours, were recorded and later transcribed. This chapter is based on information collected from 38 biotechnology companies and support organizations between December 2002 and March 2004.

Nova Scotia Biotechnology Companies

Table 1 presents a snapshot of the biotechnology companies that we interviewed. We have withheld the names of the companies for confidentiality reasons. A number of observations can be made from the data presented. First, of the 17 companies listed, four were established in the 1980s, eight in the 1990s, and five since 2000. Second, a range of scientific approaches is evident, but 14 of the companies focus on human health applications. Third, for the most part, these are fledgling companies. With workforces of 150 or more, two of the companies (I and XI[6]) might be regarded as medium-sized. The majority, however, is very small; nine have 10 or fewer employees. The small scale of the companies also is reflected in their revenues and R&D expenditures. Nine report having revenue streams, seven currently have zero revenue, and another company (IV) would not provide data. The three oldest companies report having the greatest annual sales ($13 million, $10 million, and $5 million). Four companies are spending in excess of $1 million annually on R&D activities. In terms of the development stage, eight of the companies have commercial products that generate cash flows.[7] Four others (III, V, VII, and XIII) are at the clinical trials stage, while three (VI, VII, and IX) are at an earlier stage of development. Reflecting their stage of development, five companies have annual R&D expenditures that presently exceed revenues. Finally, 15 of the 17 companies are privately owned.

Overall, we see a group of companies that have some common characteristics but also exhibit differences. The majority of the firms are small and privately funded. Some are relatively young (standing just outside the laboratory door), while others are well-established businesses with global reach. Significantly, no two companies are centered on the same scientific research, approach, or application area.

Table 1. Profile of Nova Scotia biotechnology companies

Company	Start-up	Ownership	Employees	Revenues ($m)	R&D ($m)	Stage of Development	Focus
I	1981	Private	150-300	13.00	0.50	4	Products derived from seaweeds
II	1993	Private	16	<0.50	<0.10	4	Medical device
III	1993	Private	4	0	1.30	3.3	Applications from chitin
IV	1997	Private	16	–	0.30	4	Tele-health applications
V	2001	Private	2	0	0.02	1	Medical device
VI	2000	Private	4	0	0.37	1	Drug carrier systems

Table 1. continued

VII	2000	Private	10	0	1.00	2	Vaccines for human & veterinary applications
VIII	1995	Public	37	<0.50	1.20	3.3	Rapid diagnostic testing
IX	2000	Private	1	0	–	4	Drug & vaccine delivery system
X	1999	Private	4	0	0.40	2	Gene research for Huntington's disease
XI	1987	Private	150	10.00	4.00	4	Marine-based nutraceuticals
XII	2001	Private	8	<0.50	<0.10	4	Biomedicinals & botanical based products
XIII	1997	Private	5	<0.50	0.18	3.2	Gene mapping for animal reproduction
XIV	1996	Private	2	<0.05	<0.10	1	Biotechnology derived plants & propagation systems
XV	1983	Private	22	5.00	0.05	4	Frozen human plasmas & coagulation reagents testing
XVI	1998	Private	2	<0.50	<0.10	4	Oceanographic instruments
XVII	1984	Public	41	0	10.00	4 / 2	Active pharma ingredients

Notes:

(1) Financial data are for most recent year.

(2) Stage of development: 1 = development, 2 = pre-clinical. 3.1 = initial clinical trials, 3.2 = animal trials, 3.3 = human trials, 4 = commercialization.

– information was not provided

Biotechnology Support Organizations

The 21 support organizations interviewed are profiled in Table 2. Three main observations can be made about this group of organizations. First, the organizations in question have different geographical foci—one organization is rooted in the municipality (Halifax), eight have a provincial mandate (Nova Scotia), and 12 others have a location in Halifax but serve wider areas (seven are regional [Atlantic Canada], and five are national [Canada]). Second, the 21 organizations undertake a variety of functions—seven are government agencies; six are research institutes; three are industry/civic associations; two are venture capitalists; and four provide financial, legal, and technology transfer services. This leads to the third observation that the 21 organizations provide a breadth of support services to the biotechnology industry. For example, nine of the organizations provide funding, seven support biotechnology companies with their infrastructure needs, and 18 assist biotechnology firms through advocacy activities.

Overall, there appears to be considerable overlap in terms of the jurisdictional interests of the 21 support organizations as well as in the services provided. This could be viewed either positively or negatively for biotechnology companies in Nova Scotia. For instance, having nine different organizations to approach might increase the prospects of receiving funding for clinical trials. On the other hand, the more funding sources that exist, the greater the possibility of companies (1) being confused about which organization to approach and (2) being passed from one support organization to the next.

Table 2. Profile of Nova Scotia biotechnology support organizations

Support Organization	Jurisdiction	Focus
A	Regional	Provides venture capital for technology and innovation
B	Regional	Promotes business development through funding, mentoring and business planning
C	National	Undertakes research, promotes business development and creates safeguards for the agricultural and food system
D	National	Conducts multidisciplinary research with an ocean and environmental emphasis
E	Provincial	Provides management services to biotechnology companies
F	Provincial	Facilitates networking events, communication and assists industry in meeting common needs
G	Regional	Conducts research in neurosurgery, pharmacology and bioscience health
H	Provincial	Provides legal services, including a specialty in biotechnology
I	Regional	Offers educational and research programs in medicine
J	Regional	Offers educational and research programs in pharmacology
K	Regional	Provides research services in area of infectious diseases

Table 2. continued

L	Regional	Undertakes basic and applied research, and funds investigations in genomics
M	Municipal	Facilitates economic development
N	National	Facilitates industry development
O	Provincial	Provides incubation, mentoring and investment services
P	National	Provides hardcore technical assistance, business information/networks and financing
Q	Provincial	Promotes creation of research park for biotechnology in Halifax
R	Provincial	Provides funding to bridge the gap between research grants and the market place
S	National	Conducts basic research and provides access to laboratories
T	Provincial	Facilitates the expansion of business activities in Nova Scotia
U	Provincial	Provides commercialization services for research discoveries and inventions for its members

Cluster Services, Barriers, and Outlook

In this section, we provide an analysis of data collected from the biotechnology companies and support organizations. As previously discussed, our interest is to present a case study of an industry cluster at a particular point in its development cycle. We begin by describing the services provided by the organizations that support the development of a biotechnology cluster in Halifax, Nova Scotia, as well as company usage of these services. Attention then turns to a discussion of barriers to the further development of the cluster. Companies and support organizations identified factors that were seen as impeding growth, and their responses are compared. Finally, we report on whether companies and organizations view biotechnology activity in Halifax presently to constitute a cluster.

What Services are Provided by Support Organizations?

Analysis of the interview data yielded seven types of support services or programs that are provided to biotechnology companies. These were advocacy, business development, financing, human capital, intellectual property (IP) protection, research dissemination, and research infrastructure (see Table 3 for definitions and examples).

The most frequently provided service was advocacy, with fully 18 of the support organizations (86%) active in this area (see Figure 1). For four organizations (F, K, M, and Q), advocacy was the sole function, while another (D) viewed this to be a prime function. A full range of approaches was taken to advocating on behalf of the biotechnology industry, including conferences, trade shows, and community awareness campaigns.

Twelve of the organizations (60%) provided services in the human capital domain, making it the second most frequently provided type of service. However, only one organization (J) stated that this was a prime role. Others offered a variety of human resource programs including recruitment, training and retention courses, and support (B, C, D, E, G, I, J, Y, P, S, T, and U). In fact, P had some of its own personnel on loan to one biotechnology firm. These same organizations indicated that although they were active in the human capital services area, more should be done. Specifically, a major deficiency in Halifax was that of experienced senior managers who are able to lead growth and development of the biotechnology firms.

Nine organizations (43%) provided financing programs to biotechnology companies. Together with business development services, this was the third most frequently offered type of service to Halifax companies. For four organizations (A, B, R, and T) this was the primary role played, while in the case of five others (C, E, L, N, and P), funding was provided, but so too were other services such as human capital, business development, and advocacy.

Business development services were provided by nine (43%) of the organizations. Two (B and E) stated that this was their primary function, and they offered business planning, mentoring, and partnering programs. Six other organizations offered business development programs as a complement to other offerings to biotechnology firms (A, C, L, N, O, T, and U). Interestingly, organization A made its business development programs mandatory for all biotechnology firms that applied for funding consideration. Other approaches included those with financial (T) and licensing (U) slants.

Eight organizations (38%) offered some type of program to assist with research dissemination. Two organizations (D and J) viewed this to be their primary support role for biotechnology firms. An interesting comment from D was that it had not achieved the same degree of success in disseminating to the private sector as it had to the public sector. Another six other organizations (C, F, I, L, P, and S) indicated that they also assisted biotechnology firms in

Table 3. Services provided by support organizations to Halifax biotechnology companies

Service Type	Description and Example
Advocacy	Promotion of the industry to policy makers, civic officials, and the local community (e.g., media exposure, networking events)
Business development	Provision of business intelligence and advice on strategy development to companies (e.g., competitor reports, prospects for partnering)
Financing	Supply of funding to help companies develop commercial products and achieve growth (e.g., early-stage funding, equipment financing)
Human capital	Assistance in accessing qualified technical and management personnel on a full-time or part-time basis (e.g., secondment of a scientist, appointment of a board member)
Intellectual property	Protection of IP inherent in scientific discoveries (e.g., legal advice regarding IP, patenting discovery)
Research dissemination	Publicity about research programs and findings to stimulate the interest of relevant parties (e.g., research open house, technology transfer office)
Research infrastructure	Creation of an environment that is conducive to the conduct of high quality research (e.g., funding basic science, providing research and office space)

this area. Instead of simply publicizing research findings, one organization took the findings and used them to generate possibilities for research or business partner linkages.

Research infrastructure services were provided by seven of the organizations (33%). In four cases, this was their primary support function for biotechnology firms (D, J, O, and P). Organization D stated that its initial and continuing role was to provide needed infrastructure to the academic community and incubator biotechnology firms. The services provided in this domain were quite diverse, ranging from office and research space to technical networks.

Although five organizations (23%) provided some services to companies with regard to IP protection, only one (H) was a specialist with respect to biotechnology firms. Four other support organizations (D, E, I, and U) provided some support with questions relating to patenting and technology transfer issues.

The analysis shows that a range of services is provided by support organizations to the Halifax biotechnology sector. Further, some organizations appear to specialize, whereas others offer greater program coverage. For example, organizations H, K, M, Q, and R offered only one type of support to biotechnology firms, whereas C was active in six of the seven areas (see Figure 2). Over half of the support organizations offered three or more program types (see Figure 3). Advocacy services dominated, followed by human capital, financing, business development, and research dissemination programs. The services that were least often provided were those that focus on IP protection, followed by research infrastructure and research dissemination.

What Support Services Do Biotechnology Companies Use?

The same seven types of support service were analyzed from the standpoint of biotechnology companies. Their usage of advocacy, business development, financing, human capital, IP protection, research dissemination, and research infrastructure services are shown in Figure 4. Three types of service support were most heavily used; 14 of the companies (82%) used financing, human capital, and research infrastructure support.

Figure 2. Number of support organizations providing services to Halifax biotechnology companies (n=21)

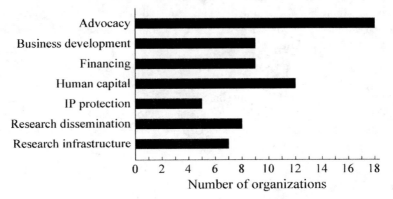

Figure 3. Number of services provided by support organizations

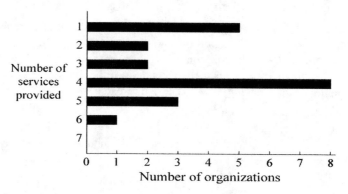

It was not surprising to find that support programs involving funding assistance were widely used. Biotechnology companies face costly and long development cycles for their scientific discoveries. The three biotechnology firms that were not users (VIII, XI, and XVI) are well-established and fund their operations from existing sales.

Human capital programs also were used frequently. Many of the firms used these programs predominantly to attract and retain technically trained employees mostly from local universities and community colleges. Companies echoed support organizations' comments about the difficulty of finding senior executives to manage growth. Those companies not using human capital services (III, IX, and XVI) explained this in terms of their small size (four, one, and two employees, respectively). Company XII linked the topic of executive talent to venture capital funds, noting that typically one was not found in the absence of the other.

Research infrastructure was the third of the services used most frequently. These firms used research space, technology networks, and other support programs to help establish their firm or to assist with its initial growth. Three companies that did not take advantage of infrastructure services were well-established (I, XII, and XV). One of these was critical of Nova Scotia's physical infrastructure (e.g., highways).

Other frequently used programs were those focusing on industry advocacy. However, although 13 companies (76%) made use of advocacy support, half of these questioned its usefulness. One interviewee stated that he was involved in order to show support for the industry rather than finding it especially helpful at an individual level. Another saw these programs to be more about social networking than about industry development. As might be expected, non-users of advocacy services (V, VII, VIII, and XVI) also were sceptical about the value produced from participation.

Eight biotechnology companies used business development services. These (I, VI, VII, IX, XI, XIII, XV, and XVI) all took advantage of such programs to develop business/marketing plans, particularly to pursue financing sources. Two firms (IV and V) did not draw upon local support organizations for business development purposes but, instead, used established partnerships that provided them with required expertise, resources, and knowledge.

Intellectual property protection services provided by local organizations were used by only six of the 17 biotechnology firms (VI, VII, IX, XII, XVI, and XVII). These companies made use of Halifax patent investigators and patent agents rather than local lawyers. As was the case with other biotechnology companies (III, V, VIII, X, XI, XIII, and XIV), these companies drew on the services of non-local patent lawyers (in Ontario, New York, and California). A main reason for this practice was the lack of a patent lawyer in Halifax until very recently.

Six companies (35%) used research dissemination services. These firms (I, V, VI, X, XI, and XII) accessed programs provided by local support organizations for publicizing scientific findings. Among the non-users were companies established by scientists who also held university appointments. In these cases, publishing research findings through academic channels was deemed sufficient for dissemination purposes. However, for competitive reasons, at least one company mentioned a reluctance to publicize research results too quickly.

In sum, these data show that Halifax biotechnology firms use a variety of services provided by local support organizations. Some companies were more active users of services than others (see Figure 5). One company (VI) made use of all seven types of support, while eight companies used five services, and five companies used four services. This is not surprising, as the majority of the biotechnology firms are relatively young and most often require capital, research space, equipment, and scientists/technicians in order to progress from the laboratory to commercial operations.

What Barriers Exist to Further Development of the Biotechnology Cluster?

Halifax-based biotechnology companies and support organizations were asked what stood in the way of further development of the cluster. Their responses are summarized in Figure 6. It is clear from the responses that some of the services that are presently provided (and discussed previously) are regarded as insufficient and/or need to be expanded. However, additional barriers were identified that are either more specific or go beyond those already mentioned. Both types of barrier are now described.

Figure 4. Number of Halifax biotechnology companies using services provided by support organizations (n=17)

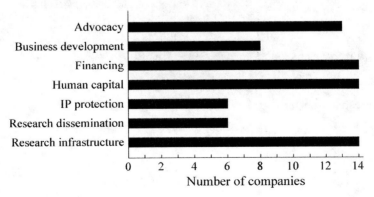

Figure 5. Number of services used by Halifax biotechnology companies

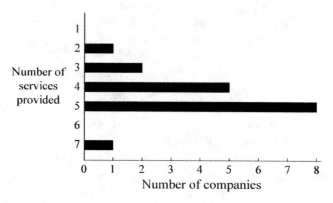

Companies and support organizations regarded adequate financing for the development of the biotechnology cluster to be the greatest barrier. Fourteen companies (82%) and 14 support organizations (67%) identified financing as a problem. Several companies stated that finding initial capital was at times almost impossible. Consequently, private funds, friends, family, and other angel investors were critical in the crucial start-up and early stages of development. Clearly, this is an acute area of need for companies.

The second most frequently identified barrier to development was human capital (by more than 60% of companies and organizations). As already noted, the attraction and retention of experienced senior managers, post-doctoral students, and skilled scientists is viewed as important to development of the cluster and not sufficiently dealt with through current support programs.

More than half the companies and support organizations viewed government programs to be inadequate, given the development task facing the cluster. These responses suggest that the industry and support organizations are looking to the federal and provincial govern-

Figure 6. Barriers to the development of the Halifax biotechnology cluster

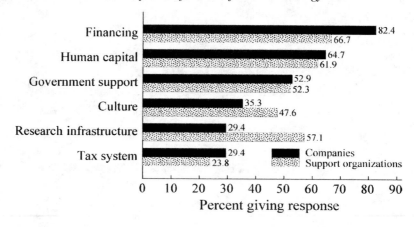

ments for greater leadership and assistance. This is not just a case of wanting more; in some cases, greater effectiveness was the issue. As one manager put it, "Government policies and programs have a completely inadequate structure to promote growth and development of the local industry".

An interesting finding was that culture is seen by some to be a roadblock to industry development. Phrases such as the following capture this point: "lack of a culture of commercialization," "resistance to change in the region," and "unresponsive research institutes." This barrier was more frequently reported by support organizations (48%) than by companies (35%).

Research infrastructure was also identified as being problematic. Once again, this was particularly the case for support organizations (57%) and somewhat less so for companies (29%). The lack of good facilities for medical research was a particular concern for support organizations. Many felt that establishing a research park with proximate firms and organizations in modern facilities was necessary to truly develop a biotechnology cluster in Halifax. Companies also viewed improved infrastructure as important to their development and growth.

A final issue mentioned by companies and support organizations concerned the tax system. Although the R&D tax credit was viewed to be an important development, several suggestions were made that would increase its value to companies. One view was that the federal portion of the R&D tax credit should be available at the same time as the provincial portion. The tax barrier was cited more often by companies (29%) but seems validated by the endorsement of 24% of support organizations.

A large number of other barriers to development of the Halifax biotechnology cluster was provided, but those achieving wide endorsement already have been identified. The scale of responses suggests that these represent serious impediments. In the case of culture and research infrastructure, differing responses are evident but, for the most part, companies and support organizations appear to be in agreement about factors that are hindering progress. Finally, it should be noted that four of the seven support service types—advocacy, business development, IP protection, and research dissemination—were not reported to be barriers to development.

Does Halifax Have a Biotechnology Cluster?

Although we have used the term *cluster*, we are interested in the fundamental question of whether the companies and support organizations interviewed considered that a biotechnology cluster did indeed exist in Halifax.[8] Respondents had contrasting viewpoints. Nine of the 21 support organizations (43%) felt that there was a cluster, albeit one that is small and nascent. Eight (38%) did not view a cluster to exist, while another four (19%) were unsure. Among the organizations that replied in the negative, this was usually explained in terms of the smallness and niche nature of the companies, their different areas of scientific and business interest, a resulting lack of interaction with each other, and the absence of an anchor firm. All of the support organizations, however, felt that potential existed for a cluster to develop if given appropriate time and support. Turning to the 17 biotechnology firms, nine (53%) felt that a cluster did exist, although it was at an early development stage. For similar reasons to those mentioned by support organizations, eight companies (47%) did not regard a cluster presently to exist. Once again, however, a cluster was seen as a distinct possibility in the future.

Discussion

Assessment of the Cluster

Data collected from biotechnology companies and support organizations in Halifax point to the beginnings of an industry cluster. There is a core of companies that is active and a range of supporting organizations (research institutes, government agencies, venture capitalists, and trade/civic associations). Some of the firms are running commercial operations, whereas others are attempting to move beyond the laboratory. The support organizations in question provide numerous services to companies, which we grouped into seven types. The mandate of support organizations was reflected in the number and type of services offered; some were very focused (venture capitalists), whereas others offered a variety of possibilities to firms (federal government departments). As might be expected, given the predominantly small nature of the firms studied, quite extensive usage was made of these services by firms. The picture that emerges is that a relatively small number of biotechnology companies in Halifax makes use of the support programs provided by what is, perhaps, a surprisingly large number of organizations. As already noted, all of the required cluster participants (identified in Figure 1) are present in Halifax, although the institutions for collaboration (IFCs) are not numerous. In a sense, it could be said that everyone in a cluster has a responsibility for its promotion. At the same time, it appears that there is a more central and full-time job to done in this regard.

Although many services are provided and used, barriers exist to the further development of biotechnology in Halifax. Chief among these are financing, human capital, government support, culture, research infrastructure, and the tax system. Securing adequate capital appears to be the highest barrier for this cluster to overcome. It is also a double-edged sword for the industry. Without sufficient capital, firms are unable to move beyond the laboratory, and thus, the cluster does not grow; on the other hand, financiers are more likely to invest in a cluster if it is growing. So, for the Halifax biotechnology cluster, money is not being attracted to the area because there is not a threshold number of companies, and the cluster is below the threshold level because there is no money being attracted to the area. The development of specialized investment funds that provide some cofinancing might be a good start to overcoming this barrier.

Hand in hand with the lack of financing is the difficulty in securing and retaining appropriate human capital. In essence, the Halifax biotechnology cluster is unable to compete on a salary basis with other large urban areas in Canada and is even less able to attract US-based scientists. Given this, local biotechnology firms will need to compete less on the basis of salary and more on life-style factors in order to attract the necessary managerial and scientific talent.

This, then, leads us directly to the third barrier: insufficient government support. As was stated previously, more than half of the companies and support organizations stated that government support of the cluster was insufficient. Support organizations at the federal, provincial, and municipal levels all pointed to other levels in the government as providing programs that were deficient in some way. With a 1:1.2 company/support organization ratio, one would think that there would be adequate programming for the cluster. This raises the question of whether we are seeing additionality or simply a crowding-out effect. A coordinated effort needs to be made to ensure that appropriate comprehensive support programs are put in place at the federal, provincial, and municipal levels, but not at all three levels at once. These programs must be mutually exclusive and collectively exhaustive in their nature.

The next barrier is a cultural reluctance to innovation/change. If true, then this is the barrier that will take the longest to overcome. Support organizations stated that a major stumbling block to cluster development in Halifax was a poor attitude toward commercialization. It is difficult to try to prescribe a cure for this condition, but it would appear that this is a perfect opportunity for the support organizations to step in with programs designed to aid commercialization. Showcasing local biotechnology firm success stories may prove useful for nascent firms.

The issue of research infrastructure was highlighted by almost 60% of the support organizations as a barrier to development. A lack of sufficient research space was most problematic. Recent construction has alleviated this concern to a degree, but a dedicated research park may be necessary. Such a park also would help to address the necessary requirement of a cluster: proximity.

Finally, a restructuring of the tax system has been called for if the biotechnology cluster in Halifax is to move to the next stage of the life cycle. Unlike the issue of changing the culture of the cluster, this issue is remedied much more easily. The call for concurrent availability of the federal and provincial R&D tax credits seems straightforward but requires some political will at both levels of government. In essence, in order to lower this barrier, a champion must be identified and supported to solve the issue.

Enhanced levels of support are required if the biotechnology industry is to move to the next levels. As is the case in most jurisdictions, venture capital, people, and facilities are critical to commercializing scientific discoveries, and more is better than less. However, there are other barriers that require attention; there is first a need for people and institutions to more explicitly embrace innovation and to be more open to the need to commercialize discoveries, and second, a need for governments to tailor their programs (including tax regimes) in order to support innovation activities more effectively.

This discussion leads to questions about the current development state of biotechnology in Halifax. Although firms and support organizations are active and engaged, there are barriers that are impeding progress. Given this situation, the fact that about half of the 38 organizations did not believe a true cluster exists was hardly surprising.[9] Nonetheless, potential was seen, and some respondents spoke in terms of Halifax being at an early stage in a development or life cycle. In terms of the cluster life cycle model shown in Figure 7, Halifax probably has moved beyond the latent stage and is at the developing stage. Why the guarded statement? Most requirements for the latent stage have been realized, but cooperation around a core activity is not evident, and linkages between firms are minimal. The Halifax companies operate in quite different fields, which reduces the gains that might accrue in the short term from collaboration and exchange. The pressure involved in establishing a business, commercializing an innovation, and growing the firm means that most owners/entrepreneurs tend to concentrate on immediate issues and concerns rather than on exploring areas with less obvious benefits. This appears to be a major challenge for those who are interested in innovation and cluster development in Halifax.

Cluster Development

Although it is dangerous to offer prescriptions for cluster development, in this section, we extend the discussion to identify possibilities for biotechnology cluster development in Halifax. This draws on experiences from other industries and jurisdictions. We note contributions of a general kind as well as those dealing with the special case of peripheral regions.

The *Cluster Policies Whitebook* provides a comprehensive assessment of cluster studies and initiatives around the world. Andersson, Serger, Sörvik, and Hansson (2004) discuss the role of cluster participants (Figure 1) in the cluster life cycle development process. A feature that is not uncommon in the early stages of cluster development is that firms, research institutes, and venture capitalists respectively may be preoccupied, disinterested, or absent. This means that the task of governments and IFCs is more significant. Governments often are called upon to provide a strategic view, support infrastructure, create policies, and act as a broker between relevant parties. But others must support government if cluster development is to occur, including IFCs. "Clusterpreneurs" and hybrid organizations (e.g., incubators, trade associations) are concrete examples of entities that often emerge to link other organizations and to encourage collaboration. The key to success here is the building of social capital and trust among the parties involved. Governments usually focus considerable attention on the improvement of cluster dynamics and the cluster environment. Sölvell, Lindqvist, and Ketels

Figure 7. Cluster lifecycle

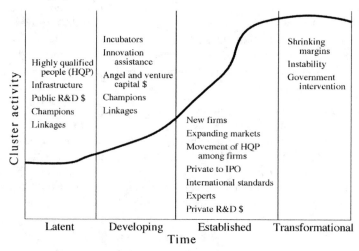

Adapted from: Wolfe, Davis and Lucas (2005)

Table 4. Cluster initiative (CI) objectives and actions [Source: Adapted from Sölvell, Lindqvist and Ketels (2003)]

CI Objective	Most Important Action (found in 75% of CIs or more)	Important Action (found in 50% of CIs or more)
Research and Networking	Establish networks among firms Foster networks among people	Make firms aware of their cluster
Policy Action	–	Lobby government for infrastructure
Commercial Cooperation	–	Promote exports from cluster Provide business assistance to cluster firms Assemble market intelligence
Education and Training	–	Provide technical training Provide management training
Innovation and Technology	Facilitate higher innovativeness Promote innovation, new technologies	Analyze technical trends Diffuse technology within cluster Enhance production processes
Cluster Expansion	Promote expansion of existing firms	Attract new firms and talent to region Create brand for region Promote spin-off formation

(2003) list examples of actions that have been taken in this regard (see Table 4). Some of the initiatives and actions that have been used quite widely around the world are evident in Halifax, but it appears that there is room for additional measures to be pursued.

Regarding the more particular case of cluster development in peripheral areas, we return to works cited previously. Tödtling and Trippl (2004) elaborate on policy approaches that might be undertaken in regions that are peripheral and suffer from organizational thinness (see Table 5). The policy agenda is usually one of strengthening and upgrading the regional economy through catch-up learning that focuses on innovation within SMEs. A variety of actions may be taken to achieve this goal. Inward investment often is pursued, as is linking companies within and outside the regions. Both actions are meant to spur innovation either through anchoring local firms to those with leading practices or to other business partners and knowledge sources. Institution building is also critical with improvement of the regional knowledge infrastructure usually emphasized. Attracting relevant research institutions to the region can be beneficial; mid-level training and mobility programs also have been used to good effect. The enhancement of social capital and networks is also important in order to improve regional innovation performance. Ties among firms and local knowledge providers are needed with a focus on demand-led activities. In some cases, however, extra-regional linkages are important, because the key ideas and technologies may not be present locally. This may be particularly relevant in biotechnology (Gertler & Levitte, 2003). In this case, the absorptive capacity of firms often must be enhanced so that benefits flow from the linkages made.

The main problems with peripheral regions "are a low level of R&D and innovation due to a dominance of SMEs in traditional industries, weakly developed firm clusters, few knowl-

Table 5. Innovation policy approaches for peripheral regions [Source: Tödtling and Trippl (2004)]

Characteristics	Policy Approaches
Strategic Orientation of Regional Economy	Strengthening/upgrading of regional economy
Innovation Strategy	"Catching up learning" (management, organization, technology) Improve strategic and innovation capabilities of SMEs
Firms and Regional Clusters	Strengthen potential clusters in the region Link firms to clusters outside the region Attract innovative companies New firm formation
Knowledge Providers	Attract branches of national research organizations with relevance to the regional economy
Education/Skills	Build up medium-level skills (e.g., technical colleges, engineering schools, management schools) Mobility schemes (e.g., innovation assistants for SMEs)
Networks	Link firms to knowledge providers and agencies inside the region and beyond, demand-led approach

edge providers and a weak endowment with innovation support institutions" (Tödtling & Trippl, 2004, p. 21). To a certain extent, these problems are found in Halifax, and so the suggested policy approaches are food for thought in the development of a stronger biotechnology cluster.

Rosenfeld (2002a) identifies a variety of actions that have been found useful in supporting cluster development in less-favored regions. The actions (with examples) are as follows:

- Understand and benchmark regional economies (e.g., identify clusters, model and map systemic relationships)
- Engage employers and institutions (e.g., recognize or form cluster associations, foster interfirm collaboration)
- Organize and deliver services (e.g., establish one-stop cluster hubs, create cluster branches of government)
- Build a specialized workforce (e.g., use clusters as a context for learning, form partnerships between educational institutions and clusters)
- Stimulate innovation and entrepreneurship (e.g., support cluster-based incubators, encourage entrepreneur networks)
- Brand and market the region (e.g., look for opportunities to brand the region, target inward investment)
- Allocate and attract resources and investments (e.g., fund critical foundation factors, invest in cluster R&D)

The full list of action items offered by Rosenfeld provides additional ideas for development of the Halifax biotechnology cluster.

Concluding Comments

We have presented a case study of an industry cluster that is at an early stage in its development. The companies and supporting organizations that make up the biotechnology cluster were profiled, and their interactions were assessed through an examination of the services provided and used. Although an array of services is offered by support organizations and companies make quite extensive use of these services, these are deemed insufficient and act as a barrier to further development of the cluster. In fact, the presence of a cluster was questioned. The analysis led us to conclude that the Halifax biotechnology cluster has progressed beyond the latent stage and is presently at an early point in the developing stage. Critical questions flow from this assessment: Is it likely that Halifax can grow its cluster to the next level (i.e., be established)? What is required for such development?

It would be foolhardy to provide a categorical response to either question. However, Halifax is not alone in being a peripheral region or in targeting biotechnology, and so the experience of others is informative. Like other less-favored regions, Halifax has some shortcomings that need to be addressed if it is to achieve its objectives. It may well be that policy measures used or proposed by others bear serious consideration. The fact that it is a biotechnology cluster that is being attempted raises other concerns. The first of these is that because of its potential for high growth, quality employment, and minimal environmental impact, almost every government is establishing a biotechnology cluster. Clearly, many of these initiatives will fail unless more precise targeting takes place. Another concern is that a recent study argues that regions with populations of fewer than one million have little chance of generating the critical mass to support a strong biotechnology cluster (Griller & Viger, 2004). Halifax does not meet this yardstick. Collectively, the case study suggests that there is a considerable challenge facing those who are attempting to build a viable biotechnology cluster in Halifax, Nova Scotia.

If we turn to the work of Andersen, et al. (2004), we may find some assistance in addressing this challenge and the barriers to growth previously identified. Five actions discussed in *The Cluster Policies Whitebook* provide some guidance for overcoming the barriers in the biotechnology cluster in Halifax. The first addresses the barrier of insufficient financing and is termed capital market failure. Suggested courses of action include attracting new venture capital firms, developing specialized investment funds, and improving foreign direct investment incentives overall. The second barrier was a lack of human capital, and Andersen, et al. (2004) label this "shortage in specialized labor supply". They propose providing management and technical training, establishing cluster skill centers, and using clusters themselves as a context for learning. Another serious barrier for the development of the cluster in Halifax is government support and infrastructure challenges. As *The Whitebook* identifies, there is a "mismatch between (public) knowledge/infrastructure and market needs." This is resolved through development of industry—research centers of excellence. A Halifax center of excellence would facilitate joint research between industry and academic players, support specialization and linkages between these players, develop in-house human capital, and initiate technology transfer programs between agencies and firms. At the same time, an adequate and appropriate infrastructure (including transportation and communication) needs to be put in place. Finally, it is suggested that the promotion of spin-offs and expansion of existing firms plus the provision of preseed venture capital will help biotechnology in Halifax to achieve a critical mass and promote continued firm growth.

Two caveats deserve to be mentioned in closing. Most writers on clusters and their development make the observation that each regional and industrial situation is different. Therefore, it is dangerous to assume that what has worked in one location will do the same elsewhere. Ultimately, clusters emerge in a location because of innovation and entrepreneurship. Funding and other forms of assistance certainly help but cannot guarantee success. Thus, clusters cannot be designed to occur. Finally, we must remind ourselves that clusters do not happen overnight but usually take decades to develop, often in a serendipitous manner through the planned and unplanned interaction of numerous players (Waluszewski, 2003).

References

Andersson, T., Serger, S., Sörvik, J., & Hansson, E. (2004). *The cluster policies whitebook.* Malmo, IKED.

Audretsch, D. (2003). Innovation and spatial externalities. *International Regional Science Review, 26*(2), 167-174.

Brusco, S. (1990). *The idea of the industrial district: Industrial districts and interfirm cooperation in Italy.* Geneva: International Institute for Labour Studies.

Conference Board of Canada, The. (2004). The economic contribution of the Nova Scotia life sciences sector, Ottawa.

Cooke, P., & Morgan, K. (1990). *Learning through networking: Regional innovation and the lessons of Baden-Wurttemberg* [Regional Industrial Research Report No. 5]. Cardiff: University of Wales.

Cortright, J., & Meyer, H. (2002). *Signs of life: The growth of biotechnology centers in the US.* Washington, DC: Brookings Institution Center on Urban and Metropolitan Policy.

De la Mothe, J., & Paquet, G. (1998). *Local and regional systems of innovation.* Boston: Kluwer Academic Publishers.

Deloitte Touche Tomatsu. (2005). *The future of the life sciences industries.* Deloitte, New York.

Gertler, M., & Levitte, Y. (2003). *Local nodes in global networks: The geography of knowledge flows in biotechnology innovation.* Paper presented at the Proceedings of the DRUID Summer Conference, Elsinore, Denmark. Retrieved from http://www.druid. dkconferences/summer2003/papers/gertler_levitte.pdf

Griller, D., & Viger, D. (2004). *Where are Canada's biotechnology clusters?* Ottawa: National Research Council.

Hotz-Hart, B. (2000). Innovation networks, regions and globalization. In G. Clark, M. Feldman, & M. Gertler (Eds.), *The Oxford handbook of economic geography* (pp. 432-450). Oxford: Oxford University Press.

Isaksen, A. (2001). Building regional innovation systems: Is endogenous industrial development possible in the global economy? *Canadian Journal of Regional Science, 1*, 101-120.

Life Sciences Development Association. (2002). *Strategy for the commercialization of life sciences research*. Halifax, Nova Scotia: Life Sciences Development Association.

Longhi, C. (1999). Networks, collective learning and technology development in innovative high technology regions: The case of Sophia-Antopolis. *Regional Studies, 33*, 333-342.

Lorenzoni, G., & Baden-Fuller, C. (1995). Creating a strategic center to manage a web of partners. *California Management Review, 37*(3), 146-163.

Malmberg, A., & Maskell, P. (2002). The elusive concept of localization economies: Towards a knowledge-based theory of spatial clustering. *Environment and Planning, 34*, 429-449.

Martin, R., & Sunley, P. (2003). Deconstructing clusters: Chaotic concept of policy panacea? *Journal of Economic Geography, 3*, 5-35.

Mytelka, L. (2001). *Clustering, long distance partnerships and the SME: A study of the French biotechnology sector.* Retrieved from http://www.utoronto.ca/isrn/documents/Mytelka_Clustering%20Long%20Distance.pdf

Nauwelaers, C., & Wintjes, R. (2003). The new wave of innovation-oriented regional policies; Policies and prospects. In B. Asheim, A. Isaksen, C. Nauwelaers, & F. Tödtling (Eds.), *Regional innovation policy for small-medium enterprises* (pp. 193-220). Cheltenham: Edward Elgar.

Niosi, J., & Bas, T. (1999). The competencies of regions: Canada's clusters in biotechnology. *Small Business Economics, 17*(1), 31-42.

OECD. (2003). OECD science, technology and industry scorecard 2003. Retrieved from http://www1.oecd.org/publications/e-book/92-2003-04-1-7294

Porter, M. (1990). *The competitive advantage of nations.* London: Macmillan.

Porter, M. (1998a). *On competition.* Cambridge, MA: Harvard Business School Press.

Porter, M. (1998b, December). Clusters and the new economics of competitiveness. *Harvard Business Review,* 77-90.

Rosenfeld, S. (2002a). *Creating smart systems: A guide to cluster strategies in less favoured regions.* Proceedings of the Conference on European Union-Regional Innovation Strategies, Brussels. Retrieved from http://www.rtsinc.org/rosenfeld.html

Rosenfeld, S. (2002b). *Just clusters: Economic development strategies that reach more people and places.* Retrieved from http://www.rtsinc.org/rosenfeld.html

Rosson, P., & McLarney, C. (2004). Biotechnology companies and clustering in Nova Scotia. In D. Wolfe, & M. Lucas (Eds.), *Clusters in a cold climate: Innovation dynamics in a diverse economy* (pp. 73-94.). Montreal: McGill-Queen's University Press.

Saxenian. A. (1994). *Regional advantage: Culture and competition in Silicon Valley and Route 128.* Cambridge, MA: Harvard University Press.

Smith, K. (1995). Interactions in knowledge systems: Foundations, policy implications and empirical methods. *STI Review, 16,* 69-102.

Sölvell, Ö, Lindqvist, G., & Ketels, C. (2003). *The cluster initiative greenbook.* Retrieved from www.ivorytower.se/greenbook

Staber, U. (2001). The structure of networks in industrial districts. *International Journal of Urban and Regional Research, 25*(3), 537-532.

Swann, G., & Prevezer, M. (1996). A comparison of the dynamics of industrial clustering in computing and biotechnology. In G. Swann, M. Prevezer, & D. Stout (Eds.), *The dynamics of industrial clustering: International comparisons in computing and biotechnology* (pp. 1139-1157). Oxford: Oxford University Press.

Tödtling, F., & Trippl, M. (2004). *One size fits all? Towards a differentiated policy approach with respect to regional innovation systems.* Paper presented at the Proceedings of the Conference on Regionalization of Innovation Policy—Options and Experiences, Berlin. Retrieved from http://epub.wu-wien.ac.at/dyn/virlib/wp/showentry?ID=epub-wu-01_749

Waluszewski, A. (2003). *What's behind a prospering biotech valley? A competing or co-operating cluster or seven decades of combinatory resources?* [unpublished paper]. Uppsala University.

Wolfe, D., Davis, C., & Lucas, M. (2005). Global networks and local linkages: An introduction. In D. Wolfe, & M. Lucas (Eds.), *Global networks and local linkages: The paradox of cluster development in an open economy.* Montreal and Kingston: School of Policy Studies, Queen's University Press.

Wolfe, D., & Lucas, M. (Eds.). (2005). *Global networks and local linkages: The paradox of cluster development in an open economy.* Montreal: McGill-Queen's University Press.

Endnotes

[1]   Two other types of less-favored regions also are identified: neighborhoods of inner cities and poor and peripheral rural areas (Rosenfeld, 2002b).

[2]   The OECD (2003) defines biotechnology as "the application of science and technology to living organisms as well as parts, products and models thereof, to alter living or non-living materials for the production of knowledge, goods and services" (Section A.6.1).

[3]   Global revenues for pharmaceutical companies were estimated at $466 billion in 2003, and those for medical device companies were estimated at $183 billion (Deloitte Touche Tomatsu, 2005).

[4]   A biotechnology innovator firm is one that uses biotechnology for developing new products and processes and is engaged in biotechnology related R&D activities.

5   Following the lead of others, the SSHRC-funded studies use 100 kms to define the limits of a local or regional cluster. Almost all biotechnology activity in Nova Scotia takes place within 100 kms of Halifax.

6   Company I is shown as having 150 to 300 employees. The larger number reflects seasonal employment required for harvesting seaweed.

7   Company XVII manufactures a commercial product for its parent and is in the process of developing a new formulation.

8   Elsewhere, we examined the importance of firms' local linkages with respect to customers, suppliers, knowledge relationships, and financing as an indication of whether a biotechnology cluster existed (Rosson & McLarney, 2004).

9   *Clutter* and *clump* were offered as alternative terms to describe the industry in Halifax.

Section III

Management
and Economics

Chapter VI

Cluster Development:
Issues, Progress and
Key Success Factors

Alev M. Efendioglu, University of San Francisco, USA

Abstract

Over the years, industry clusters have been touted to have economic and strategic advantages and have been used to develop embryonic industries. The cluster development process/methodology generally has taken two distinct approaches: laissez-faire, or economic system-driven; or planned/sponsored, or driven by government policy and intent. This chapter looks at two biotech clusters that are representative of each of these methodologies—the San Francisco Bay Area (California, U.S.) cluster and the Hsinchu (Taiwan) cluster—to identify the evolution and success of these two methodologies. The chapter also identifies and discusses key success factors that impact the development and growth of business clusters.

Introduction

The idea that national economic success depends in part, at least, on the development of localized concentrations of industrial specialization can be traced back more than 100 years to Alfred Marshall (1890). He argued that Britain's economic growth and leadership during the 19th century was founded on the development of several examples of localized industries. This concept was further developed and linked directly to the theory of the international firm by Markusen (1995), which has been shown to strongly impact the potential for business firms' strategic advantages (Porter, 1998).

The impact and use of clusters in the development of embryonic industries are well documented. As previous research has shown, clusters of related industries have formed around promising industries, becoming a part of the overall business activity and further feeding the embryonic industry's development and growth and contributing to its eventual success. These clusters have resulted in both internally derived and externally derived economies of scale, have reduced the transactions costs of dealing with suppliers and customers, and are evidenced by extensive knowledge spillovers, enabling a geographic region to capture additional economic benefits (Bahrami & Evans, 1995; Braunerhjelm & Johansson, 2003; Brown, 2003; Mathieu & Gibson, 1993).

Even though clustering always has involved some kind of cooperation and coordination between economic systems and governmental policies, different economic environments have utilized and depended more on one (the economic system with an organic and laissez-faire approach) or the other (governmental policies and efforts with a planned approach) supporting system. Generally, organic approaches have been the primary development methodology in economically advanced countries and around major metropolitan areas. (Orton, 2001) There are many examples, such as entertainment in and around Los Angeles, household furniture and synthetic fibers in North Carolina, insurance in Connecticut, and major manufacturing clusters in Japan around Tokyo and Osaka. In most other countries, clustering primarily has been initiated, encouraged, and partially sustained by governmental policies and support.

Interest in clusters has not been confined to academic research, and over the years, the cluster concept has found a ready audience amongst policymakers at all levels, from the World Bank to national governments, regional development bodies, and city authorities. These groups have sought new forms of industrial policy or activism in which the focus has been firmly on the promotion of successful, competitive economies. Porter's (1998a, 1998b) work has been a major impetus in stimulating this policy interest, and his writings have suggested that governments and other policy bodies may have a role to play in facilitating and supporting the development of competitive industrial clusters. An excellent example of this is the information technology industry development in Taiwan.

Given these two primary development methodologies and support systems, the objective of this study was to determine if any time-based outcome differences can be identified to exist between an organic (via an economic system) and a planned (via governmental policies and support) cluster. In order to identify the evolutionary and outcome differences between cluster developments supported by these different systems, two representative clusters (one in the San Francisco Bay Area (SF Cluster) in California, representing the organic process; and the other Hsinchu Cluster in Taiwan, representing the planned process) were identified and studied. The following sections will present and discuss the development and evolution of these two clusters and will focus on an industry (biotech) that is common to both clusters.

The biotech clustering evolved in the San Francisco Bay Area (SF Cluster) through an economic system-supported organic process that utilized a laissez-faire strategy and became one of the world's largest biotechnology clusters. On the other side, for the past 15 years, the Taiwanese government has instituted dramatic policy changes and developed support systems and infrastructures to replicate the success of the SF Cluster. This chapter compares the evolution of Taiwan and the Hsinchu Cluster to the SF Cluster in order to determine whether government planning and support can replicate the success of the organic model and looks at the outcomes and success of these two different approaches and support systems in the development of a technology-based (biotech) cluster in an embryonic industry. In order to determine if there are any significant differences in the successful progress of the cluster, firm growth rates, number of employees, and patent data are used to compare the two models. For the purposes of the study, Bonifant's (2001) definition of a biotech firm is adopted and used in analyzing the data. He defines a biotech firm as a company that researches human therapeutics by deriving from a naturally occurring substance or biological (e.g., human, animal, plant) substance. The company must apply genetic engineering or recombinant DNA technology, and its therapeutic products must be intended for sale through prescription. Based on the identified characteristics of the SF and Hsinchu Clusters and other business clusters, a set of key success factors that impact the successful formation of a business cluster also is stated and presented in the chapter.

San Francisco Bay Area (California) Cluster

The SF Cluster is comprised of Marin, Contra Cost, Alameda, Santa Clara, San Francisco, and San Mateo counties, which cover an area of 4,149 square miles and extend along a 50-mile corridor from San Francisco to San Jose. The population of the region is 5,837,915, yielding an average density of 1,407 persons per square mile. The SF Cluster employs more than 52,000 people.

The SF Cluster has more than 570 biotech companies. Thirty-four percent of firms are located in the East Bay, 55% in San Mateo/Santa Clara, and 11% in the North Bay (including San Francisco County). Eighteen of the world's 100 largest publicly traded biotechnology companies are located in the SF Cluster, and during 2002; these 18 public companies employed more than 15,020 people and spent in excess of $2 billion U.S. on research and development (Biotechnology Industry Organization, 2004). The largest company in the SF Cluster, Genentech, was founded in 1976, spends more than $600 million U.S. per year, and employs more than 3,100 people.

The organic development of the biotech cluster in the San Francisco Bay Area was no accident. The region embodies all the characteristics necessary for such a development and includes a very high concentration of research centers; it is home to venture capitalists, merchant banks, commercial banks, investment houses, and big pharmaceutical technology shoppers. The area's business culture encourages development of new ideas and the establishment of new firms to commercialize such ideas. There is a complex infrastructure offering contracting

Figure 1. U.S. biotech clusters (Source: DeVol, Wong, Ki, Bedroussian, & Koep, 2004)

and outsourcing opportunities tailored to individual bioscience company needs, there are numerous universities that have programs in bioscience, and there are programs that are designed to train biotech workforce of all levels.

Hsinchu (Taiwan) Cluster

The Hsinchu region is located in a rustic farming area in northwestern Taiwan and is comprised of one city, three towns, and nine villages. In 2003, Hsinchu's population was 439,713 with an average population density of approximately 750 persons per square mile. Two universities and a technology institute facilitate the higher education development in the Hsinchu region. In 1961, the number of higher education graduates was less than 10,000, but by 1996, this soared to nearly 200,000 with 40% having a degree in engineering (Saxenian, 2001). The 1,100-hectare Hsinchu Science Park (HSP) is home to many of Taiwan's largest and most famous IT and semiconductor companies, including Taiwan Semiconductor, the world's largest made-to-order IC manufacturer (Voyer, 2003). To the north and south of the park are two special biomedical zones.

After the first National Science Technology Conference in 1978, the Taiwanese government established the Hsinchu Cluster in 1980 to emulate Silicon Valley and to lure back Taiwanese researchers working abroad. To encourage the development of the science park and the technology cluster, major incentives were offered, including five-year tax exemptions, prefabricated factories, and generous grants, among others. The government's efforts to develop and promote the science park were very successful, and the Hsinchu science park was praised as an example of intelligent government intervention (Micklethwait, 1996).

Figure 2. Clusters in Taiwan

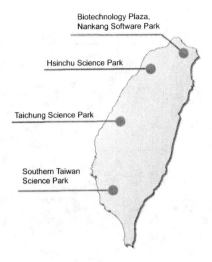

Even though biotech firms were being established in the Hsinchu Cluster since 1980, in order to develop a larger specialized biotech cluster, the Taiwanese Cabinet-Level Council for Economic Planning and Development (CEPD) approved in February 2003 a proposal to set up a biomedical park, and on February 18, 2004, the nation's first biomedical science park was officially established in Hsinchu County. This more concentrated cluster within the Hsinchu technology cluster area, fully operational in 2006, was developed around the 600-bed National Taiwan University Medical Center and houses an incubation center, joint research centers, an information network center, and a biotechnology center. In addition to the public infrastructure projects, it is home to private businesses and research facilities. By the time it was completed, the Taiwanese government had injected $27.3 billion NT ($844.66 million U.S.) into the project (The China Post, 2003; Taiwan Economic News, 2003).

Because the Hsinchu science park specializes in computers, semiconductors, and telecommunications, the Hsinchu biotech cluster, although still in its infancy, has benefited from the same effects as the SF Cluster, and it already has experienced a significant growth in the number of firms. According to the statistics compiled by Taiwan, in 2003, there were 27 biotech companies based in the park, posting $1.84 billion NT ($56.93 million U.S.) in revenues for 2003 (up by 30% over 2002), and 12 additional biotech companies had won approval (bringing in $4.4 billion NT in capital) to set up in the park; eight more were waiting for approval (Taiwan News, 2004). Even though at the time of this study these firms were in the process of being established, those approved and waiting for approval firms were included in the data set when generating the graph on Figure 3 in order to get a more accurate trend line.

Figure 3. Comparative growth patterns (Source: Data distilled from multiple sources)

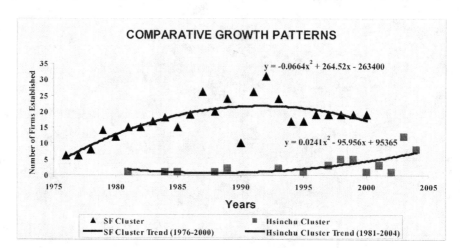

Comaparative Discussion of San Francisco and Hsinchu Clusters

Cluster Growth Rates

As can be seen in Figure 3, the Hsinchu biotech cluster has been experiencing a growth rate of new firms that is much slower than the one for the SF Cluster. During the first 25 years (1980 to 2005), there were 27 firms established in the Hsinchu Cluster compared to more than 550 in the SF Cluster since Genentech was established in 1976 (this date is considered to mark the birth year of the biotech industry in the U.S.).

Bresnahan, Gambardella, and Saxenian (2001, p. 850) suggest that "growth of companies, and not just the growth in the number of firms, is a signal of the success of the cluster." If we use a firm's employment as a measure of the firm's growth, we find that the number of persons employed in the two clusters also show a dramatic difference. Taiwan has 60,400 employees nationwide in the biotechnology industry, whereas the SF Cluster alone employs 52,000. The number of employees in the Hsinchu biotech cluster is 1,242. Genentech in the SF Cluster employs more than 3,000, far exceeding the number of employees in the entire Hsinchu Cluster. Even though there are similar percentages of small-sized firms (i.e., less than 50 employees), because of quite a few very large firms, the relative size of firms in the Hsinchu Cluster is also much smaller in comparison to the SF Cluster. For example, in the San Francisco Bay Area biotechnology cluster, 62.5% of the companies has less than 50 employees, 32.5% has 50 to 499 employees, and 5% has more than 500 employees (Day, 2000). In comparison, the Hsinchu Cluster is composed of 27 companies, of which 62.67% has less than 50 employees, 22.22% has 50 to 100 employees, 14.8% has 100 to 200 employees, and none has more than 200 employees.

New Patents Awarded

In 1980, Taiwan was ranked 21st in the number of U.S. patents received, coincident with the development of the Hsinchu Science Park. By 1990, Taiwan ranked 11th and currently has moved into 3rd place behind the U.S. and Japan (Saxenian, 2001; Wu & Lin, 2000). From 1976 to the end of 2002, there were 20,000 patents in the fields of biotechnology and related areas for all of Taiwan. Of those, 56 were for Chinese herbs, 8,019 for biotechnology innovations, and 10,669 for medicines (Heaney, 2003). In contrast, between 1975 and 1999, there were more than 5,000 patents issued to the companies that were in the SF Cluster alone (Schiller, 2002). Figure 4 illustrates the number of U.S. patents issued yearly and clearly shows the success of the biotech firms in the SF Cluster.

Key Success Factors for Cluster Formation and Development

There seems to be some unique characteristics that enable a cluster, especially a biotech cluster, to be sustainable and successful. These conditions include appropriate infrastructures (conditions conducive to enterprise development, including regulation, real estate, appropriate educational programs, and minimal barriers to associative activity within the cluster); an environment that encourages and fosters links between university/research institutions and the private sector; the availability of appropriate types of consulting, training, and mentoring; an environment that encourages and promotes linkages among companies

Figure 4. Comparative patents: U.S. vs. Taiwan (Source: Data distilled from multiple sources)

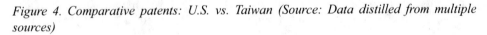

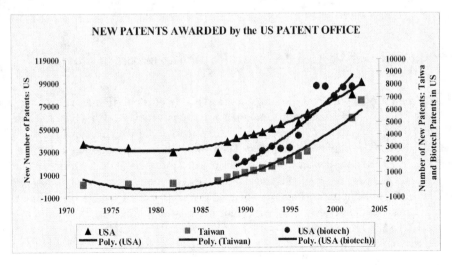

within the cluster (between industries and between firms and supporting institutions); and an environment in which financing (either directly from government agencies or from private sources) is available and in which financial incentives are in place to encourage investment in newly forming cluster firms. Even though some of these conditions require direct involvement from regional or national governments, it seems that having the private sector in the driving seat of the cluster development and minimizing governmental involvement and intervention in the process enhances the sustainability and growth of the cluster. When one looks at the SF Cluster, it is clear that most of the aforementioned conditions are in place and have contributed significantly to its success for 25 years; however, many of these conditions either are lacking or are in a very formative stage and may be impediments to the progress and growth of the Hsinchu Cluster.

Availability and Focus of Educational Institutions

The San Francisco Bay Area has more than 15 universities, and there are many programs that are focused on entrepreneurial education. There is a tradition of businesses sponsoring mini-company start-ups at the high school level and international business plan competitions at the university level. For example, the annual business-plan competition at the University of San Francisco draws more than 250 teams and business plans from all over the world. These university programs have encouraged and supported many start-up companies.

Spin-offs from educational institutions and new business start-ups are considered to be a significant measure of effectiveness for research institutions as incubators and for entrepreneurial education. The SF Cluster region has numerous academic institutions, including Stanford University and the University of California institutions at Berkeley, Davis, San Francisco, and Santa Cruz. These academic research institutions employ more than 10,000 people, contribute directly and indirectly to the development of biotechnology in the region, and have spun off 221 biotech firms in the SF Cluster. In comparison, there is a lack of biotech spin-offs from Taiwanese educational institutions, which portrays an inadequate entrepreneurial education infrastructure in the biosciences. As such, the Hsinchu Cluster has exhibited slow growth in the number of new firms created and has no reported spin-offs from academic institutions.

Availability of Venture Capital and Investment Patterns

Venture capital (VC) firms and venture capital funds seek out opportunities to fund and support most of the business start-ups and ongoing operations at their growth stages. Availability of such companies and funds provide an environment within which innovative but risky ideas can be put forth, funded, and tested. The United States, especially the San Francisco Bay Area is an environment in which such firms (i.e., more than 100 VC firms) exist and flourish, and their impact on the SF Cluster has been enormously positive. For example, in 2002, the total amount of VC funds available in the SF Bay Area was $4.125 billion U.S., and the investment in biotech in the San Francisco Bay Area was $660.00 million U.S. as compared to $628.08 million U.S. for all of Taiwan from all sources (95% from government) (Biotechnology Industry Organization, 2004; The China Post, 2003; Pao, 2003). During second quarter of 2004, the San Francisco Bay Area continued to be the biggest recipient of VC spending with $2.13 billion U.S. invested by VCs, which amounted to 38.2% of all the VC funds invested in the United States. This trend (availability of VC funds) continued, and during the second quarter of 2005, 43 VC firms raised $6.1 billion U.S., an increase of 88% from the previous year (Said, 2005). This infusion of money into VC funds is very good news for entrepreneurs and for the development of future clusters, and represents a distinct advantage for the area businesses (existing as well as new).

Because the United States excels in its ability to fund innovative companies at an early stage, new U.S. companies, especially the ones in technology and sciences, have had a significant advantage over other similar companies in Europe and Asia. U.S. VC spending doubled to more than $40 billion U.S. in 1999, with each dollar of venture capital producing three to five times more patents than each dollar of research and development spending by existing firms (Mandel, 2000). Unfortunately, similar benefits are not derived from the new venture funds in Asia, where these funds often have corporate or government affiliations. This association, because of the level of risk tolerance of the funding companies and the accompanying government oversight, provides much less autonomy than the one associated with the U.S. VC firms, thus making them much less effective.

To encourage entrepreneurship and support its progress toward a possible cluster, among other characteristics, the local economy has to have well-functioning institutions and capital markets. In order to measure this capability and to evaluate the ability of new and existing businesses to access capital, the Milken Institute (DeVol et al., 2004) has developed a measure called Capital Access Index (CAI) and has applied it to different countries. Its findings show that the United Kingdom is the country in which there is the greatest opportunity and ability for entrepreneurs to access capital, and 17 of the 20 countries ranked lowest were located in Africa. Among the countries listed in the top half of the CAI, New Zealand showed the greatest improvement from 2004 to 2005, and Mexico and Bulgaria moved up eight places in the ranking (Barth et al., 2005). The countries that measure low on CAI exhibit a precondition that is a major impediment not only to entrepreneurs who hope to start new businesses or to support their newly formed ones but also to the eventual formation of clusters that support these businesses. These countries need to institute major political and institutional changes in order to create conditions in which conditions conducive to entrepreneurial-based clusters can be established and sustained.

Entrepreneurial Spirit and Commensurate Risk-Reward Systems

Clusters that have their foundations on entrepreneurial activity are very much dependent upon and impacted by cultural factors and ethnicity. A study done by the Ewing Marion Kauffman Foundation has found some unique demographic characteristics associated with the degree of entrepreneurial activity in the United States. The foundation's findings show that entrepreneurial activity is substantially higher among men than among women, immigrants have substantially higher rates of entrepreneurship than U.S.-born individuals, and entrepreneurial activity is highest in the Western region of the country (Fairlie, 2005). These findings demonstrate some constraints and challenges not only for overall entrepreneurial activity but also for clusters that are based on this entrepreneurial activity, and may act as preconditions that are significant limitations to the formation of entrepreneurial clusters.

In order for start-up companies to form and create clusters, there has to be a culture of entrepreneurial sprit (an attitude that encourages and values risk and independence). California (a Western U.S. state) and especially the San Francisco Bay Area are known for such social and demographic characteristics and have provided a fertile environment for new companies and clusters. For example, during the first nine months of 2003, there were more than 62,000 new businesses incorporated in California (California Department of Finance, 2003). This social characteristic, coupled with the availability and focus of educational programs and commensurate reward systems (e.g., stock options in lieu of salaries), have further supported these new businesses and clusters. Seventy-three percent of the 567 San Francisco Bay Area companies with annual revenues exceeding $50 million U.S. in 2000 were started since 1985. The closest European region was the London area, in which there were 1,954 companies founded since 1985, out of which only 31% had $50 million U.S. revenues in 2000. Of the eight regions studied by Kluge, Meffert, and Stein (2000), the top three were in the United States and were identified as the San Francisco Bay area (73%), the Boston area (69%), and the Austin (Texas) area (58%).

When one looks at the number of business start-ups by ethnic Chinese, it is very easy to see the level of the region's entrepreneurial sprint and risk-taking behavior. Forty percent of the companies located in the Hsinchu Science Park (110 of 284) in 1999 were started by U.S.-educated engineers. In contrast, in the same year, Chinese engineers were CEOs of 2,001 San Francisco Bay Area high-tech companies (Saxenian & Hsu, 2000). In addition to the prevailing entrepreneurial spirit, Taiwanese regulations on importing foreign talent, especially from China, and the practice of taxing stock payments (given as a partial compensation by the start-ups in lieu of cash) have made it very difficult to lure the 4,500 U.S. biotech specialists back to Taiwan, where such payments are very popular (Chung, 2004). In contrast, California, which hosts 31% of U.S. biotech companies, has been a particularly vibrant biotech R&D base and has helped the U.S. sector to mature. Availability of talent, entrepreneurial sprint, risk-oriented compensation systems, and risk-taking funding mechanisms have fueled the formation of new biotech companies (in the SF Cluster, there are 221 spin-offs/new firms from local educational institutions) and, through a trial-and-error (risk) approach in biotech research, have created a successful industry and regional cluster.

Infrastructure and Support of Cluster Activities

Clustered businesses, especially at their embryonic stages, need and significantly benefit from an infrastructure that offers contracting and outsourcing opportunities tailored to their basic operational needs and especially supports back-office operations. Among them are insurance agencies; legal, accounting, management, and public relations firms; clinical research organizations; strategic planners; scientific writers; headhunters and placement agencies; science park developers; and webmasters. All of these related businesses and organizations have had a significant impact on the biotech cluster development in the San Francisco Bay Area and continue to support its growth. Over time, the critical mass of cluster companies attracts additional support businesses and further enhances the cluster and supports its growth. Furthermore, in the San Francisco Bay Area, a large concentration of high-tech firms has attracted biotech firms and has supported the growth of this cluster; one of the major reasons for Taiwan's selection of the Hsinchu area for a biotech cluster was the existence of a very sophisticated and fully functioning collection of IT firms and an IT cluster.

In order for clustered firms to share experiences, knowledge, and skills to fuel their growth, these experiences and knowledge have to be disseminated and publicized. This publicity and dissemination of knowledge continues to attract more firms that populate the cluster and contribute to its operational success and growth. For example, the San Francisco Bay Area is home to BioCentury, Medical Technology Stock Letter, Red Herring, Upside, Biospace. com, and Signals. More than 80 regional reporters cover Northern California's bioscience community. In addition to the media, Ernst & Young and Burrill & Company research and publish their annual analyses on the biotech sector. These reports are accepted worldwide as a means to track the industry. The German Aerospace Center in Oberpfaffenhofen (near Munich, Germany) recently set up a department to transfer the institute's know-how to potential start-ups, revitalizing established local industries that use them as suppliers of technology. Their primary objective is to support a cluster of technology-based businesses in order to enhance their future vitality and growth as this cluster develops and grows.

Size of Supporting Community

As technology and information have become more commoditized, the advantage of making things faster, cheaper, and better locally has diminished, and the profit margins have declined. With this commoditization, business core advantages (mainly in the form of manufacturing) have been shipped abroad from the United States and Western Europe mainly to India, China, and Eastern Europe, in some cases creating government-sponsored, planned clusters in these countries. This transformation has caused local businesses (existing as well as start-ups) to focus on design and service-based differentiation that is based on understanding the consumer experience and creating products that address consumers' unmet and often unarticulated desires. This increased importance on design and service requires companies to form clusters in and around large population areas where there are enough potential customers (individual or institutional) and a good supply of trained labor. Most of the organic (laissez-faire) clusters exhibit this characteristic, among which are entertainment in and around Los Angeles; household furniture and synthetic fibers in North Carolina; insurance in Connecticut; major manufacturing clusters in Japan located around Tokyo and Osaka; and the fourth-largest information technology center in the world (after Silicon Valley, Boston, and London) in Munich, one of the largest cities in Germany and the capital of Bavaria.

Conclusion

Because of some of the similarities and cross-pollination in equipment, educational backgrounds of employees, and high R&D requirements, most of the biotech clusters have been formed around and in the same areas in which there already exist electronics and software clusters. This is true for the SF Cluster and the Hsinchu biotech cluster. Furthermore, even in laissez-faire cluster formations, as in the SF Cluster, there have been some governmental influences and help. For example, in July 2003, the U.S. House of Representatives introduced the Biotechnology Future Investment Expansion (BIOFIX) Act (H.R. 2968), a piece of legislation designed to change the U.S. Tax Code in order to encourage further investments and innovations in the biotech industry. In primarily government-sponsored clusters, there is continued investment by government entities and direct involvement by various government organizations. For example, the Taiwan Ministry of Economic Affairs (MOEA) has publicly stated its support and has earmarked a total investment of $150 billion NT ($4.64 billion U.S.) in biotech during the five-year period between 2002 and 2006.

Some researchers have argued that starting a cluster requires different economics than sustaining a cluster (Bresnahan et al., 2001). Among the major issues that negatively impact the ability to successfully sustain and promote the cluster's growth seem to be lack of investment in education; relatively limited open market institutions; inability to curb brain drain; lack of infrastructure (e.g., supporting institutions, medical research, and hospital facilities for biotech); and government policies and procedures that lack coordination, especially in clusters that are primarily supported by government efforts and financing. As a result, one could argue that even though Taiwan's interventionist government policies were able to jump-start the biotech cluster formation, some of the conditions required to sustain a biotech cluster may have been lacking. This could have contributed to the limited growth experienced by the Hsinchu biotech cluster, and the late development or continued existence of factors that limit cluster sustainability might be the biggest difference between the Hsinchu Cluster (a government-planned and supported cluster) and the SF Cluster (an organic laissez-faire cluster).

It might be somewhat unwise to read too much into generalizations about a given region's (in different countries) biotech cluster and to draw broad concrete conclusions and assume that they also will be similar under conditions presented by other national environments. In order to eliminate some of the country-specific influences and characteristics, it might be much more appropriate to examine how biotech clusters in different areas of a country compare with each other. We can gain a much better understanding of issues associated with cluster development and develop insights, if we could compare clusters with different sources for foundation (organic and laissez-faire vs. government-sponsored, planned, and supported) and with similar setups within a given national boundary rather than comparing them over different national boundaries. Future studies that pursue and use such environments and can account for cross-national and cultural issues will enhance our understanding of this concept that seem to be a major competitive advantage for the firms involved in clusters.

References

Bahrami, H., & Evans, S. (1995). Flexible re-cycling and high-technology entrepreneurship. *California Management Review, 37*(3), 62-98.

Barth, J. R., et al. (2005). *2005 capital access index: Securitization in financing economic activities*. Milken Institute.

Biotech industry plays bigger role in Hsinchu Park. (n.d.). TaiwanNews.com. Retrieved September 18, 2004, from http://www.etaiwannews.com/Taiwan/2004/09/18/1095475297.htm

Biotech: What's all the fuss? (2003, October 22). *The China Post*. Retrieved September 25, 2004, from http://www.chinapost.com.tw/p_detail.asp?id=42425&GRP=i&onNews

Biotechnology Industry Organization. (n.d.). *Biotechnology industry facts*. Retrieved October 20, 2004, from http://www.bio.org/speeches/pubs/er/statistics.asp?p=yes&

Biotechnology Industry Organization. (2004, June 16). *Impact of biotechnology to California*. Retrieved August 3, 2006, from http://www.bio.org/events/2004/media/cabio.asp

Bonifant, B. (2001). New playing fields: Emerging arenas are challenging the blockbuster model dominating the pharmaceutical industry for the last 20 yrs. *Pharmaceutical Executive, 21*(9). Retrieved from http://www.pharmexec.com/pharmexec/article/articleDetail.jsp?id=781

Braunerhjelm, P., & Carlsson, B. (1999). Industry clusters in Ohio and Sweden, 1975-1995. *Small Business Economics, 12*(4), 279-293.

Bresnahan, T., Gambardella, A., & Saxenian, A. (2001). "Old economy" inputs for "new economy" outcomes: Cluster formation in the new Silicon Valleys. *Industrial and Corporate Change, 10*(1), 835–860.

Brown, J. (2003, March 24). Dublin things big over biotech. *Financial Times*, 13.

Cabinet OKs biotech, medical park in Hsinchu. (2003, March 28). *The Taiwan Economic News*. Retrieved October 10, 2004, from http://th.gio.tw/show.cfm?news_id=17211

California Department of Finance. (2003, September-October). *California economic indicators*. Retrieved June 7, 2004, from http://www.dof.ca.gov/html/fs%5Fdata/indicatr/2003/cei%5Fsept%2Doct%5Fweb.pdf

Chung, A. (2004, May 13). Biotech talent lacking, industry says. *Taipei Times*, p. 10.

Day, S. M. (2000, June). The Bay area: Best place in the world to do biotech. *BayBio Publications* (1).

Fairlie, R. W. (2005). *Kauffman Index of Entrepreneurial Activity*. Kansas City, MO: Ewing Marion Kauffman Foundation.

Heaney, B. (2003, October 3). Taiwan's biotech industry could leap ahead to success. *Taipei Times*, pg. 10.

Industry leaders say Taiwan biotech gaining traction. (2003, November 28). *Taiwan News.com*. Retrieved from http://www.etaiwannews.com/Business/2003/11/28/1069986695.htm

Kluge, J., Meffert, J., & Stein, L. (2000). Germany has an entrepreneurship gap. *The McKinsey Quarterly, Special Edition: Europe in Transition*. Retrieved September 20, 2004, from http://www.mckinseyquarterly.com/article_print.aspx?L2=21&L3=35&ar=829

Mandel, M.J. (2000, January 31). The new economy. *Business Week*, 73–77.

Markusen, J.R. (1995). Incorporating the multinational enterprise into the theory of international trade. *Journal of Economic Perspectives, 9*, 169–189.

Marshall, A. (1920). *Principles of economics*. (8th ed.). London: Macmillan and Co.

Mathieu, R., & Gibson, J. (1993). A methodology for large-scale R&D planning based on cluster analysis. *IEEE Transactions on Engineering Management, 40*(3), 283-292.

Micklethwait, J. (1996, March 9). Bits and bytes. *The Economist*, 15.

DeVol, R., Wong, P., Ki, J., Bedroussian, A., & Koepp, R. (2004, June). *America's biotech and life science clusters: San Diego's position and economic contributions*. Milken Institute.

Orton, C.W. (2001). Fertile ground in the Southwest U.S.. *World Trade, 14*(5), 68.

Pao, W.C. (2003, January 8). Cabinet calls for 79 biotech projects. *The China Post*, p. 3.

Porter, M. (1998, November-December). Clusters and the new economics of competition. *Harvard Business Review, 76*(6), 77–90.

Said, C. (2005, July 19). New money flocks to VC funds. *San Francisco Chronicle*, p. D1.

Saxenian, A.L. (2001, June 16). *Taiwan's Hsinchu region: Imitator and partner for Silicon Valley* (SIEPR Discussion Paper No. 00-44). Stanford Institute for Economic Policy Research.

Saxenian, A.L., & Hsu, J.-Y. (2000). *The Silicon Valley-Hsinchu connection: Technical communities and industrial upgrading*. Retrieved from http://www.sims.berkeley.edu/~anno/papers/

Schiller, T. (2002). From laboratory to market: The biotechnology industry in the third district. *Business Review, Q4*, 6–17.

Voyer, R. (2003). *Clustering: A contact sport*. Proceedings of the Research Money Conference, Technology Clusters: By Accident or Design? Impact Group.

Wu, R.-I., & Lin, H. (2000, August 23-24). A study on industrial technology competitiveness in Taiwan. *The measurement of industrial technological competitiveness in the knowledge-based economy in Taipei* Retrieved from http://www.tier.org.tw/07publication/president/25.htm

Chapter VII

Regional Clusters:
Classification and Overlap of Wine and Tourism Microclusters

Pamela McRae-Williams, University of Ballarat, Australia

Abstract

This chapter examines the application of cluster theory to small groups of collocated wine and tourism enterprises. It explores how traditional notions of cluster theory apply in the microcontext and whether such interpretations can be used as a valid tool for understanding how collocated regional businesses interact. The chapter describes three case studies of regional wine- and tourism-related businesses to illustrate how these microclusters might be identified and to determine the significance of interrelationships within and between collocated clusters. Such findings provide evidence of the strength or otherwise of these clusters. The chapter suggests that at the microscale, collocated clusters share some complementarity or overlap with each other through geography, resources, and levels of activity, which may be a factor that propels these clusters forward or sparks new cluster development.

Introduction

Many studies of performance, innovation, and clustering note that industry matters (Porter, 1998; Rosenfeld, 1996; Swann, Prevezer & Stout, 1998). It is well documented that industry together with cooperative behavior is important in cluster development (Porter, 1998). In some industry sectors such as wine and tourism, this may be of particular relevance because of the size of dominant enterprises, the nature of knowledge and knowledge transfer, the diverse makeup of these sectors and their competitive rules, and path dependencies.

The study reported on in this chapter concerns the wine and tourism industries and the interaction between them in the form of wine tourism. It draws from four bodies of literature; clusters, the tourism industry, the Australian wine industry, and wine tourism. Although the focus is industry-specific, the concepts of cluster classification, interaction, or overlap, and the comparative economic significance of clusters are not, and there may be some parallels between these industries and other regional industries. In discussing wine and tourism, attention is drawn specifically to the nature of the industries, the implications for regional cluster development, and finally, the convergence in wine tourism. Understanding industry-specific cluster preconditions may influence the development of certain industries in a given region and may be important in the formation of regional and industry-based clusters.

Using regionally based wine and tourism industries as exemplars, this study explores whether clusters differ in different industries and, if so, whether the processes of clustering also vary. In addition, can the industry type, the extent of clustering activity, the location, or a combination of these factors influence the level of cluster activity and the extent of cluster overlap?

An insight into how regional cluster theory applies in the different industries of wine and tourism may prove useful in the study of how other collated industries interact. Using the diamond advantage framework proposed by Porter (1990), the California wine cluster study evaluated its competitiveness in order to improve productivity and to help determine its position in the global wine market. It identified key issues facing the cluster and compared these with other wine clusters in Chile, France, and Italy (Alexander, Arney, Black, Frost & Shivananda, 1997). The resultant cluster map illustrated the interconnectedness of elements that make up this wine industry cluster. This schematic representation of a wine cluster indicates across firm linkages, together with linkages with other clusters. These linkages were identified with the tourism cluster, the food cluster, and the agricultural cluster; however, there was no exploration of the nature of these intracluster linkages (Porter, 1998). There also has been less emphasis in the traditional cluster literature on identifying and classifying clusters in situations in which the level of economic activity of an individual industry may not be significant in isolation but is more important when there is overlap among collated industries. It is therefore important to understanding what is meant by industry, regions, and clusters in this context if the application of this theory is to be broadened.

Industries, Regions, and Clusters

The concepts of an industry, a region, and a cluster are ways to describe and understand how enterprises are organized in specific geographic locations. In regional wine and tourism enterprises, exploring these concepts is important in determining what is important for the development of wine tourism as a new industry in specific regions. The emergence of wine tourism as a vibrant industry in some regions and its limited development in others has highlighted a variance in the way these industries operate and interact across different locations.

First, what is meant by an industry? In this chapter, industry is meant as essentially a group of establishments or businesses that produce related goods or services (Jackson, 1989a). Thus, in this context, an industry is not interpreted on the basis of how it is classified statistically (i.e., for standard industry classification) but rather on interrelationships and similarities between products and activities. However, in order to measure economic inputs and outputs, a clearly identified industry is required, which is a challenge when applied in particular to tourism. The diverse ranges of establishments that engage in tourism are included in a number of recognized industries (Jackson, 1989b). For this reason, standard industry definitions that are used for economic analysis fail to fully capture tourism endeavors. By comparison, the wine industry poses fewer problems, as it is narrower and has a more easily identified range of establishments involved. It is, however, not purely within the agricultural sector or, indeed, the manufacturing sector, so again, standard industry classification is unclear (Chapman, 2000). Consequently, the notion of a clearly defined industry as identified by Standard Industry Classification data, the basis on which many tradition clusters have been identified, does not necessarily apply in all cases.

Second, the nature of much of the tourism and wine industry means that often it is located in regional parts of Australia. A region in this study means non-metropolitan and generally has links with primary industries and associated or decentralized secondary industries (Black, 2000). Regions can have both tourism resources and wine resources, and in some instances, regions may have some similarities in their wine and tourism industry development. This suggests a degree of industry overlap whereby these two industries may share a number of common attributes such as geographic collation and economic, social, and natural resource assets. In some cases, the industries compete for land, capital, and skilled labor. However, they also have significant demand and supply side complementarities that create better conditions for the development and performance of both industries. This complementarity, however, in terms of its nature and economic significance, varies considerably from one region to another.

Finally, because of the nature and scope of both industries and regions, this means that the term *cluster* is interpreted from a broad perspective. Within the cluster literature, there is some ambiguity in the definition of clusters (Bergman & Feser, 1996; Feser, 1998; Jacobs & De Man, 1996; Porter, 1998; Rosenfeld, 1997). Porter (1998) provides the most commonly quoted definition; however, it does not specify the particular application of clusters at a microscale or in rural settings. Therefore, the following definition (although less commonly used) was adopted for this study, because it identifies relevant aspects of microclusters. Rosenfeld (1997) contends that clusters need not be economically significant in order to exist, for "a cluster is very simply used to represent concentrations of firms that are able to produce synergy because of their geographic proximity and interdependence, even though their scale of employment may not be pronounced or prominent" (p. 4). In this context, the term *microcluster* is used to identify those small, often regional or industry-specific clusters that may or may not have been formally identified.

This definition of clusters, which interprets clusters as a group of establishments that are collated and interact with each other and have some interdependency that may or may not be recognized economically or strategically, seems most applicable when applied to sometimes small and regionally specific centers of wine or tourism activity. This means that clusters can be loosely formed by simple collation and passive interaction or may be the result of actively sought collation benefits, such as joint marketing, or focused around a dominant player or a center of excellence. The existence of passive and active externalities referred to by Brown (1999) can determine the level of dynamism that a cluster generates. These externalities are part of the cluster classification process and reflect the types of clustering processes that are present. Passive cluster processes occur when businesses collate; they occur without any conscious effort on the part of the individual businesses but provide positive benefits to the businesses. These benefits generally relate to traditional cluster externalities and include specialist inputs, spillovers of knowledge, the existence of skilled labor, or local knowledge and infrastructure development that occurs outside the sphere of influence of the individual business. Rather, they occur by passive interaction of businesses within a cluster or between clusters. As these passive processes become stronger, active cluster processes such as joint marketing and production activities, innovation, and infrastructure support may begin to develop. These active processes relate to the dynamism of clusters; they are different from passive cluster externalities in that they depend on those benefits gained only through conscious activity by businesses within the cluster (Brown, 1999). The dynamism created is a consequence of highly developed interrelationships among businesses in the cluster and may occur between clusters. These relationships involve competition, collaboration, and joint activity.

There are other cluster classification approaches that are less about levels of activity and more about types of production. For example, Verbeek (1999) and Roelandt and Hertog (1999) classify clusters into two distinct categories based on similarity or interdependency of production, which reflects a static approach. This form of classification may restrict the ability to describe clusters in the microcontext, because it largely depends on concentration of enterprises. However, it also reflects how interdependent cluster members are on one another while, in turn, has implications for cluster complementarity. The import of interrelationships among firms in a cluster is recognized by both Rosenfeld (1996) and Enright (2000a, 2000b); when classifying clusters, they consider the level of firm interaction. This level of interaction may become a key factor in determining the shape and strength of the cluster.

Brown (1999) introduces another concept in classifying clusters: preconditions. Preconditions are those factors that are present in cluster development; they may spark this development or add incrementally to such development. These conditions will be explored in relation to each of the clusters identified in the case studies reported on in this chapter.

The Tourism Industry and Clusters

The growth of the Australian tourism industry and its continued expansion into regional and rural parts of Australia has implications for the economic future of many rural and regional areas (Blamey & Hatch, 1998; Prosser, 2001). A number of important industry-specific features of the tourism industry influences the way in which it operates in the regional economy. Understanding issues associated with the tourism industry and whether these influence how regional businesses engaged in tourism may contribute to how regional tourism clusters form are structured and the processes that are active within them.

This understanding is complicated by the nature of tourism and by the breadth of this industry. Because this chapter focuses on clustering in an industry, it is important to understand the issues associated with identifying components of this industry and measuring their relationships and activity. The discussion emerges from the debate on a standard definition for tourism that can be used in meaningful comparative studies (French, Craig-Smith, & Collier, 1995; Hall, 1995; Jackson, 1989b; Leiper, 1979, 1990, 1995; Leiper & Carlsen, 1998; Williams, 1998). The literature demonstrates that definitions vary according to the purpose of the specific study undertaken, and the term *tourism* is used loosely and represents a multidisciplinary and complex phenomenon (Leiper, 1990). As a complex network of value-generating relationships, it is a rare phenomenon.

Tourism is an industry that has been recognized but is not easily measured and is an industry with such a broad scope that it limits intraindustry cooperative behavior (Jackson, 1989b; Leiper, 1990). This suggests that clustering is less likely in tourism than in industries with a narrower scope. Difficulty in identifying tourism clusters stems from both the broad industry base and the limited data available that delineate this industry from others.

Analysis of the economic impact of tourism using a tourism satellite accounting system has been an attempt to provide data that reflect where and how much tourism contributes to the economy (Australian Bureau of Statistics, 2002). This system, however, falls short of identifying industry participants and the relationships among these participants. The shortfall in data on supply-side activities and data identifying the businesses that are actively supplying tourism product creates some difficulties when identifying clusters and understanding the processes that occur within them. Another complicating factor is that many tourism enterprises are at the microlevel. This leads to difficulties in identifying, classifying, and measuring the components of the tourism industry. This difficulty in defining tourism and the data limitations may require the use of other approaches that represent this industry better. Clusters, value chains, and value nets are alternative classifications to industry. These measures may capture the complexities associated with a diverse range of businesses and relationships involved in a fragmented industry such as tourism.

It seems that there are several characteristics of the tourism industry that are important when considering how and, indeed, if clusters apply in this industry. Most cluster studies rely on broad industry definitions, and the more traditional and statistically based cluster analysis often may use standardized industry data (Institute for Strategy and Competitiveness, 2004). There are difficulties in applying traditional cluster analysis to tourism, which stem largely from the limited availability of this type of data and the nature of the tourism industry. Other aspects of tourism also may challenge the notion of clustering. A key component of clusters is that competition and cooperation can be mutually beneficial (Enright, 1996; Jorge, 1978). In tourism, the prevalence of a competitive approach by managers and organizations within the industry is well-recognized. Businesses involved in tourism are more likely to see themselves as competitors rather than potential partners or allies (Smith, 1998). This indeed may restrict the productivity and potential of regional tourism clusters (Leiper, 1995).

Cooperation does occur within the tourism industry and is generally driven by marketing and is demonstrated when specific partnerships are forged; for example, resort associations and destination-marketing associations. However, this is not always viewed as functional industry cooperation in the tourism context (Smith, 1998). Smith (1998) suggests that within these industry-based organizations, "[i]t is rare to find integrated, industry-wide, cooperative marketing strategies with a commitment to sharing data and research and a willingness to work together on industry-wide challenges" (p. 33). Consequently, the benefits of cooperation may not be fully realized, which is perhaps why few successful tourism clusters have been reported in the literature.

There are, however, a number of characteristics of the tourism industry that may benefit from a cluster approach. By recognizing that tourism is a fragmented industry in which some participants do not realize they are part of the industry, Leiper (1995) suggests that tourism extends beyond the scope of markets and industries and should be viewed as part of a whole system. This includes economic, cultural, and physical aspects (Jackson, 1989b; Leiper, 1990). The notion of a system is akin to that of a cluster and may be a powerful tool in helping to understand the structure, conduct, and performance of tourism in regions.

Other aspects of the tourism industry, such as horizontal integration, economies of scale, innovation through information technology, branding en masse and niche markets, and networks based on strategic alliances, are also relevant to cluster research (Nordin, 2003; Porter, 1990, 1998; Rosenfeld, 1997). These have become part of the travel industry rationale in order to maintain a competitive advantage in the marketplace (Ioannides & Debbage, 1998; Porter, 1990). Also, the confluence of economic and spatial interrelationships in tourism through regional destination planning can provide an impetus for regional tourism cluster developments (Enright & Ffowcs-Williams, 2000; Gunn, 1994).

These apparent similarities in tourism development and clustering do not mean that identification of tourism clusters is easy. This is reflected in the absence of certain cluster requirements, and tourism clusters may be obscured by their involvement in several overlapping industry categories (Porter, 1998). Porter (1998) sees tourism as a good example of complementarity in clusters, because the quality of visitor experience depends not only on the primary attraction but also on other related facilities. This is exemplified where the quality of a visit can be influenced by one of many seemingly unrelated experiences that can have an influence on the tourism experience as a whole. This notion of complementarity in tourism and clusters is significant and may be a means by which tourism clusters can be understood. By relating tourism clusters to other industry clusters such as wine, there is an opportunity to explore if this is, in fact, the case.

The challenges associated with tourism cluster development, however, largely reflect the difficulty in measuring economic impacts using standard statistical sources and the often small scale of regional tourism that results in a lack of critical mass, geographic isolation, infrastructure shortfalls, and shortages of skilled resources (Smith, Denton & Crinion, 1999). Attempts at tourism cluster identification and analysis have been undertaken using a range of approaches and reflect these difficulties (Roehl, 1998). Within Australia, attempts by state governments to identify particular tourism clusters have shown varying levels of success. The first of these initiatives was to identify an international tourism cluster in South Australia (Blandy, 2001; Smith et al., 1999). Using a collaborative approach to industry cluster development, this program identified an international tourism cluster, but the development of this cluster met with limited success (Blandy, 2001). In the tropical north Queensland region, there has been some success in developing a tourism cluster (Nordin, 2003). The Cairns Regional Economic Development Corporation (CREDC) cluster development formula is based on collaborative marketing and development of the Cairns tourism destination precinct (Cairns Regional Economic Development Corporation [CREDC], 2002).

These government-initiated approaches to creating clusters may be more about intent and hope than about real cooperation and relationships. Hence, these types of cluster approaches often rely on seeding by government development initiatives and are initiated by consultants. Consequently, they initially are driven from the top down rather than emerging organically. This may have some impact on how these essentially market-driven destination strategies function as clusters in the long term. There are other examples of cluster developments beginning to emerge within the Australian tourism market, but there is limited assessment of these approaches reported in the literature. It is noted at this point that not all industries approach clusters in the same way; an example of this is the Australian wine cluster.

The Wine Industry and Clusters

Wine, unlike tourism, is a fairly narrowly based industry category. As an industry, wine has a number of characteristics that have influenced its growth as an Australian exporter and its competitiveness on the world market. The location of the industry over regional Australia's agricultural land has meant that this industry continues to have significant implications for the economic circumstances of these regions. The industry, however, faces a number of challenges from changing world markets and a changing industry structure.

The changing structure of the industry from a dominance of small to medium producers to fewer large companies has led to the 20 top companies controlling almost 95% of the wine output. This is very different to tourism, which is dominated by small businesses in which no one enterprise owns or controls the most popular destinations. In the wine industry, the change in structure has implications for domestic producers and particularly for small to medium wine producers. A report recently commissioned by the Commonwealth Government identified strategies for smaller wine producers based on regional branding for niche marketing for the long-term growth and profitability of these businesses (ACIL, 2002).

The Australian wine industry today is largely made up of two components: the large multinational exporters that depend less on the domestic market, and the large number of small to medium operators that make up the bulk of the domestic wine industry. Many existing and developing wine regions are dominated by these smaller enterprises that often become engaged either intentionally or by necessity in regional tourism-based activities.

There are a number of attributes demonstrated by the Australian wine industry that make it particularly amenable to cluster behavior. One of the key preconditions for the current success of the Australian wine industry has been attributed to the industry's capacity to collaborate (Marsh & Shaw, 2000). Rivalry and fierce competition exist between producers, but it is argued that collaboration around shared concerns of future competitiveness and profitability has drawn this industry together (Anderson, 2001a). In addition, preconditions associated with natural advantages present in many Australian wine regions extend beyond the resource base and suitability of the region for wine production to include the importance of recognized boundaries for the various wine-growing regions and subregions (Anderson, 1999). This differentiation between wine regions promotes localization in a way that is not readily achieved by other regional products in Australia (Anderson, 2001b). This creates a direct means of generic branding and promotion of wines from these regions (Anderson, 1999). Branding, usually regionally based, has strong links to tourism destination marketing, which is also regionally based with strong local identity.

A number of accounts have been given of the Australian wine industry and its propensity to exhibit strong clustering characteristics (Anderson, 2001a; Bond, 2000; Chapman, 2000; Marceau, 1997; Marsh & Shaw, 1999). Not surprisingly, it has been identified as a successful industry cluster (Blandy, 2001; Chapman, 2000; Marceau, 1997; Marsh & Shaw, 2000). There is, however, limited documentation and analysis of this industry using cluster methodologies. Marsh and Shaw (2000) suggest that synergy between collaboration and competition is the key driver for this cluster. Importantly, these types of cluster processes are not as evident within the tourism industry.

Marceau (1997) described the Australian wine industry as a natural resource-based cluster and identified three contributory factors: producers are geographically concentrated, producers have common interests in technology and oenology; and education, research, and development have provided common training facilities at a world-class standard, creating a highly skilled and highly technical industry. Anderson (2000) and Marsh and Shaw (2000) have labeled the industry as a knowledge-driven cluster with cluster linkages, embedded capabilities, and knowledge infrastructure. There are some indications, however, that this cluster potential may not continue, and Marceau (1997) suggests that the sense of common purpose within the wine industry has been diluted by a rapid increase in the number of new winegrowers with little in common with existing growers.

Understanding how wine and tourism industries might cluster creates an opportunity to look at linkages between these regional industries. This approach provides an opportunity to explore wine tourism and how it stands in relation to regional clusters. Using the lens of clusters in this way brings to light some interesting complementarities associated with wine tourism.

Wine-Tourism Clusters

Geographic collation based on natural advantage, proximity to existing tourism centers or population centers, and regional or brand recognition is seen as a significant precondition for wine tourism (Fuller, 1997; Hall, Johnson, & Mitchell, 2000; Salter, 1998). It is not simply the wine that makes a wine-tourism destination but that it comes from a special place (Salter, 1998).

Crittenden (1999) suggests that the wine-tourism company should be involved in wine tourism, suggesting that in order for wine tourism to be successful, it needs to be at the forefront of the enterprise. As a result, the main preconditions for wine tourism based on Crittenden's (1999) analysis would include those enterprises with limited export focus or overseas sales, limited wholesale/retail off-site sales, and a reliance on cellar-door sales. Consequently, the increasing dominance of the major wine corporations in Australia and their continued focus on export markets (Marceau, 1997) means that wine tourism increasingly is becoming the arena of the smaller boutique producer.

How to recognize the potential impacts of wine tourism on regional wine and tourism industries is something that only recently is being explored. Wine tourism is in the early stages of its life cycle within the Australian context, and perhaps later in the cycle, when wine tourism has been successful, some negative impacts may emerge. An example of this has occurred in Napa Valley, California, where wine tourism is now limiting the success of the wine industry upon which it was founded (Nordin, 2003; Skinner, 2000). Providing a sustainable wine-tourism product depends on the survival of the local wine industry and a commitment to cooperation, slow planned growth, and the establishment of partnerships (Skinner, 2000). These developmental stages also are linked with how relationships between the wine and tourism industries are manifested within a region. It is at this point that the significance of clusters becomes most relevant. The discussion has suggested that there are differences between how the wine and tourism industries behave in terms of clusters, and these now play a role in how a region's wine-tourism activities develop.

Applying cluster concepts to wine tourism has not been the focus of major research; however, some wine-tourism research has identified and described some of the key components of clusters. Perhaps the most well researched wine-tourism cluster is Napa Valley, where Porter's Californian wine clusters sparked the use of this methodology. Nordin (2003) provides an overview of how the wine cluster and tourism and hospitality cluster are working together. She suggests that the interaction of a comparatively well-developed and recognized wine industry cluster with a less understood tourism cluster can provide an opportunity for increasing the competitive advantage of each industry through the development of wine tourism. Geographic collation (agglomeration), competition and cooperation, collaboration and networks, niche creation, innovation, and knowledge transfer all play a role in wine-tourism development. All of these are important cluster factors that are particularly evident in wine clusters and not so evident in tourism clusters.

On the domestic market, the "formal definition of regions is leading to more information-sharing among producers within the region, and to better coordination with regional tourism activities" (Anderson, 2001b, p. 13). This is perhaps one of the more prominent opportunities for wine-tourism cluster development. However, in order for clusters to be active, there is a number of factors that are important. There seems little doubt in the literature that wine tourism has the potential to benefit from cooperation and collaboration, whether vertical, horizontal, or diagonal networks (Hall & Jenkins, 1998; Johnson, 1998; Michael, 2001), and through value chains in which each stage adds economic value (Getz, 1998).

Not withstanding the potential for positive cluster development in wine tourism, there are recognized barriers to its successful development. These simply may stem from the nature of the relationship between these two industries. The development of networks in wine tourism can be difficult due to the information gaps about the perceived benefits of such linkages (Hall & Johnson, 1997) and the apparent lack of interindustry linkages and cooperation (Macionis & Cambourne, 2000).

From a winery perspective, both the wine and tourism industries suffer from a lack of sectoral linkages, which has resulted in a lack of cohesion and interorganizational cooperation (Johnson, 1998; Macionis, 1997). On the other hand, Macionis (1997) suggests that barriers to the wine industry stem from a lack of experience and entrepreneurial skill regarding tourism, particularly amongst smaller wineries, and that tourism often is seen as a secondary or tertiary activity in the wine industry. Conversely, Johnson (1998) sees these barriers in relation to the tourism industry, which has a lack of understanding of viticultural practices and the demands of wine making and, on occasion, a conflicting demand for scarce resources.

The difficulty in developing relationships between the wine and tourism industries is most likely the consequence of a number of factors specific to these industries rather than how they manifest in regional settings. It is important to note that differences between these industries include structure, breadth, the degree of collaborative behavior, and the level of innovation and knowledge sharing. These cluster preconditions are important when considering their impact on cluster behavior, both passive and active. Clusters in wine tourism bring with them the intricacies of these different industries and cluster types and provide insight into the interaction between clusters in distinct industries that often overlap geographically. In addition, the case studies described in this chapter provide valuable insight into the importance of common preconditions that might revolve around location and the very nature of the industries concerned.

Three Case Studies

This chapter discusses some outcomes of research on three regional case studies in Regional Victoria, Australia. Each case study comprised a wine and tourism cluster and investigated their characteristics and interaction between the two collated clusters. The regional case studies were examined using qualitative and quantitative data. This chapter reports on the qualitative information derived from secondary data and semi-structured interviews. The sample population for each of the three regions was drawn from key stakeholder representatives in the wine and tourism industries, local government, local industry group, education providers, and other stakeholder representatives identified as the extent of the cluster was identified. The sample selecting was based on snowball or networking (Hussey & Hussey, 1997). For each region, the number of key representatives initially identified varied due to the extent of industry/government/educational involvement in the region. In total, 32 interviews were conducted across the three case studies.

Using a question-answer reporting format described by Yin (1994) for reporting on multiple case studies, the following questions were asked for each of the three case studies:

- Which elements are important in classifying regional wine and tourism clusters?
- Are cluster preconditions important in these clusters?
- How important are passive processes in these clusters?
- How important are active processes in these clusters?

- Do these wine and tourism clusters overlap?
- Do these clusters complement each other?

This information provides an assessment of the context and activities of each case, which is used later to categorize the cluster by reference to the level of clustering activity, complementarity, and overlap. Each question addresses a particular component or activity of clusters.

Cluster elements include the geographic, economic, and social aspects of a cluster. The focus of the study is essentially rural and regional microclusters, which one might expect to have some impact on the role and strength of cluster elements that might not be evident in larger and more established clusters (Rosenfeld, 1996).

Cluster preconditions are those conditions that need to be present in order to initiate or sustain a cluster. In this research, preconditions are implied in the reasons why businesses choose to locate in a particular region. This approach has not been reported widely in the literature, al though it was adopted by Brown (1999) for his work on the electronics cluster in Christchurch, New Zealand. This approach allows key cluster strengths to be identified in the absence of other data sources.

The concept of passive cluster processes is an outcome of business collation that is not sought actively. In this study, specific questions provide a measure of the extent to which businesses derive goods and services locally, have local customers, and acquire technology through spillover, skill, and knowledge transfer from within the cluster. These are considered the result of collation and are not specifically the result of the cluster's existence.

Active cluster processes are of particular interest in cluster research because they help to describe the dynamism of clusters. They depend on those benefits gained only through the deliberate decisions made by businesses within the cluster (Brown, 1999). Active processes are also a feature of cross-cluster activity. These processes typically result from strong relationships among businesses within the cluster and among clusters. In this study, the strength of these relationships was ascertained by asking respondents to map the cluster relationships. The relationships that businesses have with other local businesses or agencies vary; they may be informal in nature and may become more formal over time. The data collected in this study include formal and informal relationships.

Cluster overlap was identified by Porter (2001, 2003) and is essentially a measure based on industry category, strength of cross-industry activities, and relationships. According to Porter (2003), both clusters need to demonstrate industry overlap by undertaking the same activity or by having some of the same components and sectors contributing to the cluster. This reciprocity of cluster overlap is an important factor when determining cluster overlap in relation to this study.

The study uses the concept of cluster complementarity, which is gauged through the importance of reputation, regional recognition, and cross-cluster relationships to cluster members. The data collected in this study reflect the level of complementarity achieved by identifying whether businesses have working relationships with other businesses and the nature of those relationships. The study determines that if most of those interviewed regarded the level of complementarity between businesses as important for a range of cluster activities and relationships, then these clusters are regarded as displaying active complementarity. These working relationships are sought actively by most businesses in order to gain benefits from each other. If, on the other hand, most of these activates and relationships were seen as of little importance by most interviewees, then these clusters are described as displaying passive complementarity; that is to say, this complementarity may be a matter of chance rather than actively sought. These measures of complementarity, though not conclusive, have been chosen in order to provide an understanding of the extent of cluster activity in the absence of other more quantitative methods.

Characteristics of the Regional Wine and Tourism Cluster Case Studies

Does any one of the cluster elements (i.e., geographic, economic social) become more important than the others in determining cluster type? The relative importance of these elements in each cluster is summarised in Table 1, which reflects the qualitative data gathered.

The information gleaned through the interviews suggests that cluster elements, whether they are geographically-based, economically-based, or social, vary in importance. The importance of geographic and social elements in the case studies appears to be most variable and seemingly of less importance in many of the clusters studied. It may be that these elements create the differences among the clusters in this study.

Cluster preconditions are related to cluster elements. For example, geographic preconditions include distance from markets, infrastructure, climate, and landscape. Economic precondi-

Table 1. The comparative importance of cluster elements

Cluster Elements	Case Study One: Wine Tourism		Case Study Two: Wine Tourism		Case Study Three: Wine Tourism	
Geographic	X	XXX	XX	XXX	XXX	XXX
Economic	X	XXX	XXX	XXX	XXX	XXX
Social	XX	XX	XXX	X	XXX	XX

Note: X not important; XX important; XXX very important

Table 2. The comparative importance of cluster elements as cluster preconditions

Cluster Preconditions	Case Study One: Wine Tourism		Case Study Two: Wine Tourism		Case Study Three: Wine Tourism	
Geographic	XX	XX	XXX	XXX	XX	X
Economic	X	XXX	XXX	XXX	X	XX
Social	XX	XXX	XXX	XXX	XX	XX

Note: X not important; XX important; XXX very important

Table 3. Comparative importance of passive cluster processes in each cluster

Cluster Processes	Case Study One: Wine Tourism		Case Study Two: Wine Tourism		Case Study Three: Wine Tourism	
Passive cluster processes	X	X	XXX	X	XXX	X

Note: X not important; XX important; XXX very important

tions concern the significance of the cluster in the region's economy, its export activity, the size and structure of enterprises within the cluster, and the degree of vertical and horizontal integration within and beyond the region's economy. Social preconditions include the presence of industry associations, collaborative activity, and life-style factors. Table 2 indicates the relative importance of a range of preconditions in each cluster and, again, is derived from qualitative data gathered. The data indicate that the types of preconditions important to clusters vary between clusters and regions.

These findings suggest that the importance of preconditions varies across the clusters with some regions (case study two), showing that geographic, economic, and social preconditions are very important. The relative importance of social preconditions suggests that clusters are not necessarily formed by economic or geographic preconditions in isolation.

Passive cluster processes are diverse, and identifying if they are important in each cluster provides an indication of their level of development. Table 3 summarizes the data obtained from the case studies and identifies that not all clusters demonstrate benefits associated with passive cluster processes.

For example, in case study one, the clusters show little benefit from passive cluster processes. These data suggest that tourism clusters, in particular, have limited recognized passive eternality development; this may be a function of tourism clusters in general (Braun, 2003) and might reflect the broad scope and fragmented nature of this industry.

Active cluster processes are those that determine the level of cluster dynamism and should be well-developed in successful clusters. Table 4 summarizes the relative strength of active cluster processes in each cluster.

These data show that only some clusters demonstrate strong active cluster process, and these, with the exception of case study one, are more commonly wine clusters.

In this study, cluster overlap implies that both clusters need to share activities or businesses; none of the case studies demonstrated cluster overlap between their wine and tourism clusters.

Table 4. Comparative importance of active cluster processes in each cluster

Cluster Processes	Case Study One: Wine Tourism		Case Study Two: Wine Tourism		Case Study Three: Wine Tourism	
Active cluster processes	X	XX	XXX	X	XXXX	XX

Note: X not important; XX important; XXX very important

Table 5. Complementarity between clusters

Clusters	Case Study One		Case Study Two		Case Study Three	
	Wine	Tourism	Wine	Tourism	Wine	Tourism
Cluster Complementarity	Active	Passive	Active	Passive	Active	Active

The use of this measure of cluster overlap may prove to be problematic in other applications, but it remains important in this context, because it is indicative of reciprocal interactivity among these clusters. In all cases in this study, the tourism clusters did not demonstrate sufficient levels of joint activity or engagement with wine businesses in order to constitute overlap as it is defined in this study. Conversely, there appears to be a tendency for the wine clusters to be engaged in joint activities with business in the tourism cluster.

Assumptions on how to determine cluster complementarity were required, and the measures of active and passive complementarity have been adopted. These aspects of clusters were derived using a relationship map that indicated the importance of cluster interaction with other components of the region's economy. These components were divided into those that are derived simply by collation (i.e., passive processes), while active processes involved the wine and tourism clusters actively developing relationships and business opportunities as a consequence of collation.

It appears that it is generally the wine clusters that demonstrate more active complementarity toward the tourism clusters than tourism clusters with the wine clusters; case study three is the exception. Understanding cluster complementarity between wine and tourism clusters is complex, and this study has relied on data gained from a range of stakeholders within each region and industry sector. With this in mind, case study three demonstrates reciprocal cluster complementarity, which sets this region apart in terms of its potential for wine-tourism development. Why this is so remains unclear; however the wine and tourism clusters in case study three share strong economic, geographic, and, to a lesser extent, social elements and appear less reliant on cluster preconditions but exhibit stronger active cluster processes than the other case studies described.

Conclusion

This chapter has provided an overview of several characteristics peculiar to both wine and tourism industries. Perhaps the most notable of these relates to the nature and structure of these industries and the implications for the development of regional clusters; namely, the implications of the broadly based tourism industry on how it is defined and described both as an industry and as a factor in regional economies. In addition, preconditions for tourism development can be contradictory. They rely on resources, relationships between stakeholders, and bottom-up and top-down factors that can result in positive competitive advantage but may also cause negative competitive behavior or community rejection. Using clusters as a marketing tool or a strategy for economic development and not as a means to determine and strengthen preconditions that are important for the development of regional tourism activity may be partly the cause of limited successful tourism cluster development in regional Australia.

Conversely, the wine industry appears more easily identified but still has a diverse base. It has been recognized as having preconditions that mean it is readily viewed as a cluster in Australia. There are, however, aspects of the industry that are changing how it functions in many regions. These changes are diverting some of the clustering energies of particularly smaller operators in the wine sector to becoming more focused on domestic sales through tourism and life-style markets. This appears to be generating some cluster activity through the medium of wine tourism.

Clusters can be used with caution as an analysis tool in the tourism industry, but the impact of top-down tourism approaches modify how clusters actually can function, particularly the active processes of clustering that involve collaboration, shared knowledge, and interaction. These are evidences that suggest that the essence of clustering is undeveloped, and there is opportunity to investigate further the reasons for this. The wine industry is based on a collaborative joint-marketing approach that has provided the impetus for effective wine clusters to emerge. The opportunities that this might provide for sectors of the tourism industry to gain clustering expertise through interaction with a wine cluster is worthy of note. Using clusters as a tool to understand how these industries are organized and function does appear to have merit by achieving a better understanding of wine tourism, in particular, and to identify those aspects that are barriers to expansion.

The implications of this are reflected in the realization that wine and tourism industries are different and require approaches that normally might not be used to measure their success or potential for success when considering wine tourism. It seems that by taking a more holistic approach, realizing strengths and weakness in both the wine and tourism industries through a cluster approach might highlight new and innovative ways in order to advance regional wine tourism.

This chapter has introduced the concept that cluster studies can reveal characteristics of regional wine and tourism industries, but there is now a need for this discussion to be explored more fully. It appears that the nature of the industry does matter, and it is the wine industry that plays the most significant role in cluster activities associated with wine tourism. The study also shows that location may play a significant role in how collated clusters might interact and actively complement each other. This qualitative exploration of microclusters across three regional locations has provided an insight into the interaction among collated industries that have the potential to spark new enterprises and, in so doing, broaden the economic base of regional economies. It has also highlighted that not all industries or locations behave in the same way. This reflects the commonly observed phenomenon that, in some regions, wine tourism is more successful than in other regions, even though the regional attributes may be similar. It also highlights the important role that the wine industry plays in the development of wine tourism. These findings identify the importance of active cluster processes across regions and industries and can inform regional economic development and industry-based strategies.

References

ACIL. (2002). *Pathways to profitability for small and medium wineries*. Canberra, Australia: ACIL Consulting Pty. Ltd. Commissioned by the Commonwealth Government.

Alexander, R., Arney, R., Black, N., Frost, E., & Shivananda, A. (1997). *The Californian wine cluster* [unpublished report]. Boston: Harvard School of Business.

Anderson, K. (1999). *Economic briefing report*. Adelaide, Australia: S.A. Centre for Economic Studies.

Anderson, K. (2000). *Export-led growth lessons from Australia's wine industry*. Canberra, Australia: Rural Industries Research and Development Corporation.

Anderson, K. (2001a). Prospects ahead for the wine industry. *The Australian Grapegrower and Winemaker*, *448*, 67–74.

Anderson, K. (2001b). *The globalization (and regionalization) of wine*. Adelaide, Australia: University of Adelaide.

Australian Bureau of Statistics. (2002). *Tourism satellite account* [ABS document 5249.0]. Canberra, Australia: ABS.

Bergman, E., & Feser, E. (1996). *The economic development logic of strategic cluster targeting*. Paper presented at the Proceedings of the ACSP-AESOP Conference, Toronto, Canada.

Black, A. (2000). *Rural communities and rural social issues: Priorities for research*. Canberra, Australia: Rural Industries Research and Development Corporation.

Blamey, R., & Hatch, D. (1998). *Profiles and motivations of nature-based tourist visiting Australia* [occasional paper number 25]. Canberra, Australia: Bureau of Tourism Research.

Blandy, R. (2001). *South Australian business vision 2010 industry cluster program: A review*. Adelaide, Australia: University of South Australia.

Bond, G. (2000). *The California wine cluster*. Boston: Harvard School of Business.

Braun, P. (2003). *.comUnity: A study of the adoption and diffusion of Internet technologies in a regional tourism network* [unpublished doctoral dissertation]. Ballarat, Australia: University of Ballarat.

Brown, P. (1999). *Industrial clusters and market externalities: The impact of co-location on the marketing activities of the firm* [unpublished master's thesis]. Dunedin, New Zealand: University of Otago.

Cairns Regional Economic Development Corporation (CREDC). (2002). *Clusters*. Retrieved December 2, 2003, from http://www.credc.com.au/clusters.html

Chapman, P. (2000). *Assisting cluster development and networking in regional economies of South Australia*. Adelaide, Australia: Centre for Labour Research, Adelaide University.

Crittenden, G. (1999). *Finding out about your customers*. Paper presented at the Proceedings of the Second Australian Wine Tourism Conference, Rutherglen, Australia.

Enright, M. J. (1996). Regional clusters and economic development: A research agenda. In U. H. Staber, N. V. Schaefer, & B. Sharma (Eds.), *Business networks prospects for regional development* (pp. 190–231). Berlin: Walter de Gruyter.

Enright, M. J. (2000a). The globalization of competition and the localization of competitive advantage: Policies towards regional clustering. In N. Hood, & S. Young (Eds.), *The globalization of multinational enterprise activity and economic development* (pp. 303–326). Houndsmill, England: Macmillan Press.

Enright, M. J. (2000b). *Survey on the characterisation of regional clusters.* Honk Kong: University of Hong Kong.

Enright, M. J., & Ffowcs-Williams, I. (2000). *Local partnerships, clusters and SME globalisation.* Paris: Local Economic and Employment Program of the OECD Territorial Development Service.

Feser, E. (1998). Old and new theories of industry clusters. In M. Steiner (Ed.), *Clusters and regional specialisation on geography, technology and networks* (pp. 18-40). London: Pion.

French, C., Craig-Smith, S., & Collier, A. (1995). *Principles of tourism.* Melbourne: Addison Wesley Longman Australia Pty.

Fuller, P. (1997). Value adding the regional wine experience. *The Australian and New Zealand Wine Industry Journal, 12*(1), 35–39.

Getz, D. (1998). *Wine tourism: Global overview and perspectives on its development.* Proceedings of the First Australian Wine Tourism Conference, Margaret River, Western Australia.

Gunn, C. (1994). *Tourism planning basics concepts cases* (3rd ed.). Washington, DC: Taylor & Francis.

Hall, C.M. (1995). *Introduction to tourism in Australia* (2nd ed.). Melbourne, Australia: Longman.

Hall, C. M., & Jenkins, J. (1998). The policy dimensions of rural tourism and recreation. In W. R. Butler, C. M. Hall, & J. Jenkins (Eds.), *Tourism and recreation in rural areas* (pp. 19–42). Milton, Australia: John Wiley & Sons.

Hall, C.M., & Johnson, G. (1997). *Wine tourism in New Zealand: Larger bottles or better relationships?* Paper presented at the Proceedings of the Trails, Tourism and Regional Development Conference, Dunedin, New Zealand.

Hall, M., Johnson, G., & Mitchell, R. (2000). Wine tourism and regional development. In C. M. Hall, L. Sharples, B. Cambourne, N. Macionis, R. Mitchell, & G. Johnson (Eds.), *Wine tourism around the world development, management and markets* (pp. 196–225). Oxford: Butterworth-Heinemann.

Hussey, J., & Hussey, R. (1997). *Business research: A practical guide for undergraduate and postgraduate students.* London: Macmillan.

Institute for Strategy and Competitiveness. (2004). *Cluster mapping project.* Harvard Business School. Retrieved March 10, 2004, from http://data.isc.hbs.edu/isc/cmp_overview.jsp

Ioannides, D., & Debbage, K. G. (1998). Neo-fordism and flexible specialization in the travel industry. In D. Ioannides, & K. G. Debbage (Eds.), *The economic geography of the tourist industry* (pp. 99–122). London: Routledge.

Jackson, D. (1989a). *The Australian economy.* South Melbourne: Macmillan.

Jacobs, D., & De Man, A.P. (1996). Clusters, industrial policy and firm strategy: A menu approach. *Technology Analysis and Strategic Management, 8*(4), 425–437.

Jackson, I. (1989b). *An introduction to tourism.* Elsternwick, Australia: Hospitality Press Pty.

Johnson, G. (1998). *Wine tourism in New Zealand: A national survey of wineries 1997* [unpublished thesis for postgraduate diploma in tourism]. Dunedin, New Zealand: University of Otago.

Jorge, A. (1978). *Competition, cooperation, eficiency, and social organisation introduction to a political economy.* Cranbury, NJ: Associated University Presses.

Leiper, N. (1979). The framework of tourism: Towards a definition of tourism, tourist and the tourist industry. *Annals of Tourism Research, 2,* 69–84.

Leiper, N. (1990). *Tourism systems an interdisciplinary perspective.* Palmerston North, New Zealand: Massey University.

Leiper, N. (1995). *Tourism management.* Melbourne: RMIT Press.

Leiper, N., & Carlsen, J. (1998). *Strategies for winery managers contemplating tourist markets a case history: What happened to a winery positioned to remain on the fringe?* Paper presented at the Proceedings of the First Australian Wine Tourism Conference, Margaret River, Western Australia.

Macionis, N. (1997). *Wine tourism in Australia: Emergence, development, and critical issues* [unpublished masters thesis]. Canberra, Australia: University of Canberra.

Macionis, N., & Cambourne, B. (2000). Towards a national wine tourism plan: Wine tourism organisations and development in Australia. In C.M. Hall, et al. (Eds.), *Wine tourism around the world development, management and markets* (pp. 226–252). Boston: Butterworth-Heinemann.

Marceau, J. (1997). *The disappearing trick: Clusters in the Australian economy.* Paper presented at the Proceedings of the Boosting Innovation the Cluster Approach OECD, Amsterdam, The Netherlands.

Marsh, I., & Shaw, B. (1999). Collaboration and learning in Australia's wine industry. *The Australian and New Zealand Wine Industry Journal, 14*(5), 105–119.

Marsh, I., & Shaw, B. (2000). *Australian wine industry: Collaboration and learning as causes of competitive success* [unpublished report]. Adelaide, Australia: Australian Wine Industry.

Michael, E. (2001). *Tourism growth and the development of micro-market clusters.* Melbourne: Victorian University of Technology.

Nordin, S. (2003). Tourism clustering and innovation—paths to economic growth and development. *Etour Analysis and Statistics.* Ostersund, Sweden: Mid Sweden University.

Porter, M. (1990). *The competitive advantage of nations*. New York: Free Press.

Porter, M. (1998). *On competition*. Boston: Harvard Business School.

Porter, M. (2001). *Clusters of innovation: Regional foundations of U.S. competitiveness*. Paper presented at the Proceedings of the National Clusters of Innovation Meeting, Washington, D.C.

Porter, M. (2003). *Clusters and regional competitiveness: Recent learnings*. Paper presented at the Proceedings of the International Conference on Technology Clusters, Montreal, Canada.

Prosser, G. (2001). Regional tourism. In N. Douglas, N. Douglas, & R. Derrett (Eds.), *Special interest tourism* (pp. 86–110). Brisbane, Australia: John Wiley & Sons.

Roehl, W. (1998). The tourism production system: The logic of industrial classification. In D. Ioannides, & K. G. Debbage (Eds.), *The economic geography of the tourism industry: A supply-side analysis* (pp. 53–76). London: Routledge.

Roelandt, T., & Hertog, P. (1999). *Summary report of the focus group on clusters* [unpublished report]. Paris: OECD.

Rosenfeld, S. A. (1996). *Overachievers—business clusters that work: Prospects for regional development*. Chapel Hill, NC: Regional Technology Strategy.

Rosenfeld, S. A. (1997). Bringing business clusters into the mainstream of economic development. *European Planning Studies, 5*(1), 3–23.

Salter, B. (1998). *The synergy of wine, tourism and events*. Paper presented at the Proceedings of the First Australian Wine Tourism Conference, Margaret River, Western Australia.

Skinner, A. (2000). Napa Valley, California: A model of wine region development. In C.M. Hall, L. et al. (Eds.), *Wine Tourism around the world development, management and markets* (pp. 283–296). Boston: Butterworth-Heinemann.

Smith, S., Denton, S., & Crinion, D. (1999). *South Australian international tourism industry cluster background paper*. Adelaide: South Australian Tourism Commission.

Smith, S.L.J. (1998). Tourism as an industry. In D. Ioannides, & K.G. Debbage (Eds.), *The economic geography of the tourist industry* (pp. 31–52). London: Routledge.

Swann, P., Prevezer, M., & Stout, D. (Eds.). (1998). *The dynamics of industrial clustering international comparisons in computing and biotechnology*. London: Oxford University Press.

Verbeek, H. (1999). *Innovative clusters: Identification of value-adding production chains and their networks of innovation, an international study* [upublished doctoral thesis]. Rotterdam: Erasmus University.

Williams, S. (1998). *Tourism geography*. London: Routledge.

Yin, R.K. (1994). *Case study research—design and methods* (2nd ed.). Newbury Park, CA: Sage Publications.

Chapter VIII

From Networks to Clusters and Back Again:
A Decade of Unsatisfied Policy Aspiration in New Zealand

Martin Perry, Massey University, New Zealand

Abstract

Since the mid-1990s, trade promotion and regional development policy in New Zealand has aimed to promote business growth by encouraging various forms of interfirm coopera-tion. This chapter reviews the case for public policy intervention in cluster formation and highlights policy insight, drawing on the author's evaluations of the ways that New Zealand policymakers have sought to encourage business cooperation through networks, alliances, and clusters. The chapter makes a case for cluster intervention but cautions against too much optimism in the contribution that clusters can make to business development. By explain-ing the particular influences behind successful projects in New Zealand, it is hoped that researchers and policymakers can obtain a better understanding of the conditions needed for effective cluster-based cooperation.

Introduction

Encouraging enterprise owners to recognize their existing or potential membership in a business cluster has been one of the most influential business development ideas of the last decade (Isaksen & Hauge, 2002; Martin and Sunley, 2003; Raines, 2002). This frequently is attributed to the influence of Michael Porter, whose claims about business clusters suggest that they create near-perfect conditions for business growth.

A concentration of visible rivals encourages the search for ways of competing that are not head on. Niche opportunities overlooked by others can reveal themselves. Ready access to suppliers and partners provides flexibility to configure the value chain in a variety of ways. A more positive-sum form of competition can result when customer choice is widened and different customers are served most efficiently. (Porter, 2000, pp. 265–266)

In contrast to the optimism of cluster advocates such as Porter (2000), the outcomes of public agency efforts to encourage business participation in cluster groups are frequently disappointing (Huggins, 2000; Kotval & Mullin, 1998; Perry, 2004a; Schmitz, 1999; Tarn-bunan, 2005). This chapter examines the contrast between policy ambition and outcome in the context of three policy initiatives in New Zealand.

Strictly, the initiatives examined focus on various forms of business cooperation rather than specifically on business clusters. The first program linked directly to Michael Porter but involved efforts to encourage the formation of joint action groups (JAGs), which were envisaged as loose networks of relatively large groups of firms that would work together to develop new export markets. The second program involved the promotion of hard networks in the form of formal business alliances among small groups of firms. The third and most recent initiative is the Cluster Development Program that was introduced to shift the focus of support to groups of businesses located within the same region. This program has the most claim to be consistent with the idea of business clusters, but for several reasons, all three programs are presented in this chapter as relevant to the debate about small business clustering.

Networks, alliances, and clusters are variations on a theme rather than wholly different species (Rosenfeld, 2005). All may be seen as aspects of the associative economy in which businesses are thought to gain an advantage by making more use of the resources of other businesses and industry support agencies than they did in the past. It can be important to recognize that the precise mechanisms that connect businesses imply particular economic relationships and opportunities for encouraging their formation. For example, it is suggested that networks and alliances require some form of membership, whereas clusters are not based on membership (Rosenfeld, 2005). In practice, this kind of distinction tends to break down. New Zealand's Cluster Development Programme (CDP), for example, is essentially about encouraging membership groups, some of which had support as joint action groups. Part of the popularity of clusters lies in their vagueness and lack of definitional rigor (Martin & Sunley, 2003). Another reason for the overlap is that clusters, networks, and alliances can be seen to be embedded within each other. A cluster is a geographic concentration of inter-related companies and institutions. Belonging to a cluster may not require any membership of a formal association, but it might be expected that one outcome will be that such groups form. Similarly, the benefits of a cluster frequently are expressed in terms of the opportunities for deliberate acts of cooperation and collaboration that give individual companies the strength of numbers to influence customers, markets, or policies (Rosenfeld, 2005).

This chapter links networks, alliances, and clusters from the perspective that the lessons learned from seeking to promote alliances and networks have relevance to larger task of promoting business clusters. Policy in New Zealand has tended to turn full circle without making this reflection. The larger interest in this experience is in demonstrating how the transition from policies to build networks to policies to build clusters demonstrates minimal evolution in the understanding of economic development practice. Whatever the precise target of intervention, policy has tended to progress from a perspective that large-scale changes in technology, organizational behavior, and markets have given widespread scope for businesses to gain from cooperation. The perspective developed in this chapter is that more attention needs to be paid to the conditions required for effective business cooperation than hitherto has been given. These findings are considered significant, as there are some aspects of New Zealand's business environment that are supportive of cooperation. To commence this discussion, the chapter examines whether a convincing case for public policy support for cluster promotion has yet been made, and if so what it is. New Zealand's policy experiences are then summarised and effort made to distil wider 'policy insight'. The policy experience then is reviewed, drawing on evaluations conducted at varying stages of each policy's implementation (Perry, 1995; 2001; 2004a; 2005). This chapter combines the evidence obtained from the individual evaluations in order to draw out the major lessons for business cluster promotion.

Can Business Cooperation Be Promoted?

Before examining New Zealand's particular policy experiences, it is important to consider whether policy intervention of any form can be justified. One assessment concludes that there is no evidence to justify efforts to promote business clusters (Martin & Sunley 2003). The definition of clusters is too elastic to provide a basis for making any rigorous claims about the significance of agglomeration for regional and local economic development. The concept needs to be nailed down in a way that sets specific parameters for distinguishing a cluster from lesser forms of concentration. Meanwhile, with no precise rules for establishing when a cluster exists, it has been possible to pick and mix research evidence too freely. Even though there is an association among some high-growth industries and a tendency for geographical concentration, this is not a basis for claiming that concentration is a cause of high growth. The enthusiasm for clusters has jumped too quickly from a few particular experiences to a belief in the universal capacity for concentration to generate growth.

Given widespread advocacy of the advantages of business clusters, the depiction of clusters as merely a chaotic conception needs to explain how they have attained the status that they have. One suggestion is that clusters appeal because they apparently check the drift of much economic and business activity into a footloose existence without allegiance to any single location (Peters & Hood 2000). The apparent ability to adopt any position along the intervention spectrum, from simply recognizing the presence of a cluster to the microman-agement of business relations among cluster participants, is a further appeal. More than its flexibility, cluster advocacy has been interpreted as an example of brand management rather than intellectual discourse (Martin & Sunley 2003). Just as commercial organizations use a brand image to seek to differentiate an otherwise ordinary product, the cluster label has been attached to a set of ideas that essentially are little different from standard business agglomeration theory and associated policy recommendations. Tired academic arguments have gained a new lease on life through the cluster brand, partly through its skillful link-age to an image of high productivity, knowledge richness, and decentralization, with its entrepreneurial and socially progressive local economies being within the reach of any location. As a brand, a cluster has five essential attributes: (1) accordance with strongly held aspirations; in this case, innovation and competitiveness; (2) expressed in language that is flexible enough to permit a wide range of interpretations; (3) backed by authority; in this case, Michael Porter's expert knowledge of competition and business strategy; (4) capable of continual and consistent renewal to keep pace with changing environments, as achieved with cluster applications to the dot.com and knowledge economies; and (5) permits practical action; in this case, the replication of cluster successes.

Further investigation of the branding of academic theory is justified, but to focus on cluster evangelism alone overlooks that clustering of some form is a real phenomenon. There is a tendency for economic activity to concentrate in remarkably few locations and for individual locations to develop some degree of specialization distinctive to other concentrations of like activity (Sorenson & Audia, 2000; Stuart & Sorenson, 2003). There is a justifiable interest in learning how these experiences might be used to inform local economic strategies. At the same time, the doubts raised by Martin and Sunley (2003) do require recognition that there is no universally agreed upon explanation of why clusters exist or agreement about how policymakers might be able to encourage their development.

At the broadest level, there are two versions of a business cluster. One version presents clusters as self-organizing entities that do not require and are largely unresponsive to efforts to deliberately mold the behavior of individual participants. Porter (1990, 2000) originally drew attention to clusters on this basis as a way of explaining the export specialization of industrialized economies. He argued that a country's successful export-orientated industries emerged as a result of interactions across groups of interrelated firms and industries that were especially effective where activity was collocated. Market processes, assisted by factor endowments and fortuitous circumstances rather than deliberate intervention, explained the growth of these clusters. Similarly, many economic geographers see clusters in high-income economies as resulting from untraded dependencies that promote localized learning through informal channels and the operation of external labor markets (Leamer and Storper 2001; Malmberg, Malmberg & Lundequist, 2000; Pinch, Henry, Jenkins & Taliman, 2003).

The other version of a cluster sees public intervention as a requirement for maintaining the existence of a cluster (Schmitz & Nadvi, 1999). This interpretation is based on the evalua-tion of clusters in developing countries but also has support from research that has drawn attention to the changing composition of Italy's industrial districts (Rabellotti & Schmitz, 1999). It argues that cluster characteristics change as a few dominant businesses emerge, based on their greater entrepreneurial capacity than on ordinary cluster firms. Unplanned benefits from geographical concentration can explain how a cluster first comes into being, but sustained growth relies on deliberate joint action to exploit the resources of the cluster

(Schmitz, 1995). When some cluster firms start to engage in joint action, the benefits brought by the cluster concentrate in those firms that directly participate in joint action rather than being freely available to all simply by virtue of a location in the cluster. Differences emerge among enterprises with respect to their size, resources, markets, and pursuit of growth that compound and ultimately cause the breakdown of the cluster. Maintaining the life of a cluster depends on broadening the opportunity to participate in planned action, which is a role that public agencies can perform. By diffusing opportunities across enterprises that are unable or unwilling to join private planned action, it is claimed that there is more likelihood of the cluster sustaining a diversity of interconnected enterprises than otherwise would be the case.

One contradiction surrounding much of the public policy interest in clusters, including that in New Zealand, is that public intervention exists alongside a preference for Porter's interpretations of cluster development. This contradiction exists partly because Porter's emphasis on self-organizing clusters is not consistent. For example, he has drawn attention to a cluster of 400 medical device companies in Massachusetts that employ nearly 40,000 workers; the cluster laid dormant until revealed through a search for potential clusters (Porter, 1998). Once revealed, Porter reported that business executives came together to consciously exploit the advantage of belonging to a cluster. Similarly, he recently has developed a cluster-mapping procedure to help regional agencies monitor and influence cluster development (Porter, 2003). This mapping methodology is intended to be rolled out across other countries as part of the "missionary" work by Porter and the associated Monitor Consultancy in order to spread interest in cluster promotion (Benneworth, Danson, Raines, & Williams, 2003).

Porter's mapping project gives a basis for the development of cluster policy, but it is worth noting that other researchers using similar methodologies sound a note of caution about this (Feser & Bergman, 2000; Feser & Luger, 2003). Porter's (2003) claims about the importance of clustering need to be understood as a way of analyzing economic activity rather than supporing any specific location pattern. The importance of clustering is merely the recognition that tight connections can bind certain firms and industries and that this makes it meaningful to study groups of interconnected activity. It offers a mode of inquiry that results in cluster templates rather than pinning clusters to a specific level of agglomeration. Feser and Luger (2003) draw an analogy with cost-benefit analysis, a technique that became popular in the 1970s and 1980s as a way to understand the complex trade-offs between up-front investments and long-term benefits. Cost-benefit analysis was promoted originally as a technique in order to provide objective and precise judgments on development proposals. In practice, data inputs were often incomplete and surrounded by assumptions, and the technique ceased to be accepted as a precise measurement tool. So, cluster analysis is viewed appropriately as a mode of inquiry that "is simply not capable of producing a single right answer about the industries and businesses a region should seek to support or grow" (Feser & Luger, 2003, p. 16).

The implication is that public policy intervention should use cluster analysis to help identify public policy goals rather than starting out with a predetermined vision of a cluster. In practice, cluster promotion frequently is driven by the image of Silicon Valley, Italy's industrial districts, and other exemplar clusters rather than by what is appropriate to the particular locality (Benneworth, 2002). The use of existing clusters as role models of how other local economies can develop is questionable for three main reasons.

First, many of the clusters that have excited policy interest are located in economically advantaged regions, as with England's Motor Sport Valley, the Öresund medical cluster spanning Denmark and Sweden, biotechnology in Rhône-Alpes, and medical technology around Baltimore (Benneworth, 2002; Lagendijk, 1999). High levels of selectively disbursed public funds have contributed to the modern-day reputations and capabilities of such clusters. Exemplar clusters that are centered on public institutions are necessarily exceptions. As pointed out from the experience of Sophia-Antipolis, it simply is not possible to multiply the benefits of accumulated exceptional levels of public funding over many locations (Longhi, 1999).

Second, catching up with established concentrations of innovative activity may not be feasible. There are now many clusters of IT expertise around the world, for example, but a large gap tends to remain between them and Silicon Valley (Bresnahan, Gambardella, & Saxenian, 2001). First, mover advantages require that subsequent clusters need to focus on new technology and market opportunities with high growth potential that have not been captured by any other cluster. Identifying a technology with exceptional market opportunity involves luck as well as foresight. Bresnahan et al. (2001) further argue that old-economy processes associated with years of firm and market building effort and regional investments in educational institutions and skill development underscore clusters.

Third, high profile clusters arise from multiple causes, some of which are more open to replication than others. In the case of Silicon Valley, the impetus from war-related investments (Prevezer, 1998); social networks (Saxenian, 1994); labor market intermediaries (Benner, 2002; Cappelli, 1999) and venture capital availability (Kenney, 2000; Prevezer, 1998) all have been claimed as the key source of advantage. Other research points to contingent influences that restrict the opportunity to replicate the development experience. In computing, the key links and information flows were between engineers in different companies; in biotechnology, the important relationships have been between the science base and the companies (Prevezer, 1998). Computing the time window between invention and innovation was frequently narrow, encouraging close geographic location between large established companies and new ventures. In biotechnology, research alliances between geographically dispersed organizations have been more characteristic of the industry than start-ups that cluster around established participants. The full context of Silicon Valley's emergence and growth draws attention to its uniqueness and dangers of viewing it as a development model (Kenney, 2000). Equally, the ability to find biotechnology clusters in many regions reflects features particular to this activity rather than incipient concentrations that public policy can grow into new Silicon Valleys (Sharp, 1990, 1999).

If the ambition to replicate high-profile clusters is misplaced, a surviving rationalization for policy intervention is to provide public goods that are missing due to market failure. Four types of such goods have been identified as relevant to cluster promotion (Martin & Sunley, 2003).

- The creation of cooperative networks that encourage dialogue between firms and other agencies with the result that firms more easily can pool resources, design collective solutions to shared problems, and develop a strong collective identity.

- The development of collective marketing of an industry specialization and shared investment in the opening of new markets.

- The local provision of services for firms such as financial services, marketing, design and component production in place of remotely obtained services. Through local provision, such services can become customized to the particular industrial specialization of the cluster.

- Weaknesses in existing cluster value chains can be addressed by helping to rationalize activity among existing firms and by efforts to attract investment and businesses to fill the gaps and to strengthen demand and supply links.

These justifications for cluster intervention leave unresolved the scale of the public benefit required to justify intervention and how much attention needs to be paid to the distribution of the benefit obtained. Rosenfeld (2003) has argued that unless distributional issues are addressed in policy initiatives, there is a risk of cluster promotion widening economic disparities. Clusters create a capacity for industry participants to network and learn from one another but potentially raise the barriers for firms outside the cluster. The more that clusters are defined by formal membership and the more that business activity depends on personal networking, the higher the hurdles can become for outsiders to gain entry. To enable clusters to reach and serve the interests of weaker economies and small businesses, Rosenfeld (2003) suggests that cluster policy should have low entry requirements and should impose conditions on the access to cluster assistance. These recommendations are unlikely to appeal to policymakers. Low entry requirements imply a flexible definition of clusters in order to encompass a wide range of situations, whereas policymakers are likely to prefer a precise definition that imparts a specific status to resulting interventions. The suggested conditions include representation from labor unions and third-sector organizations with interests in the environment, civil society, and equity.

The debate about business clusters has tended to move quickly from claims of business advantage to calls for cluster promotion. The implication of this brief review is that public agencies need to be explicit about at least three matters prior to launching any form of cluster promotion. First, the interpretation of cluster development guiding the proposed intervention needs to be resolved and checked for its consistency with the proposed measures. Second, investigation of the particular existing opportunities is needed rather than a justification based on replicating the development of exemplar clusters. Third, public agencies need to respond to the potential distributional consequences of cluster promotion, explaining how unequal gains will be mitigated or how the intervention has been designed to allow for a wide range of participation. Not unusually, policy has progressed in New Zealand without this careful prior consideration. The review of the outcomes given next shows how this has left a large gap between expected and actual outcomes. More constructively, the efforts to encourage various forms of business cooperation have provided novel experiences and insights from which other policymakers may be able to learn.

Cluster Promotion in New Zealand

As in many countries, Porter has had a large influence on encouraging policymakers to promote various forms of business clusters. This influence commenced at the start of the

1990s, when he was commissioned by Trade New Zealand (now New Zealand Trade and Enterprise [NZTE]) to provide guidance on how that agency could engage with industry. Trade New Zealand (or the Market Development Board, as it was originally called) had previously delivered export assistance to groups in its efforts to accelerate export capacity following a trade agreement with Australia in the early 1980s. It sought Porter's assistance to set its industry support on a systematic basis. The resulting report on how to upgrade New Zealand's competitiveness followed the diamond model that was then Porter's standard tool for assessing national competitive strengths and weaknesses (Crocombe, Enright & Porter, 1991).

In Porter's diamond model, local conditions shaped international competitiveness mainly through the following four attributes:

- Factor conditions, such as a specialized labor pool, specialized infrastructure, and sometimes selective disadvantages that drive innovation.

- Home demand or demanding local customers who push companies to innovate, especially if their tastes or needs anticipate global or local demand.

- Related and supporting industries, internationally competitive local supplier industries that create business infrastructure and spur innovation and spin-off industries.

- Industry strategy, structure, and rivalry; intense local rivalry among local industries that is more motivating than foreign competition and a local culture that influences attitudes within individual industries to innovation and competition.

When it appeared, this framework was criticized for its doubtful relevance to small, open economies such as New Zealand's or other high income resource-based economies such as Australia and Canada (Dunning, 1993; Yetton, Craig, Davis & Hilmer, 1992). It overlooked that prominent exporters from these countries often sustained successful strategies of offshore production and value adding. This rendered domestic buyer-supplier relations less critical to national economic success than those built by the subsidiaries of domestic companies in their export markets. In essence, the single diamond model applied to New Zealand was biased because it favored economies with businesses that export from a home base rather than from investing overseas. This criticism had no impact on Trade New Zealand whose resulting policy intervention in the form of the joint action program was only loosely connected to the report of the Porter Project. Trade New Zealand simply took the message that business advantage partly resides in clusters of related activity and applied this by encouraging existing and potential exporters to work collectively to develop overseas markets.

The second policy intervention was linked to the Danish Technological Institute (DTI) rather than Porter. This was the hard networks program that had been promoted as a successful model for network development, partly as evidenced by its diffusion to other countries including Australia (Bureau of Industry Economics, 1995), the UK (Chaston, 1996) and other European countries (OECD, 1995). The origins of the program were in the DTI's own efforts to fit business network experiences in North America, Germany, and Italy to Danish conditions. In those countries, the DTI concluded that a large firm typically acted as the initiator of business networks, while in Denmark, there were no large firms available for this role. In the DTI scheme, independent network brokers filled the gap with their role being to identify network opportunities, seek potential network members, and act as a facilitator of the new entity. As well as the adaptation to Denmark's small business environment, the DTI was influenced by Johnston and Lawrence's (1988) concept of value added partnerships. Such partnerships, it was argued, could bring trading partners close together and thus generate savings in the costs of transferring goods and services (Chaston, 1996).

Evidence of the program being taken up in other countries, the apparent fit with the small business dominance of the New Zealand economy, plus a small-scale trial convinced Trade New Zealand to implement the program (DTI, 1994; Ffowcs Williams, 1996). It was presented as a complementary initiative to the JAG program that was restyled as a soft way to encourage business cooperation. Promoting business alliances and joint ventures differed in producing formal (hard) connections between businesses. Launched in late 1994, the hard networks program worked on the simple notion that an individual small firm had many resource challenges to becoming an exporter that could be overcome if networks of four to six companies shared their resources and cooperated to develop export capacity. There was no evaluation of this proposition prior to the transfer of the program, but it was necessary to modify the program compared with how it had been administered in Denmark.

The third policy initiative examined is the Cluster Development Program. This particular program was launched in 2002 initially under the administration of Industry New Zealand and subsequently transferred to NZTE. The origins can be traced back to the Porter Project (Crocombe, Enright, & Porter, 1991). The investigation had been concerned mainly with national competitiveness, but it had drawn attention to the possibility of industry clusters being concentrated in a region. In particular, it profiled a fishing industry cluster in Nelson as New Zealand's most developed regional cluster and claimed that geographical concentration strengthened the cluster (Ffowcs Williams 1997a). This gave Trade New Zealand the inspiration for a series of cluster musters in which individual localities were encouraged to search out their local specializations and promote their growth (Ffowcs Williams 1997b). In the major cities where local authorities sponsored economic development agencies, support was given to encourage businesses to form cluster groups. Whereas some regional specializations had long been known to exist, it appeared that many latent clusters were based on previously unrecognized specializations such as earthquake technology in Wellington, aviation in Marlborough, and boat building in Auckland. With policy advisors who were encouraged to think that these clusters had the potential to become like small-scale Silicon Valleys, the central government launched its cluster development program (Cluster Navigators, 2001).

Before reviewing the outcomes of each of these initiatives, it is worth commenting on whether there is anything about New Zealand that should make cluster promotion unusually hard or unusually easy. Based on Nordic experience, it has been suggested that small economies such as New Zealand's should benefit from shared trust (Maskell, Eskelin, Hannibalsson, Malmberg & Vatne, 1998). Just as in a village compared with a city, it may be difficult to act opportunistically without being sanctioned, so in a small economy, the pressure to play by the rules is said to increase (Maskell, 1998). Shared backgrounds and the likelihood of participation in joint activities (social, political, or professional), if not present in the past, means that information flows quickly and widely across business communities. With confidence that disruptive or dishonest behavior will be transparent and that business has a common interest in punishing malfeasance, barriers to cooperation are thought to be low.

Assuming that shared trust actually exists in the way described, the New Zealand environment for business cooperation is different than that of Nordic economies. Business managers in New Zealand confirm that there is a high degree of personal familiarity and shared culture among participants in an industry, but it is doubted that this in itself makes cooperation easy to establish (Perry, 2001). The weakness of informal sanctions for punishing abuse of trust is one reason given for cooperative relations being hard to establish. As well, most managers agree that big players have little interest in developing mutual development opportunities with small firms. Overall, it may be concluded that New Zealand is not particularly distinct in its business culture, which affects the willingness to act collaboratively. Some features of the country suggest that it should be comparatively easy to gain support for cluster activity; others suggest that there would be significant resistance to overcome.

Joint Action Groups

The perceived benefits of a group approach to export market promotion provided the underlying rationale behind the JAG program. Especially when developing new markets, there was believed to be a need for basic information gathering and generic promotional and research activity in order to raise awareness of New Zealand's products or services. As well, pooled marketing budgets could maximize the impact of individual resources as through a joint trade stand at an exhibition or shared marketing agents. It was also hoped that the JAGs would foster an "NZ Inc" outlook with mutual support among exporters recognizing their shared goal of strengthening New Zealand's business community. If these incentives to join a group were not sufficient, Trade New Zealand sought to extend interest by giving group members priority in the allocation of export assistance. As well, financial support to the costs of operating a group, including employment of a coordinator, was offered as a further inducement to group formation.

From 1993 to 1999, JAGs remained the cornerstone of the effort to encourage a collective approach to export development (Trade New Zealand, 1996). More than 30 JAGs were active at the peak of the program in the mid-1990s (Perry, 1995). In most cases, activity or membership or both reduced after an initial period of enthusiasm. Around 20 groups remained when Trade New Zealand's funding for group coordinators was withdrawn in 1999. A small number of these survivors were given the status of industry groups and received ongoing funding. This included three groups that continued to operate: the New Zealand Marine Export Group (Marex), the Pine Manufacturers Association, and the New Zealand Organic Products Exporters Group (OPEG). Most JAGs either wound up with the loss of funding or survived only a short time in some other form. Those linked to a larger industry association were absorbed back into that association or continued as a separate group with their parent association's sponsorship. For example, the New Zealand Wine Guild JAG was established for marketing in the UK when few members of the New Zealand Wine Institute supplied this market. This work shifted back to the Wine Institute after the winding up of the Wine Guild.

The program was wound up because of four weaknesses, as assessed by its administrators. First, JAGs did not sustain industrywide support and tended to become comparatively exclusive cliques. This made it hard to justify the priority in export assistance given to JAGs over businesses outside a group. Second, a large proportion of program resources (perhaps a third or more) were being diverted into group management and domestic activities rather than export development, a problem that was accentuated by the multiplication of small groups. With the fragmentation of groups, firms that operated across several activities needed to stay in touch with several groups. This created unrealistic demands for potential participants as each group had its own fees and obligations. Third, there was much variability between groups in the relative financial inputs from Trade New Zealand and group members, partly reflected in large differences in their membership fees. This lack of consistency suggested weak commitment in some groups or a lack of consistent treatment, which raised public accountability issues for Trade New Zealand. Four, there was little cooperation among JAGs when market development sometimes required groups to work together.

In essence, the group approach to export development proved to have less potential than had been expected. A shortfall had been evident from an early stage of the program (Perry, 1995). As might be expected, firms participated if they saw direct benefit to their own organizations. Trade New Zealand's hope that experienced exporters would be motivated to mentor would-be exporters proved to be too optimistic. This occurred in the textile and apparel sector but only because a major exporter recognized that industry survival was at stake; if small firms did not survive, even large experienced exporters would be damaged by the loss of supporting activity. Typically, experienced exporters preferred to work with like organizations rather than mentor aspiring exporters. They sought confidence of comparable commitment, ability, and potential rewards. Even then, there was a general reluctance among experienced exporters to support projects in markets in which they had already established a presence. Generally, firms with knowledge of particular export markets preferred to protect their investments and did not want to share their export experiences with others. This left JAGs the challenge of identifying wholly new markets of common interest. Such efforts could be stymied by the unwillingness of key industry participants to join groups. In some cases, there were even accusations of outsiders actively seeking to disrupt projects proposed by JAGs.

The general pattern was that any scope for collective activity existed among only a few of the firms that initially came together in a group. Consequently, fragmentation into smaller and more specialized groups was the norm. At the outset, this looked like the program was succeeding as more and more groups came into existence, but really it reflected the limited basis for cooperation. In sectors in which firms relied on project work, such as construction and engineering, competing contractors typically would not work together, and so groups only became effective once one or more competitors had left the group. Fragmentation also was explained by the context in which the program was introduced. It started in the wake of the massive cutback in New Zealand's trade and industry protection that made exporting a matter of survival for many enterprises (Silverstone, Bollard & Lattimore, 1996). Companies joined a group in order to explore opportunities and identify their target markets. Typical participants were small companies with limited capacity and ambition. They benefited from undertaking market exploration collectively, but once they had resolved their market priorities and had established customer contacts, the group could cease to be so important to them.

These developments are partly illustrated in the case of the Building Industry Export Group, which at one time promised to be a highly effective group but fell apart within three years of its launch. Research prior to the group's establishment, including a survey of potential members and a review of other JAGs, was intended to set it on a firm basis and to guide the work of the full-time coordinator appointed in 1993. Responding to the market priorities indicated by members, Australia and Southeast Asia were selected to focus on. Despite the initial declarations of interest, the Australian program attracted little support. Subsequent investigation revealed that members did not favour working as a group in Australia, partly because it was seen as an extension of the domestic market and many companies already had experience of selling there. As well, it transpired that companies perceived that their New Zealand connection was a disadvantage in Australia, whereas the group association risked drawing attention to it.

In Southeast Asia, participation reduced as it became evident that the region had to be addressed as separate national markets, and the group fragmented once individual countries were targeted. For example around six of the 50 members joined a mission to Vietnam. After several years, the group had effectively become a dozen or more subgroups, each with a different sector or geographic market focus or both. With encouragement from Trade New Zealand, some subgroups became JAGs in their own right (including airport technologies, food systems and kitset homes). This trend suited specialists, but for multi-activity companies, it resulted in a loss of attachment to any single group and reduced sectorwide activities. The original group was refashioned as Constructive Solutions and retained about 20 members. These were mainly specialist companies, resolving the difficulties of gaining agreement between direct competitors that had been a further constraint on the original group. Even so, with varying degrees of commitment and little consistent participation, the efforts of the coordinator were essential in sustaining a program of activities. From Trade New Zealand's perspective, too little of its support was being devoted to actual export promotion as compared with the effort invested in maintaining membership. After Trade New Zealand's funding was withdrawn, some interest was expressed in keeping the group going, but this was partly to capture any activity from earlier promotion, and no trace of the group now survives.

Special conditions existed for those JAGs that survived the winding up of the support program. A Defence Technologies group survived because members supplied or wanted to supply the New Zealand Defence Force and Ministry of Defence, which required all members to conform to defense procurement protocols and procedures. The Marine Export Group and the Organic Product Exporters Group survived, partly because they represented new activity without an established industry association. Similarly, the Pine Exporters Group survived because it provided an alternative industry association to membership of the Timber Industry Federation or the Forest Owners Association by targeting companies that were dissatisfied with their existing industry group or not represented by them.

Policy Insight

Reflecting the sponsoring agency, the effectiveness of JAGs was evaluated solely in terms of the direct contribution to export growth. The experience was that it was hard for groups to maintain this focus. There was a need to engage in group-building exercises, and sometimes market development activity spilled over into the domestic market. Limiting the purpose of joint activity proved unrealistic and suggested the importance of integrating export promotion with business development support. This was recognized by the creation of New Zealand Trade and Enterprise in 2003 that merged the two agencies that previously specialized in each role.

The JAG program was highly flexible in allowing activity to be shaped to the characteristics of individual business groups. This proved to be a strength and a weakness of the program. Groups varied in their organization, size, motivation, and activities. The freedom to mold the program to group preferences helped participation, but the flexibility became a problem for policy administrators as well as for businesses seeking access to trade promotion assistance. Of particular interest was the ability to link the nature of group activities with the membership profile of the group (Perry, 1995).

Groups comprised of comparatively similar-sized organizations were most likely to conform to the policy agency's expectations. In dualistic industries that comprised a few dominant firms and a large number of small firms, joint activities relied on the large firms' having some strong reason to engage with firms whose experience in and capacity for exporting was considerably less than theirs. Typically, this was either when there was a threat of new entry into the industry or when the industry as a whole was under severe pressure. In the former case, large firms sought to protect their established marketing strategies. In the case of industry-wide pressure, large firms were motivated to help small firms to survive in order to protect the industry's supply base. Depending on which of these motives was present, various collective actions resulted. This experience suggests that public agencies could learn how to tailor assistance to the makeup of individual groups.

Hard Networks

There has been no formal evaluation of the hard networks' programs that ran from 1994 to 1999. Late in the program, it was reported that 95 networks were in formation (Healy, 1997). Although subsidies to participants were modest, especially compared with the original Danish program, they were concentrated at the feasibility investigation stage. The initial impact, therefore, was not a good indicator of commitment and viability. Efforts to trace impacts of the project in 2000 led to the conclusion that few, if any, sustainable business groups of any significance resulted (Perry, 2001).

The program's limited impact holds lessons for intervention that is designed to influence business cooperation. The assumption behind the program was that small firms would want to join a network because joining would be easier and less risky than entering export markets alone (Ffowcs Williams, 1996). By sharing resources and undertaking joint investments, small firms could compete as if they were a large firm while still retaining their own identities and core competencies. Optimistically, it was also noted that there was no constraint on the number of networks that might join. In practice, such possibilities need to be balanced against the motivations for being in business and the difficulty of maintaining agreement over inputs and returns from a venture on which individual participants are likely to have differing degrees of dependence.

At the outset of the program, there was some discussion that its implementation in New Zealand might prove to be more effective than in Denmark. In Denmark, the Ministry of

Industry appointed 40 full-time network brokers, who were employed for the duration of the program while the UK government agency staff fulfilled the role. With fewer administrative resources, the New Zealand version relied on part-time brokers who combined this role with their main occupation as accountants, management consultants, and other professionals. It was thought that this would give an incentive to search out network opportunities, but in practice, broker interest in the scheme tended to lapse quickly, partly because more lucrative fees could be earned from their other activities (Maher, 1996).

Policy Insight

One message may have been that greater note needed to be taken of the cost of the program in Denmark before attempting its replication. In Denmark, networks received an average public subsidy of more than US$260,000 out of a maximum availability of US$1 million (Henriksen, 1995; OECD, 1995), whereas in New Zealand, the maximum subsidy available was US$30,000 (at prevailing exchange rates). More importantly, the evidence in Denmark was that once public subsidies were withdrawn, networks rapidly ceased to function (Amphion Report, 1996; Huggins, 1996). Consequently, it appears that the relative effectiveness of different program modalities was not the issue. The limited impact of the scheme in New Zealand probably says little about the business environment and more about the need for public policy to be guided by realistic assessments of the scope to accelerate business cooperation. Getting small firms to cooperate is highly problematic wherever you are. Even in Denmark, an evaluation linked to the DTI program concluded that attempting to accelerate cooperation among businesses that have little prior familiarity with each other likely was to be fraught with serious problems (Henriksen, 1995).

Publicity material from New Zealand's hard network program suggests that interest came mainly from small-scale producers or service providers that saw potential in adopting a common identity and in sharing business publicity. Such horizontal networks bring together participants that have similar skills and resource needs. This form of network addresses marketing weaknesses and responds to the increased concentration of market control; indeed, several of the networks started prior to the network program. Obtaining cooperation among firms operating in different parts of the value chain represents a more significant development than horizontal integration, but it is harder to establish. At the outset, there may be few areas of common experience, different perspectives on the aspects of their business critical to performance, and possibly a history of adversarial relationships with the businesses in their value chain. When projects are identified, implementation exposes networks to even greater challenges. Perhaps inevitably, firms will have different dependencies on the network and different perceptions of the potential returns and barriers to going it alone.

Business Clusters

The Cluster Development Program (see Table 1), started by Industry New Zealand and subsequently transferred to NZTE, was the main focus of cluster support from 2003 to 2005.

Table 1. Features of the cluster development program (Source: www.nzte.govt.nz)

Definition a cluster group:
Clusters are groups of companies and related organizations that collaborate to grow their businesses.

Expected cluster activity:
Using this collaborative team approach allows businesses, regions, and interest groups to develop greater speed, quality, innovation, and critical mass. This assists in resolving practical issues like training, infrastructure, and procurement.

The 2003-2004 CDP funding round identified the following four types of qualifying projects:

- **Commercial clusters:** Small groups of firms that form a hard business network or strategic alliance. Their joint activity might be directed toward developing an individual market, improving their supply chain, or addressing other shared business issues. This form of cluster might comprise business organizations only.
- **Special interest clusters:** Developed and managed by Mäori, Pacific Peoples, or women, and directed primarily at advancing development opportunities for their affiliated population.
- **Regional clusters:** Seek to enhance the economic specializations of a locality by helping to build a supportive environment as well as by developing linkages among participating firms.
- **National clusters:** May be based on any of the previous three types, with membership opened nationally to provide a critical mass, or they might address whole industry issues and include the participation of industry associations.

Eligible projects:
A minimum combined revenue generation of $30 million NZ by businesses linked to the cluster has become a rough benchmark for eligibility.

It followed earlier initiatives by both central and local government agencies to encourage cooperation among geographically concentrated groups of related businesses. Local economic development agencies continue to support clusters outside that program, but they now tend to view their role as assisting clusters that gain support from the program. Consequently, whatever the sponsoring agency is, common conceptions exist about how business clusters can be most effectively promoted and how eligibility is determined (Perry, 2005).

- Clusters are envisaged as membership associations. This might be an informal association, but public agency preference is typically to see groups develop some form of legal entity with a specific membership structure.

- Eligibility has not been based on any prior cluster-mapping exercise or strict guidelines regarding the selection and scope of activity. This has allowed groups of variable significance to gain recognition as clusters.

- The main forms of support provided by public agencies are in identifying and bringing together potential clusters and then providing administration and facilitation to help develop and maintain activity.

- The level of direct public support typically enables a part-time facilitator and, occasionally, a full-time person to be appointed. For group activities, clusters rely on membership fees or project-specific contributions, possibly assisted by funding separate business development programs.

The policy context has tended to result in the encouragement of a large number of clusters covering typically no more than 30 enterprises and frequently significantly fewer than this (Perry 2004a). This means that groups are of comparable size to the former JAGs. Potential differences exist, but in reality, there is not a clear-cut differentiation. Clusters do not require a formal membership structure, but public agencies tend to prefer that they develop one. Clusters do not have to focus on export market development, but some do (e.g., the Wellington-based Earthquake Engineering and Natural Hazards clusters). Clusters are more likely to draw participation from a restricted geographical area, but this is no longer a requirement of the CDP (see the following). Even where the cluster is supported by an economic development agency, extraterritorial membership of a cluster may be allowed to bring in additional expertise (e.g., the case of Wellington's Earthquake Engineering and Natural Hazards clusters supported by the regional development agency).

A review of 25 clusters out of the approximately 90 projects existing in 2004 identified some significant initiatives (see Table 2). The clusters selected for this review sought to examine the most well-developed projects. The extent to which this was achieved cannot be verified, since little independent information exists about the projects. A subsequent and more detailed study of four timber industry clusters (Perry, 2005) suggests that the sample is consistent with larger experience, and thus, there are reasons to claim that a reliable insight was obtained. From the 25 projects examined, the following six limits on the ability to lever significant business advantage were identified (Perry, 2004a).

- **Value chain division:** Encouraging value chain integration frequently is identified as a main benefit of business cluster development. An obvious constraint on this goal is the absence of complete value chains located in New Zealand. Commodities tend to be exported for further processing, which, as noted previously, is partly why Porter's original methods for identifying clusters were considered inappropriate. Either for this reason or for other reasons connected to the smallness of the economy, cluster projects

Table 2. New Zealand cluster innovations (Source: Perry, 2004a)

Electronics South has developed an on-sale component market for members. Small firms, it is believed, often are forced to buy components in larger volumes than they need. This provides a surplus that other firms might wish to buy. The market network has been established in order to facilitate the exchange of these surplus components.

Three members of the Canterbury Electronics Group established a joint Web site in order to promote employment opportunities in their companies to engineers that reside outside New Zealand.

Creative Capital established a separate legal entity to allow those members wishing to participate in the Singapore market to operate as a single commercial business.

Kapiti Horowhenua Apparel & Textile cluster designed a scheme in negotiation with the local benefit agency and training providers to attract local unemployed into the apparel industry. Firms committed to employ 30 trainees, but the project lapsed when redundancies created a surplus of trained workers.

Health IT has negotiated a Sector Collaboration Framework with the Ministry of Health in order to secure a role for the cluster in recommending and reviewing health IT standards.

---

are unable to encompass whole or even large segments of a value chain. Health IT is a partial exception to the extent that it encompasses software development companies, health industry regulators, and representatives of user organizations. On this basis, the cluster is of some significance in encouraging dialogue among providers and users. This achievement arises in the particular context of the health sector. Users are mainly public health sector providers whose activities are coordinated centrally. The Ministry of Health responsible for administering the health sector sees potentially substantial efficiency and medical service benefits from the increased application of IT in the health sector. Software developments must adhere to standards set by the Ministry of Health and health providers. There is no equivalent conjunction of forces in other industries.

- **Conditions on cooperation:** Controls on who gets to join a cluster are a feature of groups in the forestry and other sectors. The Tertiary Education Cluster comprised seven public sector tertiary establishments that decided against inviting private-sector tertiary institutions to join the group. The Canterbury Electronics Group (CEG) represents the region's six largest electronics companies, which required the regional development corporation to establish a separate cluster for SMEs. CEG considers that their interests do not coincide with those of small companies and that lobbying by the big six would be more effective than working through a diffuse group or voicing concerns individually. Placing conditions on who joins a group can have justification, but it does indicate that business support for cooperation frequently is circumscribed.

- **Facilitator dependence:** The number and size of individual clusters present a misleading impression of collaborative activity. In reality, projects such as Film South and Nelson Bays Arts Marketing exist only because of the presence of a business development agency. A minority of the 25 clusters examined appears to have developed to a point that the clusters would survive the loss of their publicly funded facilitator. Facilitator dependence is significant for the nature of the activity pursued as well as for its sustainability. Where the dependence is high, it tends to result in a cluster characterized by customized support to individual members rather than the development of projects that require changes in behavior by individual members or a commitment to joint activity.

- **Need for a leader:** Among clusters that have sought to help develop export activity, experiences similar to the JAG program are evident. The Earthquake Engineering cluster is focused on export market development to a greater extent than any other cluster that was examined. Membership from New Zealand's largest engineering consultancy firm has provided the critical resource to enter overseas markets. A collective approach has worked, because the lead firm needs the specialist expertise of other members in order to deliver projects. The Creative Capital cluster, on the other hand, shows how small firms working together cannot make up for the absence of a lead contractor. To exploit opportunities in Singapore, a commercial entity was formed in which individual members would participate according to their interest in that market and the combination of expertise needed for individual contracts. Still lacking was the financial capital to enable that new entity to secure government contracts in its own right. This forced it to act as a subcontractor to a Singapore-based company. Contracts were won on this basis, but the position as a subcontractor exposed cluster members to the uncertainties of being dependent on other parties for project delivery and payment. Ultimately, key businesses felt that there was insufficient control and too much risk. In 2004, the decision was made to cease trading through their joint entity, and the cluster has reverted to a focus on activity in New Zealand with a reduced membership compared with when there was optimism about export growth (Perry, 2004b). The general message is that the scope for a group approach to export markets is less than policymakers have assumed.

- **Missing clusters:** The location of cluster projects indicates that projects do not coincide with important centers of activity. The Auckland region accounts for about one-third of the national economy but has few cluster initiatives. One reason for this is that the drift of economic activity to Auckland has given greater support for local economic projects in other parts of the country. The distribution of clusters, therefore, is indicative of promotional effort rather than business development potential. Similarly, in respect to land-based activity, clusters are largely absent in the food sector. In the forestry sector, cluster groups have emerged outside the region with the largest concentrations of activity.

- **Need to go national:** In the search for projects judged to engage enterprises with potential to generate significant revenue, the CDP has opened participation to national industry groups. This shift can be interpreted as a realistic approach to promoting collaboration in a small economy, but there are reasons for believing that it will not resolve the policy dilemmas. One outcome is that policy distinctiveness from the JAG program is reduced. This implies that at least some of the problems that challenged the survival of JAGs will be encountered again. For example, there is already evidence from one cluster that was enlarged to cover two regions (i.e., the Canterbury and Nelson Neutraceuticals cluster) that geographical extensiveness raises barriers to the participation of small firms. Participation in national clusters tends to favor comparatively well-resourced organizations. This may not be a concern if the goal is to assist national economic growth, but cluster promotion also is intended to address regional development and entrepreneurship, as well.

Policy Insight

It is possible to understand some of the weaknesses in the present approach to cluster promotion by looking at the sectors that have generated most projects. Nearly all regions, for example, have been able to identify an education cluster (although not all have been classed as clusters for the purpose of seeking government support) because of unique conditions existing for this sector. Promotion of New Zealand to international students has been coordinated nationally, but individual institutions wish to maintain their own marketing, as well. The costs of this are reduced through collaboration with neighboring institutions, and in this case, there are few barriers to marketing cooperation. It generally is recognized that other countries rather than neighboring institutions are the main competitors. Each education provider tends to have a point of difference from its immediate neighbors. For example, secondary schools may differ according to whether they are public or private, boarding or non-boarding, single-sex or coeducational, or affiliated to a religious persuasion or non-religious. There is a common interest in needing to work with local communities to ensure international students have a positive experience and to manage accommodation standards. Through this community dependence, large institutions are linked to smaller institutions and are willing to use their resources for joint as well as individual activities. Individual institutions have a common regulator (i.e., the Ministry of Education) and benefit from sharing experience in maintaining compliance to an industry code of practice.

Earthquake Engineering is a one-off cluster and also is unusual in that it is among the few to have sustained export market cooperation and some contract successes over several years. As well as the presence of a single lead contractor, the group has other attributes that mean that other groups are unlikely to be able to match it. Overseas work opportunities for New Zealand are mainly in low-income countries on government-controlled projects funded by international agencies such as the World Bank. This means that there is a long and uncertain process for winning contracts, which imposes market costs beyond the reach of individual cluster members. The option of firms becoming significant exporters in their own rights is considerably more limited than for suppliers to business or consumer markets. The nature of the work and the specialization of member firms mean that members offer complementary skills and that there is mutual recognition of the role played by the lead contractor. Even so, rules of engagement have been developed to minimize the risk of conflict. Annual membership fees have been kept low in order to ensure that firms involved in individual bids rather than the group as a whole fund that activity. When information is shared, it is expected to be in full and open for others to act upon, but there is no requirement for individual members to share information on market opportunities or other industry intelligence.

Multiple influences have enabled the Earthquake Engineering cluster to maintain a cooperative approach to overseas marketing. The contrast is seen with a group such as the Canterbury Electronics Group. Among the projects examined, it is one of the few others with a high degree of self-management. The six members have their own international marketing capacities, particular specializations, and business relationships. This restricts the group to lobbying government agencies, benchmarking, and one-off projects such as sharing resources for international recruitment. Consequently, as well as the need to understand the conditions conducive to cluster formation, public policy interest needs to be guided by appreciation of the different forms of collective action likely to be supported.

Conclusion

The research interest in business cooperation has translated rapidly into a policy interest in promoting various forms of cooperation within business communities or, at least, in providing resources to facilitate such cooperation. The perspective of this chapter is that policy influenced by the perceived ability to replicate natural clustering experiences does not reflect real-world complexity. The main policy lesson to be drawn from exemplar clusters is that some activities have more of a tendency to cluster than others and that the history of places and industry matters for the location patterns that result. Some companies can benefit by clustering with others that make similar or closely related products. Equally, there are other companies that operate successfully in a location amidst a broad range of activities and that even might benefit from the proximity to unconnected businesses as well as to the services supplied to industry in general. In line with this, the consistent message of New Zealand's policy intervention is that unusual conditions are required in order for businesses to obtain sustained advantage from the forms of cluster cooperation that have been promoted.

In the case of the hard networks program, in theory, small firms can combine resources to gain strength. In practice, it is hard to combine individual companies, as each tends to have its own priorities, perspectives, and experiences. The networks most frequently formed were joint marketing projects among firms that shared the same customers (e.g., incoming tourists). A condition for these projects is that individual firms recognize that they have no likelihood of attracting significant visitors alone or of capturing all the visitors that arrive. In the case of JAG and cluster promotion, sustained cooperation relies on member firms having similar backgrounds, resources, and objectives. Business populations rarely have this equality. Otherwise, projects have relied on special conditions such as a perceived need among incumbents to control new entrants or to manage a threat to industry survival.

These experiences contrast with cluster advocacy based on the perception that there is widespread interest in and ability to gain from cooperation within business clusters. Policy intervention commencing with this perspective leads to selective gains and requires policymakers to examine whether the distribution and extent of advantage is sufficient to justify continued involvement. Ideally, such a judgment would encompass an evaluation of the relative gains and losses from alternative forms of collective association. To date, government agencies have sought to encourage relatively small-scale forms of business cooperation without demonstrating that this will bring additional benefit to supporting larger forms of collective association. Consideration needs to be given to the relative benefits of fragmenting collective association vs. the benefits of concentrating collective activity. Firms have limited resources to devote to participation in collective groups. The policy programs tried in New Zealand can be seen as competing with business participation in an existing industry association. One justification for the JAG program was that existing industry groups were directed to lobbying government rather than to promoting business development. Since then, greater awareness has grown among industry groups of their potential role in promoting business growth, partly as other areas of government policy such as training have called for them to make a contribution. Going forward, it is important to reconsider whether government support would not be best directed at industry associations rather than at smaller-scale groupings. This is particularly so in a small industrial country such as New Zealand, where even broadly based industry groups potentially encompass a small population of businesses.

References

Amphion Report. (1996). *Evaluation of the network co-operation programme 1989–1992.* Copenhagen: Department of Trade and Industry.

Benner, C. (2002). *Work in the new economy: Flexible labour markets in Silicon Valley.* Oxford: Blackwell.

Benneworth, P. (2002). Creating new industries and service clusters on Tyneside. *Local Economy, 17*(4), 313–27.

Benneworth, P., Danson, M., Raines, P., & Whittam, G. (2003). Confusing clusters: Making sense of the cluster approach in theory and practice. *European Planning Studies, 11*(5), 511–520.

Bresnahan, T., Gambardella, A., & Saxenian, A. (2001). "Old economy" inputs for "new economy" outcomes: Cluster formation in the new Silicon Valleys. *Industrial and Corporate Change, 10*(4), 835–860.

Bureau of Industry Economics. (1995). *Beyond the firm: An assessment of business linkages and networks in Australia.* Canberra: Australian Government Publishing Service.

Cappelli, P. (1999). *The new deal at work: Managing the market driven workforce.* Boston: Harvard Business School Press.

Chaston, I. (1996). Critical events and process gaps in the Danish Technological Institute SME structured networking model. *International Small Business Journal, 14*(3), 71–84.

Cluster Navigators. (2001). *Cluster building a toolkit,* Wellington: Industry New Zealand.

Crocombe, G., Enright, M., & Porter, M. (1991). *Upgrading New Zealand's competitive advantage.* Auckland: Oxford University Press.

Danish Technological Institute (DTI). (1994). *First assessment and recommendations on a business network programme in New Zealand* [unpublished report]. Wellington: Danish Technological Institute for the New Zealand Trade Development Board.

Dunning, J. (1993). Internationalizing Porter's diamond. *Management International Review, 33*(2), 7–15.

Feser, E., & Bergman, E. (2000). National industry cluster templates: A framework for regional cluster analysis. *Regional Studies, 34*(1), 1–20.

Feser, E., & Luger, M. (2003). Cluster analysis as a mode of inquiry: Its use in science and technology policymaking in North Carolina. *European Planning Studies, 11*(1), 11–24.

Ffowcs Williams, I. (1996). New Zealand: The internationalisation of competition and the emergence of networks. In Local Economic and Employment Development (OECD) (Ed.), *Networks of Enterprises and Local Development.* Paris: Organisation for Economic Cooperation and Development.

Ffowcs Williams, I. (1997a, June). Upgrading Nelson, New Zealand's seafood capital. *Seafood New Zealand,* 35–39.

Ffowcs Williams, I. (1997b, Summer). Local clusters and local export growth. *New Zealand Strategic Management,* 24–30.

Healy, P. (1997). *Hard Business Networks Newsletter.* Wellington: New Zealand Trade Development Board.

Henriksen, L.B. (1995). Formal cooperation among firms in networks: The case of Danish joint ventures and strategic alliances. *European Planning Studies, 3*(2), 254–260.

Huggins, R. (1996). Technology policy, networks and small firms in Denmark. *Regional Studies, 30*(5), 523–552.

Huggins, R. (2000). The success and failure of policy-implanted inter-firm network initiatives: Motivations, processes and structure. *Entrepreneurship & Regional Development, 12,* 111–135.

Isaksen, A., & Hauge, E. (2002). *Observatory of European SMEs 3*. Luxembourg: European Commission.

Johnston, R., & Lawrence, P. (1988, July-August). Beyond vertical integration—the rise of value-adding partnerships. *Harvard Business Review, 66*(4), 54–68.

Kenney, M. (Ed.). (2000). *Understanding Silicon Valley: The anatomy of an entrepreneurial region*. Stanford: Stanford University Press.

Kotval, Z., & Mullin, J. (1998). The potential for planning an industrial cluster in Barre, Vermont: A case of "hard rock" resistance in the granite industry. *Planning Practice & Research, 13*(3), 311–318.

Lagendijk, A. (1999). Learning in non-core regions: Towards intelligent clusters addressing business and regional needs. In R. Rutten, S. Bakkers, K. Morgan, & F. Boekem (Eds.), *Learning regions: Theory, policy and practice*. Cheltenham: Edward Elgar.

Leamer, E., & Storper, M. (2001). *The economic geography of the Internet age* [working paper 8450]. Cambridge, MA: NBER.

Longhi, C. (1999). Networks, collective learning and technology development in innovative high technology regions: The case of Sophia-Antipolis. *Regional Studies, 33*(4), 333–342.

Maher, P. (1996). Hard business networks: A comparative study [unpublished master's thesis]. Auckland: University of Auckland.

Malmberg, A., Malmberg, B., & Lundequist, P. (2000). Agglomeration and firm performance: Economies of scale, localisation, and urbanisation among Swedish export firms. *Environment and Planning A, 32*, 305–321.

Martin, R., & Sunley, P. (2003). Deconstructing clusters: Chaotic concept or policy panacea? *Journal of Economic Geography, 3*, 5–35.

Maskell, P. (1998). Learning in the village economy of Denmark: The role of institutions and policy in sustaining competitiveness. In H. J. Braczyk, P. Cooke, & M. Heidenreich (Eds). *Regional innovation systems* (pp. 190-213). London: UCL Press.

Maskell, P., Eskelin, H., Hannibalsson, I., Malmberg, A., & Vatne, E. (1998). *Competitiveness localised learning and regional development*. London: Routledge.

OECD. (1995). *Boosting business advisory services*. Paris: Organisation of Economic Cooperation and Development.

Perry, M. (1995). Industry structures, networks and joint action groups. *Regional Studies, 29*(3), 208–217.

Perry, M. (2001). *Shared trust strategies for small industrial countries*. Wellington: Victoria University of Wellington.

Perry, M. (2004a). Business cluster promotion in New Zealand and the limits of exemplar clusters. *Policy and Society, 23*(4), 82–103.

Perry, M. (2004b). Creative capital, New Zealand, LEDIS Overseas E254. *Agenda for Local Economic Development, 68*, 9–10.

Perry, M. (2005). *Conditions for business cluster development*. Wellington: New Zealand Centre for SME Research.

Peters, E., & Hood, N. (2000). Implementing the cluster approach. *International Studies of Management & Organization, 30*(2), 68–92.

Pinch, S., Henry, N., Jenkins, M., & Tallman, S. (2003). From "industrial districts" to "knowledge clusters": A model of knowledge dissemination and competitive advantage in industrial agglomerations. *Journal of Economic Geography, 3*, 373–388.

Porter, M. (1990). *The competitive advantage of nations.* New York: Free Press.

Porter, M. (1998). Clusters and the new economics of competition. *Harvard Business Review, 76*(6), 77–90.

Porter, M. (2000). Locations, clusters and company strategy. In G. Clark, M. Feldman, & M. Gertler (Eds.), *The oxford handbook of economic geography* (pp. 253-274). Oxford: Oxford University Press.

Porter, M. (2003). The economic performance of regions. *Regional Studies, 37*(6-7), 549–578.

Prevezer. (1998). Clustering in biotechnology in the USA. In G. Swann, M. Prevezer, & D. Stout (Eds.), *The dynamics of industrial clustering: International comparisons in computing and biotechnology* (pp. 124-193). Oxford: Oxford University Press.

Rabellotti, R., & Schmitz, H. (1999). The internal heterogeneity of industrial districts in Italy, Brazil and Mexico. *Regional Studies, 33*(2), 97–108.

Raines, P. (2002). *Cluster development and policy.* Aldershot, UK: Ashgate.

Rosenfeld, S. (2003). Expanding opportunities: Cluster strategies that reach more people and more places. *European Planning Studies, 11*(4), 359–377.

Rosenfeld, S. (2005). Industry clusters: Business choice, policy outcome, or branding strategy? *Journal of New Business Ideas and Trends, 3*(2), 4–13.

Saxenian, A. (1994). *Regional advantage: Culture and competition in Silicon Valley and Route 128.* Cambridge, MA: Harvard University Press.

Schmitz, H. (1995). Collective efficiency: Growth path for small-scale industry. *Journal of Development Studies, 31*, 529–566.

Schmitz, H. (1999). Global competition and local cooperation: Success and failure in the Sinos Valley, Brazil. *World Development, 27*, 1627–1650.

Schmitz, H., & Nadvi, K. (1999). Clustering and industrialization: Introduction. *World Development, 27*, 1503–1514.

Sharp, M. (1990). European countries in science-based competition: The case of biotechnology. In D. Hague (Ed.), *The management of science.* Basingstoke: Macmillan.

Sharp, M. (1999). The science of nations: European multinationals and American biotechnology. *Biotechnology, 1*(1), 132–162.

Silverstone, B., Bollard, A., & Lattimore, R. (Eds.). (1996). *A study of economic reform: The case of New Zealand.* Amsterdam: Elsevier.

Sorenson, O., & Audia, P. (2000). The social structure of entrepreneurial activity: Ggeographic concentration of footwear production in the United States, 1940–1989. *American Journal of Sociology, 106*(2), 424–462.

Stuart, T., & Sorenson, O. (2003). The geography of opportunity: Spatial heterogeneity in founding rates and the performance of biotechnology firms. *Research Policy, 32*, 229–253.

Tarnbunan, T. (2005). Promoting small and medium enterprises with a clustering approach: A policy experience from Indonesia. *Journal of Small Business Management, 43*(2), 138–154.

Trade New Zealand. (1996). *Stretching for growth: Two years into an eight year journey.* Wellington: New Zealand Trade Development Board.

Yetton, P, Craig, J., Davis, J., & Hilmer, F. (1992). Are diamonds a country's best friend? A critique of Porter's theory of national competition as applied to Canada, New Zealand and Australia. *Australian Journal of Management, 17*(1), 1–32.

Chapter IX

The Analysis of Tourism Cluster Development of Istanbul:
A Longitudinal Study in Sultanahmet District (Old Town)

Aslihan Nasir, Bogazici University, Turkey

Melih Bulu, International Competitiveness Research Institute (URAK), Turkey

Hakki Eraslan, International Competitiveness Research Institute (URAK), Turkey

Abstract

The Sultanahmet district in Turkey has a distinct and unique historical characteristic that includes both Byzantine and Ottoman styles in the design of historical shopping centers, architecture in general, and mosques. Competitive Advantage of Turkey (CAT) conducted a comprehensive cluster study in this historical district in 2001 and initiated the cluster development project. Therefore, the main aim of this research is to identify the analysis of tourism cluster development in the Sultanahmet district (old town). For this purpose, a longitudinal study was realized. Along with secondary research, semi-structured questionnaires, semi-structured interviews, and expert opinions were used as the primary data collection method. A questionnaire was given to members of civil societies, governmental organizations, entrepreneurs (e.g., travel agents, hotel owners, shopping centers owners, etc.), local governments, and suppliers located in the Sultanahmet district.

Introduction

Industrial cluster is one of the latest agendas in today's organizational researches; it can be characterized as networks of production of strongly interdependent firms (including specialized suppliers), knowledge-producing agents (universities, research institutes, engineering companies, R&D centers), bridging institutions (brokers, consultants), competitors, NGOs, governmental organizations, specialized institutions, local governments, inspection and control bodies, and customers, all linked to each other in a value-adding production chain (Bulu & Eraslan, 2004; Roelandt & Hertog, 1998). Porter (1998) defines clusters as the derivers of new economics of competition. After his pioneering study, a number of theoretical and empirical studies initiated all over the world. As a result of these attempts, many research centers were launched in different countries, and many countries, including member countries of the EU, accepted cluster-based economic development. On the other side, Harvard University founded a center for mapping all clusters in the US, and the UK initiated 15 regional development agencies in the country managed by the central government. The Sweden Competitiveness Institute started an independent center that worked for the country's clusters, and Italy initiated various cluster centers in industrial districts. The cluster approach also has been studied and utilized as a strategic tool by Competitive Advantage of Turkey (CAT), which was established as an NGO by private sector leaders of Turkey together with the cooperation of Porter's intellectual support since 1999 for increasing the competitiveness power of Turkey. CAT realized a number of cluster studies and field researches in different industries, including the tourism sector.

Turkey is a middle-income country with a GNP per capita of $4,617 and a population of 70 million in 2004 (SIS, 2005). The Turkish Republic is a social, democratic, secular state and is one of the most developed East European countries, industrializing at a rapid rate. Trade has been increasing, and Turkey has become more open to the world both economically and socially. Turkey is bordered by six countries and is at the crossroads between Asia and Europe; it serves as a link and a strategic barrier between the Southern Caucasus and the northern Middle East. Its area is 779,452 sq. km., and is surrounded by three seas—the Black Sea to the north, the Mediterranean Sea to the south, and the Aegean Sea to the west—which presents good sea tourism opportunities. Turkey is also a member of various international political, social, economic, cultural, and military organizations, which include the Council of Europe, the UN, the World Bank, the IMF, the OECD, the WTO, the Multilateral Investment Guarantee Agency (MIGA), and NATO. Turkey has had a history of cooperation with the European integration movement since the movement's early beginnings. In 1963, Turkey and the European Community (EC) signed the Turkey-EC Association Agreement. In 1987, Turkey formally applied for accession to the EC. Nevertheless, the Commission recommended continuing cooperation with Turkey, which eventually led to the formation of an EU customs union with Turkey in 1995. In April 1997, at the EU Intergovernmental Conference, the EU announced that Turkey would remain eligible for accession on the same political criteria as other applicant countries (Banani, 2003). The Helsinki European Council formally recognized Turkey as a candidate for accession to the European Union in December 1999. In December 2002, the Copenhagen European Council resolved to decide on the launching of accession negotiations with Turkey at the end of 2004. As a result, the negotiation progress with EU was initiated on October 3, 2005. Along with the wind of relationship between EU and Turkey and the globalization and liberalization progress of

Turkey, tourism industry has achieved great success both qualitatively and quantitatively. As a result of this enhancement, the industry has become one of the most important economic values for Turkish economy.

Tourism Industry

The Turkish tourism industry consistently has enhanced since the 1990s. Today, the industry can be regarded as a shining star and defined as the admiral ship of Turkish economy. Apart from the manufacturing industry, the sector contributed $13.1 billion US annual revenues for the Turkish economy alone in 2004. Due to its economic and social importance, early cluster research has been initiated by CAT in tourism industry, and the Sultanahmet tourism district has been chosen for our research area.

International tourism has been influenced negatively by several factors: the Iraq conflict, the tsunami in the Indian Ocean, the SARS disease, and the terrorist attacks in different regions of the world in the last two decades (WTO, 2004, 2005). However, 2004 was obviously a better year than 2003 (WTO, 2005). According to the same report, there will be an increasing trend in international tourism in 2006. Moreover, the experts assert that international tourist arrivals will grow by approximately 5% in 2006 (WTO, 2005). The declining effect of terrorist shocks on the travel industry, the positive impact of emerging economies (i.e., China) on demand, the realization of the tsunami as a one-time event, and the successful recovery process after SARS are among the factors that will lead to an upward trend in international tourism. Furthermore, price-cutting strategies and promotional campaigns are the marketing tools that can be used to attract tourists to the destinations that are affected most heavily by the aforementioned negative factors.

Table 1 illustrates the international tourist arrivals (ITA) rank and international tourism receipts (ITR) rank for the years 2002 and 2003. According to WTO (2005), international tourist arrivals reached an all-time record of 760 million, corresponding to an increase of 10%. In addition, international tourist arrivals all over the world increased by 69 million, and

Table 1. World's top 10 ITA and ITR ranks (2002–2003) Source: WTO (2004)

International Tourist Arrivals (million) Rank			International Tourism Receipts ($ billion US) Rank		
	2002	2003		2002	2003
1 France	77.0	75.0	1 United States	66.7	64.5
2 Spain	52.3	51.8	2 Spain	33.8	41.8
3 United States	43.5	41.2	3 France	32.7	37.0
4 Italy	39.8	39.6	4 Italy	26.9	31.2
5 China	36.8	33.0	5 Germany	19.0	23.0
6 United Kingdom	24.2	24.7	6 United Kingdom	20.5	22.8
7 Austria	18.6	19.1	7 China	20.4	17.4
8 Mexico	19.7	18.7	8 Austria	11.2	14.1
9 Germany	18.0	18.4	9 Turkey	11.9	13.2
10 Canada	20.1	17.5	10 Greece	9.7	10.7

Figure 1. New arrivals 2004 by region (worldwide 69 million) (Source: World Tourism Organization (WTO) (2005))

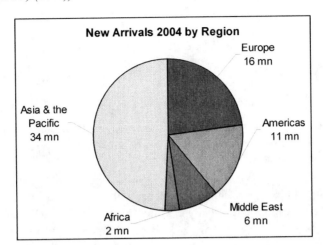

all the tourism regions share this increase in varying degrees. As can be seen from Figure 1, Asia and the Pacific gained almost half of all the new arrivals, followed by Europe and the Americas, respectively.

WTO tourism panel experts envisaged a worldwide growth between 5% and 8% for international tourism in 2005. This meant that 2005 would be a year with growth at significantly above the long-term average rate for worldwide international tourism of 4.1%. Additionally, leisure tourism was expected to continue its growth, while business tourism would recover further. WTO's Tourism 2020 Vision anticipates that international arrivals should reach more than 1.56 billion by the year 2020. Moreover, it is estimated that by 2020, the top three tourist-receiving regions will be Europe (717 million), East Asia and the Pacific (397 million), and the Americas (282 million).

Turkish Tourism Industry

According to the WTO (2004) report, the increase in Turkey's international tourist arrivals between the years 2002 and 2003 was more than 4%, whereas the increase in international tourism receipts in the same period was around 11%. Some important destinations in Europe were affected negatively from the Iraq war, economic slowdown, and the strong euro. However, during 2004, Turkey demonstrated a 27% increase in international tourist arrivals, and its tourism boom is expected to continue, which will be driven by an attractive product combined with attractive prices. The possible integration to the European Union also can be an important factor that contributes to the inclining tendency of the Turkish tourism industry. Table 2 shows Turkey's tourist arrivals and receipts between the years 2000 and 2004.

The distribution of tourists according to their purpose of visit is also another crucial indicator of the structure of the Turkish tourism industry. Table 3 demonstrates the purposes of visits

Table 2. Turkey's tourism arrivals and receipts between 2000 and 2004 [Source: Turkey's Statistical Yearbook (2004)]

	2000	2001	2002	2003	2004
Tourism Arrivals	10.4 mn	11.6 mn	13.2 mn	13.9 mn	17.5 mn
Tourism Receipts	-	7.3 bn $	9.0 bn $	9.6 bn $	13.1 bn $

of tourists between the years 2001 and 2004. According to Table 3, the majority of tourists prefers Turkey for the purpose of travel and entertainment, while another important group comes for cultural and sporting purposes.

Table 3 also presents the varieties of Turkish tourism sectors including sports, culture, travel, entertainment, health, religion, shopping, science (meetings, conferences, and seminars), commerce, and education. Historical and cultural heritages especially dominate overall tourism varieties. In other words, historical places offer genuine tourism clusters in different parts of Turkey.

The Cluster Approach

The concept of clusters is fairly a new orthodoxy among researchers and has become the new mantra for economic development policy. Despite this, it has been fascinated by a number of studies since Porter's *Competitive Advantage of Nations* (1990) and has become one of the most popular concepts in competitiveness. Thus, the cluster concept is a powerful metaphor that is used routinely to guide industrial and developmental planning and competitive advantage throughout the US, European countries, and Turkey.

However, the notion of industrial complexes and the regional concentration of networks of specialized suppliers, producers, and users is by no means new in economic theory. This approach has its roots in Marshall's (1890) analysis of textile and metalworking districts

Table 3. Turkey's tourist arrivals by purpose of visit between 2001 and 2004 [Source: Turkey's Statistical Yearbook (2004)]

Purpose of Visit	2001	2002	2003	2004
Travel Entertainment	5.2 mn	6.4 mn	6.8 mn	8.2 mn
Culture	0.9 mn	1.0 mn	1.0 mn	1.1 mn
Sport Events	0.1 mn	0.1 mn	0.15 mn	0.2 mn
Visiting Relatives	0.7 mn	0.9 mn	0.8 mn	1.0 mn
Heath Reasons	0.09 mn	0.08 mn	0.1 mn	0.13 mn
Religious	0.03 mn	0.06 mn	0.05 mn	0.06 mn
Shopping	0.8 mn	0.7 mn	0.9 mn	1.0 mn
Meeting, Conference and Seminars	0.2 mn	0.2 mn	0.2 mn	0.3 mn
Job-Related Reasons	0.5 mn	0.5 mn	0.7 mn	0.8 mn
Commercial Relations and Exhibitions	0.5 mn	0.3 mn	0.4 mn	0.6 mn
Transit	0.3 mn	0.2 mn	0.2 mn	0.1 mn
Education	-	0.1 mn	0.07 mn	0.1 mn
Other	0.4 mn	0.1 mn	0.3 mn	0.5 mn

of England, Germany, and France during the latter half of the 19th century. Porter (1990) popularized the concept of industry clusters in his book titled *The Competitive Advantage of Nations.*

Clusters are geographical and sectoral concentrations of interconnected companies, enterprises, and institutions in a particular field (Porter, 1998). Clusters can be characterized as a network of production of strongly interdependent firms (including specialized suppliers), knowledge-producing agents (universities, research institutes, engineering companies), bridging institutions (brokers, consultants), and customers that are linked to each other in a value-adding production chain (Roelandt & Hertog, 1998). According to the National Governors Association (2002), most experts define an industry cluster as a geographically bounded concentration of similar, related, or complementary businesses with active channels for business transactions, communications, and dialogue that share specialized infrastructure, labor markets, and services and that are faced with common opportunities and threats. Hence, a cluster develops when enough similar, related, or complementary businesses locate in a region in order to give firms a collective advantage.

After the Porter study, a case study method was used mainly for cluster analyses for different issues of clusters all over the world, including supply chain networks for inventory control (Srinivasan & Moon, 1999), high-tech cluster creation and cluster reconfiguration (Andersen & Teubal, 1999), a network of relationships between the economic environment and the entrepreneurial culture in small firms (Minguzzi & Passaro, 2000), innovative clusters (Bergman, 2001; Hertog, 2001), Singapore electronic cluster (Best, 1999), Northeast Ohio clusters (Kleinhenz, 2000), networks and linkages in African manufacturing cluster in Nigeria (Oyeyinka, 2001), and identifying microcluster (Bulu, 2003).

All studies concluded that a network of relationships between firm and market is the main factor external to the firm. Powell (1990) stated:

[M]any firms are no longer structured like medieval kingdoms, walled off and protected from hostile outside forces. Instead, we find companies involved in an intricate latticework of collaborative ventures with other firms, most of whom are ostensibly competitors. (p. 300)

Powell also gives examples of auto and biotechnology industries for network formation of firms. Network form also offers advantages specific to entrepreneurial firms. The use of a network exchange structure represents a critical leveraging opportunity whereby resources can be gained and competitive advantages realized without incurring the capital investments of vertical integration (Larson, 1992).

Levels of Clusters

Roelandt, Hertog, Sinderen, and Vollard (1997) define clusters in three groups: national level (macro), branch or industry level (meso), and firm level (micro). At the micro level of analysis, clusters can be described as networks of various suppliers around a core enterprise (Hagendoorn & Schakenraad, 1990). This kind of analysis can be used to make a strategic analysis of the firm and to identify missing links or strategic partners when innovation projects encompass the whole production chain. It also is used to analyze the different stages in the production chain when analyzing environmental innovations (e.g., waste management, energy use, emissions, materials management). In this case, cluster analysis often is used in combination with case study material (Roelandt, Hertog, Sinderen, Vollaard, 1997). The meso level concentrates mostly on a branch or industry scope. Mesoclusters can be defined if there is inter- and intra-industry linkages in the different stages of the production chain of similar end products in a cluster formation area. Most of the Porter studies carried out in different countries (Finland, Sweden, US, Denmark, Netherlands) used this level of analysis. In the macro level, some countries' contributions focus on linkages between industry groups (megaclusters like Finland and Netherlands) and mapping specialization patterns of a country or region economy-wide (Roelandt, Gilsing & Sinderen, 2000).

The Importance and Benefits of Clusters and Their Effect on Competitiveness

The incentives for cluster formation differ quite considerably. The principle incentives for cluster formation are (1) to gain access to new and complementary technology, (2) to capture economics of synergy or economics of interdependent activities, (3) to spread risks, (4) to promote joint R&D efforts with suppliers and users, (5) to reduce competition as a defensive strategy, (6) to obtain reciprocal benefits from the combined use of complementary assets and knowledge, (7) to speed up the learning process, (8) to lower transaction costs, and (9) to overcome (or create) entry barriers in markets (Roelandt, Gilsing & Sinderen, 2000).

Cluster Initiatives in Turkey and the CAT Platform

Studies using the clustering approach also were made in Turkey in the last few years. Öz (1999, 2001, 2002) mainly applied Porter's framework for National Competitive Advantage to Turkey. Kumral, Akgüngör, and Lenger (2001) examined the national industry clusters of Turkey, whereas Eraydın (2002) studied the relation between economic growth and clusters. Moreover, Akgüngör (2003) made an input-output (I/O) analysis in order to define Turkey's meso-level clusters.

The cluster approach also has been used by CAT, which was established as a nongovernmental organization (NGO) by private sector leaders of Turkey, together with the cooperation of Porter's intellectual support in 1999, as a tool for increasing competitiveness of the Turkish economy in the global arena. By using Porter's methodology, CAT defined the sectors in which Turkey may have competitive advantage in the global market. These sectors were textile, construction, food, automobile, and tourism; they began to be analyzed by using the cluster approach.

As already explained, CAT attempted its first cluster project in the Sultanahmet district for tourism cluster due to its importance. The tourism cluster consisted of industries that provide services to tourists, both local residents and travelers, in the areas of scenic transportation, travel arrangement, and amusement- and recreation-related activities. This study grouped industries in the tourism cluster into three divisions: cultural, scenic, and sightseeing transportation. The Sultanahmet district encompasses entire features of these types because it was the capital of the Byzantine and Ottoman Empires.

Methodology of the Research

The main aim of this research is to identify the analysis of the tourism cluster development of the Sultanahmet district (old town). This is the first and only study that was conducted to examine the results of cluster advancement in the tourism industry.

This research project was a longitudinal, empirically based study of a carefully selected sample of tourism players in the Sultanahmet tourism district. The longitudinal study designs are the key to examine and understand changes of competences over the lifespan. In order to examine the result of the first project of cluster development, the second research was realized by a longitudinal study.

For the CAT tourism cluster project in 2001, a semi-structured questionnaire was conducted to 44 major players of the tourism industry in the Sultanahmet district. This sample was selected by expert opinion and by semi-structured in-depth interviews with sector leaders and related civil societies that mainly were located in this zone. The same method was used by the CAT team in 2005. In this case, the semi-structured questionnaire was given to the same players in order to determine the results of cluster developments.

Determining Sample Size

The sample size was determined by doing in-depth interviews with the sector leaders and the managers of NGOs by selecting and determining major players in 2001. Initially, 89 players (e.g., travel agents, shopping centers owners, hotel and motel owners, restaurant owners, etc.) were evaluated as major players of the district. After these players were evaluated by their annual revenues and employees, some of them were eliminated from the research. Finally, 44 major players were identified by experts and CAT team members.

Data Collection Method

A semi-structured questionnaire was conducted by the snowball method for this study. The questionnaire was designed by CAT's members by seeking major players' suppliers, competitors, clients, related institutions (e.g., universities, civil societies, research centers, etc.) in order to determine the fundamental roots of the tourism cluster and its links to this district.

The second questionnaire was conducted to the same members of the cluster by CAT members in 2005 in order to determine the advancements and enhancements of the first project. The data contained in this report also were collected from a series of in-depth interviews with individuals who had engaged in the tourism sector for a long time in this area. The results of the interviews were used for interpretation of the cluster map.

The Analysis of Research

After collecting the data by questionnaire, the first cluster map was drawn in 2001. The second map also was drawn by using same token in 2005. As a result, two cluster maps were created (Figure 2 and Figure 3). Nodes show the members of the cluster, whereas the links show the relationship between the members (e.g., trade, innovation, knowledge-flow relations, etc.)

As shown in Figure 2, which was drawn in 2001, 85 links were defined between 44 players of the cluster. At that time, the members did not come together in order to make common projects such as marketing, R&D, and purchasing activities. On the other hand, because of capital scarcity, members needed to make common marketing activities such as participating international tourism fairs, which required a budget that one firm could not afford alone. Actually, firm owners said that they did not have trust in each other; therefore, common projects were very difficult to realize.

Another important issue was the skill level of the people working in the tourism sector. In 2001, there was no firm that had an Internet connection. Naturally, none of the employees working either at hotels or travel agencies had Internet usage skill.

The cluster development study started in 2001 and continued until 2005. From the initial analysis, all the vital members of the value system were available in the Sultanahmet area (e.g., hotels, travel agencies, tourist handicraft shops, museums, historical places, restaurants, etc.). Two major problems were defined regarding the cluster: (1) links among members were rather low; and (2) the intellectual level of the employees was under qualification standards.

A local development committee was founded from the local cluster members. The representatives of the cluster that had leadership characteristics were preferred for the committee.

Figure 2. Sultanahmet tourism cluster map 2001

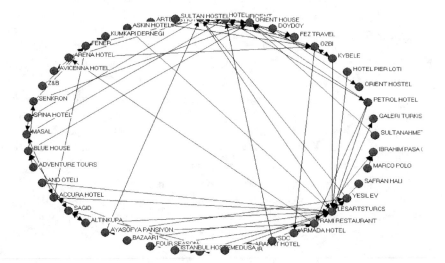

Figure 3. Sultanahmet tourism cluster map 2005

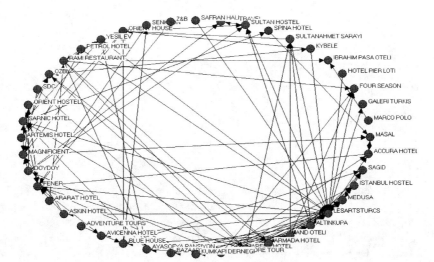

The Local Committee defined various projects in order to increase employee qualifications and links among cluster members. These projects were realized until 2005 and continue to be realized.

In 2005, the Sultanahmet cluster was analyzed again in order to see the difference in the cluster development program. The members that were surveyed in 2001 were surveyed again, and a new cluster map was drawn (Figure 3).

From the analysis of surveys, it was found that the number of links was 85 in 2001. This number increased to 147 in 2005, which was a 73% increase in the number of links during a four-year period. The increase in the number of links has two main components. First, members of the cluster increased common projects that were naturally in need of cooperation. For example, a travel agency has the responsibility supplying regular tourists to a hotel. Second, cluster members defined and participated common projects. For example, similar hotels came together and established a fund for participating international tourism fairs, seminars, and so forth. Each time, a hotel participated in the fair and distributed other hotels' brochures. Moreover, new travel packages were defined as a result of cluster members' cooperation (e.g., a travel agency used a hotel in Sultanahmet for accommodation needs and a handicraft shop for touristic shopping requirements in its travel package). In addition, a new newspaper, the *Sultanahmet News*, began printing in the region, and a Web site was designed (www.sultanahmetonline.org). These two results were very helpful and showed the members what was going on in the cluster and how they could participate the new projects.

The analysis in 2005 demonstrates that the average annual revenue of the firms increased from $400,000 to $1,000,000 in the Sultanahmet cluster. This is an overperformance when compared to the increase in Turkish tourism revenues over the same period. Furthermore, the data show that the average number of employees in the firms increased from 12 to 18. This information is evidence that supports the enlargement of the cluster members.

Table 4. The improvements in the Sultanahmet district after the initiation of the cluster project

	2001	2005
Average revenues of the cluster members	$400,000	$1,000,000
Average employees of the cluster members	12	18
Number of links among cluster members	85	147
Average stay of tourists	2 days	3 days
Average daily spending of tourists	$50	$80
Average hotel room rates	$20	$40

The figures related to tourists coming to Sultanahmet also developed positively. Days spent in the area and average daily spending for tourists increased significantly. The average stay increased from two days to three days, which means that tourists began to stay one more day in the region. This took place because tourists were given new touristic products that were developed by cluster member cooperation. Travel agencies and domestic tour operators cooperated and designed new products (e.g.. city tours with sultan ships, etc.) that attracted tourists' interests. In addition, the average daily spending of tourists increased from $50 to $80, which was due mainly to an increase in hotel room prices. Due to the boost in demand to the Sultanahmet region, average hotel room rates increased from $20 to $40.

Table 4 illustrates a summary of the improvements that were seen after the initialization of the cluster project in the Sultanahmet region in 2001 and 2005, respectively.

Research Results and Conclusion

The Cluster Development Project was initiated to devise a unified, regionwide strategy in order to enhance competitiveness of the Sultanahmet tourism industry. A broad range of industry stakeholders participated in the cluster's strategy work and initiative development, including universities, academic experts, community groups, regional tourism associations, and several public sector agencies. These players established a Cluster Development Committee in order to manage the project. Two years after the initiation of the project, this committee established an NGO. Thus, the steadiness and future of the cluster development project was guaranteed. Through this NGO, the Sultanahmet tourism cluster gained a strong tool to manage future challenges to the cluster. Because the committee was composed of leader cluster members, they had the ability to sense the upcoming challenges and organize defense strategies. Since the committee had management power on cluster members, advance strategies could be applied easily within the cluster in the development progress.

An increase in average staying time can be attributed mostly to the new products developed within the cluster. This success is the result of cooperation among cluster members. Mainly travel agencies and tour operators designed new touristic products, which attracted people to stay one more day in the region.

Training and specialized education programs were given to cluster member employees, which contributed to the whole cluster. For example, as a result of IT information and training, hotels initiated Internet service and started to follow up with their customers via e-mail. This followup provided a significant return to these hotels.

The cluster development study shows that this kind of development program can be a vital model for tourism industries that have problems with average staying time and average revenue amounts. In addition, cooperation among cluster members constitutes a more competitive industry in both the domestic and the international arenas. Finally, all these improvements obviously lead to more revenue for cluster firms and employment for the region's people, which are very crucial outputs for both the sector and the country.

This research shows that the cluster development project gives a significant enhancement for the tourism sector in the Sultanahmet District. The annual revenue of firms and employment figures increased, communication among players was enhanced, marketing capabilities of players expanded, and human resources of the region developed. The Cluster Development Committee, which was composed of cluster leader players, became the administrative body of the cluster; thus, a self-improving cluster management system was established.

As a result, there has been strong evidence from the local leaders, who have confessed that there have been enhancements in various areas of the Sultanahmet tourism cluster during the last four year period. The Sultanahmet Tourism Cluster Development Project can be seen as a successful example of tourism industry development for other world tourism clusters. The experience gained during this project can be very useful for tourism clusters that are similar to Sultanahmet. In particular, the handling of the trust issue among potential cluster members; the upgrade of the labor skill level; dexterity in the industry; and development of common marketing activities, which enlarges the market share of the cluster, should be examined for other clusters that have a development target.

In summary, the findings of this research reveal that there are improvements in both the number of players in the cluster and the links among the players. Furthermore, the average number of employees, the average accommodation period of tourists, and their average daily spending are among other variables that indicate an increasing tendency. It is also equally important to see advancement in the skill and capability levels of employees of the cluster member organizations and institutions. Another finding of the current study is the significant increase in the revenues of the cluster members. Finally, since the initialization of the cluster project in 2001, the average hotel rates in the district were also boosted. The following part of this study was devoted to introduction, in which it is possible to see a general framework of Turkey and its current situation.

References

Andersen, E. S., & Teubal, M. (1999). *High tech cluster creation and cluster re-configuration: A system and policy perspective.* Paper presented at the DRUID Conference on Innovation Systems, Rebild.

Akgüngör, S. (2003, April 12-15). *Exploring regional specializations in Turkey's manufacturing industry.* Paper presented at the Regional Studies Association International Conference, Pisa, Italy.

Banani, D.D. (2003). Reforming history: Turkey's legal regime and its potential accession to the European Union. *Boston College International & Comparative Law Review,* *26*(1), 113-127.

Bergman, E. (2001). *In pursuit of innovative clusters*. Paper presented at the NIS Conference on Network- and Cluster oriented Policies, Vienna.

Best, M. H. (1999). *Cluster dynamics in theory and practice: Singapore/Johor and Penang electronics*. Lowell: University of Massachusetts, Lowell.

Bulu M. (2003). *Profiling micro clusters: identification of value-adding production and service chains by using graph theoretical approach* (PhD thesis). Istanbul, Turkey: Boğaziçi University: .

Bulu, M., ve Eraslan, İ. H. (2004). In K. Yaklaşımı & İ. Bakan (Eds.), *Çağdaş Yönetim Yaklaşımları: İlkeler, Kavramlar ve Yaklaşımlar*. Beta Basım Yayım Dağıtım A.Ş.: İstanbul.

Eraydın, A. (2002). *Yeni Sanayii Odakları: Yerel Kalkınmanın Yeniden Kavramlaştırılması*. Ankara: METU Architecture Press.

Hagendoorn, J., & Schakenraad, J. (1990). Interfirm partnerships and cooperative strategies in core technologies. In C. Freeman & L. Stoete (Eds.), *Information technology and employment: An assessment*. University of Sussex.

Hertog, P. (2001), *In pursuit of innovative clusters*. Paper presented at the Proceedings of Measuring and Evaluating Industrial R&D and Innovation in the Knowledge Economy, Taipei.

Kleinhenz, J. (2000). An introduction to the northeast Ohio clusters project. *Economic Development Quarterly, 14*(1), 63–64.

Kumral, N., Akungor, S., & Lenger, A. (2001). *National industry clusters: The case of Turkey*. Paper prepared for Regional Transitions: European Regions and the Challenges of Development, Integration and Enlargement. Presentation at the Regional Studies Association.

Marshall, A. (1890). *Principles of economics*. London: Macmillan.

Minguzzi, A., & Passaro, R. (2000). The network of relationships between the economic environment and the entrepreneurial culture in small firms. *Journal of Business Venturing,* (16), 181-207.

National Governors Association. (2002, August). *A governor's guide to cluster-based economic development*. Retrieved from http://www.nga.org/Files/pdf/AM02CLUSTER.pdf

Öz, Ö. (1999). *The competitive advantage of nations: The case of Turkey*. Ashgate Publishing.

Öz, Ö. (2001). Sources of competitive advantage of Turkish construction companies in international markets. *Construction Management and Economics, 19*, 135-144.

Öz, Ö. (2002). Assesing Porter's framework for national advantage: The case of Turkey. *Journal of Business Research, 55*, 509-515.

Oyeyinka, B.O. (2001, September). *Networks and linkages in African manufacturing cluster: A Nigerian case study* (Discussion Papers Series No. 2001-5). Helsinki: The United Nations University.

Porter, M. (1998, November-December). Clusters and the new economics of competition. *Harvard Business Review, 76*(6), 77-90.

Porter, M. (1990). *Competitive advantage of nations*. Harvard University Press.

Powell, W. (1990). Neither market nor hierarchy: Network forms of organization. *Research in Organizational Behavior, 12*, 295-336.

Roelandt, T. J. A., & Den Hertog, P. (1998). Cluster analysis and cluster-based policy in OECD-countries: Various approaches, early results and policy implications. In *Draft Synthesis Report on Phase 1, OECD-focus Group on Cluster Analysis and Cluster-Based Policy* (pp. 1-76). The Hague; Utrecht.

Roelandt, T. J. A., Den Hertog, P., Van Sinderen J., and Vollaard, B. (1997, October 10-11). *Cluster analysis and cluster policy in The Netherlands.* Paper presented at tge OECD-Workshop on Cluster Analysis and Cluster Based Policy, Amsterdam, The Netherlands.

Roelandt, T. J. A., Gilsing, V. A., & Van Sinderen, J. (2000). *Cluster-based innovation policy: International experiences.* Paper presented at the 4th Annual EUNIP Conference, Tilburg, The Netherlands.

Srinivasan, M., & Moon, Y. B. (1999). A comprehensive clustering algorithm for strategic analysis of supply chain networks. *Computers and Industrial Engineering, (36)*, 615-633.

State Institute of Statistics of Turkey (SIS). (2005). *Statistical indicators 1923-2004.* Retrieved from http://www.tuik.gov.tr/yillik/Ist_gostergeler.pdf

Turkey's Statistical Yearbook. (2004). Retrieved from http://www.die.gov.tr/yillik/yillik_2004_eng.pdf

World Tourism Organization (WTO). (2004). *Tourism highlights* (2004 ed.). Retrieved from http://thesius.wtoelibrary.org/vl=24788595/cl=11/nw=1/rpsv/journal/publication9284407915_home.htm

World Tourism Organization (WTO). (2005). *World Tourism Barometer, 3*(1). Retrieved from http://www.world-tourism.org/facts/eng/pdf/barometer/january2005.pdf

Chapter X

Uppsala BIO – The Life Science Initiative:
Experiences of and Reflections on Starting a Regional Competitiveness Initiative

Robin Teigland, Stockholm School of Economics, Sweden

Daniel Hallencreutz, Uppsala University, Sweden

Per Lundequist, Uppsala University, Sweden

Abstract

Numerous regions around the globe are implementing initiatives designed to improve their competitiveness by promoting interaction and innovation among their regional organizations. This chapter presents one such initiative, Uppsala BIO–The Life Science Initiative, that was created by local representatives from government, industry, and academia in Uppsala, Sweden. The purpose of this chapter is to describe Uppsala BIO's activities during its first 18 months, to present some reflections on the organization that were gathered through a longitudinal study, and to discuss the initiative's impact on the region. Thus, this chapter is relevant to both practitioners and policymakers involved in regional initiatives as well as researchers working to understand the dynamics of such initiatives.

Introduction

The life sciences industry and, even more so, the biotechnology industry are knowledge- and R&D-intensive industries in which new products and innovations develop at the interface between electronics, information technology, biomedicine, and drug discovery. Due to the possibility of value creation through high returns and increased employment, some regions around the globe are competing to become world leaders in life sciences by implementing government-supported initiatives. For example, 41 states in the U.S. recently launched their own life science initiative as have other areas of the world such as Germany, Singapore, the United Kingdom, Saudi Arabia, and the Netherlands (Ketels, 2005). Often, the primary intent of these initiatives is to improve competitiveness by promoting the region's innovative capability and interaction between the region's local firms, public and private research organizations, financial institutions, governmental organizations, institutions for collaboration, and specialized service companies. Yet, while regions continue to increase their efforts and new regions are constantly entering the arena, there has been little effort to transfer knowledge and learning from one initiative to another.

In this chapter, we present an in-depth study of one such initiative, Uppsala BIO–The Life Science Initiative, located in Uppsala, Sweden. The Uppsala region is appoximately 50 miles (65 kilometers) to the north of Stockholm, and it has been increasingly receiving recognition during the past five years as one of the world's strongest and most dynamic biotechnology regions (Cooke, 2004a, 2004b). In order to further support the region's development and competitiveness, local representatives from government, industry, and academia came together to create Uppsala BIO–The Life Science Initiative. This initiative received considerable government and local funding in Swedish standards in the second half of 2003. The purpose of this chapter is to describe the activities of this initiative during its first 18 months, to present some reflections on the organization itself gathered through a longitudinal study involving participant observations by the authors, and to discuss the initiative's impact on the region. Thus, this chapter is relevant to both practitioners and policymakers who are involved in regional initiatives as well as researchers working to understand the dynamics of such initiatives.

This chapter is organized as follows. First, we present a discussion of the relevant cluster and regional innovation systems' concepts in order to provide some background regarding why the interest and implementation of such initiatives have grown in recent years. Second, we provide a brief history and overview of Uppsala and its biotech industry. The third section presents the background of Uppsala BIO–The Life Science Initiative, while the fourth section discusses Uppsala BIO's four primary areas of activities during its first 18 months. The next section focuses on some observations and reflections on Uppsala BIO's organization. Finally, before concluding the chapter, we discuss how Uppsala BIO and its activities have impacted the development and competitiveness of the Uppsala biotech cluster and its firms.

The Importance of Clusters and Regional Innovation Systems

Since the publication in 1990 of Michael Porter's book, *The Competitive Advantage of Nations*, the cluster concept has been circulated widely and used in both academic as well as policy circles. However, while the term *cluster* is widespread, no one universal definition of the term exists. Thus, for the purposes of this chapter, we define a cluster as a spatial agglomeration of similar and related economic- and knowledge-creating activities.

The work on clusters is based on four broad assertions. First, in today's knowledge-based economy, the ability to innovate is more important than cost efficiency in determining the long-term ability of firms to prosper. Innovation is defined broadly here as the ability to develop new and better ways of organizing the production and marketing of new and better products (Grant, 1996; Lundvall, 1992; Nelson, 1993; Nonaka, 1994; Porter, 1990). This does not mean that cost considerations are not important but simply that the combined forces of the globalization of markets and the deepening divisions of labor make it increasingly difficult to base a competitive position on cost advantage only.

Second, innovations predominantly occur as a result of interactions among various actors rather than as a result of a solitary genius (Håkansson, 1987 Lundvall, 1992; von Hippel, 1988). This fits with a Schumpeterian view of innovations as new combinations of already existing knowledge, ideas, and artifacts (Schumpeter, 1934). Additionally, most innovations are based on some form of problem solving in which someone generally perceives a problem and turns to someone else for help and advice. In an industrial context, these interactions often follow the value chain. A firm facing a particular problem turns to a supplier, a customer, a competitor, or some other related actor in order to get help in specifying the problem and defining the terms for its solution. From this, it follows that the level of analysis for understanding the processes of industrial innovation and change is some notion of an industrial system or network of actors carrying out similar and related economic activities. The cluster, then, is basically an attempt to conceptualize an industrial system.

Third, and this is where geography enters the picture, there are a number of reasons why interactive learning and innovation processes are not spaceless or global; on the contrary, they unfold in a way in which geographical space plays an active role. Spatial proximity carries with it, among other things, the potential for intensified face-to-face interactions, short cognitive distance, common language, trustful relations among various actors, easy observations, and immediate comparisons (Malmberg & Maskell, 2002). In short, spatial proximity seems to enhance the processes of interactive learning and innovation; therefore, it should be assumed that industrial systems have a distinctly localized component.

Fourth and finally, an implication of the previous is that there are reasons to believe that the knowledge structures of a given geographical territory are more important than other characteristics such as general factor supply, production costs, and so forth, when it comes to determining where we should expect economic growth and prosperity in today's world economy (Malmberg & Maskell, 2002).

Thus, the cluster perspective provides a way to describe the systemic nature of an economy; in other words, how various types of industrial activities are related. This way of approaching the systemic nature of economic activity has much in its favor. It opens up a scope for analyzing interactions and interdependencies among firms and industries across a wide spectrum of economic activities. An additional advantage is that it contributes to the bridging of a number of more or less artificial and chaotic conceptual divides that characterize so much work in economic geography and related disciplines. These include, for example, manufacturing vs. services, high technology vs. low technology, large vs. small-to-medium-sized companies, public vs. private activities, and so forth. Thus, a single cluster defined as a functional industrial system may embrace firms, actors, and activities on both sides of each of these divides.

Regional Innovation Systems

Much related to clusters is the concept of regional innovation systems, or the networks of organizations, institutions, and individuals within which the creation, dissemination, and exploitation of new knowledge and innovations occur (Cooke, Heidenreich, & Braczyk, 2004). The regional innovation system concept has been introduced in order to describe how the industrial and institutional structure of a given national or regional economy tends to steer technological and industrial development onto certain trajectories. As such, there is a stronger focus on innovation and on the way the research system and the regulations for immaterial property rights are organized in the regional innovation system perspective rather than in the cluster perspective.

While there are differences between clusters and regional innovation systems, there are also many similarities. Groups of similar and related firms (e.g., large and small firms, suppliers, service providers, customers, rivals, etc.) comprise the core of the cluster, while academic and research organizations, policy institutions, authorities, financial actors, and various institutions for collaboration and networks make up the innovation system of which the cluster is a part. Both concepts have as their point of departure that innovation and industrial transformation are the result of interactions across sets of actors, and they both adopt a geographical starting point by emphasizing that this interaction takes place in a spatially defined territory, such as countries and regions.

Much of the extant literature on regional innovation systems and clusters tends to focus on formal interactions among actors; however, there is increasing evidence of the importance of informal interactions, as well. For example, Saxenian (1996) proposes in a well-known study that one of the primary reasons for the relative success of the Silicon Valley area over that of Route 128 in Boston is that knowledge is easily shared through informal relationships among individuals belonging to competing firms as well as other organizations in the Silicon Valley region. This is in direct contrast to the Route 128 area in Boston, where informal interorganizational fraternization was discouraged.

In response to this increasing interest in clusters and regional innovation systems, many governments and industry organizations around the globe have turned to these concepts in recent years as a means to stimulate urban and regional economic growth. As a result, a large number of regional competitiveness or cluster initiatives was started during the 1990s, and the trend continues, as evidenced by the 2005 Global Cluster Initiative Survey in which more than 1,400 such cluster initiatives around the globe were identified (Ketels, Lindqvist & Sölvell, n.d.). In the next section, we provide a brief history and overview of Uppsala, Sweden, before we present the region's cluster initiative, Uppsala BIO.

Uppsala and the Uppsala Biotech Industry

Similar to other biotechnology-intensive regions around the globe, Uppsala is the result of a close historical relationship between industry and academia, and it traces its origin back to a number of researchers and research findings at Uppsala University. These include the development of the ultracentrifuge by Nobel Laureate Theodor (The) Svedberg (1926), research on serum proteins by Nobel Laureate Arne Tiselius (1948), and the discovery and development by Gunnar O. Johansson, Hans Bennich, and Leif Wide of the immunoglobulin E (IgE antibody) used in allergy diagnosis and treatment. Additionally, in order to be located physically near leading research, one of the leading pharmaceutical companies at the time, Pharmacia, relocated its business from Stockholm to Uppsala in the 1950s. Today, the development and production of biotechnology methods, instruments, and research tools is considered to be the traditional core of the Uppsala cluster, leading to an international reputation as "the city of methods."

The Uppsala region employs approximately 5,000 individuals in almost 100 active biotech companies, of which more than one-third have been founded since 1995. Moreover, almost 10% of the total Uppsala workforce is employed in biotech-related activities in industry, academia, or government organizations. In terms of the research environment, Uppsala University and the Swedish University of Agricultural Sciences (SLU) encompass more than 900 researchers and graduate 900 students each year in biotechnology-related areas. An academic hospital as well as several research centers serve as customers, suppliers, and knowledge resources for Uppsala's biotech companies. Additionally, the universities have created business centers and holding companies that work specifically with the commercialization of research results, while there are a number of related national government authorities, such as the National Veterinary Institute, the Medical Products Agency, and the National Food Administration, that together employ around 1,200 individuals.

Recently, Uppsala has seen the growth of an extensive sector of specialized services firms, such as patenting, legal advice, business development, recruiting, auditing, and marketing. Finally, a number of local organizations has as an explicit objective to stimulate the development of the region (e.g., STUNS [Foundation for Collaboration between Uppsala's Universities, the Business Community, and Society], the Uppsvenska Chamber of Com-

Table 1. Estimated number of actors in the Uppsala biotech cluster in 2002/2003 (Waxell, 2005)

Cluster Components	No. of Firms/ Organizations	Estimated No. of Employees
Biotech firms	83	5,000
Public and private research organizations	18	2,500
Financial organizations	11	200
Supporting and complementary organizations	48	300
Total	160	8,000

merce, and Invest in Uppsala). These organizations act as meeting points for representatives from industry, academia, and local and regional authorities (Waxell, 2005). As presented in Table 1, the life science sector as a whole is estimated to employ 8,000 people in Uppsala, which accounts for almost 18% of the total employment in the life sciences sector in Sweden (Waxell, 2005).[1]

In addition, the Uppsala region has a sound basis for being a strong, dynamic biotechnology cluster. For example, the region continues to produce outstanding research in terms of both quantity and quality, and it has a long tradition of successfully commercializing this research. There is a relatively large number of startups and established companies across the whole span of the biotech sector, several of which are world leaders in their fields. Moreover, Uppsala is a region that is used to rapid change, since it has weathered the dismantling of Pharmacia in Uppsala. This dismantling has led to numerous startups and seasoned entrepreneurs who have experienced all aspects of the biotech sector and have a strong customer and market focus and understanding.

Uppsala BIO: The Life Science Initiative for Improving Regional Competitiveness

In 2002, the Vinnväxt program run by the Swedish Agency for Innovation Systems (Vinnova) was initiated when the first call for regional development proposals was launched. Vinnväxt's primary objective is to promote sustainable growth and international competitiveness in functionally defined regions by supporting initiatives that result from the coordinated actions of companies, academia, and the public sector. The program is designed as a competition in which regional teams compete for financial support of up to $100 million SEK, or approximately $13 million U.S., over a period of 10 years. While the program offers government support, a prerequisite is that the region has local sponsors that match the Vinnväxt funding. In other words, the money paid by Vinnväxt to the regional initiative must be matched by equal support from the region's organizations either in the form of cash or hourly labor. For example, if the local initiative is successful in raising only $8 million SEK (approx. US$1 million) one year, then Vinnväxt will pay only $8 million SEK (approx. US$1 million) for that year. More information on Vinnova and Vinnväxt can be found at www.vinnova.se.

In the first Vinnväxt call in 2002, Vinnova received 150 Vinnväxt proposals across Sweden, and of these, 25 proposals made the first cut and received a planning grant to be spent on developing a full Vinnväxt application. In June 2003, Vinnova then selected from a pool of these 25 applicants plus a handful of additional Vinnväxt pilot projects three recipients of the Vinnväxt grants, of which Uppsala BIO was one. (While Uppsala BIO won the Vinnväxt 2002 competition, the initiative actually dates back to 2001, when a pilot project headed by Uppsala University's Holding Company [UU AB] found that the collaboration among industry, academia, and the public sector needed to be increased in order to promote the long-term growth of the region in biotechnology.) As a recipient of Vinnväxt, Uppsala BIO received the necessary added resources to support this collaboration.

Uppsala BIO is organized not as a legal entity but as a project under STUNS—the Foundation for Collaboration between Uppsala's Universities, the Business Community, and Society. As such, it does not have a board, but rather a steering committee. This steering

Figure 1. The Uppsala BIO organization (December 2004)

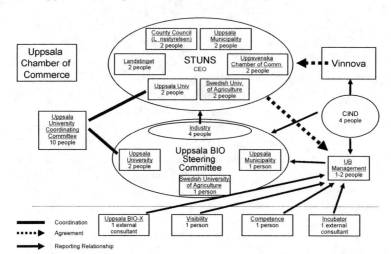

committee reflects the initiative's commitment to increasing collaboration among academia, industry, and government, and it comprises senior executives and leading figures from Uppsala's leading biotech companies, top county officials, and influential individuals within Uppsala's universities (Figure 1). More information on Uppsala BIO can be found at www.uppsalabio.com .

Uppsala BIO's underlying driving goal is to enhance value creation for the region by increasing the number of new, qualified jobs within the life sciences sector, improving economic growth, and strengthening the region's academic and industrial attractiveness and competitiveness. The vision for the initiative, as stated in the original Vinnväxt application, is the following:

Within a period of five years, the Uppsala-Stockholm region will be one of the world's five leading biotechnology regions supported by a sustainable competitive industrial base, world-class research and education, and a good climate for companies, academics, and employees. In this region, Uppsala will be the center for the research and development of research methods, models, and tools within biotechnology research.

One of the conditions of the Vinnväxt program was that grant recipients work together with academia in order to ensure that learning and knowledge created during the 10 years could be captured and disseminated to other Vinnväxt participants. As a result, Uppsala BIO contracted CIND, the Centre for Research on Innovation and Industrial Development, at Uppsala University (www.cind.se) to facilitate this process by monitoring, analyzing, reflecting upon, and giving advice regarding all aspects of Uppsala BIO's activities. This chapter is the result of this cooperation. During the period of June 2003 to December 2004, the CIND team conducted 29 interviews with individuals in Uppsala BIO, academia, industry, and government in the Uppsala region, as well as participant observation in 29 meetings, such as steering committee and project management meetings. In addition, the team conducted an online questionnaire of the region's various actors during the winter of 2004 in order to collect baseline statistical and social network interaction data.[2]

Uppsala BIO: The First 18 Months

As previously mentioned, Uppsala BIO's vision is that within a period of five years, the Uppsala-Stockholm region will be one of the world's five leading biotechnology regions. However, this is a very broad goal, so one of the first steps of Uppsala BIO was to break down the vision into clear, attainable, and measurable goals. In order to do so, the Uppsala BIO team performed an analysis of the challenges facing the region and found the following:

- Difficulty in attracting capital for investment and growth in the region's small and medium-sized companies and a poor international collaboration network to attract investment to Uppsala.

- Tendency in recent years for commercial ideas to disappear from the region through sales and licensing.

- An unstable pipeline of new and realistic product ideas arising from innovative individuals and research.

- A declining supply of skilled and specialized labor for current and future companies of all sizes.

The region and Uppsala BIO faced a further challenge in that Uppsala is small, and as a result, resources are limited. Thus, Uppsala BIO established the guiding principle that while it should initiate and support new activities, all of these activities should be owned and operated by already established regional actors. Thus, Uppsala BIO's primary role in the region's development is a facilitator rather than an operator of various activities. Uppsala BIO may act as an external coordinator when no other natural coordinator exists, and it provides funding for activities that would contribute significantly to the end goal. Thus, Uppsala BIO supports and collaborates with existing regional actors who initiate, run, and own Uppsala BIO activities. In this manner, Uppsala BIO aspires to leverage and use efficiently the region's resources so that the region becomes strong in every aspect—an industry that attracts the most skilled individuals, universities that attract the best students, and a local community and infrastructure that attracts people to settle in Uppsala.

In addition, Uppsala BIO also decided to determine a focus in terms of what kind of life science activities it primarily should support or prioritize. It was decided that this focus would build upon the main strengths of Uppsala—methods, models, and tools for biotechnological research. This was not to imply that this would be the only area in which Uppsala would excel, since in Uppsala, there are several successful companies providing products in other areas such as drug development. However, in order to ensure the maximum return on expended resources in the shortest term, Uppsala BIO felt that it was important to focus, wherever relevant, on its areas of existing strength.

Figure 2. Four focus areas and their relationships

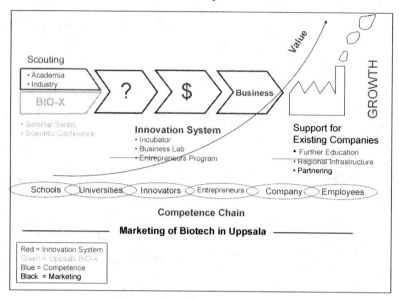

Four Focus Areas

Uppsala BIO's guiding principle in determining its primary focus areas was to examine the region's innovation and commercialization chain and to determine which areas needed support in order to ensure a dynamic and productive value creation chain. Based on this underlying principle and the initiative's analysis of challenges and resources, Uppsala BIO defined the following four focus areas that would best help it to move toward its vision (Figure 2):

1.   To promote cross-disciplinary biotech research with a strong product focus through the establishment of Uppsala BIO-X, a cross-disciplinary center for research on methods, models, and tools (green area in Figure 2).

2.   To strengthen the region's innovation system through activities such as the development of an incubator (red area in Figure 2).

3.   To ensure a long-term supply of relevant competence to the region (blue area in Figure 2).

4.   To improve the region's national and international visibility in order to attract investment and competence (black area in Figure 2).

Next, we discuss the goal, strategy, and initial activities of each of these four areas.

1.   *To promote cross-disciplinary biotech research with a strong product focus through the establishment of Uppsala BIO-X, a cross-disciplinary center for research on methods, models, and tools.*

As mentioned previously, Uppsala BIO-X is the cross-disciplinary research effort focused on Tools for Life Science. Its projects are based on cutting-edge science with the potential to generate new product opportunities for today's and tomorrow's life sciences industry.

Goals

The overriding goal of Uppsala BIO-X is to initiate and support ambitious, world-class, cross-disciplinary research projects in the region by making available supplementary funding and resources. In line with this is the goal to develop a working model for a viable interface between research and industry. This relies, in turn, on developing a mindset among researchers that involves understanding the principles of market needs and product development as well as increasing the opportunities for contacts between industrialists and researchers.

Strategy

The strategy of Uppsala BIO-X involves funding a small number of cross-disciplinary research projects that then will be commercialized through local startups. In addition to being cross-disciplinary, potential projects also must (1) engage in problems of relevance to society, industry, and research, (2) be commercially viable, and (3) reflect areas of strengths in the region. Uppsala BIO's management selects the projects with support from a scientific advisory board comprised of five internationally recognized scientists from both academia and industry.

The Swedish University of Agricultural Sciences and Uppsala University constitute the foundation of the effort. Local life science companies also lend their active support by making industrial researchers and infrastructure available to Uppsala BIO-X projects. The strategy for the future development of Uppsala BIO-X includes building upon the base that already exists; for example, by organizing research seminars and conferences with a focus on market need by publicizing progress and activities and by extending networks of collaborators.

Activities

The first step was for the leader of Uppsala BIO-X, a hired consultant, to develop a strategy and project plan that was based on the original guidelines in the Vinnväxt application. Once this plan was approved and the scientific advisory board was appointed in the first half of 2004, the next step was to run a call for proposals. The first project was initiated in June 2004 (Tools for High-throughput Analyses of Microbial Communities) in close collaboration with an existing Uppsala biotech company, Olink AB. This project then worked to develop a bioanalytical microchip designed to receive a blood sample from a patient and be able to communicate the test results to expert systems via the Internet or cell phones.

After the initial project, Uppsala BIO spent considerable time developing routines among Uppsala BIO-X and the involved universities, such as budgeting, follow-up, and so forth. The second Uppsala BIO-X project then was chosen in late fall of 2004 (Lab on Chip—Point

Figure 3. The innovation system

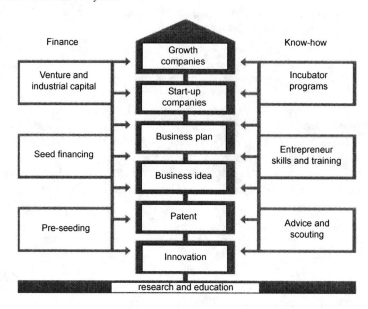

of Care). This process was much quicker, since the majority of routines was already in place. More information on the first two projects can be found at www.uppsalabio.com.

2.   *To strengthen the regional innovation system.*

An innovation system is a chain of support for business ideas (Figure 3), which includes the transfer of knowledge from experienced individuals and organizations (right-hand side of the figure) and the possibility of financing (left-hand side) at each stage of a value chain.

Goal

The goal of the innovation system focus area is to develop a complete, unbroken chain of support for business projects, from a professional and thorough analysis of their potential to a stage in which they can be valued and commercialized (as either a new company, a project within an existing company, or an outlicensing). Ideas may emerge from research (Uppsala BIO-X is one such source) or from private individuals, or they may be ideas or projects that cannot be supported within local industry. Individuals with business ideas and entrepreneurial ambitions then should be directed to an appropriate instance of support and advice to develop their ideas.

Strategy

Uppsala BIO's role in the innovation system is to be a central coordinator. Uppsala traditionally has had a significant number of organizations and individuals involved in scouting for and supporting of business ideas. The sheer variety and number of these prevents the system from being transparent and causes the dilution of valuable resources. Thus, Uppsala BIO needed to find points of symbiosis and to gather critical mass in support, advice, and financing.

Activities

During the spring of 2004, Uppsala BIO conducted three activities directed at the initial steps of the innovation system: (1) execution of a benchmarking study of scouting in several areas of Sweden; (2) patent strategy advising; and (3) designing the contents of a business lab and entrepreneurs program together with CEF of Uppsala University (the Centre for Entrepreneurship and Enterprise Development, www.cef.uu.se). The scouting project was commissioned to CIND and was designed to improve the ability to scout for new ideas at universities and in industry that were worthy of commercializing in Uppsala. The purpose of the business lab was to improve the early business development processes in startups with a focus on developing complete business plans; the first group of business lab companies was accepted in November 2004. Additionally, the entrepreneurs program was directed at individuals who were interested in starting companies yet were unsure as to the commercial viability of their ideas. The first group of students entered in the spring of 2005.

In December 2004, the local incubator, Uppsala Innovation Centre (UIC), succeeded in obtaining four years of financing. As a result, the aforementioned three activities were handed over to UIC's management, and Uppsala BIO decided to focus its resources on further strengthening and building upon UIC's structure. More information on UIC can be found at www.uic.se.

3.   *To ensure a long-term supply of relevant competence to the region*

The focus area of ensuring a supply of relevant competence to the Uppsala region involves the entire chain of competence supply, from primary schools to higher education.

Goal

Securing the availability of suitably trained and skilled people for the biotech industry as well as for the academic sector is a long-term strategic goal of Uppsala BIO. This involves the entire chain of competence supply from attracting young people to science subjects in grammar schools to offering state-of-the art, higher education programs and providing leadership programs and further education that are vital both for existing and budding biotech companies.

Strategy

In line with its overall operating strategy, Uppsala BIO decided to provide services for networking and coordination as well as to offer financing in order for well-planned and effective activities to facilitate collaboration and communication between the important players, such as schools, universities, and industry.

Activities

Uppsala BIO has identified several activities within this area.

- **Attracting students to science:** To provide a continuous supply of competence, individuals of all ages need to be attracted to science. One of the first places to start is primary education. It is of fundamental importance to educate primary school teachers in creating useful, inspiring education in biotechnology. Uppsala BIO supported a biotechnology week for primary school teachers in October 2004. Additionally, it cooperated with Uppsala University in organizing activities for attracting youngsters to university education. Industry also plays a very important part both in attracting youngsters to select the natural sciences in school as well as providing input into the content of university courses, and one of Uppsala BIO's activities is, thus, to coordinate many of the industry-led activities that occur today.

- **Empowering entrepreneurship and leadership:** As an important part in building the industry of the future, Uppsala BIO supports and stimulates budding entrepreneurs primarily through UIC-organized training courses (see previous section) but also by drawing attention to activities organized by others. Uppsala BIO plans to conduct a project-leadership training program in the fall of 2005 in response to the acute need for experienced project leaders by the region's biotech companies.

- **Supporting infrastructure development:** Through a cofinancing agreement with the City Council in Uppsala, a number of resources has been reserved for representing the needs of the biotech sector in developing the infrastructure in Uppsala. Issues include local transportation, accommodation, and development of a local high school.

- **Promoting gender management as a tool for improving competitiveness:** An important issue for the success of companies is to empower employees to achieve their very best. Uppsala BIO will take part in a government-funded gender initiative that is built on the premise that an active gender management program can contribute to a company's overall profitability.

4.   *To improve the region's national and international visibility in order to attract investment and competence*

One important aspect of a region's competitiveness is the visibility and reputation of the region in national, European, and global arenas.

Goals

The overall goals of Uppsala BIO's visibility program involve marketing Uppsala as an internationally attractive and leading biotech region in order to (1) attract international investment in the form of capital and competence to Uppsala's biotech sector; (2) support existing biotech companies and organizations, particularly foreign-owned ones, so that they retain their operations in Uppsala; (3) secure long-term, local support of Uppsala BIO's action plan by communicating Uppsala BIO's activities to its partners; and (4) increase the general awareness of the importance of biotechnology in Uppsala.

Strategy

The strategy for achieving the above goals included identifying the relevant target group(s) for each of the goals and defining the specific and unique strengths and competitive advantages of Uppsala, as further described in the following section.

Table 2. Summary of types of activities for specific visibility goals

Goal	Target Groups	Activities
Attract capital and competence to Uppsala's biotech sector	Investors Industry leaders Key international researchers	PR and media Exhibitions, trade shows (e.g., Biotech Forum) Partnering with Invest in Sweden Agency, Business Arena Stockholm, and Invest in Uppsala BIO-X Science Conference Web site (www.uppsalabio.com) Newsletter, subscription available through Web site Brochure "Biotech Hotbed? Uppsala BIO!"
Support existing biotech activities; make them stay	Investors Industry leaders Uppsala biotech customers Research groups' partners Key international researchers	PR and media Partnering with Invest in Sweden Agency, Business Arena Stockholm, and Invest in Uppsala Information kits Web site
Secure partners' long-term interest in and support of Uppsala BIO's action plan	Cofinancers Other biotech parties in Uppsala	PR and media BIO-Pubs, monthly informal gatherings based on a theme (e.g., risk, the deal of the year, together with CONNECT) Web site Newsletter
Increase general awareness of biotechnology in Uppsala	Uppsala locals Politicians	Biotech in Town, a one-day annual open house activity for people of all ages

Activities

One of the primary activities initially was to secure long-term support by improving the internal information to the cofinancers of Uppsala BIO. This activity proved to be quite time-consuming, since the project had to develop the proper meeting and communication form with almost 90 organizations and individuals. One major event organized for the co-financers was a strategy day in January 2004, in which cofinancers were invited to discuss the operational strategy of Uppsala BIO. Table 2 provides an overview of the other activities conducted by Uppsala BIO that related to its specific visibility focus area.

Creating an Effective Regional Competitiveness Initiative: Observations of and Reflections on Uppsala BIO

Having presented Uppsala BIO and its first 18 months of activities, we now turn to our re-flections on the organization of Uppsala BIO that we gathered during our role as participant observers during this time.

An Effective Organization: An Internal Perspective

Within the organizational development and leadership literatures, there is a number of fac-tors that are necessary in order to ensure the long-term effectiveness of an organization that has many different types of actors through fulfilling both its strategic and operational goals as well as through satisfying the goals and demands of the actors involved within a limited time frame (Katzenbach & Smith, 1993; Mankins et al., 2004). In brief, these include the following:

- An open and trusting culture
- Shared language and values
- An appropriate legal organizational form
- An appropriately staffed organization
- Strong leadership
- A well-formulated work plan
- An effective decision process
- A long-term communication strategy

In the following section, we use these to structure our discussion on some of the factors for success for an effective regional initiative. Our intention is not to provide a how-to list but rather to provide a few points for consideration. To do so, we highlight our discussion with some examples from Uppsala BIO as well as pose one or more questions at the end of each point that regional initiatives similar to Uppsala BIO should consider.

An Open and Trusting Culture

In order for any project organization to be successful, it is important that there is an environment in which different opinions can be raised and discussed. While discussions in Uppsala BIO's steering committee were open and included many different actors, initially a number of decisions appeared to have been made already in closed, informal situations before the meetings began. This can be seen as an indicator of the strong social network in which many, but not all, of Uppsala BIO's steering committee members participate. As a result, the challenge was for those who were not members of this network to make their opinions heard. Thus, there is a danger that a strong informal network may dominate the formal management of such a regional initiative, especially when the purpose of such an initiative is to bring together people from different organizations who might not have worked together previously.

- How can an initiative ensure that the pre-existing social network among different actors does not hinder openness in the management of a regional initiative?
- How can the initiative ensure that new blood and new opinions are incorporated into the initiative's management?

Shared Language and Values

Regional development projects that are successful often are well-anchored in both the region's industry and key opinion leaders before they begin. Uppsala BIO fulfilled both these criteria, which enabled the project to get started quickly. However, once the project was initiated, it was discovered that the members of the steering committee differed in their understandings of several things. Interestingly, one of these areas was in terms of the time perspective of the project. Generally speaking (and perhaps unexpectedly), the industry representatives had a longer time perspective than did the public sector representatives. The public sector actors were interested in seeing more immediate results, such as increased employment. Additionally, different actors had different definitions of the same concept; for example, a work plan. In this case, there was some confusion as to whether a work plan should be a living document underway with room for changes or a document in which activities were set in stone. These different definitions and time perspectives led to time-consuming discussions, and activities sometimes heading in different directions.

- Do the different members of the initiative have a common understanding of the initiative's strategy as well as the time perspective and central terminology?

An Appropriate Legal Organizational Form

As already mentioned, STUNS (the Foundation for Collaboration between Uppsala's Universities, the Business Community, and Society) is the project owner of Uppsala BIO.

In this manner, Uppsala BIO differs from other regional initiatives in Sweden, since it is not a legal entity but rather one project within a larger organization. As a result, STUNS is responsible for Uppsala BIO's management and is the employer of the project's personnel. However, STUNS has delegated the strategic operations of the project to Uppsala BIO's steering committee and the day-to-day operations to Uppsala BIO's management. While this legal arrangement works fine in terms of Uppsala BIO's management, an unforeseen taxation issue unrelated to its legal organizational form has arisen. The government questions whether Uppsala BIO really is providing a commercial service or if it is just working for the common good of the region. To date, the government maintains that Uppsala BIO is the latter and, thus, not entitled to deduct the sales tax (25%) that it pays on a number of expenses that it has, such as external consulting and supplies. This is an issue that is still not resolved, despite several discussions with the tax authorities and, unfortunately, one that could have a considerable negative effect on the already limited resources of the project.

- What form of legal organization is the most appropriate for the initiative's activities?
- What taxation and other financial issues need to be considered?

An Appropriately Staffed Organization

A long-term perspective and continuity in Uppsala BIO are ensured though involving leading companies and other key players with significant resources in the region. Experiences from several other regional initiatives in Sweden have shown that local heroes, top executives, and key opinion leaders are often necessary initially in order to raise awareness of the initiative as well as to ensure its longevity. However, these individuals may not be able to fulfill the day-to-day needs of an initiative due to considerable demands on their time. Thus, one criterion for success is to recruit one or more middle-level managers from industry and involve them in both the strategic and operational activities. These individuals should have the knowledge as well as the energy and legitimacy to drive the process forward.

Additionally, Uppsala BIO's recruitment of its management, for the most part, was based on using existing local networks. While these tight networks support trusting and open relationships, as mentioned previously, there is a risk that these relationships may close out individuals not in these networks, and as a result, the introduction of new ideas may be hindered.

- What mix of individuals should be incorporated in the initiative's management (key opinion leaders vs. people who have time to involve themselves)?
- How should individuals be recruited for the initiative?

A second point for discussion is the role that external consultants play. Uppsala BIO was heavily dependent on external consultants with several going in and out of the project's management team in the initial phases. On the whole, this arrangement did provide some value in terms of management being able to accomplish several activities initially. However, it is important to question how this turnover affected the knowledge accumulated by the project over time, since when these consultants left, they took their knowledge with them. Additionally, this turnover might have affected the impression that other actors in Uppsala had of Uppsala BIO (i.e., is Uppsala BIO just a temporary organization)?

- Which initiative activities should be kept in-house so that knowledge remains with the organization?
- If external consultants are to be used, how can an initiative ensure that their knowledge is retained by the initiative?

Strong Leadership

Due to the often conflicting goals of the initiative's supporters (academia, industry, and government), management must be strong enough to follow its own lines while ensuring that all stakeholders' demands are handled adequately. Additionally, the management's members should be able to work together in a team. These teams, however, should not be seen as static, but rather they should be flexible in order to accommodate the development or discontinuation of initiative activities. Finally, as in the startup of almost any organization, it is important that management has a broad network and is able to command the required resources from this network.

- What is the right profile of the initiative's management?

A Well-Formulated Work Plan

A project plan should not be set in stone. A significant part of the dynamics of an effective organization is the ability to take a step back, reflect, and make necessary changes. Uppsala BIO's workplan was continuously under construction during the first 18 months. At one point, however, it hired an external consultant to perform some of the work, because there was a feeling that a final document needed to be produced. This proved to be unproductive, since this external person had not been involved in the project's activities. As a result, Uppsala BIO now understands that it is necessary to have someone on the management team to complete this task, since it is not necessarily the document itself but the process that is the most important.

- What purpose should a workplan serve?
- What format should it have (e.g., how often should it be updated, who should be involved)?

An Effective Decision Process

Both the overarching management (e.g., the steering committee or the board) and the daily management fill important roles for any initiative. However, in order to ensure an effective decision process, strategic issues and operational issues should be discussed separately. In the case of Uppsala BIO, many operational issues were discussed in the steering committee meetings, which often led to very long and inefficient meetings. For example, project leaders would inform the steering committee in detail of their daily activities, and as a result, the steering committee members often would ask detailed, low-level questions. Thus, it is important to ensure that the right questions and topics are presented in the right forum.

- What questions are the appropriate ones for the steering committee or board?

A Long-Term Communication Strategy

As previously discussed, it is important that management focuses its communication efforts on actively marketing and making visible the initiative both internally within the region and to the outside world. In this manner, the initiative can both gain support from local actors and encourage investment from organizations in other areas of the world.

- What efforts should the initiative make to market itself internally as well as externally and what is the appropriate balance between the two?
- How can the initiative ensure that realistic expectations are communicated without risking a decline in external interest in the initiative?

In summary, while Uppsala BIO did meet several obstacles during its first 18 months, the organization was able to put many of the aforementioned factors in place and, as such, appears to be on its way to fulfilling its vision and goals. Next, we take a closer look at the outcomes and impacts of Uppsala BIO's initial activities.

Impact of the Uppsala BIO Initiative on the Development and Competitiveness of the Uppsala Biotech Cluster

As mentioned in the previous section on clusters and regional innovation systems, some of the main factors underlying economic development and competitiveness include the level of formal and informal interaction among actors, the learning and knowledge sharing that occurs through these interactions, as well as the degree of innovation within the cluster. As a result, many cluster initiatives tend to focus on promoting interaction among actors with the hope of improving learning and knowledge sharing in addition to improving the conditions necessary for innovation, and Uppsala BIO is no exception. Next, we discuss Uppsala BIO's activities in terms of its effects on interaction and innovation within the cluster. We also take a look at cluster performance indicators. It is important to note, however, that the first 18 months of Uppsala BIO have been a period of setting up the structure for Uppsala BIO-X and organizing its other activities; thus, it is still too early for Uppsala BIO to have had any significant impact on the cluster's economic development and competitiveness.

Promoting Interaction

As mentioned earlier, Uppsala BIO is embedded in an environment characterized by strong local networks and a high degree of interaction among its actors. While on the one hand this may lead to openness and trust among the actors in these networks, these networks tend to include actors from similar backgrounds and/or organizations. Previous research has shown that such closed networks can lead to core rigidities or inappropriate knowledge sets that preserve the status quo and limit new insights, which result in gaps between the knowledge of the region and the changing market conditions (Leonard-Barton, 1992; Levitt & March, 1988), thus negatively impacting the development of a cluster.

While not explicitly stated in Uppsala BIO's vision or four activity focus areas, one of the underlying outcomes of Uppsala BIO's various activities is the promotion of interaction between previously poorly connected sets of diverse actors in the cluster (e.g., firms, public and private research organizations, financial institutions, governmental organizations, specialized service companies). In terms of formal interaction, to begin with Uppsala BIO in itself is a rather unique organization, a public-private partnership bringing together actors from industry, academia, and the public sector. These different actors tend to have conflicting goals and values and a relatively low level of trust for one another (Klijn & Teisman, 2003). However, bringing them together under the umbrella of one organization facilitates the development of a common language, a shared understanding, and trustful relations among them. The creation of Uppsala BIO has led to an increased common understanding among its members of the cluster's underlying strengths and weaknesses as well as what needs to be done to improve its competitiveness.[3] Additionally, Uppsala BIO-X promotes an increased level of formal interaction between Uppsala's two major universities by bringing together researchers as well as an increased level of interaction between academia and commercial firms through its focus on project commercialization.

In terms of informal interaction, Uppsala BIO's activities bring together actors in a variety of settings in which individuals may interact and network informally with one another. For example, the strategy day in January 2004 brought together approximately 100 individuals from industry, academia, and the public sector. Some of the day's activities included group work and discussions that led to numerous new connections among individuals. Other activities that led to new connections and increased interaction across sets of actors are Uppsala BIO's entrepreneurship, project-leadership training and educational programs, and biotech open houses. One of its most popular activities has been the Uppsala BIO-X research seminar series and monthly pubs, which present a variety of biotech topics and are open to anyone.

While this focuses primarily on promoting interaction among local actors, this local interaction should be put into perspective. A cluster's boundaries are difficult to define, and Uppsala is no exception to this. Since it is only approximately 41 miles (65 km) to the north of Stockholm, Uppsala could be considered to be a part of the greater Stockholm area, if one were to think in Silicon Valley terms. In addition to the Uppsala BIO initiative, there is also a biotech initiative in Stockholm as well as in Mälardalen, the region just east of Stockholm. To date, however, Uppsala BIO has focused primarily on promoting interaction within the narrowly defined Uppsala area; thus, a matter for discussion is to what degree and in what manner Uppsala BIO should cooperate and promote interaction with the other regions.

Interestingly, however, one of the underlying goals of Uppsala BIO's visibility and marketing efforts is an increased level of interaction with organizations and individuals from outside of Sweden, since one of its main activities is to attract capital and competence to Uppsala's biotech sector from Europe, the U.S., and, to some extent, Asia. Uppsala BIO's first 18 months of activities in these efforts have led to valuable learning about how to attract outside interest:

- Examples of interesting and successful individuals who learned valuable lessons and had an interesting story to tell were found to be more powerful in attracting interest than providing facts and numbers about Uppsala BIO.

- The image of Uppsala as a region with dynamic and modern, front-line developments was just as important as describing the region's long tradition of a world-class research standard.

- Focusing attention on the message was more important than focusing on the messenger, Uppsala BIO. The name of a provider or the appearance of a product is meaningless if the product itself and its benefits are not clearly understood. Source: Uppsala BIO, Strategy meeting January 2004

Promoting Innovation

The second primary means in which to improve a cluster's economic development and competitiveness is to promote the degree of innovation within the cluster. The following two Uppsala BIO focus areas are related specifically to this area: (1) to promote cross-disciplinary research through Uppsala BIO-X and (2) to strengthen the regional innovation system by being a central coordinator. In order to successfully promote innovation, these efforts need to lead to an increased degree and heightened speed of commercialized research. On a small scale, Uppsala BIO-X has been successful in achieving this, since it has successfully funded and started two research projects to be commercialized through local startups, and the number of applicants for new Uppsala BIO-X projects continues to increase. However, one of the main objectives of Uppsala BIO-X is to fund radically new cross-disciplinary projects that traditionally have difficulty receiving funding, because they often fall between departments and universities, and Uppsala BIO has been struggling with whether the first two Uppsala BIO-X projects really are something novel and cross-disciplinary or just more of the same.

As noted above, Uppsala BIO does promote innovation; however, the region seems to lack an overall strategy for the commercialization of its intellectual property. For example, in some instances, intellectual property may be commercialized within a firm in the region; however, it just as likely might be sold or licensed to a firm outside Uppsala or even outside Sweden all together. Already, a considerable amount of intellectual property has been bought by firms outside Sweden and, as a result, has been taken from Uppsala. One of the most well-known events is the sale of the successful company NeoPharma to Solvay Pharmaceuticals and the subsequent decision to move NeoPharma's operations out of Uppsala to Belgium. The question thus remains whether this exodus of intellectual property is beneficial for the Uppsala region in terms of economic development and increased competitiveness due to side effects such as an increased inflow of capital and success stories. Moreover, Uppsala BIO needs to make sure that its activities ensure the most beneficial outcomes of its innovation efforts for the cluster.

Relevant Performance Indicators

While the previous discussion provides an indication that the degree of interaction and innovation has increased due to Uppsala BIO, we are unable to determine how and if this has impacted Uppsala's competitiveness. A further important principle of Uppsala BIO's operating strategy, however, is to develop a means of measuring progress in its key activities, since measurable project goals are a critical part of assessing progress and success. In its original strategy document, Uppsala BIO specified a few quantitative goals: (1) doubled employment in biotech-related positions from 4,000 to 8,000 employees; (2) an increase in the number of biotech researchers at Uppsala University and SLU from 900 to 1,500; and (3) an increase in the region's gross regional product of 6% on average per year. However, while these may be relevant performance indicators for the cluster as a whole, it is difficult to determine what effect Uppsala BIO has on the numbers measured by these indicators. This is especially so since Uppsala BIO typically collaborates with and supports an already established actor in the cluster through the providing of resources in return for the ability to place certain demands on the actor's activities as opposed to initiating and leading its own activities.

Thus, the challenge for Uppsala BIO is to develop relevant performance indicators that can be measured. These may not necessarily be based only on results, but they also might be based on Uppsala BIO's activities. One action Uppsala BIO has taken was to create a baseline set of data through conducting a survey in 2004 of the region's actors. The survey included areas that looked at the degree of informal and formal interaction between various sets of actors; the perception of the cluster's competitiveness, strengths, and weaknesses; and expectations on Uppsala BIO. It is of interest to note that this survey found that respondents have quite high expectations of Uppsala BIO in terms of its improving the cluster's competitiveness. A second follow-up survey was conducted in 2006 with the objective of measuring how effective Uppsala BIO has been in improving the competitiveness of the cluster by comparing results from the two time periods in the aforementioned areas.[4]

Conclusion

In conclusion, the objective of this chapter was to present the initial activities of one regional competitiveness initiative, Uppsala BIO–The Life Science Initiative, and a set of reflections on this organization made by a group of participant researchers as well as a discussion of the initiative's impact on cluster development. As the number of these initiatives continues to grow, it is important that the learning from ongoing initiatives be disseminated to others so that valuable resources are not wasted through the reinvention of the wheel. In the case of Uppsala BIO, the initiative's management decided to focus on using its limited resources primarily to initiate regional activities in collaboration with existing cluster actors as opposed to initiating and leading its own activities. Through an analysis of the challenges and resources in the region's innovation and commercialization value chain, Uppsala BIO defined four focus areas: (1) promoting cross-disciplinary biotech research with a strong product focus through the establishment of a cross-disciplinary research center; (2) strengthening the region's innovation system through the development of an incubator in order to provide operative support for the commercialization of research findings; (3) ensuring the long-term supply of relevant competence to the region; and (4) improving the region's national and international visibility in order to attract investment and competence. Thus, our hope was that this chapter was relevant and provided insights into both practitioners and policymakers involved in cluster initiatives as well as researchers working to understand the dynamics of such initiatives.

Acknowledgments

The authors would like to acknowledge the extremely valuable encouragement and help they received from Madeleine Neil, Rhiannon Sanders, and Jonas Åström of Uppsala BIO in performing this research. They also would like to thank Dr. Anders Malmberg of CIND at Uppsala University for his significant input on the chapter's discussion of the relevant cluster and regional innovation systems concepts as well as guidance and support throughout this project and comments on previous versions of this chapter. Funding for this study and chapter were provided by Uppsala BIO, CIND, and the Jan Wallanders and Tom Hedelius Foundation.

References

Cooke, P. (2004a). Life sciences clusters and regional science policy. *Urban Studies*, *41*(5/6), 1113–1131.

Cooke, P. (2004b). The accelerating evolution of biotechnology clusters. *European Planning Studies*, *12*(7), 915–920.

Cooke, P., Heidenreich, M., & Braczyk, H.-J. (Eds.). (2004). *Regional innovation systems: The role of governances in a globalized world* (2nd ed.). London: Routledge.

Grant, R.M. (1996). Prospering in dynamically-competitive environments: Organizational capability as knowledge integration. *Organization Science, 7*(4), 375–387.

Håkansson, H. (1987). *Corporate technological behaviour: Co-operation and networks.* London: Routledge.

Katzenbach, J.R., & Smith, D.K. (1993). *The wisdom of teams: Creating the high-performance organization.* Boston: Harvard Business School Press.

Ketels, C. (2005). *Life sciences in the Nordic countries.* Proceedings of the Issues Shaping Nordic Competitiveness in Biotechnology Symposium, Stockholm.

Ketels, C., Lindqvist, G., & Sölvell, Ö. (n.d.). *Cluster initiatives in transition and developing economies.* United States Agency for Economic Development.

Klijn, E-H., & Teisman, G.R. (2003). Institutional and strategic barriers to public-private partnership: An analysis of Dutch cases. *Public Money & Management, 23*, 137-146.

Leonard-Barton, D. (1992). Core capabilities and core rigidities: A paradox in managing new product development. *Strategic Management Journal, 13* (Summer Special Issue), 111–126.

Levitt, B., & March, J.G. (1988). Organizational learning. *Annual Review of Sociology, 14*, 319–340.

Lundvall, B.-Å. (Ed.). (1992). *National systems of innovation: Towards a theory of innovation and interactive learning.* London: Pinter.

Malmberg, A., & Maskell, P. (2002). The elusive concept of localisation economies: Towards a knowledge-based theory of spatial clustering. *Environment and Planning, 34*(3), 429–449.

Mankins, M.C., et al. (2004). *What makes a decisive leadership team.* Boston: Harvard Business School Press.

Nelson, R. (Ed.). (1993). *National innovation systems: A comparative analysis.* Oxford: Oxford University Press.

Nonaka, I. (1994). A dynamic theory of organizational knowledge creation. *Organization Science, 5*, 14–37.

Porter, M.E. (1990). *The competitive advantage of nations.* Basingstoke: Macmillan.

Saxenian, A. (1996). *Regional advantage: Culture, competition in Silicon Valley and Route 128* (2nd ed.). Cambridge, MA: Harvard University Press.

Schumpeter, J. (1934). *The theory of economic development: An inquiry into profits, capital, credit, interest, and the business cycle.* Cambridge, MA: Harvard University Press.

Teigland, R., & Lindqvist, G. (n.d.). Seeing eye-to-eye: How do public and private sector views of a biotech cluster and its cluster initiative differ? *European Planning Studies.*

Teigland, R., Lindqvist, G., Malmberg, A., & Waxell, A. (2004). Investigating the Uppsala Biotech cluster. Uppsala: Uppsala University.

von Hippel, E. (1988). *The sources of innovation.* Oxford: Oxford University Press.

Waxell, A. (2005). *The Uppsala Biotech custer—Economic-geographical studies of inter-action, knowledge spillover, and labor mobility* [doctoral thesis]. Uppsala: Uppsala University.

Endnotes

[1]   For an in-depth description of the Uppsala Biotech Cluster, see Waxell (2005).

[2]   For the results of this questionnaire, see Teigland and Lindqvist (n.d.) and Teigland, Lindqvist, Malmberg, and Waxell (2004).

[3]   For an in-depth study of this, see Teigland and Lindqvist (n.d.).

[4]   More information on this survey can be found in Teigland et al. (2004) and Teigland and Lindqvist (n.d.).

Section IV

Information Technology

Chapter XI

Clustering, Collaborative Networks and Collaborative Commerce in Small and Medium Enterprises

Michelle Rowe, Edith Cowan University, Australia

Janice Burn, Edith Cowan University, Australia

Abstract

Information technology (IT), which underpins the information society, has brought with it a number of changes that have far-reaching consequences for business, especially small and medium enterprises (SMEs). One such change is IT-facilitated collaboration and the sharing of information by organizations, which has implications for the processes within and among those organizations. The focus here is on collaborative networks of SMEs and collaboration around IT. Of particular interest is collaborative commerce (c-commerce). The relationship among collaborative networks, including c-commerce and clustering, is explored, and factors necessary for c-commerce adoption by SMEs are outlined. Finally, an overview of the results of a Delphi study, the first phase in a longitudinal study into the adoption of c-commerce by Australian SMEs, is provided.

Introduction

Information and communication technologies (ICT) have had profound effects on business relationships and the way in which business is conducted. Markets have globalized; technology has become all-embracing; and relationships with suppliers, customers, and competitors have undergone constant change (Walters, 2004). These developments potentially enable SMEs to compete globally and to enter into more complex, collaborative relationships (Jarratt 1998).

Typically, SMEs are characterized by features of limited resources and experience (Blili & Raymond, 1993; Cragg & King, 1993; MacGregor & Vrazalic, 2005) and are less able to exert control or influence over their environments (Hill & Stewart, 2000; Westhead & Storey, 1996). These factors limit the ability of SMEs on their own to grow or to take advantage of opportunities that might arise. The premise behind the formation of relationships by SMEs is the realization that individually, SMEs cannot cope with an increasingly complex environment (Cravens, Shipp & Cravens, 1993) nor do they possess the resources, skills, and expertise needed to compete. Cooperative and network approaches by firms have resulted in many benefits relating to competitive advantage that not possible if firms work alone (Fuller-Love & Thomas, 2004).

This chapter sets out to explain these phenomena in relation to SMEs. First, an overview of collaborative networks, clustering, and c-commerce is provided. The differences between these concepts and the impact of ICT are highlighted. The relevance of c-commerce to and adoption by SMEs also is examined, and the critical issues for successful c-commerce are identified. Finally, an overview of expert opinion as the first phase of a set of studies into c-commerce adoption and the critical factors underpinning c-commerce adoption by Australian SMEs is reviewed.

What is a Small and Medium Enterprise?

It is important to define what an SME is, which varies according to country. Definitions adopted by the European Commission, the UK Department of Trade and Industry (DTI, 2000) and Australia (ABS, 2002) are set out in Table 1.

Variation in definitions needs to be borne in mind when reviewing literature from around the world, given the different size classifications.

Ownership is also important; to be classified as an SME, the business must be at least 25% owned by one enterprise and not jointly owned by several enterprises.

Collaborative Networks

There have been rapid developments in collaborative networks in the last two decades and involvement in networks contributing to knowledge and productivity. New business patterns have resulted and are characterized by inter alia, diminishing geographical and time

Table 1. Definitions of SMEs

FIRM	DTI EMPLOYEES	EUROPEAN COMMISSION # MAX. EMPLOYEES	MAX. TURNOVER	MAX. ASSETS	AUSTRALIA *
MICRO	0–9	9			0–5
SMALL	0–49	49	7M EUROS	5m euros	5–20
MEDIUM	50–249	249	40M EUROS	27M EUROS	20-200
LARGE	250+				200+

* The Australian Bureau of Statistics (ABS) does include agricultural enterprises in its definition of SMEs as enterprises with less than $400,000 per annum turnover.

boundaries, globalization of the labor market, increased connectivity, and extended or virtual companies. There has been a shift to the knowledge era (European Community, 2000), and as global competition intensifies, SMEs are realizing the need to form symbiotic collaborative relationships in order to keep up, to access unique resources, and to achieve efficiencies and access markets. C-commerce and clustering facilitate the coming together of firms, including competitors, to exploit opportunities that arise in the marketplace.

Collaborative networks are "collaborative relationships that firms enter into with their competitors for strategic reasons" (Fuller-Love & Thomas, 2004, p. 245) (de Wit & Meyer, 1998); however, firms often are reluctant to share information and knowledge formally for fear of their competitive position being undermined. This has been termed Negative Reverse Impact (NRI), the deleterious effect that the receiver's use of exchanged knowledge has on the sender, where partners are also competitors (Levy, Loebbecke, & Powell, 2003; Pease & Rowe, 2005).

In the absence of a collaborative approach, SMEs could find themselves "spending more and more resources administering and guarding information silos rather than using them effectively" (Badii & Sharif, 2003, p. 146), as evident in a proliferation of small and ineffective Web sites that are inadequately maintained (Bode & Burn, 2002; Pease & Rowe, 2005).

Collaborative networks, including c-commerce, demand a new approach by firms that are incorporating new relationships, new assumptions, trust, and a shift in culture that values partnerships and sharing (Peterson, 2002). Without these, it is not likely that SMEs will recognize or consider the benefits of collaboration. Collaboration is built on relationships (O'Keefe, 2001). Relationalism departs from purely economic motives and becomes overlaid with social content that carries strong expectations of cooperation and abstention from opportunistic behavior (Grover, Teng & Fiedler, 2002). The realization of the importance of a social or relational perspective is particularly pertinent with respect to approaches to clustering, as discussed shortly.

ICT also has brought about a shift in the phenomenon of clusters, subjugating the importance of proximity and location by virtual proximity. Additionally, ICT fosters interregional collaboration so the boundaries between regions are no longer as distinct as they once were (Joo, 2002). This has significant implications for the notion of clustering and is borne out in contemporary approaches to clustering, which reflects a shift from mere focus on geographic proximity.

Clusters, Networks, and C-Commerce

It is important to denote the distinction between clusters, networks, and c-commerce in order to ensure that various mechanisms for business-to-business transactions are not confused. In simple terms, the differences between these are detailed next.

Clusters

There are a number of definitions of a cluster. A cluster may be considered a group of firms from the same or related industries located geographically near each other (Becattini, 1990; Brusco, 1990; Harrison, Kelley, & Gant, 1996; Storper & Harrison, 1991). Porter (1998, p. 199) defines a cluster as "a geographic proximate group of interconnected companies and associated institutions in a particular field, linked by commonalities and complementarities." Rosenfeld, (2001) states that being in a cluster "is a function of geography and relationships, not membership," which provides access to economies of scale otherwise not possible if the firm operated individually (p. 15).

Clusters refer to an aggregation of SMEs located in a relatively delimited geographic area, engaged in the production of related or complementary products. This traditional notion of clustering sees geographic proximity as a driver for competition and collaboration of firms in the production process, often resulting in clusters of specialized SMEs. SME clusters are important as local government authorities (LGAs) use economic development to leverage competitive advantage to attract businesses to their region.

Porter (1990) and Harrison (1994) argue that firms located in a cluster are more productive due to two effects: (1) agglomeration economies, which enables access to suppliers; and observation of competitors, which enables tapping into collective knowledge; and (2) network-based effects, particularly enhancements in interactions among firms (Bell, 2005).

Modern approaches to clustering, however, acknowledge the role of social capital (Putnam, 2000), the social dimension rather than just the economic dimension on which Porter's (1998) model is based. The traditional view of clusters omits the social context and the role of and need to generate relationship and trust among firms. In addition, the role of infrastructure providers, such as government, educational institutions, and so forth, is important and is not captured by the traditional notion of clusters. Rather, these providers increasingly are recognized as playing a critical role in contemporary clusters (Humphreys, 2004; Putnam, 2000).

Humphreys (2004, p. 17) defines a cluster as "a system of inter-related companies, institutions and networks with common understandings, a desire for continual growth, and a level of trust which enhances the flow of knowledge." This broader definition is considered to be more relevant to the notion of clusters today and encompasses virtual clusters (Enright, 2001). Geographic proximity is no longer essential, as is evident in corridor-type developments as well as relationships that are interregional, international, or virtual. This definition recognizes the critical role of relationships, with clusters depending on community (OECD, 2001), trust, and social capital.

Networks

A network encompasses a firm's set of relationships—its relations and contacts—with other organizations (Burt, 1992; Martin, 2000). Networks essentially are arrangements that reflect interfirm collaboration or cooperation "in which two or more independent firms cooperate to perform business activities" (BarNir & Smith, 2002, p. 220). This facilitates the exchange of goods and services or information, which may relate to technology, products, or resources (Auster, 1994). Social network theory and the theoretical framework of social embeddedness propose that economic activity cannot occur, let alone be analysed, without due consideration of the social context within which such activity takes place (Granovetter, 1985). This is imperative because of the following:

- The intertwining of economic and noneconomic activities and objectives,
- The impact of the social context, which influences motives of economic actors,
- The social construction of economic institutions. (BarNir & Smith, 2002)

Strategic networks include ties that are more enduring and that have strategic significance for firms entering them (Martin, 2000). Strategic alliances are dynamic arrangements constantly evolving and adjusting in order to accommodate changes in the business environment. Yeung (1994) argues that strategic alliances are "an integrated and coordinated set of ongoing economic and non-economic relations embedded with, among and outside business firms" (p. 476). Strategic alliances not only are a structure but also reflect common processes among partners with links being formal and informal, conscious and unconscious (Dennis, 2000; MacGregor & Vrazalic, 2005).

Martin (2000) classifies three forms of SME networks—personal, support, and industrial—which, he argues, are fundamental to the existence of many SMEs. Interfirm arrangements generate positive benefits such as cost sharing, technology transfer, and sharing of information. This assists SMEs as they take on larger competitors, which enables entry into markets. Networks are important entrepreneurial tools that can aid in the establishment and development of SMEs (Shaw & Conway, 2000). The challenge for SMEs is to make themselves attractive to potential alliance partners. Using a network lens enables SMEs to seek out "value creating resources and capabilities to extend beyond the boundary of the firm"

(Gulati, Nohria, & Zaheer, 2000, p. 207). A firm's network can be thought of as "creating an imitable and non-sustainable value as a resource in its own right and as a means of accessing other capabilities" (Martin, 2000, p. 14).

Social networks are defined as a manager's relations and contacts with others (Burt, 1992). For SMEs, this relates to relationships that the proprietor has developed. Birley, Cromie, and Myers (1991) proposed that the importance of social networks for SMEs is fourfold: the information they provide; the support engendered as a consequence of interactions; credibility that ensures membership of high-status networks (Rowe, Burn & Walker, 2005); and the governance mechanism it provides; which regulate the behaviors of network participants. Executive networks particularly benefit SMEs, since the network itself becomes a resource that, in part, overcomes resource constraints. In a study of 149 US SMEs involved in the electronics components industry and medical instrument and supplies industry, the following aspects of executive networks were studied: "propensity to network, scope of the network, strength of the ties with network members, and prestige of network members" (BarNir & Smith, 2002, p. 222).

The content of network and the nature of the contacts were found to be important factors that influence formation and entry into networks. Also of importance was the source of information and reliability of the network, which act as a safety net, as well as governance structures that were agreed to by network members. These factors also serve to reduce risk; that is, entry into networks may be perceived to be risky, but, on the other hand, entry into such alliances also serves to reduce risk.

Bell (2005) tried to unravel the impact of clustering and networks on innovation of an organization. While he found that clustering tended to have a stronger impact on innovation, largely because it increases access to firms that tended to be more innovative, he concluded that networking also had a role to play in innovation. Bell suggested that managers need to manage informal networks as well as strategic networks in order to achieve benefits from both of these mechanisms.

Rosenfeld (2001) suggests that interest in the success of clustering in Italy (Piore & Sabel, 1984) was, in fact, an example of networking supported by the provision of specialized services generated by government and trade associations. Rosenfeld (2001) argues that social infrastructure underpins cooperation and is essential to market-driven interfirm cooperation. He distinguishes between networks and clusters as in Table 2.

Further, Rosenfeld (2005) distinguishes between hard and soft networks. Hard networks, he asserts, are small, closed, and often formally allied groups of firms working together toward common bottom-line objectives. Soft networks, on the other hand, are a looser membership-based group formed to address general issues of concern to members in order to seek lower costs, to facilitate learning from each other, or to access information collectively or via information sharing. Networks, Rosenfeld believes, are naturally occurring and are spawned by clusters, or they may occur outside of a cluster. Table 3 is a typology of relationships among firms proposed by Rosenfeld (2005).

Table 3 shows that the distinction between clusters and hard and soft networks is apparent. Clusters require no membership and may occur as a result of collocation with proximity, at least in the traditional sense, generating externalities. Embeddedness of relationships and

Table 2. Distinction between networks and clusters (Rosenfeld, 2001, p. 3)

Comparing Networks To Clusters
Networks allow firms access to specialized services at lower costs
Clusters attract needed specialized services to a region
Networks have restricted membership
Clusters have open "membership"
Networks are based on contractual agreements
Clusters are based on social values that foster trust and encourage reciprocity
Networks make it easier for firms to engage in complex production
Clusters generate demand for more firms with similar and related capabilities
Networks are based on cooperation
Clusters require both cooperation and competition
Networks have common business goals
Clusters have collective visions

Table 3. A typology of various networks

TYPE	HARD NETWORK	SOFT NETWORK	CLUSTER
RELATIONSHIP	Cooperation	Collegial	Competitive and cooperative
MEMBERSHIP	Closed	Open	None
BASIS FOR DECISIONS	Clusters	Majority	Social norms
BASIS OF EXTERNALITIES	Shared functions	Membership	Proximity

many of the issues discussed in relation to networks are not necessarily present in clusters, as firms remain more independent and as interfirm cooperation or collaboration may not occur. While cooperation or collegiality may arise among firms situated within a cluster, generally, competition and business imperative are the key drivers. Collective activity may not arise if firms do not see themselves as interdependent.

Collaborative Commerce

Collaborative commerce (c-commerce) effectively is a soft network in which firms openly enter into a relationship in pursuit of benefits or advantages that they believe will accrue to their businesses. Members (i.e., firms that enter into c-commerce relationships) recognize that these benefits would not occur if they operated alone. A coming together around IT (i.e., membership) enables them to operate and take advantage of opportunities that arise. Geographic proximity is not essential to this collaboration. Decision making is based on mutual agreement, requiring members to negotiate endogenous systems to guide and enforce behavior and to minimize negative reverse impact (NRI) (Levy, Loebbecke & Powell, 2003). Trust and commitment are at the heart of the c-commerce relationship, as are other factors to be outlined.

C-commerce consists of all of an organization's ICT bases, knowledge management, and business interactions with its customers, suppliers, and partners in the business communities in which it interacts. Essentially, it is the coming together of collaborators around IT in order to exploit opportunities when they arise (GartnerGroup, 1999; McCarthy, 1999). As global competition intensifies, many organizations are forming partnerships as an expeditious way in which to keep up or to access unique or pioneering resources (Ring & Van de Ven, 1992, 1994). Collaboration around IT is a response to an increasingly complex and dynamic market (Cravens, Schipp, & Cravens, 1993).

C-commerce represents the coming together of both ICT and social networks. Collaborations between business and community depend upon the willingness of businesses to network and share information as well as their ability to accept business cultural change. Technology networks depend upon the hard and soft infrastructure available and the willingness of businesses to adopt new business methods involving business technological changes (Braun, 2002).

The phenomenon of c-commerce is one means by which organizations can share information and resources. This is especially beneficial for SMEs, since it means that "it may no longer be necessary for a firm to own a process in order to control it" (Clayton & Criscuolo, 2002, p. 62) but rather can share resources. Control can be achieved via the establishment of relationships among organizations. Normann (2001) called this new approach a new strategic logic, suggesting that managers need to be good at mobilizing, managing, and using resources rather than formally acquiring and necessarily owning resources.

Why Collaborate around ICT?

The definitions of c-commerce emphasize the importance of the exchange of information between collaborators (Fairchild & Peterson, 2003; Holsapple & Singh, 2000) and signifies an organizational shift in focus from transactions and exchange to one of relationships among firms (Sheth, 1996). This is underpinned by a realization that information does much more than support the value-adding process and that the information itself has value and can result in a competitive advantage. The adoption of IT has been identified as a possible source of strategic competitive advantage for SMEs (Yetton & Johnston, 1994) and potentially generates innovation, which results in further competitive advantage (Ryssel, Ritter & Gemunden, 2004).

This sharing of resources that is central to c-commerce potentially can "improve performance, increase knowledge and competitive position" (More & McGrath, 2003a, p. 1). Moreover, More and McGrath (2003b) assert that collaboration is a critical tool for enterprises in the 21st century, with benefits accruing if collaborators "learn to work together as well as to work to learn together" (Ireland, Hitt, & Vaidyanath, 2002, p. 427).

C-commerce enables firms to grow their assets and access markets (Holsapple & Singh, 2000; Ring & Van de Ven, 1994) and facilitates innovation, information, and knowledge and systems sharing and exchange (Holsapple & Singh, 2000), which may lead to increases in efficiency. Internal efficiencies also can be generated by the sharing of information via IT in inter-organizational relationships (IORs) (Ryssel et al., 2004). Bititci, Martinez, Albores, and Parung (2004) observed that collaborative enterprises or networks "create new and unique value propositions by complementing, integrating and leveraging each other's capabilities and competencies" (p. 266).

This collaboration generates "relational rents" through "relation-specific assets, knowledge-sharing routines, complementary resource endowments, and effective governance" (Dyer & Singh, 1998, p. 674). Most SMEs, however, have not considered c-commerce, let alone taken a strategic approach; formed appropriate relationships; or dedicated assets, resources, and routines to enable its introduction.

The absence of relationships, network competence, and social identity among SMEs impedes c-commerce adoption. This chapter serves to document what is considered to be important antecedents to c-commerce adoption, based on the literature and supported by expert opinion.

What Does C-Commerce Require?

In order to enable SMEs to make the most of the opportunities afforded by the Web (Grover et al., 2002) and changes identified by Walters (2004) in relation to new business models required by the new economy, a new way of thinking, planning, and operating is required. SMEs need to "adopt an entirely different approach to strategic planning and management which can enable them to deploy an extensive infrastructure network based on shared resources with other firms" (Tetteh & Burn, 2001, p. 171). This requires strategic thinking, trust, and a realization of the importance of co-opting or collaboration rather than competition, which typically exists among individual firms.

In order for c-commerce to be successfully adopted, social interaction is the key preceding adoption of technology. An understanding of the importance of relationships is required. Relationships are critical to successful implementation and are developed via networking; hence, the importance of relationship quality factors and network competence. A coming together around IT is secondary to the formation and existence of relationships between firms, since they underpin collaborative relationships (O'Keefe, 2001).

While technology is central to c-commerce, it is the willingness to share information rather than the technology per se that potentially constrains the relationship (Mason, Castleman & Parker, 2004; O'Keefe, 2001). Attitudes to knowledge and the willingness to share information with others are critical. Yet the knowledge gained by cooperation may be used for competition (Levy et al., 2003, p. 3). This can only be overcome through the generation of trust, commitment to the relationship, and an agreement to not act opportunistically, which are enforced by endogenous systems.

In addition to relationship quality issues, as encompassed in the discussion of network theory (Pease & Rowe, 2005; Rowe et al., 2005), c-commerce requires a view that sees other firms as an extension of itself—a co-opting approach rather than one of competition (Levy et al., 2003). Essentially, if SMEs see that their identities are more important than a collective identity, then cooperation and collaboration are not likely to occur. This is explained by social network theory (Kramer, 1993; Tajfel, 1982; Tajfel & Turner, 1979). Cooperation requires a strong social or collective identity (Kramer, 1993) and the adoption of a relational perspective, not a mere focus on economics and transactions. This collective view is an important precursor to the level of cooperation demanded by c-commerce.

Grover, et al., (2002) suggests that the decision to use IT within the dyad can encourage a commitment to establishing relational behavior. IT is an enabler of knowledge sharing in that it facilitates the flow of information and plays an important role in the control and coordination of joint ventures (Birnberg, 1998).

The management of knowledge sharing is critical when considering c-commerce adoption. The decision about what and how much information to share is an important one (Choo & Bontis, 2002). This question is more complex with respect to collaborative structures compared to traditionally structured organizations due to the interplay of culture and trust.

In summary, then, c-commerce requires firms to develop a strategy, both short- and long-term; adopt appropriate business models; develop and sustain appropriate collaborative cultures engendering trust; invest in ICT to facilitate information and knowledge sharing; and set in place appropriate organizational structures to enable collaboration (Kalakota & Robinson, 1999). A deficiency of the elements outlined here prevents the consideration and/or adoption of c-commerce.

The Research Study

A multi-phase research study is underway that is investigating how and why SMEs become involved in c-commerce and the facilitators and impediments to the same. Also of interest in this research is the relationship between clustering and c-commerce. The study to date

Table 4. Summary of drivers/enablers and inhibitors of c-commerce

DRIVERS/ENABLERS OF C-COMMERCE FOR SMEs	INHIBITORS OF C-COMMERCE FOR SMEs
• Technological awareness/ICT affinity • Open to consider alternatives; aware of opportunities • Opportunistic/entrepreneurial • Economic benefits/rationale for collaboration; business imperative • Willingness to collaborate, either to achieve competitive advantage or to survive • Need for human contact; isolated • Relationships are a driver; IT is a tool • Development of trust is an important precursor • Proactive government or educational providers/external support	• Limited time and resources; operational focus • Lack of awareness and knowledge of IT and how it can benefit the business; IT is a tool; not strategic • Lack of integration of IT and business strategy • Lack of planning or strategy • Lack of knowledge and skills • Lack of tradition to collaborate • Independence • Lack of innovation/creativity • Fear of sharing information; NRI (negative reverse impact) • Lack of trust/confidence in others • Infrastructure such as broadband • Lack of perceived value of collaboration • Absence of government support; no external facilitator • Lack of social identity or realization of the value of social capital; operate from economic viewpoint • Mindset of SME proprietor

has incorporated two stages: (1) a Delphi study involving academics, practitioners, and policymakers from the fields of IT, e-commerce, and SMEs; and (2) an in-depth examination of actual c-commerce exemplars from Australia. This chapter reports the findings of the first phase of the study.

The aforementioned Delphi study has confirmed the drivers, enablers, and inhibitors to c-commerce adoption that have been deduced from the literature. An analysis of the issues emerging from this phase of the study reveals the following.

Sectoral/Regional Influences

Two opposing views emerged from this Delphi study: those who believed c-commerce adoption was not sectoral or regional and that growth could be pursued in any industry or region with entrepreneurial SMEs located anywhere; and those, on the other hand, who argued that industry or region was an important factor in explaining c-commerce adoption.

These respondents believed that funding on an ongoing basis had proven itself to be critical to portals, for example, and cited initiatives occurring in Victoria where the state government

Table 5. Important traits of the SME proprietor for c-commerce adoption

- Entrepreneurial; boundary span; look to growth; risk-taking; look beyond organization for new ideas; optimistic and positive; visionary
- IT champion or driver or defer to same
- Adopt a relational/social view rather than a purely economic perspective; see value in sharing and networking; may be evident in a cooperative or coopetition approach
- Flexible and responsive
- Innovative and open to and considers alternatives
- Realize opportunities from c-commerce
- Willing to adopt systems and approaches to better manage firm; may be interorganizational
- Think strategically and smart

Table 6. Propositions relating to c-commerce adoption by SMEs

SME/SME PROPRIETOR	ENVIRONMENT	TASK ENVIRONMENT
• Innovative, entrepreneurial • Wanting to grow; recognizes alternatives • Visionary proprietor; sees opportunities and is willing to take risks • Not limited by lack of resources • Coopetition approach accepted; see synergy and benefits from collaborating • Strategic approach rather than operational view • Integration of IT with business strategy • Experience and expertise re IT; IT not just an operational tool • Deference to IT champion • Boundary spanning, high NQ, and actively networks (intra- and intersectoral)	• Supportive environment • Active supportive role taken by government, business associations, and/or educational institutions; this support takes the form of advice and financial assistance and has to be ongoing • Visionary driver in external environment • Source of funding to support initiatives	• Industry has a tradition of information sharing and collaboration • Innovative industry or one under threat where need for collaboration is recognized • Industry tends to be information-centric; knowledge and information sharing central to the nature of the industry • Collaboration is recognized as critical to the industry and its future • Industry that is open to new ways of operating or doing things, including the adoption of technology to improve business processes

supported SMEs and technology uptake with some examples of c-commerce having emerged. Since government involvement and support differs across regions and states, this difference may explain in part the successful adoption of c-commerce. Also, some respondents argued that the role of educational institutions acted as a driver, which varies by region/state.

Some believed that c-commerce adoption and success were a function of the nature of the industry generally, insofar as it tends to be information-centric and has a tradition of collaboration, and where collaboration was at the heart of the way the industry operated. Information sharing and a willingness of SMEs to do so were considered to be fundamental to c-commerce adoption. Other experts discussed differences among regional, rural, and metropolitan regions and even metropolitan and outer-metropolitan regions.

Important Traits of the SME Proprietor for C-Commerce Adoption

Respondents also identified important traits of SME proprietors that they considered motivators for c-commerce. These are essentially linked to the enablers/drivers and are as shown above.

Propositions

Consideration of the literature and the results of the first phase of the research indicate that there are three broad groups of factors that are critical to c-commerce adoption by SMEs. These are listed as a series of propositions in Table 6.

These factors are considered to be critical to c-commerce adoption. These propositions are to be tested in subsequent phases of the research study. Further analysis of the results so far is required in light of the second and subsequent phases of the research study in order to develop a conceptual framework. Preliminary results from the second phase of the research bears out the aforementioned propositions.

Discussion

C-commerce is a type of collaborative network. Firms engaged in c-commerce do so because they recognize the strategic benefits; however, c-commerce demands a significant investment in inter-organizational systems (IOS). A commitment to the relationship requiring investment in IT from a long-term perspective is critical for collaborative networks, including c-commerce. For c-commerce adoption, firms require a strategic view, integrating IT with their business planning processes, and a strategic approach generally in their businesses and toward IT.

This chapter asserts that organizations must possess certain characteristics for effective c-commerce adoption based on the literature and findings from an ongoing research study. The lack of these characteristics and the low level of awareness of the benefits of c-commerce are believed to explain partly the low rate of adoption in Australia. These characteristics, though, are not required for entry into a cluster.

Further research is required in order to determine factors that are critical antecedents to c-commerce adoption. As stated, this chapter reports on the results of the first phase in a suite of research studies that seeks to do this. The relationship among factors identified here and other factors identified by subsequent research studies needs to be investigated generally and in the context of the specific industries, both in Australia and overseas. Also, further investigation of the connection between clustering and collaborative networks is required.

Consideration of the impact that external and task environments have on c-commerce adoption is important, especially comparing the Australian context with environments in which c-commerce is more entrenched, in order to identify significant differences. Given that the majority of research regarding collaborative IORs and c-commerce has taken place in Europe, the impact of the cultural and institutional settings needs to be acknowledged as well as differences in social psychology that exist there.

Conclusion

Collaborative networks and c-commerce are emerging phenomena in Australia. Little evidence exists about their connection with clusters from the SME perspective. This chapter seeks to identify these concepts and the factors that are critical to c-commerce adoption by SMEs. The relationships among collaborative networks, of which c-commerce is one example, and clustering have been overviewed.

It is important to clarify these concepts so that policymakers are clear about the interplay between collaborative networks and clustering, and to identify the impact of social theory and relationalism as well as IT on traditional notions of clustering.

References

Auster, E. (1994). Macro and strategic perspectives on inter-organisational linkages: A comparative analysis and review with suggestions for reorientation. In P. Shrivastave, A. Huff, & J. Dutton (Eds.), *Advances in strategic management* (pp. 3-39). Greenwich, CT: JAI Press.

Australian Bureau of Statistics. (2002). *Small business in Australia (cat. 1321)*. Canberra: Australian Bureau of Statistics.

Badii, A., & Sharif, A.M. (2003). *Enterprise innovation challenges: Information management, knowledge integration and deployment.* Presented at the Proceedings of the 2nd International Conference on Systems Thinking in Management (ICSTM2002), Manchester, UK.

BarNir, A., & Smith, K. (2002). Inter-firm alliances in the small business: The role of social networks. *Journal of Small Business Management, 40*(3), 219-231.

Becattini, G. (1990). The Marshallian industrial district as a socio-economic notion. In F. Pyke, G. Bettacini, & W. Segenberger (Eds.), *Industrial districts and inter-firm co-operation in Italy* (pp. 37-51). Geneva: International Institute for Labour Studies.

Bell, G. (2005). Clusters, networks and firm innovativeness. *Strategic Business Journal, 26*, 287–295.

Birley, S., Cromie, S., & Myers, A. (1991). Entrepreneurial networks: Their emergence in Ireland and oversees. *International Small Business Journal, 9*(4), 56-73.

Birnberg, J. (1998). Control in inter-firm co-operative relationships. *Journal of Management Studies, 35*(4), 421-428.

Bititci, U., Martinez, V., Albores, P., & Parung, J. (2004). Creating and managing value in collaborative networks. *International Journal of Physical Distribution and Logistics Management, 34*(3), 251-268.

Blili, S., & Raymond, L. (1993). Threats and opportunities for small and medium enterprises. *International Journal of Information Management, 13*, 439-448.

Bode, S., & Burn, J.M. (2002). Strategies for consultancy engagement for e-business development — a case analysis of Australian SMEs. In S. Burgess (Ed.), *Managing information technology in small businesses: Challenges and solutions.* Hershey, PA: Idea Group Publishing.

Braun, P. (2002). *Regional connectivity and virtual clustering: Networking SMEs for competitive advantage.* Presented at the Proceedings of the 5th Global Competitiveness Institute Conference, Cairns, Australia.

Brusco, S. (1990). The idea of the industrial district: Its genesis. In F. Pyke, G. Bettacini, & W. Segenberger (Eds.), *Industrial districts and inter-firm co-operation in Italy* (pp. 10–19). Geneva: International Institute for Labour Studies.

Burt, R. (1992). *Structural holes: The social structure of competition.* Cambridge, MA: Harvard University Press.

Choo, C.W., & Bontis, N. (Eds.) (2002). Knowledge, intellectual capital and strategy: Themes and tensions. In *The Strategic Management of Intellectual Capital and Organisational Knowledge* (pp. 3–19). Oxford: Oxford University Press.

Clayton, T., & Criscuolo, C. (2002). *Electronic commerce and business change.* National Statistics. Retrieved April 16, 2005, from <http://www.statistics.gov.uk/cci/article.asp?ID=139>

Cragg, P., & King, M. (1993). Small-firm computing: Motivators and inhibitors. *MIS Quarterly, 17*(1), 47–60.

Cravens, D.W., Shipp, S.H., & Cravens, K.S. (1993). Analysis of co-operative interorganizational relationships, strategic alliance formation, and strategic alliance effectiveness. *Journal of Strategic Marketing, 1*(1), 55–70.

Department of Trade and Industry. (2000). *Small and medium enterprise (SME) — Definitions.* Retrieved from http://www.dti.gov.uk/SME4/define.htm

De Wit, B., & Meyer, R. (1998). *Strategy, process, content, context.* London: International Thomson Business Press.

Dyer, J.H., & Singh, H. (1998). The relational view: Ccooperative strategy and sources of interorganisational competitive advantage. *The Academy of Management Review, 23*(4), 660-680.

Enright, M. (2001). *Regional clusters: What we know and what we should know.* Presented at the Proceedings of the Kiel Institute International Workshop, Kiel, Germany.

European Community. (2000). *Business networks and the knowledge-driven economy.* Geneva: Enterprise Directorate General.

Fairchild, A.M., & Peterson, R.R. (2003). *Business-to-business value drivers and ebusiness infrastructures in financial services: Collaborative commerce across global markets and networks.* Presented at the Proceedings of the 36th Hawaii International Conferences on System Sciences (HICSS 36), Waikoloa, Hawaii.

Fuller-Love, N., & Thomas, E. (2004). Networks in small manufacturing firms. *Journal of Small Business and Enterprise Development, 11*(2), 244-253.

GartnerGroup. (1999). Gartner Group identifies c-commerce supply chain movement: An emerging trend in collaborative Web communities. *GartnerInteractive.* Retrieved from http://gartner5.gartnerweb.com/public/static/aboutgg/presrel/

Granovetter, M. (1985). Economic action and social structure: The problem of embeddedness. *American Journal of Sociology, 91*(3), 481-510.

Grover, V., Teng, J.T.C., & Fiedler, K.D. (2002). Investigating the role of information technology in building buyer-supplier relationships. *Journal of the Association for Information Systems, 3,* 217–245.

Gulati, R., Nohria, N., & Zaheer, A. (2000). Strategic networks. *Strategic Management Journal, 21*(3), 203-215.

Harrison, B. (1994). *Lean and mean: The changing landscape of corporate power in the age of flexibility.* New York: Basic Books.

Harrison, B., Kelley, M., & Gant, J. (1996). Innovative firm behaviour and local milieu: Exploring the intersection of agglomeration, firm effects, and technological change. *Economic Geography, 72*(3), 233-258.

Hill, R., & Stewart, J. (2000). Human resource development in small organisations. *Journal of European Industrial Training, 24*(2/3/4), 105-117.

Holsapple, C.W., & Singh, M. (2000) Toward a unified view of electronic commerce, electronic business, and collaborative commerce: A knowledge management approach. *Knowledge and Process Management, 7*(3), 151-164.

Humphreys, J. (2004). *Enhancing national economic benefits through a new cluster paradigm.* AAEMA Final Report prepared under the Innovation Access Program — Industry for the Department of Industry Tourism and Resource, January, Brisbane, Australia.

Ireland, R.D., Hitt, M.A., & Vaidyanath, D. (2002). Alliance management as a source of competitive advantage. *Journal of Management, 28*(3), 413-446.

Jarratt, D.G. (1998). A strategic classification of business alliances: A qualitative perspective built from a study of small and medium-sized enterprises. *Qualitative Market Research: An International Journal*, *1*(1), 39-49.

Joo, J. (2002, Summer). A business model and its development strategies for electronic tourism markets. *Information Systems Management*, 58–69.

Kalakota, R., & Robinson, M. (1999). *Frontiers of electronic commerce*. Reading, MA: Addison-Wesley.

Kramer, R.M. (1993). Cooperation and organisational identification. In J.K. Murninghan (Ed.), *Social psychology in organisations—Advances in theory and research* (pp. 244-268). London: Prentice Hall.

Levy, M., Loebbecke, C., & Powell, P. (2003). SMEs, co-opetition and knowledge sharing: The role of information systems. *European Journal of Information Systems*, *12*(1), 3-17.

Mason, C., Castleman, T., & Parker, C. (2004). *Knowledge management for SME-based regional clusters*. Presented at the Proceedings of the CollECTeR, Adelaide, Australia.

MacGregor, R., & Vrazalic, L. (2005). The effects of strategic alliance membership on the disadvantages of electronic-commerce adoption. *Journal of Global Information Management*. Hershey, PA: Idea Group.

Martin, C., (2000). *International and strategic networks: An SME perspective*. Presented at the Proceedings of the 5th International Manufacturing Research Symposium, International and Strategic Network Development, Cambridge.

McCarthy, J. (1999). *Gartner foretells of collaborative commerce*. Breaking News: IDG. net. Retrieved from http://www.idg.net/idgns/1999/08/16/GartnerFortellsOfCollaborativeCommerce.shtml

More, E., & McGrath, G.M. (2003a). *Encouraging e-commerce collaboration through seed funding consortia*. Presented at the Proceedings of the 2003 European Applied Business Research Conference, Venice, Italy.

More, E., & McGrath, G.M. (2003b). Organisational collaboration in an e-commerce context: Australia's ITOL project. *The E-Business Review*, *3*, 121-124.

Normann, R. (2001). *Reframing business: When the map changes the landscape*. Chichester: John Wiley & Sons.

OECD. (2001). *The new economy: Beyond the hype Final report on the OECD growth project*. Presented at the meeting of the OECD Council at the Ministerial Level.

O'Keefe, M. (2001). Building intellectual capital in the supply chain — the role of e-commerce. *Supply Chain Management: An International Journal*, *6*(4), 148-151.

Pease, W., & Rowe, M. (2005). *Collaborative commerce in the tourism industry*. Presented at the Proceedings of the Tourism Enterprise Strategies: Thriving — and surviving — in an online era (TES2005), Melbourne, Australia.

Peterson, R.R. (2002). *Information governance*. Tilberg, The Netherlands: Tilberg University Press.

Piore, M., & Sabel, C. (1984). *The second industrial divide*. New York: Basic Books.

Porter, M.E. (1990). *The competitive advantage of nations*. New York: Free Press.

Porter, M.E. (1998). On competition. *Harvard Business Review Book*, 77-90, 85.

Putnam, R. (2000). *Bowling alone: The collapse and revival of American community*. New York: Simon and Schuster.

Ring, P.S., & Van de Ven, A.H. (1992). Structuring cooperative relationships between organizations. *Strategic Management Journal, 13*(7), 483-498.

Ring, P.S., & Van de Ven, A.H. (1994). Developmental processes of cooperative interorganizational relationships. *Academy of Management Review, 19*(1), 90-118.

Rosenfeld, S. (2001). *Backing into clusters: Retrofitting public policies*. Proceedings of the Integration Pressures: Lessons from Around the World, Cambridge, MA.

Rosenfeld, S. (2005). *Clusters and the creative economy—Keynote address*. Presented at the Proceedings of the Beyond Clusters — Current Practices and Future Strategies, Clustering Conference, Ballarat.

Rowe, M., Burn, J., & Walker, E. (2005). *Collaborative commerce: A social, issues perspective*. Presented at the Proceedings of the Beyond Clusters — Current Practices and Future Strategies, Clustering Conference, Ballarat.

Ryssel, R., Ritter, T., & Gemunden, H.G. (2004). The impact of information technology deployment on trust, commitment and value creation in business relationships. *Journal of Business & Industrial Marketing, 19*(3), 197-207.

Shaw, W., & Conway, S. (2000). Networking and the small firm. In S. Carter, & D. Jones-Evans (Eds), *Enterprise and small business, principles, practice and policy*. Harlow: Pearson Education.

Sheth, J.N. (1996). Organizational buying behavior: Past performance and future expectations. *Journal of Business & Industrial Marketing, 11*(3/4), 7-24.

Storper, M., & Harrison, B. (1991). Flexibility, hierarchy and regional development: The changing structure of industrial production systems and their forms of governance in the 1990s. *Research Policy, 29*, 407-422.

Tajfel, H. (1982). *Social identity and intergroup relations*. Cambridge, MA: Cambridge University Press.

Tajfel, H., & Turner, J.C. (1979). *An integrative theory of intergroup conflict*. In .G. Austin, & A.S. Worchel (Eds.), *The social psychology of intergroup relations* (pp. W33–47). Monterey, CA: Brooks/Cole.

Tetteh, E., & Burn, J. (2001). Global strategies for SMe-business: Applying the SMALL framework. *Logistics Information Management, 14*(1), 171-180.

Walters, D. (2004). New economy—New business models—New approaches. *International Journal of Physical Distribution & Logistics Management, 34*(3/4) 219-229.

Westhead, P., & Storey, D. (1996). Management training and small firm performance: Why is the link so weak? *International Small Business Journal, 14*(4), 13-24.

Yetton, P.W., & Johnston, K.D. (1994). Computer-aided architects: A case study of IT and strategic change. *Sloan Management Review, 35*(4), 57-67.

Yeung, H. (1994). Critical reviews of geographical perspectives on business organisations and the organisation of production: Towards a network approach. *Progressive Human Geography, 18*(4), 460-490.

Chapter XII

The Role of Small Business Strategic Alliances in Small/Medium Enterprises (SMEs)

Robert MacGregor, University of Wollongong, Australia

Lejla Vrazalic, University of Wollongong, Australia

Abstract

Despite advances in Internet technology, small to medium enterprises (SMEs) are reporting relatively low rates of e-commerce adoption. In response to this, government organizations are putting in place a number of initiatives to promote e-commerce use by SMEs. One of these initiatives is the formation of strategic alliances between businesses in order to pool resources and facilitate e-commerce adoption. This chapter examines the role of strategic alliances in e-commerce use by SMEs by presenting the results of a study of 313 Swedish businesses and by comparing the e-commerce adoption criteria, benefits, and disadvantages among those who are members of a strategic alliance and those who are not. The results of the study indicate distinct differences between the two groups in relation to specific aspects of e-commerce.

Introduction

The diffusion and assimilation of e-commerce in small to medium enterprises (SMEs) represents a critical area of investigation. A number of studies (Donckels & Lambrecht, 1997; Miles, Preece & Baetz, 1999) suggests that more and more SMEs are confronting an environment that is increasingly complex, technologically uncertain, and globally focused. These studies have suggested that some SMEs are turning toward some form of strategic alliance in which the locus of the impact of change is interorganizational rather than organizational. Indeed, these studies have prompted government initiatives (e-Europe, 2005; NOIE, 1998) that suggest that disadvantages and difficulties associated with e-commerce adoption may be reduced through joint technical information, market expertise, and business know-how, and that the structure of the strategic alliance provides a more flexible arrangement than the hierarchy in dealing with environmental turbulence.

Yet, despite the proclaimed advantages of small business strategic alliances, little research has been carried out to determine whether these structures promote the benefits and/or cushion the disadvantages that arise from e-commerce adoption for member businesses. Indeed, few studies have examined the role of strategic alliances in the decision-making processes leading up to the adoption of e-commerce.

This chapter examines both adopters and nonadopters of e-commerce. For the nonadopters, the chapter compares the perception of barriers to e-commerce between respondents that are members of a small business strategic alliance and respondents that are not. For those respondents that have adopted e-commerce, the chapter compares the perception of the importance of criteria in the decision to adopt e-commerce as well as the perception of benefits and disadvantages derived from the adoption of e-commerce by SMEs that are part of a small business strategic alliance and those that are not.

The chapter begins by examining the nature of SMEs, which is followed by a brief overview of the adoption of e-commerce by SMEs. The chapter then examines the criteria for adoption of e-commerce, the barriers that lead to nonadoption, the benefits derived from e-commerce adoption, and the disadvantages incurred through the adoption of e-commerce. Finally, the chapter presents a study of 313 Swedish small businesses, 176 of which have adopted e-commerce and 137 have not. The study compares the rating of criteria for adoption, barriers precluding adoption, benefits derived from adoption, and disadvantages incurred through the adoption between those SMEs that are part of a small business strategic alliance and those that are not. Finally, the limitations of the study are presented along with the conclusions and future research directions.

The Nature of
Small and Medium Enterprises (SMEs)

There are a variety of definitions pertaining to what constitutes a small to medium enterprise. Some of these definitions are based on quantitative measures such as staffing levels, turnover, and assets, while others tend to employ a qualitative approach. Meredith (1994) suggests that any description or definition must include a quantitative component that takes into account staff levels, turnover, and assets, together with financial and non-financial measurements, but that the description also must include a qualitative component that reflects how the business is organized and how it operates.

Not only is there a myriad of views concerning the nature of SMEs, but from a governmental standpoint, there is a variety of definitions of small to medium enterprises. These include the following:

Small business is one in which one or two persons are required to make all of the critical decisions (such as finance, accounting, personnel, inventory, production, servicing, marketing and selling decisions) without the aid of internal (employed) specialists and with owners only having specific knowledge in one or two functional areas of management. (Meredith, 1994, p. 31)

An "SME shall be deemed to be one which is independently owned and operated and which is not dominant in its field of operation." (Small Business Act, 1953)

[H]aving fewer than 50 employees and is not a subsidiary of any other company. (United Kingdom Companies Act, 1985)

For the purposes of this study, the UK definition will be used.

Not only do the definitions of SME vary, but there are wide-ranging views on the characteristics of SMEs.

There have been many studies in the literature that have attempted to demonstrate the characteristics of SMEs. Central to all of these studies is the underlying realization that many of the processes and techniques that have been applied successfully to large businesses do not necessarily provide similar outcomes when applied to SMEs. This, perhaps, is best summed up by Barnett and Mackness (1983), who stated that SMEs are not small large businesses but rather are unique in their own right. It is appropriate that we examine some of the characteristics found in the literature.

Brigham and Smith (1967) found that SMEs tended to be more risky than their larger counterparts. This view was supported in later studies (DeLone, 1988; Walker, 1975). Cochran (1981) found that SMEs tended to be subject to higher failure rates, while Rotch (1987) suggested that SMEs had inadequate records of transactions. Welsh and White (1981), in a comparison of SMEs with their larger counterparts, found that SMEs suffered from a lack of trained staff and had a short-range management perspective. They termed these traits *resource poverty* and suggested that their net effect was to magnify the effect of environmental impact, particularly when information systems were involved.

These early suggestions have been supported by more recent studies that found that most SMEs lack technical expertise (Barry & Milner, 2002), most lack adequate capital to undertake technical enhancements (Gaskill, Van Auken & Kim, 1993; Raymond, 2001), most suffer from inadequate organizational planning (Miller & Besser, 2000; Tetteh & Burn, 2001), and many differ from their larger counterparts in the extent of the product/service range available to customers (Reynolds, Savage & Williams, 1994).

A number of recent studies (see, for example, Bunker & MacGregor (2000), Murphy (1996), and Reynolds, et al. (1994)) have examined the differences in management style between large businesses and SMEs. These studies have shown that among other characteristics, SMEs tend to have a small management team (often one or two individuals), they are strongly influenced by the owner and the owner's personal idiosyncrasies, they have little control over their environments (this is supported by the studies of Westhead and Storey (1996) and Hill and Stewart (2000)), and they have a strong desire to remain independent (this is supported by the findings of Dennis (2000) and Drakopoulou-Dodd, Jack, and Anderson (2002)).

Based on an extensive review of the literature, a summary of the features that are unique to SMEs is shown in Table 1. An analysis of the features revealed that they could be classified as being internal or external to the business. Internal features include management, decision-making and planning processes, and the acquisition of resources, while external features are related to the market (products/services and customers) and the external environment (risk taking and uncertainty). Further research is required in order to determine the validity of this classification; however, this is beyond the scope of this chapter. The intention here is to highlight the differences between the features.

Table 1. Features unique to small to medium enterprises (SMEs)

Features Unique to SMEs	Reported By
INTERNAL FEATURES	
Features Related to Management, Decision Making, and Planning Processes	
Features Unique to SMEs	**Reported by**
SMEs have small and centralized management with a short-range perspective.	Bunker & MacGregor (2000) Reynolds et al. (1994) Welsh & White (1981)
SMEs have poor management skills.	Blili & Raymond (1993)
SMEs exhibit a strong desire for independence and avoid business ventures that impinge on their independence.	Dennis (2000) Reynolds et al. (1994)
SME owners often withhold information from colleagues.	Dennis (2000)
The decision-making process in SMEs is intuitive rather than a process based on detailed planning and exhaustive study.	Bunker & MacGregor (2000) Reynolds et al. (1994)
SME owner(s) has/have a strong influence on the decision-making process.	Bunker & MacGregor (2000) Murphy (1996) Reynolds et al. (1994)
Intrusion of family values and concerns in decision-making processes.	Bunker & MacGregor (2000) Dennis (2000) Reynolds et al. (1994)

Table 1. continued

SMEs have informal and inadequate planning and recordkeeping processes.	Tetteh & Burn (2001) Miller & Besser (2000) Reynolds et al. (1994)
SMEs are more intent on improving day-to-day procedures.	MacGregor et al. (1998)
Features Related to Resource Acquisition	
SMEs face difficulties obtaining finance and other resources and, as a result, have fewer resources.	Reynolds et al. (1994) Blili & Raymond (1993) Cragg & King (1993)
SMEs are more reluctant to spend on information technology and, therefore, have limited use of technology.	Dennis (2000) Walczuch, Van Braven & Lundgren (2000) Poon & Swatman (1995) Abell & Limm (1996) MacGregor & Bunker (1996)
SMEs have a lack of technical knowledge and specialist staff and provide little IT training for staff.	Martin & Matlay (2001) Bunker & MacGregor (2000) Reynolds et al. (1994) Blili & Raymond (1993) Cragg & King (1993)
EXTERNAL FEATURES	
Features Related to Products/Services and Markets	
SMEs have a narrow product/service range.	Bunker & MacGregor (2000) Reynolds et al. (1994)
SMEs have a limited share of the market (often confined to a niche market) and, therefore, rely heavily on few customers.	Hadjimonolis (1999) Lawrence (1997) Quayle (2002) Reynolds et al. (1994)
SMEs are product-oriented, while large businesses are more customer-oriented.	Reynolds et al. (1994) Bunker & MacGregor (2000) MacGregor, Bunker & Waugh (1998)
SMEs are not interested in large shares of the market.	Reynolds et al. (1994) MacGregor et al. (1998)
SMEs are unable to compete with their larger counterparts.	Lawrence (1997)
Features Related to Risk Taking and Dealing with Uncertainty	
SMEs have lower control over their external environment than larger businesses and, therefore, face more uncertainty.	Westhead & Storey (1996) Hill & Stewart (2000)
SMEs face more risks than large businesses, because the failure rates of SMEs are higher.	Brigham & Smith (1967) DeLone (1988) Cochran (1981)
SMEs are more reluctant to take risks.	Walczuch et al. (2000) Dennis (2000)

E-Commerce

There are nearly as many definitions of e-commerce as there are contributions to the literature. Turban, Lee, King, and Chung (2002) define e-commerce as the following:

[A]n emerging concept that describes the process of buying, selling or exchanging services and information via computer networks. (Turban et al., 2002, p. 4)

Choi et al. (1997, cited in Turban et al., 2002) draw a distinction between what they term pure e-commerce and partial e-commerce. According to Choi et al. (1997), pure e-commerce has a digital product, a digital process, and a digital agent. All other interactions (including those that might have one or two of the three nominated by Choi et al., 1997) are termed *partial e-commerce.*

Raymond (2001) defines e-commerce as follows:

[F]unctions of information exchange and commercial transaction support that operate on telecommunications networks linking business partners (typically customers and suppliers). (Raymond, 2001, p. 411)

Damanpour (2001), by comparison, defines e-commerce as follows:

[A]ny "net" business activity that transforms internal and external relationships to create value and exploit market opportunities driven by new rules of the connected economy. (Damanpour, 2001, p. 18)

For the purposes of this study, which examines changes to the organization brought about by involvement in e-commerce, the definition provided by Damanpour (2001) is used. While it may be argued that other definitions do not preclude organizational transformation, only the definition of Damanpour (2001) demands those transformations, and it is consistent with the concept in the literature, generally.

As already stated, e-commerce is not just another mechanism to sustain or enhance existing business practices. It is a paradigm shift that is radically changing traditional ways of doing business. Dignum (2002) believes that although IT is an important component, the biggest mistake made by many organizations is that they believe that simply by introducing e-commerce technology, they will succeed without having to worry about their organizational structure. If, as suggested by Treacy and Wiersema (1997), e-commerce transforms a company from one geared toward production excellence to one geared toward customer intimacy, e-commerce is not about technology but about a new way of treating customers and suppliers. Achrol and Kotler (1999), in a discussion of marketing within a network economy, describe this transformation as a shift from being an agent of the seller to being an agent of the buyer. Thus, according to Lee (2001), the biggest challenge for most organizations is not how to imitate or benchmark the best e-commerce model but how to fundamentally change the mindset of management away from operating as a traditional business.

Fundamental to any changes to traditional business procedures is the realization that e-commerce, unlike any previous technological innovation, has a locus of impact not within the organization but at an interorganizational level. Thus, a traditional management focus, which included total quality management, lean manufacturing, and business process reengineering (collectively termed *economics of scarcity* by Lee (2001)), are replaced by gathering, synthesis, and distribution of information (collectively termed *economics of abundance* by Lee (2001)). Output for organizations no longer can simply be finished products but must include information and information services bundled for customer use.

Not only has e-commerce changed the rules pertaining to processes within the organization, it also has had a profound effect on the structure of organizations. The advent of e-commerce has seen a radical change away from the hierarchical-based philosophy. Organizations that were once housed within strict product-based boundaries now have to operate and compete at a global level, and strict hierarchies appear less adept in the turbulent global market. Functions such as marketing, which once were organizational and product-based (i.e., a select set of products was marketed by an individual organization), now are becoming interorganizational and knowledge-based (i.e., multiple organizations continually adjusting their operations to meet changing customer needs and passing on information rather than products to their customers). Indeed, Achrol and Kotler (1999) suggest the following:

Driven by a dynamic and knowledge-rich environment, the hierarchical organizations of the 20th century are disaggregating into a variety of strategic alliance forms. (p. 146)

Not only has e-commerce altered perceptions of organizational structure and function (Giaglis, Klein & O'Keefe, 1999; Kuljis, Macredie & Paul, 1998), it also has altered the use of technology within the organization (Fuller, 2000; Kendall & Kendall, 2001). Where once technology supported the hierarchical structure, it is now technology that is driving the evolution away from it.

For larger businesses, there has been a variety of approaches. Some businesses are moving entirely to a Web-based presence (Lee, 2001), some are establishing subsidiaries that ultimately become stand-alone, online businesses (Gulati & Garino, 2000), and others are merging with online businesses. In all cases, there has been a realization that multi-level hierarchies with their inability to react to external change need to be replaced by flatter structures that are adaptable to an ever-changing external environment.

In light of the previous discussion, the adoption and use of e-commerce in SMEs now will be considered.

E-Commerce and SMEs

Studies carried out at the onset of e-commerce (Acs, Morck, Shaver & Yeung, 1997; Auger & Gallaugher, 1997; Gessin,1996; McRea, 1996; Murphy, 1996; Nooteboom, 1994) predicted that since SMEs always had operated in an externally uncertain environment, they were more likely to benefit from e-commerce. Other authors agreed in principle with this viewpoint but did so with a degree of caution. Hutt and Speh (1998) felt that most areas of the SME sector, with the exception of those SMEs involved in the industrial market, would benefit from e-commerce. They suggested that industrial SMEs already concentrated on an established base of customers and product offerings. Swartz and Iacobucci (2000) felt that the service industries would benefit far more than other areas of the SME community. Other studies (Donckels & Lambrecht, 1997) felt that the business age was a strong predictor of relative benefit of e-commerce adoption, suggesting that older businesses would not adopt as easily as newer ones. Among the predicted benefits available to SMEs were the following:

- A global presence presenting customers with a global choice (Barry & Milner, 2002)
- Improved competitiveness (Auger & Gallaugher, 1997)
- Mass customization and "customerization," presenting customers with personalized products and services (Fuller, 2000)
- Shortening of supply chains, providing rapid response to customer needs (Barry & Milner, 2002)

Recent studies have found that these predictions have not eventuated and that it has been the larger businesses that have been more active with respect to e-commerce (Barry & Milner, 2002; Riquelme, 2002; Roberts & Wood, 2002). A number of reasons has been put forward, including poor security, high costs, and lack of requisite skills. However, some researchers have begun to examine how decisions concerning IT adoption and use are made in the SME sector.

There have been many governmental as well as privately funded projects that have attempted to further the adoption of e-commerce by SMEs. Unfortunately, many of these projects relied on pre-e-commerce criteria and focused on internal systems within the SME rather than interorganizational interaction (Fallon & Moran, 2000; Martin & Matlay, 2001; Poon & Swatman, 1995). The resulting models were stepwise or linear, beginning with e-mail, progressing through a Web site, and moving on to e-commerce adoption and finally organizational transformation. Not only are these models based on inappropriate or oversimplified criteria (Kai-Uwe Brock, 2000), but they also recommend the adoption of e-commerce prior to or without any consideration of any form of organizational change.

E-commerce brings with it changes in communication (Chellappa, Barua, & Whinston, 1996), business method (Henning, 1998), market structure and approach to marketing (Giaglis et al., 1999), as well as changes in day-to-day activities (Doukidis, Smithson, & Naoum, 1998). These changes are exacerbated in the SME sector, as many SMEs have no overall plan and, for the most part, fail to understand the need for competitive strategies (Jeffcoate, Chappell, & Feindt, 2002).

Unlike previous technological innovations, e-commerce brings with it changes to both procedures within the organization as well as changes to the structure of the organization itself. These changes include the way businesses interact; their approaches to marketing, products, and customers; and the way decisions are made and disseminated, particularly decisions concerning technology adoption and use. For SMEs, these changes can have both positive and negative effects. Those SME owners/managers who have developed an organization-wide strategy for e-commerce adoption report increases in efficiency. Those who have not often find that the changes reduce flexibility within their businesses.

Since this study is concerned with both SME adopters and nonadopters, it is appropriate to consider briefly the criteria for e-commerce adoption, the barriers to adoption, the benefits derived from adoption, and the disadvantages incurred through adoption. These will now be considered separately.

Criteria for the Adoption of E-Commerce by SMEs

In their study of 146 SMEs, Poon and Swatman (1995) provided the following five drivers or criteria leading to e-commerce adoption: new modes of direct or indirect marketing; strengthening of relationships with business partners; the ability to reach new customers; improvement to customer services; and the reduction of costs in communication. Similar studies have been carried out in a variety of SME communities. Some of the criteria for adoption and use have been similar to those found by Poon and Swatman, others have provided alternative responses. Abell and Lim (1996) found that reduction in communication costs, improvement in customer services, improvement in lead time, and improvement in sales were the major criteria for e-commerce adoption and use, adding that external technical support was considered vital to any adoption and use strategies.

Lawrence (1997), in an examination of Tasmanian SMEs, noted that improved marketing and the ability to reach new customers were the most common incentives for adopting and using e-commerce. Lawrence also noted that decisions concerning e-commerce adoption often were forced onto SMEs by their larger trading partners. This is supported by studies carried out by MacGregor and Bunker (1996), MacGregor, et al.(1998), Reimenschneider and Mykytyn (2000), and Raymond (2001). Auger and Gallaugher (1997) noted that improvement in customer services and improvement to internal control of the business were strong criteria for e-commerce adoption in SMEs. The strong desire for control also was noted in studies carried out by Reimenschneider and Mykytyn (2000), Poon and Joseph (2001), and Domke-Damonte and Levsen (2002).

A number of studies (Power & Sohal, 2002; Reimenschneider & Mykytyn, 2000) has found that some SMEs have adopted e-commerce, nominating pressure from customers as one of the motivating criteria.

Table 2 provides a summary of the findings related to the criteria used by SMEs in their decision to adopt e-commerce.

Table 2. Summary of e-commerce adoption criteria reported by previous studies

E-Commerce Adoption Criteria	Reported By
Demand and/or pressure from customers	Power and Sohal (2002) Reimenschneider and Mykytyn (2000)
Demand and/or pressure from suppliers	Raymond (2001) Reimenschneider and Mykytyn (2000) MacGregor, et al. (1998) Lawrence (1997)

Table 2. continued

Pressure from competitors	Raisch (2001) Poon and Strom (1997)
Reduced costs	Raisch (2001) Poon and Swatman (1995) Auger and Gallaugher (1997) Abell and Lim (1996)
Increased sales	Lee (2001) Phan (2001) Abell and Lim (1996)
Improvements to customer service	Power and Sohal (2002) Poon and Swatman (1995) Auger and Gallaugher (1997) Abell and Lim (1996)
E-Commerce Adoption Criteria	**Reported By**
Improvements to lead time	Power and Sohal (2002) Reimenschneider and Mykytyn (2000) Abell and Lim (1996)
Improvements to internal efficiency	Porter (2001)
Stronger relations with business partners	Raymond (2001) Evans and Wurster (1997) Poon and Swatman (1995)
Ability to reach new customers and/or markets	Power and Sohal (2002) Reimenschneider and Mykytyn (2000) Poon and Swatman (1995) Lawrence (1997)
Improved competitiveness	Raymond (2001) Turban, Lee, King, and Chung (2000)
Improved marketing	Power and Sohal (2002) Reimenschneider and Mykytyn (2000) Poon and Swatman (1995) Lawrence (1997)
Improved control	Poon and Joseph (2001) Reimenschneider and Mykytyn (2000) Auger and Gallaugher (1997)

Benefits and Disadvantages of E-Commerce in SMEs

For SMEs, the changes associated with e-commerce have produced both positive and negative effects. Studies by Raymond (2001) and Ritchie and Brindley (2000) found that while
e-commerce adoption has eroded trading barriers for SMEs, this has often come at the price
of altering or eliminating commercial relationships and exposing the business to external
risks. Lawrence (1997), Tetteh and Burn (2001), and Lee (2001) contend that e-commerce
adoption fundamentally alters the internal procedures within SMEs. Indeed, Lee (2001)

adds that the biggest challenge to SMEs is not to find the best e-commerce model but to change the mindset of the owners/managers themselves. For those who have developed an organizationwide strategy (in anticipation of e-commerce), these changes can lead to an increase in efficiency in the business for those who have not, which can reduce the flexibility of the business (Tetteh & Burn, 2001) and often lead to a duplication of the work effort (MacGregor et al., 1998). We will now examine the benefits and disadvantages of e-commerce adoption more closely.

E-Commerce Benefits

Many of the substantial benefits of e-commerce adoption fall into the category of intangible benefits and are often not realized by SMEs at the time of adoption. However, SMEs have reported various benefits in the long term following e-commerce implementation. A number of studies has examined both the tangible and intangible benefits achieved by SMEs from the adoption of e-commerce. Studies by Abell and Lim (1996), Poon and Swatman (1995), and Quayle (2002) found that the tangible benefits (e.g., reduced administration costs, reduced production costs, reduced lead time, increased sales) derived from e-commerce were marginal in terms of direct earnings. These same studies found that the intangible benefits (e.g., improvement in the quality of information, improved internal control of the business, improved relations with business partners) were of far greater value to SMEs. Poon and Swatman (1995) also found that e-commerce led to an improved relationship with customers.

It is interesting to note that various authors (Abell & Lim, 1996; Martin & Matlay, 2001; Poon & Swatman, 1995) suggest that tangible benefits are marginal in the short term, which is contrary to the expectations of SME owners/managers, and that, at best, these may be more fruitful in the longer term. This is supported in a recent article by Vrazalic, Bunker, MacGregor, Carlsson, and Magnusson (2002). For summary purposes, the actual benefits of e-commerce derived from a comprehensive review of the literature are listed in Table 3.

Disadvantages Encountered Through the Adoption and Use of E-Commerce by SMEs

E-commerce always has carried the stigma of poor security. Innumerable studies have pointed to the perceived lack of visible security as a reason for nonacceptance of the technology both by businesses and customers (Lawrence, 1997; MacGregor et al., 1998). Recent studies, however, have identified a number of other disadvantages incurred by SME operators in their day-to-day use of e-commerce technologies.

Raymond (2001), in examining the removal of business intermediaries by e-commerce, noted a deterioration of relationships with business partners and customers. He termed this effect as *disintermediation*. Similar findings have been presented by Stauber (2000), who

Table 3. Summary of e-commerce adoption benefits reported by previous studies

E-commerce Benefits	Reported By
E-commerce has led to increased sales.	Abell and Lim (1996)
E-commerce has given us access to new customers and markets.	Quayle (2002) Ritchie and Brindley (2001) Raymond (2001) Sparkes and Thomas (2001)
E-commerce has improved our competitiveness.	Vescovi (2000)
E-commerce has lowered our administration costs.	Quayle (2002) Poon and Swatman (1995) Abell and Lim (1996)
E-commerce has lowered our production costs.	Quayle (2002) Poon and Swatman (1995) Abell and Lim (1996)
E-commerce has reduced the lead time from order to delivery.	Quayle (2002) Poon and Swatman (1995) Abell and Lim (1996)
E-commerce has reduced the stock levels.	Quayle (2002)
E-commerce has increased internal efficiency.	Tetteh and Burn (2001) MacGregor, et al. (1998)
E-commerce has improved our relations with business partners.	Poon and Swatman (1995)
E-commerce has improved the quality of information in our organization.	Quayle (2002) Poon and Swatman (1995) Abell and Lim (1996)

also found that many SME operators complained that increasing costs in their business dealings were attributable to e-commerce use.

Lawrence (1997) found that e-commerce particularly, but not exclusively EDI, resulted in reduced flexibility of work practices and heavier reliance on the technology. Her findings are supported in studies by MacGregor et al. (1998), Lee (2001), and Sparkes and Thomas (2001).

MacGregor et al. (1998), in a study of 131 regional SMEs in Australia, found that many respondents complained that they were doubling their work effort, which, in part, was due to the e-commerce systems not being fully integrated into the existing business systems in the organization. They also found that many respondents complained that the technology had resulted in higher computer maintenance costs.

Again, for convenience, these studies are summarized in Table 4.

Table 4. Summary of e-commerce disadvantages reported by previous studies

Disadvantages of E-Commerce Adoption	Reported By
Adopting e-commerce has resulted in a deterioration of our organization's relations with business partners.	Raymond (2001) Stauber (2000)
Adopting e-commerce has increased our costs.	Stauber (2000)
Adopting e-commerce has increased the computer maintenance in our organization.	MacGregor, et al. (1998)
Adopting e-commerce has doubled the work in our organization.	MacGregor, et al. (1998)
Adopting e-commerce has reduced the flexibility of the work in our organization.	Lee (2001) Lawrence (1997) MacGregor, et al. (1998)
The work in our organization has become more monotonous since e-commerce was adopted.	Healy and DeLuca (2000)
Adopting e-commerce has affected the security of the IT systems in our organization.	Ritchie and Brindley (2001)
Our organization has become dependent on e-commerce following the adoption of this technology (non-e-commerce procedures having to be done through e-commerce formats).	Sparkes and Thomas (2001) MacGregor, et al. (1998) Lawrence (1997)
Demand for on-time service from our customers is greater.	Lee (2001)

Non-Adopters: Barriers to E-Commerce Adoption

Many studies have examined the barriers to e-commerce adoption in SMEs. Some studies simply have reported these barriers, and others have attempted to categorize them. Hadji-monolis (1999), in a study of e-commerce adoption in Cyprus, categorized barriers as either internal or external. She suggested that external barriers could be categorized further into supply barriers (difficulties obtaining finance and technical information), demand barriers (e-commerce not fitting with the products/services or not fitting with the way clients did business), and environmental barriers (security concerns). Internal barriers were divided further into resource barriers (lack of management and technical expertise) and system barriers (e-commerce not fitting with the current business practices). While it is not within the scope of the current study to investigate the validity of these categories, a detailed list of findings and related studies is presented in Table 5.

Strategic Alliances and SMEs

Frequently, it has been argued that multi-level hierarchical structures no longer fit the marketplace (Overby & Min, 2000; Tikkanen, 1998). Not only has this meant a reexamination of organizational structure, but many factors previously considered informal procedures, such as sharing expertise and advice, now have become prominent in day-to-day organizational procedures. This reduction in hierarchical structure together with the increasing importance of informal interorganizational links has meant that organizations not only are interacting economically but also are tied together by factors that Storper (1995) describes as untraded interdependencies. These links, which include sharing of practical experience, sharing of technical expertise, collective learning, and market knowledge (Keeble, Lawson, Moore & Wilkinson, 1999; O'Donnell, Gilmore, Cummins, & Carson, 2001; Overby & Min, 2001, Tikkanen, 1998) have been termed *strategic alliances* or *networks* and are based on relationships of trust and reciprocity.

Table 5. Summary of e-commerce adoption barriers reported by previous studies

Barriers to E-Commerce Adoption	Reported By
E-commerce is not suited to the organization's products/services.	Kendall and Kendall (2001) Walczuch, et al. (2000) Hadjimonolis (1999)
E-commerce is not suited to the organization's way of doing business.	Hadjimonolis (1999) Iacovou, Benbasat, and Dexter (1995)
E-commerce is not suited to the ways in which the organization's clients (customers and/or suppliers) do business.	Hadjimonolis (1999) Iacovou, et al. (1995)
E-commerce does not offer any advantages to the organization.	Quayle (2002) Iacovou, et al. (1995)
There is a lack of technical knowledge in the organization to implement e-commerce.	Chau and Turner (2002) Riquelme (2002) Quayle (2002) Van Akkeren and Cavaye (1999) Lawrence (1997) Iacovou (1995)
E-commerce is too complicated to implement.	Quayle (2002)
E-commerce is not secure.	Quayle (2002) Riquelme (2002) Hadjimonolis (1999) Poon and Swatman (1999) Van Akkeren and Cavaye (1999) Purao and Campbell (1998)
The financial investment required to implement e-commerce is too high.	Riquelme (2002) Quayle (2002) Van Akkeren and Cavaye (1999) Purao and Campbell (1998) Lawrence (1997) Iacovou, et al. (1995)

Table 5. continued

	Walczuch, et al. (2000)
There is a lack of time to implement e-commerce.	Van Akkeren and Cavaye (1999)
	Lawrence (1997)
It is difficult to choose the most suitable e-commerce standard with so many different options available.	Tuunainen (1998)
	Lawrence (1997)

There is a variety of reasons in the literature as to why strategic alliances have developed. Black and Porter (2000) argue that the more complex and dynamic the environment is, the more need there is for some structure to coordinate disparate groups. Christopher (1999) suggests that businesses need to achieve greater agility with supply chain partners. Gilliland and Bello (1997) point to market volatility and technological uncertainty as a source of need for some form of controlling structure, while Tikkanen (1998) suggests a need to realign organizational structure to market structure.

It could be argued that by the very nature of business, all organizations relate to others and, thus, are part of some form of strategic alliance. On the surface, these relationships may appear to be nothing more than exchanges of goods and payments, but relationships with customers, suppliers, and competitors never can be simply described in terms of financial transactions. Dennis (2000) suggests that any dealing with other organizations must impinge on the decision-making process, even if these decisions only involve the strengthening or relaxing of the relationships themselves. Nalebuff and Brandenburg (1996) state that in order for a relationship to be truly a strategic alliance, it must be conscious, interdependent, and cooperating toward a predetermined set of goals.

Eccles and Crane (1998, cited in Dennis, 2000) suggest that strategic alliances, viewed then as self-designing partnerships, are dynamic arrangements that are evolving and adjusting in order to accommodate changes in the business environment. Achrol and Kotler (1999) take this a step further by stating that strategic alliances:

... are more adaptable and flexible because of loose coupling and openness to information. Environmental disturbances transfer imperfectly through loose coupled networks and tend to dissipate in intensity as they spread through the system. (Achrol & Kotler, 1999, p. 147)

Thus, member organizations have interconnected linkages that allow more efficient movement toward predetermined objectives than would be the case if they operated as a single separate entity. By developing and organizing functional components, strategic alliances provide a better mechanism with which to learn and adapt to changes in their environment.

In addition to providing much needed information, strategic alliances often provide legitimacy to their members. For businesses that provide a service and whose products are intangible, company image and reputation becomes crucial, since customers rarely can test or inspect the service before purchase. Cropper (1996) suggests that membership of a strategic alliance very often supplies this image to potential customers.

The advent of e-commerce has given rise to a new wave of research that examines the role of strategic alliances, particularly in SMEs. Much of this research has been prompted by the realization that old hierarchical forms of company organization produced relationships that were too tightly coupled (Marchewka & Towell, 2000) and did not fit an often turbulent marketplace (Overby & Min, 2000; Tikkanen, 1998).

Schindehutte and Morris (2001) state that organizations, particularly SMEs, survive or fail as a function of their adaptability to the marketplace. Those organizations that can interpret patterns in the environment and adapt their structure and strategy to suit those changing patterns will survive. While adaptability may be a function of prior experience or business sector focus, in the SME sector, adaptability often relies on strategic alliance partners.

Properly utilized, strategic alliances can provide a number of advantages over stand-alone organizations. These include the sharing of financial risk (Jorde & Teece, 1989), technical knowledge (Marchewka & Towell, 2000), market penetration (Achrol & Kotler, 1999), and internal efficiency (Datta, 1988).

The purpose of this study was to examine the role, if any, of strategic alliances on the adoption/nonadoption of e-commerce by SMEs. The methodology and findings of this study follow.

Methodology

As can be seen in Tables 2 through 5, previous studies have given rise to 13 criteria, 10 benefits, nine disadvantages, and 10 barriers to e-commerce adoption. A series of six interviews (three with SMEs that had adopted e-commerce and three with SMEs that had rejected the adoption of e-commerce) was undertaken. For the three SMEs that had adopted e-commerce, owners/managers were asked whether the criteria in Table 2, benefits in Table 3, and disadvantages in Table 4 were pertinent to their experience with e-commerce adoption and post-adoption. Owners/managers also were asked whether any other criteria, benefits, or disadvantages should be added to those in the tables. All three owners/managers indicated that the criteria, benefits, and disadvantages were pertinent to their experience and that there were no others that needed to be added. For the SMEs that had rejected adoption of e-commerce, a similar set of interviews was carried out to determine the appropriateness and completeness of the list of barriers (Table 5). Again, all three owners/managers indicated that the barriers in Table 5 were pertinent to their decision making and that no other barriers needed to be added to the existing list.

Based on the findings of the six in-depth interviews, a survey instrument was developed for SME managers. The survey was used to collect data about criteria for adoption of e-commerce, benefits derived from adoption of e-commerce, disadvantages incurred through adoption of e-commerce, and barriers to adoption of e-commerce. Respondents were asked to rate each of the criteria and barriers in terms of the importance to the decision-making process as to whether to adopt e-commerce or not. For those that had adopted e-commerce, respondents were asked to rate the benefits and disadvantages to their own business. A standard five-point Likert scale was used to rate the importance, with 1 meaning very unimportant and 5 meaning very important. Respondents also were asked whether their businesses were part of any form of small business strategic alliance.

Since the survey was intended to examine the criteria, benefits, disadvantages, and barriers of e-commerce adoption in regional SMEs, the location of the respondents needed to be considered. The following set of location guidelines was developed:

- The location must be a large regional center rather than a capital city.

- A viable government-initiated chamber of commerce for SMEs must exist and be well patronized by the SME community.

- The location should have a full range of educational facilities.

- The business community must represent a cross-section of business ages, sizes, sectors, and market foci.

- The SME community must include those that had adopted as well as not adopted e-commerce.

The region chosen was Värmland, Sweden, at four locations (Karlstad, Filipstad, Saffle, and Arvika). The locations met all of the location guidelines and contained personnel who could assist with the distribution and regathering of survey materials. A total of 1,170 surveys were distributed by mail.

Results

Responses were obtained from 313 SME organizations in Sweden, giving a response rate of 26.8%. From these, 275 responses were considered to be valid and usable. The total number of adopters was 152, representing 55.3% of the valid responses. Of those adopters, 91 respondents (59.9%) indicated that they were not members of any form of small business strategic alliance, and 54 (35.5%) indicated that they were. An inspection of the frequencies indicated that the full range of the scales was utilized by respondents for all four of the measures (criteria for e-commerce adoption, benefits derived from e-commerce adoption, disadvantages incurred through e-commerce adoption, and barriers to e-commerce adoption). These will each be presented separately.

E-Commerce Adoption Criteria: Results

The aim of the statistical analysis was to examine the factors underlying the criteria for adoption of e-commerce.

The results of Kaiser-Meyer-Olkin MSA (.785) and Bartlett's Test of Sphericity ($\chi^2 = 614$, $p = .000$) indicated that the data set satisfied the assumptions for factorability. Principle Components Analysis was chosen as the method of extraction in order to account for maximum variance in the data using a minimum number of factors. A three-factor solution was extracted with Eigenvalues of 3.441, 2.816, and 1.667. This was supported by an inspection of the Scree Plot. These three factors accounted for 61.037% of the total variance, as shown in Table 6.

The resulting components were rotated orthogonally using the Varimax procedure, and a simple structure was achieved, as shown in the Rotated Component Matrix in Table 7. Five drivers loaded highly on the first component. These drivers are related to reaching new markets, improving competitiveness, increasing sales, and improving marketing and customer service. This component has been termed *Marketing Objectives*. The driving forces loading on the second component are termed *Internal Business* and are related to cost reduction, improved lead time, improved internal efficiency, and control. The third component is termed *Market Forces* and is related to demand/pressure from customers or competition. The three factors are independent and uncorrelated, as an orthogonal rotation was used. It is interesting to note that the driver "stronger relations with business partners" loads on both component 1 and component 2.

The data then were subdivided into two groups: members (N=61) and non-members (N=115) of a small business strategic alliance. Each of the sets of data was examined to determine the factors underlying the criteria for adoption of e-commerce.

The results of Kaiser-Meyer-Olkin MSA (.876 for non-members, .871 for members) and Bartlett's Test of Sphericity ($\chi^2 = 1028$, $p = .000$ for non-members and $\chi^2 = 692$, p = .000 for members) indicated that the data set satisfied the assumptions for factorability.

For non-member respondents, a three-factor solution was extracted with Eigenvalues 7.127, 1.366, and 1.095. These, again, are termed *Marketing Objectives, Internal Business*, and *Market Forces* and account for 68.486% of the variance (see Table 8).

For member respondents, a two-factor solution was extracted with Eigenvalues 8.101 and 1.360. These are termed *Market Forces* and *Internal Business* and account for 67.581% of variance (see Table 9).

For the non-member respondents, the resulting components were rotated using the Varimax procedure, and a simple structure was achieved, as shown in the Rotated Component matrix in Table 10. The rotated component matrix provides the level of loading of each of the criteria onto each of the factors. The largest value for each of the criteria is determined to be the factor upon which that criterion is loaded. For example, in Table 10, the criterion "demand and/or pressure from customers" is considered loaded onto component 3, as it has the highest loading (.921).

Table 6. Total variance explained (e-commerce adoption criteria)

Component	Rotation Sums of Squared Loadings		
	Eigenvalue	% of Variance	Cumulative %
1	3.441	26.473	26.473
2	2.816	21.662	48.135
3	1.667	12.903	61.037

Table 7. Rotated component matrix (e-commerce adoption criteria)

	Component 1 Marketing Objectives	Component 2 Internal Business	Component 3 Market Forces
Demand and/or pressure from customers	.208	-.005	.846
Demand and/or pressure from suppliers	-.043	.615	.239
Pressure from competitors	.080	.227	.846
Reduced costs	.072	.759	.229
Increased sales	.693	.324	.119
Improved customer service	.639	.278	.224
Improved lead time	.097	.792	-.135
Improved internal efficiency	.295	.506	-.017
Stronger relations with business partners	.507	.407	-.015
Ability to reach new customers/markets	.898	.009	.003
Improved competitiveness	.758	.322	.145
Improved marketing	.808	-.154	.119
Improved control	.331	.673	.135

As can be seen in Table 10, five criteria (demand/pressure from suppliers, reduced costs, improved lead time, improved control, and improved internal efficiency) loaded onto the internal business factor. Five criteria (improved marketing, improved competitiveness, ability to reach new customers/markets, increased sales, and improved customer service) loaded onto the marketing objectives factor. Two criteria (demand/pressure from customers and pressure from competition) loaded onto the market forces factor. One criterion (stronger relations with business partners) loaded almost equally onto the marketing objectives and internal business factors.

For the member respondents, the resulting components were rotated using the Varimax procedure, and a simple structure was achieved, as shown in the Rotated Component matrix in Table 11.

Table 8. Total variance explained (e-commerce adoption criteria—non-members)

	Rotation Sums of Squared Loadings		
Component	Eigenvalue	% of Variance	Cumulative %
1	7.127	50.909	50.909
2	1.366	9.756	60.665
3	1.095	7.821	68.486

Table 9. Total variance explained (e-commerce adoption criteria—members)

Component	Rotation Sums of Squared Loadings		
	Eigenvalue	% of Variance	Cumulative %
1	8.101	57.864	57.864
2	1.360	9.717	67.581

As can be seen in Table 11, three criteria (improved marketing, improved competitiveness, and ability to reach new customers/markets) loaded onto the marketing objectives factor. All other criteria loaded onto the internal business factor. Of interest is the fact that three criteria (improved control, stronger relations with business partners, and improved internal efficiency) loaded equally onto both factors.

E-Commerce Adoption Barriers: Results

As with the criteria, the aim of the statistical analysis was to determine the underlying factors of the barriers to e-commerce adoption.

The results of Kaiser-Meyer-Olkin MSA (.735) and Bartlett's Test of Sphericity ($\chi^2 = 343$, $p = .000$) indicated that the data set satisfied the assumptions for factorability. Principle Components Analysis was chosen as the method of extraction in order to account for maxi-

Table 10. Rotated component matrix (e-commerce adoption criteria—non-members)

	Component 1 Internal Business	Component 2 Marketing Objectives	Component 3 Market Forces
Demand and/or pressure from customers	.079	.110	.921
Demand and/or pressure from suppliers	.696	.154	.213
Pressure from competitors	.234	.329	.733
Reduced costs	.747	.292	.262
Increased sales	.436	.713	.142
Improved customer service	.451	.661	.386
Improved lead time	.771	.294	.127
Improved internal efficiency	.526	.365	.064
Stronger relations with business partners	.498	.517	.366
Ability to reach new customers/markets	.190	.895	.166
Improved competitiveness	.441	.697	.319
Improved marketing	.082	.881	.097
Improved control	.746	.243	.182

mum variance in the data using a minimum number of factors. A two-factor solution was extracted with Eigenvalues of 3.252 and 2.745 and was supported by an inspection of the Screen Plot. These two factors accounted for 59.973% of the total variance, as shown in Table 12. The factors have been termed *too difficult* and *unsuitable*.

The two resulting components were rotated using the Varimax procedure, and a simple structure was achieved, as shown in the Rotated Component Matrix in Table 13. Five barriers loaded highly on the first component. These barriers are related to the complexity of implementation techniques, range of e-commerce options, high investments, and the lack of technical knowledge and time. This component has been termed the *Too Difficult* factor. The barriers highly loaded on the second component are termed the *Unsuitable* factor and are related to the suitability of e-commerce to the respondent's business, including the extent e-commerce matched the SME's products/services, the organization's way of doing business, their clients' ways of doing business, and the lack of advantages offered by e-commerce implementation. These two factors are independent and uncorrelated, as an orthogonal rotation procedure was used. It is interesting to note that the barrier relating to security loaded on both factors, although the loading on the Too Difficult factor was slightly higher.

The data then were subdivided into two groups: members of a small business cluster (N=63) and non-members of a small business cluster (N=60). Again, the aim of the statistical analysis was to determine the underlying factors of the barriers to e-commerce adoption.

The results of Kaiser-Meyer-Olkin MSA (.856 for non-members, .852 for members) and Bartlett's Test of Sphericity ($\chi^2 = 404$, $p = .000$ for non-members and $\chi^2 = 331$, $p = .000$ for members) indicated that the data set satisfied the assumptions for factorability. For both sets of data, again, a two-factor solution was extracted. Table 14 shows the total variance.

Table 11. Rotated component matrix (e-commerce adoption criteria—members)

	Component 1 Marketing Objectives	Component 2 Internal Business
Demand and/or pressure from customers	.475	.594
Demand and/or pressure from suppliers	.154	.813
Pressure from competitors	.261	.732
Reduced costs	.422	.739
Increased sales	.828	.175
Improved customer service	.700	.368
Improved lead time	.246	.743
Improved internal efficiency	.558	.538
Stronger relations with business partners	.603	.520
Ability to reach new customers/markets	.895	.207
Improved competitiveness	.739	.479
Improved marketing	.853	.257
Improved control	.564	.592

An examination of Table 14 shows that the priority of non-members was one relating to organizational barriers. By comparison, members of a small business strategic alliance were more concerned with technical issues than with organizational ones.

E-Commerce Adoption Benefits: Results

The aim of the statistical analysis was to determine the factors underlying the benefits derived from e-commerce adoption.

The results of Kaiser-Meyer-Olkin MSA (.798) and Bartlett's Test of Sphericity ($\chi^2 = 576$, $p = .000$) indicated that the data set satisfied the assumptions for factorability. Principle Components Analysis was chosen as the method of extraction in order to account for maximum variance in the data using a minimum number of factors. A three-factor solution was extracted with Eigenvalues of 4.083, 1.657, and 1.007 and was supported by an inspection

Table 12. Total variance explained (e-commerce adoption barriers)

	Rotation Sums of Squared Loadings		
Component	Eigenvalue	% of Variance	Cumulative %
1	3.252	32.520	32.520
2	2.745	27.453	59.973

Table 13. Rotated component matrix (e-commerce adoption barriers)

	Component 1 Too Difficult	Component 2 Unsuitable
E-commerce is not suited to our products/ services.	-.086	.844
E-commerce is not suited to our way of doing business.	-.034	.909
E-commerce is not suited to the ways our clients (customers and/or suppliers) do business.	-.004	.643
E-commerce does not offer any advantages to our organization.	.076	.731
We do not have the technical knowledge in the organization to implement e-commerce.	.743	.074
E-commerce is too complicated to implement.	.852	.102
E-commerce is not secure.	.525	.385
The financial investment required to implement e-commerce is too high for us.	.703	-.092
We do not have time to implement e-commerce.	.742	-.294
It is difficult to choose the most suitable e-commerce standard with so many different options available.	.800	-.054

Table 14. Total variance explained (e-commerce adoption barriers)

	Component	Eigenvalue	% of Variance	Cumulative %
	Rotation Sums of Squared Loadings			
Non-Members	**Too difficult**	1.538	17.086	17.086
	Unsuitable	5.218	57.974	75.060
Members	**Too difficult**	4.895	54.389	54.389
	Unsuitable	1.407	15.629	70.018

of the Screen Plot. These three factors accounted for 67.476% of the total variance, as shown in Table 15.

The three resulting components were rotated using the Varimax procedure, and a simple structure was achieved, as shown in the Rotated Component Matrix in Table 16. Five benefits loaded highly on the first component. These benefits are related to internal efficiency and marketing. This component has been termed the *Efficiency* factor. Three benefits that highly loaded on the second component are termed the *Costs* factor, and two benefits that loaded onto the final factor are termed the *Sales/Inventory* factor. These three factors are independent and uncorrelated, as an orthogonal rotation procedure was used.

The data then were subdivided into two groups: members (respondents that were members of a small business strategic alliance) and non-members (respondents that were not). Again, the aim of the statistical analysis was to determine the factors underlying the benefits derived from e-commerce adoption.

The results of Kaiser-Meyer-Olkin MSA (.738, non-members and .836, members) and Bartlett's Test of Sphericity ($\chi^2 = 351, p = .000$, non-members; $\chi^2 = 292, p = .000$, members) indicated that the data set satisfied the assumptions for factorability. Principle Components Analysis was chosen as the method of extraction in order to account for maximum variance in the data using a minimum number of factors. For the non-member respondents, a three-factor solution was extracted with Eigenvalues of 3.776, 1.774, and 1.131 and was supported by an inspection of the Screen Plot. These three factors accounted for 66.817% of the total variance, as shown in Table 17. For the member respondents, a two-factor solution was extracted with Eigenvalues of 5.083 and 1.683, accounting for 67.657% of the total variance, as shown in Table 18.

Both sets of components were rotated using the Varimax procedure, and a simple structure was achieved, as shown in the Rotated Component Matrix in Table 19. In both cases, the factors are independent and uncorrelated, as an orthogonal rotation procedure was used.

E-Commerce Adoption Disadvantages: Results

The results of Kaiser-Meyer-Olkin MSA (.879) and Bartlett's Test of Sphericity ($\chi^2 = 767.73, p = .000$) indicated that the data set satisfied the assumptions for factorability. Prin-

Table 15. Total variance explained (e-commerce adoption benefits)

	Rotation Sums of Squared Loadings		
Component	Eigenvalue	% of Variance	Cumulative %
1	4.083	29.911	29.911
2	1.657	19.985	49.897
3	1.007	17.580	67.476

ciple Components Analysis was chosen as the method of extraction in order to account for maximum variance in the data using a minimum number of factors. A two-factor solution was extracted with eigenvalues of 5.274 and 1.429 and was supported by the Scree plot. The two factors have been termed *day-to-day* and *organizational* and account for 60.935% of the variance. These are shown in Table 20.

The resulting two components were rotated using a Varimax procedure, and a simple structure was achieved, as shown in the rotated component matrix in Table 21. These two factors are independent and uncorrelated, as an orthogonal rotation procedure was used.

Four disadvantages loaded onto component 1 (Organizational): higher costs, increased computer maintenance, dependence on e-commerce, and greater demand for on-time service. Five disadvantages loaded onto the second component (Day-to-Day): deterioration of relations with business partners, doubling of work, reduced flexibility of work, monotonous work, and security risks.

Again, the data then were subdivided into two groups: respondents that were members of a small business strategic alliance and respondents that were not.

Table 16. Rotated component matrix (e-commerce adoption benefits)

	Component 1 Efficiency	Component 2 Costs	Component 3 Inventory
Increased sales	.759	.271	.255
New customers and markets	.905	.106	.018
Improved competitiveness	.742	.334	.163
Lower administration costs	.022	.822	.184
Lower production costs	.133	.447	.079
Reduced lead time	.116	.255	.788
Reduced stock	.048	.081	.874
Increased internal efficiency	.221	.820	.161
Improved relations with business partners	.489	.282	.462
Improved quality of information	.850	-.025	-.004

Table 17. Total variance explained (e-commerce adoption benefits—non-members)

	Rotation Sums of Squared Loadings		
Component	Eigenvalue	% of Variance	Cumulative %
1	3.776	37.765	37.765
2	1.774	17.741	55.505
3	1.131	11.311	66.817

Table 18. Total variance explained (e-commerce adoption benefits—members)

	Rotation Sums of Squared Loadings		
Component	Eigenvalue	% of Variance	Cumulative %
1	5.083	50.830	50.830
2	1.683	16.827	67.657

For respondents who were not members of a small business strategic alliance, the results of Kaiser-Meyer-Olkin MSA (.873) and Bartlett's Test of Sphericity ($\chi^2 = 486.94$, $p = .000$) indicated that the data set satisfied the assumptions for factorability. Principle Components Analysis was chosen as the method of extraction in order to account for maximum variance in the data using a minimum number of factors. A two-factor solution was extracted with eigenvalues of 5.237 and 1.426 and was supported by the Scree plot. These two factors accounted for 60.566% of the variance, as shown in Table 22.

For respondents who were members of a small business strategic alliance, the results of Kaiser-Meyer-Olkin MSA (.749) and Bartlett's Test of Sphericity ($\chi^2 = 288.49$, $p = .000$) indicated that the data set satisfied the assumptions for factorability. Principle Components Analysis was chosen as the method of extraction in order to account for maximum variance

Table 19. Rotated component matrix (e-commerce adoption benefits—non-members & members)

	NON-MEMBERS			MEMBERS	
	Component 1 Sales	Component 2 Efficiency	Component 3 Cost	Component 1 Efficiency/ Sales	Component 2 Costs & Inventory
Increased sales	.701	.335	.184	.875	.301
New customers and markets	.898	.004	.005	.927	.122
Improved competitiveness	.637	.337	.339	.876	.124

Table 19. continued

Lower administration costs	-.004	.260	.867	.216	.771
Lower production costs	.188	.001	.452	.399	.743
Reduced lead time	.006	.860	.005	.161	.822
Reduced stock	.008	.850	.181	-.114	.501
Increased internal efficiency	.006	.187	.853	.522	.646
Improved relations with business partners	.296	.639	.232	.720	.267
Improved quality of information	.846	.002	-.002	.808	-.003

in the data using a minimum number of factors. A three-factor solution was extracted with Eigenvalues of 5.043, 1.636, and 1.005 and was supported by an inspection of the Scree Plot. These three factors, termed *organizational*, *day-to-day*, and *technical*, accounted for 65.859% of the total variance, as shown in Table 23.

In both cases, the resulting components were rotated using a Varimax procedure, and a simple structure was achieved (see Tables 24 and 25).

An examination of Tables 24 and 25 shows that where increased computer maintenance was loaded onto the organizational factor and dependence on e-commerce was loaded equally onto both factors for non-members, member respondents considered these a separate, non-related factor of disadvantages.

Discussion

Before examining the data in detail, a discussion of a number of general findings is appropriate. First, it is interesting to note that of the 152 adopters, only 54 (35.5%) indicated that they considered that their business was part of a strategic alliance. There are two possibilities for this lower than expected result:

1. While many respondents may have dealt with other businesses, these interactions were informal rather than under some form of enforced governance. This is supported by the findings of Premaratne (2001).

Table 20. Total variance explained (e-commerce adoption disadvantages)

	Rotation Sums of Squared Loadings		
Component	Eigenvalue	% of Variance	Cumulative %
1	5.274	47.923	47.923
2	1.429	12.992	60.935

Table 21. Rotated component matrix (e-commerce adoption disadvantages)

	Component 1 Organizational	Component 2 Day-to-Day
Deterioration of relations with business partners	.165	.731
Higher costs	683	.258
Increased computer maintenance	.727	.326
Doubling of work	.351	.523
Reduced flexibility of work	.137	.874
Monotonous work	.237	.778
Security risks	.271	.763
Dependence on e-commerce	.541	.440
Greater demand for on-time service	.806	-.016

2.   Since the study was conducted on regional SMEs, the ability to form and maintain any form of network was more difficult than it might have been for city-based SMEs. This is supported by the findings of Dahlstrand (1999), who suggests that geographic proximity is essential for the development and maintenance of alliances, particularly in the small business arena.

Second, for all four measures of e-commerce adoption, there are underlying factors that denote both grouping and priority. This gives researchers a powerful explanatory tool, because it reduces the noise in the data. Instead of accounting for 13 criteria, 10 benefits, 10 barriers, and nine disadvantages, each of these can be explained by their underlying factors. The Rotated Component Matrix also enables the prediction of the scores of each individual criterion, benefit, disadvantage, or barrier based on the score of the other three or four factors, and vice versa, for an SME. This makes it simpler not only to explain but also to predict measures of e-commerce adoption in SMEs.

It is now appropriate to examine the individual measures of e-commerce adoption and the differences between the respondents that are members of a strategic alliance and those that are not.

Table 22. Total variance explained (e-commerce adoption disadvantages: non-members)

Rotation Sums of Squared Loadings			
Component	Eigenvalue	% of Variance	Cumulative %
1	5.237	47.605	47.605
2	1.426	12.962	60.566

Table 23. Total variance explained (e-commerce adoption disadvantages: members)

Rotation Sums of Squared Loadings			
Component	Eigenvalue	% of Variance	Cumulative %
1	5.043	45.849	45.849
2	1.636	14.869	60.719
3	1.005	9.140	69.859

Table 24. Rotated component matrix (e-commerce adoption disadvantages: non-members)

	Component 1 Day-to-Day	Component 2 Organizational
Deterioration of relations with business partners	.716	.285
Higher costs	.240	.708
Increased computer maintenance	.339	.733
Doubling of work	.538	.295
Reduced flexibility of work	.867	.111

E-Commerce Adoption Criteria: Discussion

The results of this study indicate that correlations exist among the criteria for the adoption of e-commerce by SMEs and enable the grouping of criteria into three factors. These factors have been termed *Marketing Objectives*, *Internal Business* and *Market Forces*. The Marketing Objectives factor is related to criteria that might be termed *long-term* or *strategic*. These include improvements to customer services, increase in sales, reaching new customers and markets, improvement in competitiveness, and improvement to marketing. The Internal Business factor is related to criteria that affect the business on a day-to-day basis at a tacti-

Table 24. continued

Monotonous work	.794	.153
Security risks	.780	.223
Dependence on e-commerce	.490	.468
Greater demand for on-time service	-.004	.783

Table 25. Rotated component matrix (e-commerce adoption disadvantages—members)

	Component 1 Day-to-Day	Component 2 Organizational	Component 3 Technical
Deterioration of relations with business partners	.691	-.134	.177
Higher costs	.211	.569	.350
Increased computer maintenance	.251	.314	.770
Doubling of work	.491	.546	-.002
Reduced flexibility of work	.875	.115	.200
Monotonous Work	.766	.421	.105
Security risks	.715	.197	.292
Dependence on e-commerce	.202	.137	.870
Greater Demand for 'on-time' service	.009	.814	.341

cal level. It includes demand and pressure from suppliers, reduction of costs, shortening of lead time, improvement in control, and improvement in internal efficiency. The third factor, Market Focus, emanates from outside the business and is related to demand and pressure from customers and pressure from competition in the line of the business. Finally, the criterion Stronger Relations with Business Partners was found to be related to the internal factors Marketing Objectives and Internal Business, although the factor loading of this criterion was higher in relation to Marketing Objectives (.507).

An examination of Tables 10 and 11 shows that while the non-member respondents have maintained a three-factor split of the criteria for e-commerce adoption, respondents that are part of a small business strategic alliance have grouped the market forces criteria under the Internal Business factor. A number of authors (Datta, 1988; Jorde & Teece, 1989; Overby & Min, 2001) has suggested that small business strategic alliances assist SMEs by improving the internal efficiency of members and bring a realization that many barriers that appear to be external can be overcome by internal strategies. The data from this study appear to support this view for regional Swedish SMEs.

For the small business owner/manager, the data in Tables 10 and 11 suggest that while respondents that are not members of a small business strategic alliance consider pressure from customers and pressure from competition as outside their sphere of control (i.e., separate to the marketing and internal needs of the business), member respondents have linked these to other factors within their sphere of control. This would suggest that in line with earlier research findings (Achrol & Kotler, 1999; Dennis, 2000; Overby & Min, 2000), one of the by-products of membership of a small business strategic alliance is to better control the external environment, particularly where e-commerce is utilized in the day-to-day functioning of the business.

For the researcher, the findings in Tables 10 and 11 raise some interesting questions concerning the mechanisms by which small business strategic alliances appear to alter the perception of pressure by competition and pressure by customers, rendering them part of the marketing and internal needs of the business rather than being separate from them.

E-Commerce Adoption Barriers: Discussion

An examination of Table 12 indicates that correlations between barriers to e-commerce adoption exist and enable the grouping of barriers according to two factors. These factors have been termed *Too Difficult* and *Unsuitable*. The Too Difficult factor is related to the barriers that make e-commerce complicated to implement, including barriers such as the complexity of e-commerce implementation techniques, the difficulty in deciding which standard to implement because of the large range of e-commerce options, the difficulty obtaining funds to implement e-commerce, the lack of technical knowledge, and the difficulty in finding time to implement e-commerce. The Unsuitable factor, on the other hand, is related to the perceived unsuitability of e-commerce to SMEs. These barriers include the unsuitability of e-commerce to the SME's products and services, way of doing business, and client's way of doing business, as well as to the lack of perceived advantages of e-commerce implementation.

An examination of Table 14 shows that while the two factors Too Difficult and Unsuitable still underpin the barriers to e-commerce adoption, the priority placed on the two factors is substantially different—54.389% of members of a small business cluster indicated that their main reason for not adopting e-commerce is that the technology is too difficult; and by comparison, only 17.086% of the non-members felt that this was their primary reason for non-adoption. Likewise, while 15.629% of the member respondents felt that e-commerce was unsuitable for their particular business, 57.974% of the non-member respondents gave this as their primary concern.

A number of authors (Achrol & Kotler, 1999; Marchewka & Towell, 2000) suggests that small business clusters assist members by sharing technical knowledge, talent, and skills. An examination of the data in Table 7 would tend to refute this, at least for the respondents of this study. However, the data do tend to support the notion put forward by Schindehutte and Morris (2001), Datta (1988), and Overby and Min (2000) that membership of a small business cluster assists in internal efficiency of its members.

E-Commerce Adoption Benefits: Discussion

One of the aims of this study was to determine whether the groupings of benefits differed between respondents that were part of a small business strategic alliance and respondents that were not. An examination of Table 19 shows that for the non-member respondents, the following three benefits loaded onto Cost: reduced administration costs, reduced production costs, and increased internal efficiency. The factor accounted for 17.741% of variance in the non-member group. By comparison, two more benefits loaded onto this factor for member respondents: improved quality of information and reduced lead time. This factor accounted for 16.827% of variance for the member respondents.

For the non-member respondents, the following three benefits loaded onto the factor Inventory: increased sales, new customers/markets, and improved competitiveness. This factor accounted for 11.331% of the variance. For the member respondents, an extra benefit (improved relations with business partners) loaded onto this factor. This factor accounted for 16.827% of variance. As can be seen in Tables 17, 18, and 19, member respondents combined cost and inventory benefits into a single factor, placing all other benefits under a single factor, Efficiency. By comparison, non-member respondents considered that there were three distinct and separate benefits: Efficiency, Sales, and Cost.

While the data in Table 19 give no comparisons (member/non-member) regarding the amount of benefit e-commerce is perceived to have given the business, they do suggest that there has been a rationalization of the perception of member respondents to those benefits. While non-member respondents have separated reduced stock, reduced lead time, and improved relations with business partners from sales and cost benefits, member respondents have grouped reduced stock, reduced lead time, and improved relations with business partners with either cost-saving or sales-enhancing benefits. For the researcher, there is a clear need to understand why stand-alone SMEs (i.e., non-member respondents) separate benefits into three distinct groups. There is also a more important need to determine what the mechanisms are whereby new member respondents begin to reconsider the groupings of benefits derived from e-commerce adoption and use.

E-Commerce Adoption Disadvantages: Discussion

An examination of Table 21 shows that the following four disadvantages loaded onto the Organizational component: higher costs, increased computer maintenance, dependence on e-commerce, and greater demand for on-time service. Five disadvantages loaded onto the second component (Day-to-Day): deterioration of relations with business partners, doubling of work, reduced flexibility of work, monotonous work, and security risks.

An examination of Table 24 shows that for the non-member respondents, the following five disadvantages loaded onto the first component (Day-to-Day): deterioration of relations with business partners, doubling of work, reduced flexibility of work, monotonous work, and security. This component accounted for 47.605% of the variance. Component 2 (Organizational), which accounted for 12.962% of the variance had the following three disadvantages loaded:

higher costs, increased computer maintenance, and greater demand for on-time service. The disadvantage dependence on e-commerce loaded equally onto both components.

An examination of Table 25 shows that for member respondents, a third component (Technical) occurs. The following four disadvantages loaded onto the first component (Day-to-Day): deterioration of relations with business partners, reduced flexibility of work, monotonous work, and security. This component accounted for 45.849% of the variance. Two disadvantages loaded onto the second component (Organizational): higher costs and greater demand for on-time service. This component accounted for 14.869% of the variance. Two disadvantages loaded onto the third component (Technical): increased computer maintenance and dependence on e-commerce. This component accounted for 9.140% of the variance.

A number of authors (Achrol & Kotler, 1999; Dennis, 2000; Foy, 1994, cited in Dennis, 2000) have suggested that small business strategic alliances maximize flexibility such that problems impinging on member organizations are dissipated quickly. While the current study does not provide the amount and speed of the dissipation of disadvantages derived from e-commerce, it does show that an extra level of potential dissipation appears to be in place for respondents that are members of a small business strategic alliance.

Limitations of the Study

It should be noted that this study has several limitations. The data for the study were collected from regional SMEs in four areas of Sweden. Therefore, although conclusions can be drawn, the results may not be generalizable to SMEs in other countries. Also, the data for the study were collected from various industry sectors, and it is not possible to make sector-specific conclusions. Furthermore, according to Sohal and Ng (1998), the views expressed in the surveys are of a single individual from the responding organization, and only those interested in the study are likely to complete and return the survey. Finally, this is a quantitative study, and further qualitative research is required in order to gain a better understanding of the key issues.

Conclusion

The aim of this study was to examine whether the underlying factors of the four measures of e-commerce adoption by SMEs (i.e., criteria, barriers, benefits, and disadvantages) differed depending on whether the SME was part of a small business strategic alliance or not. For the criteria to adopt, the results showed that while non-members grouped the criteria into three factors (market forces, internal business, marketing objectives), those that were part of a small business strategic alliance considered that criteria were either market forces or internal business.

For the barriers to e-commerce adoption, the correlation matrix indicated two distinct sets of groupings, and a two-factor solution was extracted using factor analysis. It was found that 10 e-commerce barriers could be grouped according to two factors, which were termed Too Difficult and Unsuitable. The data also showed that while the two factors were appropriate to both members and non-members, there was a distinct shift in emphasis between the two groups.

For the benefits derived from e-commerce adoption, the results showed that while the number of factors remained the same, the mapping of benefits onto those factors differed, depending on whether the respondent was a member of a small business strategic alliance or not.

The disadvantages incurred because of e-commerce adoption showed that member respondents considered dependence on e-commerce and increased computer maintenance to be neither organizational nor day-to-day disadvantages, but rather a separate set of disadvantages. This result does not support earlier findings that suggest that small business strategic alliances reduce technology concerns through a sharing of skills and experiences.

The study presented in this chapter is only one part of a larger long-term project that is investigating e-commerce adoption in SMEs. Further research currently is being undertaken in order to overcome some of the limitations outlined previously and to provide an in-depth picture of e-commerce adoption in SMEs. Specifically, the survey instrument is being replicated in two regional areas in Australia, which will provide comparable results.

References

Abell, W., & Lim, L. (1996). Business use of the Internet in New Zealand: An exploratory study. In *Proceedings of the AUSWeb—the Second Australian WWW Conference.* Retrieved from http://www.scu.edu.au/sponsored/ausweb/ausweb96/business/abell/paper.html

Achrol, R. S., & Kotler, P. (1999). Marketing in the network economy. *Journal of Marketing, 63,* 146–163.

Acs, Z. J., Morck, R., Shaver, J. M., & Yeung, B. (1997). The internationalisation of small and medium sized enterprises: A policy perspective. *Small Business Economics, 9*(1), 7–20.

Auger, P., & Gallaugher, J. M. (1997). Factors affecting adoption of an Internet-based sales presence for small businesses. *The Information Society, 13*(1), 55–74.

Barnett, R. R., & Mackness, J. R. (1983). An action research study of small firm management. *Journal of Applied Systems, 10,* 63–83.

Barry, H., & Milner, B. (2002). SME's and electronic commerce: A departure from the traditional prioritisation of training? *Journal of European Industrial Training, 25*(7), 316–326.

Black, J. S., & Porter, L. W. (2000). *Management: Meeting new challenges.* NJ: Prentice Hall.

Blili, S., & Raymond, L. (1993). Threats and opportunities for small and medium-sized enterprises. *International Journal of Information Management, 13,* 439–448.

Brigham, E. F., & Smith, K. V. (1967). The cost of capital to the small firm. *The Engineering Economist, 13*(1), 1–26.

Bunker, D. J., & MacGregor, R. C. (2000). Successful generation of information technology (IT): Requirements for small/medium enterprises (SMEs)—Cases from regional Australia. In *Proceedings of SMEs in a Global Economy*, Wollongong, Australia.

Chau, S. B., & Turner, P. (2001). A four phase model of EC business transformation amongst small to medium sized enterprises. In *Proceedings of the 12th Australasian Conference on Information Systems*, Coffs Harbour, Australia.

Chellappa, R., Barua, A., & Whinston, A. (1996). Looking beyond internal corporate Web servers. In R. Kalakota, & A. Whinston (Eds.), *Readings in electronic commerce* (pp. 311–321). Reading, MA: Addison Wesley.

Christopher, M. L. (1999). Creating the agile supply chain. In D.L. Anderson (Ed.), *Achieving supply chain excellence through technology* (pp. 28–32). San Francisco: Montgomery Research.

Cochran, A. B. (1981). Small business mortality rates: A review of the literature. *Journal of Small Business Management, 19*(4), 50–59.

Cragg, P. B., & King, M. (1993). Small-firm computing: Motivators and inhibitors. *MIS Quarterly, 17*(1), 47–60.

Cropper, S. (1996). Collaborative working and the issue of sustainability. In C. Huxham (Ed.), *Creating collaborative advantage* (pp. 80–100). London: Sage.

Dahlstrand, A. L. (1999). Technology-based SMEs in the Goteborg region: Their origin and interaction with universities and large firms. *Regional Studies, 33*(4), 379–389.

Damanpour, F. (2001). E-business e-commerce evolution: Perspective and strategy. *Managerial Finance, 27*(7), 16–33.

Datta, D. (1988). International joint ventures: A framework for analysis. *Journal of General Management, 14*, 78–91.

DeLone, W. H. (1988). Determinants for success for computer usage in small business. *MIS Quarterly, 12*(1), 51–61.

Dennis, C. (2000). Networking for marketing advantage. *Management Decision, 38*(4), 287–292.

Dignum, F. (2002). E-commerce in production: Some experiences. *Integrated Manufacturing Systems, 13*(5), 283–294.

Domke-Damonte, D., & Levsen, V.B. (2002, Summer). The effect of Internet usage on cooperation and performance in small hotels. *SAM Advanced Management Journal*, 31–38.

Donckels, R., & Lambrecht, J. (1997). The network position of small businesses: An explanatory model. *Journal of Small Business Management, 35*(2), 13–28.

Doukidis, G. I., Smithson, S., & Naoum, G. (1992). Information systems management in Greece: Issues and perceptions. *Journal of Strategic Information Systems, 1*, 139–148.

Drakopoulou-Dodd, S., Jack, S., & Anderson, A. R. (2002). Scottish entrepreneurial networks in the international context. *International Small Business Journal, 20*(2), 213–219.

e-Europe. (2005). E-business. *Europe's Information Society.* Retrieved November 20, 2005, from http://europa.eu.int/information_society/eeurope/2005/all_about/ebusiness/index_en.htm

Evans, P. B., & Wurster, T. S. (1997, September-October). Strategy and the new economics of information. *Harvard Business Review*, 70–82.

Fallon, M., & Moran, P. (2000). Information communications technology (ICT) and manufacturing SMEs. In *Proceedings of the 2000 Small Business and Enterprise Development Conference*, Manchester.

Fuller, T. (2000). The small business guide to the Internet: A practical approach to going online. *International Small Business Journal, 19*(1), 105–107.

Gaskill, L. R., Van Auken, H. E., & Kim, H. (1993). The impact of operational planning on small business retail performance. *Journal of Small Business Strategy, 5*(1), 21–35.

Gessin, J. (1996, January-February). Impact of electronic commerce on small and medium sized enterprises. *Management*, 11–12.

Giaglis, G., Klein, S., & O'Keefe, R. (1999). Disintermediation, reintermediation, or cybermediation? The future of intermediaries in electronic marketplaces. In *Proceedings of the 12th Bled Electronic Commerce Conference*, Bled, Slovenia.

Gilliland, D. I., & Bello, D. C. (1997). The effect of output controls, process controls, and flexibility on export channel performance. *Journal of Marketing, 6*(1), 22–38.

Gulati, R., & Garino, J. (2000, May-June). Getting the right mix of bricks and clicks for your company. *Harvard Business Review*, 107–114.

Hadjimonolis, A. (1999). Barriers to innovation for SMEs in a small less developed country (Cyprus). *Technovation, 19*(9), 561–570.

Healy, J. L., & DeLuca, J. M. (2000). Electronic commerce: Beyond the euphoria. *Journal of Healthcare Information Management, 14*(2), 97–111.

Henning, K. (1998). *The digital enterprise: How digitisation is redefining business.* New York: Random House Business Books.

Hill, R., & Stewart, J. (2000). Human resource development in small organizations. *Journal of European Industrial Training, 24*(2/3/4), 105–117.

Hutt, M. D., & Speh, T. W. (1998). *Business marketing management: A strategic view of industrial and organisational markets.* Fort Worth, TX: Dryden Press.

Iacovou, C. L., Benbasat, I., & Dexter, A. S. (1995). Electronic data interchange and small organisations: Adoption and impact of technology. *MIS Quarterly, 19*(4), 465–485.

Jeffcoate, J., Chappell, C., & Feindt, S. (2002). Best practice in SME adoption of e-commerce. *Benchmarking: An International Journal, 9*(2), 122–132.

Jorde, T., & Teece, D. (1989). Competition and cooperation: striking the right balance. *Californian Management Review, 31*, 25–38.

Kai-Uwe Brock, J. (2000). Information and technology in the small firm. In S. Carter, & D. Jones-Evans (Eds.), *Enterprise and the small business* (pp. 384–408). Prentice Hall.

Keeble, D., Lawson, C., Moore, B., & Wilkinson, F. (1999). Collective learning processes, networking and "institutional thickness" in the Cambridge region. *Regional Studies, 33*(4), 319–332.

Kendall, J. E., & Kendall, K. E. (2001). A paradoxically peaceful coexistence between commerce and ecommerce. *Journal of Information Technology, Theory and Application, 3*(4), 1–6.

Kuljis, J., Macredie, R., & Paul, R. J. (1998). Information gathering problems in multinational banking. *Journal of Strategic Information Systems, 7*, 233–245.

Lawrence, K. L. (1997). Factors inhibiting the utilisation of electronic commerce facilities in Tasmanian small- to medium-sized enterprises. In *Proceedings of the 8th Australasian Conference on Information Systems,* Adelaide, South Australia.

Lee, C. S. (2001). An analytical framework for evaluating e-commerce business models and strategies. *Internet Research: Electronic Network Applications and Policy, 11*(4), 349–359.

MacGregor, R. C., & Bunker, D. J. (1996). The effect of priorities introduced during computer acquisition on continuing success with it in small business environments. In *Proceedings of the Information Resource Management Association International Conference,* Washington, DC.

MacGregor, R. C., Bunker, D. J., & Waugh, P. (1998). Electronic commerce and small/medium enterprises (SMEs) in Australia: An electronic data interchange (EDI) pilot study. In *Proceedings of the 11th International Bled Electronic Commerce Conference,* Slovenia.

Marchewka, J. T., & Towell, E. R. (2000). A comparison of structure and strategy in electronic commerce. *Information Technology and People, 13*(2), 137–149.

Martin, L. M., & Matlay, H. (2001). "Blanket" approaches to promoting ICT in small firms: Some lessons from the DTI ladder adoption model in the UK. *Internet Research: Electronic Networking Applications and Policy, 11*(5), 399–410.

McRea, P. (1996, Jan-Feb). Reshaping industry with the Internet. *Management,* 7–10.

Meredith, G. G. (1994). *Small business management in Australia* (4th ed.). Sydney: McGraw Hill.

Miles, G., Preece, S., & Baetz, M. C. (1999, April). Dangers of dependence: The impact of strategic alliance use by small technology based firms. *Journal of Small Business Management,* 20–29.

Miller, N. L., & Besser, T. L. (2000). The importance of community values in small business strategy formation: evidence from rural Iowa. *Journal of Small Business Management, 38*(1), 68–85.

Murphy, J. (1996). *Small business management.* London: Pitman.

Nalebuff, B. J., & Brandenburg, A. M. (1996). *Co-operation.* Philadelphia: Harper Collins Business.

NOIE—The National Office for the Information Economy. (2002). *E-business for small business*. Retrieved May 25, 2003, from http://www.noie.gov.au/projects/ebusiness/ Advancing/SME.

Nooteboom, B. (1994). Innovation and diffusion in small firms: Theory and evidence. *Small Business Economics*, *6*(5), 327–347.

O'Donnell, A., Gilmore, A., Cummins, D., & Carson, D. (2001). The network construct in entrepreneurship research: A review and critique. *Management Decision*, *39*(9), 749–760.

Overby, J. W., & Min, S. (2001). International supply chain management in an Internet environment: A network-oriented approach to internationalisation. *International Marketing Review*, *18*(4), 392–420.

Phan, D. D. (2001, Fall). E-business management strategies: A business-to-business case study. *Information Systems Management*, *18*(4), 61–69.

Poon, S., & Joseph, M. (2001). A preliminary study of product nature and electronic commerce. *Marketing Intelligence & Planning*, *19*(7), 493–499.

Poon, S., & Strom, J. (1997). Small business use of the Internet: Some realities. In *Proceedings of the Association for Information Systems Americas Conference*, Indianapolis, Indiana.

Poon, S., & Swatman, P. (1995). The Internet for small businesses: An enabling infrastructure for competitiveness. In *Proceedings of the Fifth Internet Conference of the Internet Society*, Honolulu, HI.

Poon, S., & Swatman, P. M. C. (1999). An exploratory study of small business Internet commerce issues. *Information & Management*, *35*, 9–18.

Porter, M. (2001, March). Strategy and the Internet. *Harvard Business Review*, 63–78.

Power, D. J., & Sohal, A. S. (2002). Implementation and usage of electronic commerce in managing the supply chain: A comparative study of ten Australian companies. *Benchmarking: An International Journal*, *9*(2), 190–208.

Premaratne, S.P. (2001). Networks, resources and small business growth: The experience in Sri Lanka. *Journal of Small Business Management*, *39*(4), 363–371.

Purao, S., & Campbell, B. (1998). Critical concerns for small business electronic commerce: Some reflections based on interviews of small business owners. In *Proceedings of the Association for Information Systems Americas Conference*, Baltimore.

Quayle, M. (2002). E-commerce: The challenge for UK SMEs in the twenty-first century. *International Journal of Operations and Production Management*, *22*(10), 1148–1161.

Raisch, W. D. (2001). *The e-marketplace: Strategies for success in B2B*. New York: Mc-Graw-Hill.

Raymond, L. (2001). Determinants of Web site implementation in small business. *Internet Research: Electronic Network Applications and Policy*, *11*(5), 411–422.

Reimenschneider, C. K., & Mykytyn Jr., P. P. (2000). What small business executives have learned about managing information technology. *Information & Management*, *37*, 257–267.

Reynolds, W., Savage, W., & Williams, A. (1994). *Your own business: A practical guide to success*. Melbourne, Australia: ITP.

Riquelme, H. (2002). Commercial Internet adoption in China: Comparing the experience of small, medium and large businesses. *Internet Research: Electronic Networking Applications and Policy, 12*(3), 276–286.

Ritchie, R., & Brindley, C. (2000). Disintermediation, disintegration and risk in the SME global supply chain. *Management Decision, 38*(8), 575–583.

Roberts, M., & Wood, M. (2002). The strategic use of computerised information systems by a micro enterprise. *Logistics Information Management, 15*(2), 115–125.

Rotch, W. (1987). *Management of small enterprises: Cases and readings*. University of Virginia Press.

Schindehutte, M., & Morris, M. H. (2001). Understanding strategic adaption in small firms. *International Journal of Entrepreneurial Behaviour and Research, 7*(3), 84–107.

Sohal, A. S., & Ng, L. (1998). The role and impact of information technology in Australian business. *Journal of Information Technology, 13*(3), 201-217.

Sparkes, A., & Thomas, B. (2001). The use of the Internet as a critical success factor for the marketing of Welsh agri-food SMEs in the twenty first century. *British Food Journal, 103*(4), 331–347.

Stauber, A. (2000). *A survey of the incorporation of electronic commerce in Tasmanian small and medium sized enterprises*. Tasmanian Electronic Commerce Centre.

Storper, M. (1995). The resurgence of regional economies, ten years later: The region as a nexus of untraded interdependencies. *European Urban and Regional Studies, 2*(3), 191–221.

Swartz, T. A., & Iacobucci, D. (2000). *Handbook of services marketing and management*. CA: Sage.

Tetteh, E., & Burn, J. (2001). Global strategies for SME-business: Applying the SMALL framework. *Logistics Information Management, 14*(1/2), 171–180.

Tikkanen, H. (1998). The Network approach in analysing international marketing and purchasing operations: A case study of a European SME's. *Journal of Business and Industrial Marketing, 13*(2), 109–131.

Treacy, M., & Wiersema, F. (1997). *The discipline of market leaders*. Cambridge, MA: Perseus Press.

Turban, E., Lee, J. K., King, D., & Chung, M. (2002). *Electronic commerce: Managerial perspective*. NJ: Prentice Hall.

Tuunainen, V. K. (1998). Opportunities of effective integration of EDI for small businesses in the automotive industry. *Information & Management, 36*(6), 361–375.

United States Small Business Administration. (2005). *What is a small business?* Retrieved November 15, 2005, from http://www.sba.gov/size

Van Akkeren, J., & Cavaye, A. L. M. (1999). Factors affecting entry-level Internet technology adoption by small business in Australia: An empirical study. In *Proceedings of the 10th Australasian Conference on Information Systems*, Wellington, New Zealand.

Vescovi, T. (2000). Internet communication: The Italian SME case. *Corporate Communications: An International Journal, 5*(2), 107–112.

Vrazalic, L., Bunker, D., MacGregor, R. C., Carlsson, S., & Magnusson, M. (2002). Electronic commerce and market focus: Some findings from a study of Swedish small to medium enterprises. *Australian Journal of Information Systems, 10*(1), 110–119.

Walczuch, R., Van Braven, G., & Lundgren, H. (2000). Internet adoption barriers for small firms in the Netherlands. *European Management Journal, 18*(5), 561–572.

Walker, E. W. (1975). Investment and capital structure decision making in small business. In E. W. Walker (Ed.), *The dynamic small firm: Selected readings*. TX: Austin Press.

Welsh, J. A., & White, J. F. (1981). A small business is not a little big business. *Harvard Business Review, 59*(4), 46–58.

Westhead, P., & Storey, D. J. (1996). Management training and small firm performance: Why is the link so weak? *International Small Business Journal, 14*(4), 13–24.

Chapter XIII

E-Business Standardization in the Automotive Sector:
Role and Situation of SMEs

Martina Gerst, The University of Edinburgh, UK

Kai Jakobs, Aachen University, Germany

Abstract

Successful cooperation between large manufacturers and their suppliers is a crucial aspect, especially in the automotive industry. Such mutually beneficial cooperation requires at least a certain level of integration and interoperation of the partners' IT and e-business systems. This chapter looks at two approaches in order to achieve this goal: sector-specific harmonization (in the form of electronic marketplaces) and international, committee-based standardization. This chapter shows that SMEs are facing a severe disadvantage in both cases. This is, however, less pronounced in a formal standards setting, in which capabilities of the individual representatives are more important, at least at the working level.

Introduction

The automotive industry is facing a number of challenges to the established relations among its players. Issues to be addressed include, for instance, shorter product life cycles, increasing cost pressure in stagnant markets, and higher complexity of the embedded electronic systems. In order to meet the associated production requirements, standardization of processes, systems, and data is inevitable. This industry is characterized by vertical integration in terms of the business relationship structures between OEMs[1] and suppliers (Adolphs, 1996; Lamming, 1993). A current trend in manufacturing is that OEMs attempt to cooperate with fewer suppliers but on a worldwide scale. As a result, small and medium-sized suppliers become suppliers to tier 1 or tier 2 suppliers rather than directly to the OEMs.

The use of ICT-related technologies, particularly e-business systems, facilitates the creation of a network of relationships within a supply chain. Yet such interorganizational integration requires interoperability that cannot be achieved without widely agreed upon standards. But who has a say in the standardization process? This already has led to a range of transformations in the structure of the automotive supply chain. Large OEMs have been forced to create networks to replace the existing one-to-one relations with their suppliers, which are typically SMEs[2]. According to a study of Nexolab in 2001, standards were a major headache for SMEs, and 75% of the suppliers saw the lack of standardization as a major obstacle for closer collaboration. Therefore, it might be useful for companies to rethink their standardization strategies.

In many cases, an SME supplier does business with more than one OEM. In this situation, bilateral standardization to improve cooperation between OEMs and suppliers and between different suppliers, respectively, is inefficient. Still, this has been the approach of choice in many cases. However, possible alternatives are available, including sector-specific harmonization (e.g., in the form of an electronic marketplace) and, particularly, international committee-based standardization.

However, the challenges and the pressure for collaboration have led organizations in the automotive sector to become involved in a range of projects by means of interorganizational systems (IOS). Examples include electronic collaboration projects, the integration of engineering processes, and electronic catalogue projects to present product and service data. Such IOSs are adopted not only to achieve operational effectiveness by reducing coordination costs and transaction risks (Kumar & van Dissel, 1996) but also to improve communication and information presentation. Collaboration and integration shift the emphasis from stand-alone initiatives to the development of standardized and integrated solutions (Koch & Gerst, 2003). In this context, one form of IOS that fulfills the criteria of collaboration and integration is business-to-business/supplier portals that incorporate standardized business processes. Covisint, an e-marketplace founded in 2000 by large OEMs, is a very good example to analyze the standardization process in an industry, which is characterized by a large number of SMEs.

The remainder of the chapter is structured as follows: using the automotive industry as an example, this chapter looks at two approaches toward standardization, both of which involve large companies and SMEs. One approach is based on the use of international standards, and proactive participation in the open standards-setting process by all relevant stakeholders. The alternative comprises a standardized, albeit sector-specific, electronic marketplace.

The design and development was pushed by a group of large car manufacturers. It turned out that the situation of SMEs was not very favorable in either case—both processes were largely dominated by the big guys. Nonetheless, the chapter makes some recommendations how this situation may be changed for open standards setting.

Some Background

The Automotive Industry

According to a study by McKinsey (2003), the automotive industry in the next 10 years will be shattered by a third revolution that follows the invention of assembly-line production by Henry Ford and the lean production of Toyota. Customers are expecting better value for the same money, resulting in continuous cost pressure and innovation marathons for OEMs.

This has led to a range of transformations in the automotive supply chain. For example, in order to improve customer satisfaction and to increase revenue growth and shareholder value, large OEMs and their suppliers started establishing large automotive networks. Yet, the added value of these collaborative networks is beginning to shift from the OEMs to suppliers and to other business partners such as system integrators (see Figure 1).

In the 1980s, the relations between an OEM and its suppliers were similar. In the 1990s, this changed to a tier-x structure in which the main collaboration partners of an OEM were the tier-1 suppliers that, in turn, collaborated through tier-2 suppliers, and so forth. Today, OEMs are collaborating not only with their supply base but also with other business partners; for

Figure 1. Automotive networks determine future collaboration. (Source: BMW)

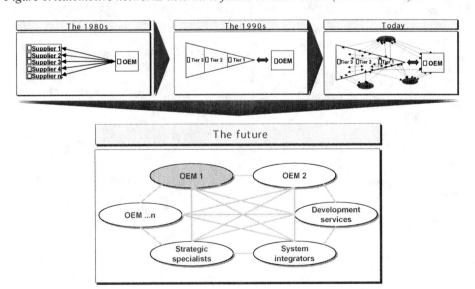

example, system integrators. In the future, the relations between OEMs and their suppliers are expected to change dramatically (Gerst & Bunduchi, 2004).

Apart from shifts in the value chain, the industry is confronted with a number of transformations that challenge the established relations among industry players. The automotive industry is characterized by extremely complex processes, and the standardization of processes and data is inevitable in order to meet production requirements. Driven by challenges such as shorter product life cycles, increasing cost pressure in stagnant markets, and higher complexity of the electronics embedded in modules and systems, OEMs gradually increase the outsourcing of manufacturing, which is expected to rise from 25% to 35% within the next 10 years (McKinsey, 2003).

The supplier community also is undergoing major changes as the result of this pressure. Increasingly, platforms and model varieties require advanced deals and project management capabilities, which means that in terms of innovation management, suppliers have to be able to provide leading-edge technology and efficient simultaneous engineering processes. This change primarily affects the tier-1 suppliers, which are taking over systems integration responsibility and management of the supply chain from the OEMs. At the same time, they also take an increasing share of risk, which used to be incurred by the OEMs. As a result, the industry is forced to collaborate more closely (e.g., by adopting portal) technology.

Standardization

Standards Setting in General

Over the last three decades, the world of IT standardization has become extremely complex. Figure 2 gives an impression of the situation in the 1970s (not complete, though). Back then, standards-setting bodies were few, national bodies contributed to the work of CEN/CENELC[3] at the European level and to ISO/IEC[4] at the international level. These bodies were responsible for all areas of standards setting, with the exception of the then highly regulated telecommunication sector, which was the realm of the CCITT[5]. The only other international organization of some importance was ECMA.[6]

Figure 2. The IT standardization universe in 1970 (excerpt)

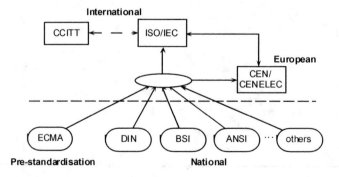

Since then, the situation has changed dramatically, especially for the IT and e-business sectors. Figure 3 depicts an excerpt of the situation that today may be found in these sectors. In addition to the newly established regional Standards Developing Organizations (SDOs; e.g. ETSI[7] in Europe, TIA[8] in the U.S., etc.), a considerable number of standards-setting industry for a and consortia have been founded as well (W3C[9], OASIS[10], etc.); a recent survey found around 190 such entities (ISSS, 2004). In a way, these organizations have successfully created a parallel universe of standards setting that is partly in competition with the older, formal bodies, partly in cooperation and partly without any relations to them at all.

The complexity of this environment represents a major obstacle for those who are considering active participation in standardization and, most notably, for SMEs. In most cases, they have neither the resources nor the knowledge necessary for a meaningful participation in this highly complex process. Questions they need to address include why, how, where, and when to participate.

At first glance, "Why participate at all?" seems to be a very valid question. After all, standardization is a costly business and is time-consuming, and the return on investment is uncertain in many cases. This normally is not a major problem for large vendors and manufacturers, who may want to push their own ideas, prevent success of competing specifications, or are just driven by the desire to gather intelligence in the work groups.

Things look very different for user companies and SMEs. They cannot easily commit considerable resources to activities with very intangible direct benefits. Yet, all users need to recognize that they will suffer most from inadequate standards. Such standards will leave them struggling with incompatibilities, which, at the end of the day, may well drive them out of business. On the other hand, they will reap major benefits from well-designed standards that address real needs. In addition, at least large and/or well-off users may find a standards committee to be a very suitable platform for cooperation with vendors and manufacturers.

Figure 3. The IT standardization universe today (excerpt)

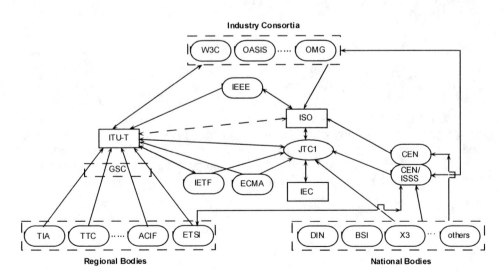

Here, technical requirements can be mapped onto system capabilities at a very early design stage (in fact, this is rather more a pre-design stage), thus making the process far more efficient.

Accordingly, (SME) users who participate in standards setting will be driven by the desire to (Jakobs, 2003).

Avoid Technological Dead-Ends

Users want to avoid purchasing products that eventually leave them stranded with an incompatible technology. A number of issues need to be considered in this context. For instance, it has to be decided if and when a new technology should be purchased and which one should be selected. Too early adoptions not only bear the risk of adopting a technology that eventually fails in being successful in the market but also ignore the considerable time and money that have gone into the old technology. It has to be decided if and when to switch from a well-established technology to a new one. Investments in the old technology need to be balanced with the prospective benefits potentially to be gained from this move. On the other hand, late adopters may lose competitive advantage while being stuck with outdated technology.

Reduce Dependency on Vendors

Being locked in into a vendor-specific environment increasingly is becoming a major risk for a user, despite the advantages that can be associated with integrated proprietary solutions. In particular, problems occur if a vendor misses an emerging development and its users are forced to switch to completely new (and different) systems, which is a very costly exercise. Accordingly, standard compliant products from a choice of vendors appeal to the users, who can pursue a pick-and-mix purchasing strategy and also stand to benefit from price cuts as a result of increased competition.

Promote Universality

Ultimately, users would like to see seamless interoperability among all hardware and software, both internally (between different departments and sites) and externally (with customers and business partners). With the ongoing globalization of markets, this only can be achieved through international standards. Clearly, this holds especially for communications products. Ideally, it should not matter at all which vendor or service provider has been selected; interoperability always should be guaranteed, which implies that user needs and requirements are met by the standards (and the implementations). In addition to seamless communication and the business value that lies herein alone, there is another major economic benefit to be gained: the cost of incompatibility may be tremendous.

The next issue to be considered is "how to participate." In general, there seems to be consensus that large users, especially those with an urgent need for standardized systems or services, should participate directly in the technical work. In fact, some do. However, especially for smaller companies, there are obvious barriers to this form of participation, which are largely rooted in the lack of sufficient financial resources and knowledgeable personnel. Here, participation via umbrella organizations would be an option, as would be participation at the national level with a mandate for national representatives to act as the voice of these SMEs in the international arena.

Considering the complexity of the IT standardization universe, "where to participate" is another relevant issue. Equivalent systems may well be standardized in parallel by different SDOs and consortia, and participation in all these work groups is well beyond the means of all but the biggest players. The correct decision here is crucial, as backing the wrong horse may leave a company stranded with systems based on the wrong (i.e., non-standard) technology. This holds for both users and manufacturers.

Especially SMEs and users should also ask themselves, "When should we participate?" In most cases, the standardization process is viewed as an atomic entity that cannot be subdivided any further. Yet, the standards life cycle depicted in Figure 4 suggests otherwise. Participation in profile development, for example, would be the option of choice, if interoperability of implementations were to be assured. On the other hand, there is little point in specifying a profile for a base standard that does not meet the requirements in the first place.

Standards in the Automotive Industry

Standardization in the automotive industry has a long tradition. According to Thompson (1954), engineers and industrialists in the American automobile industry initiated in 1910 for the first time an extensive program of intercompany technical standards. Technical standards made parts interchangeable so that mass production was facilitated, which led to production economies. In relating the growth of intercompany technical standards in the

Figure 4. Summary of the comprehensive standards life cycle (According to Cargill, 1995)

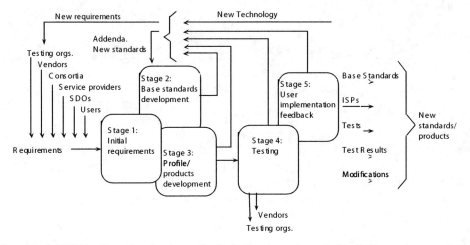

automotive industry up to about 1930, the study of Thompson (1954) attempts to show the influence of changing business conditions on standardization and, hence, on the mechanical technology of a car.

Some decades later, in the rising technology age, the launch of Electronic Data Interchange (EDI), was the next step of the automotive industry in order to collaborate more closely with suppliers by means of Interorganizational Systems (IOS) (Graham, Spinardi, Williams & Webster, 1995). IOS refers to the computer and telecommunications infrastructure developed, operated, and/or used by two or more companies for the purpose of exchanging information that supports a business application or process (Cunningham & Tynan, 1993). These companies can be suppliers and customers in the same value chain, strategic partners, or even competitors in the same or a related market. The integrative potential of networked computer systems that enabled information sharing and facilitated collaboration of hitherto competing organizations was well recognized (Monse & Reimers, 1995; Webster, 1995; Williams, Graham, & Spinardi, 1995).

Contemporary IOSs are complex Information and Communication Technology (ICT) systems that incorporate a multitude of standards. Consequently, for a company, the decision to integrate business partners with IOS requires an initial strategic decision whether to implement standardized technology that supports standardized business processes or to implement and customize off-the-shelf proprietary systems. The latter, of course, means to stick to the homemade processes and systems. This decision is influenced by various factors (e.g., economical, organizational, technical, social) and actors (e.g., players of internal business units, software suppliers, consultants) situated in a highly dynamic environment.

Today, SMEs in this sector are under enormous pressure from their frequently large customers to deploy e-business systems (and the necessary underlying ICT infrastructure) that are compatible with the customers' respective systems. Yet, as these systems typically differ, SMEs accordingly would have to set up and maintain a number of different systems. This is hardly a realistic option, and the use of standards-based systems is an SME's only chance to keep both its ICT environment manageable and all its customers happy.

Unfortunately, few standards take into account SMEs' unique requirements. Major standards setting initiatives already have failed because of this[11]. Thus, it seems to be about time to have a closer look at the current standardization practice with respect to SMEs' needs.

SMEs Between a Rock and a Hard Place

SMEs in Standards-Setting Bodies

For SMEs, a potential route toward standards that also cover their specific needs and requirements would be through participation standards setting bodies (SSBs) that produce open specifications. In the following, we will have a closer look at the prospects of SMEs in this environment. This section, therefore, will analyze what would have to be done in order to make standards setting in the ICT domain more accessible and useful for small and medium enterprises.

The study on the role of SMEs in committee-based standardization is based on desk research and several (small) studies. Here, data were collected through different questionnaires, each comprising a number of open-ended questions. Qualitative methods have been deployed to analyze the data.

Motivation

Today, the standards-setting processes in the Information and Communication Technologies (ICT) and e-business sectors are dominated very much by the large companies and other financially potent stakeholders. As a consequence, there is a real danger that standards, and thus, ultimately, policies, are based on the needs and requirements of a comparably small, albeit powerful, group of stakeholders. The action plan for innovation, Innovate for a Competitive Europe, rightly says, "Voluntary standards, properly used, can help establish the compatibility of innovative concepts and products with related products and so can be a key enabler for innovation. … SMEs should be more involved in standardization in order to exploit their potential for innovation and to enhance the accountability, openness, and consensus-based character of the European standardization system" (European Commission, 2004).

Yet, the working groups (WGs) of almost all standards-setting bodies are populated by representatives of large, multinational companies. The comparably few representatives of SMEs typically come from highly specialized vendors or manufacturers. SME users (i.e., those who merely deploy ICT systems) are hardly represented at all, and neither are their umbrella organizations.

Today, SMEs are under enormous pressure from their frequently large customers to deploy e-business systems (including the necessary underlying ICT infrastructure) that are compatible with the customer's respective systems. Yet, as these systems typically differ, SMEs accordingly have to set up and maintain a number of different systems. This is hardly a sustainable option, and the use of standards-based systems is an SME's only chance to keep both its ICT environment manageable and all its customers happy.

Some Background

There seems to be general agreement that participation of all stakeholders, particularly users, is a *sine qua non* in order for an ICT standardization activity to be successful. In fact, increased user participation often is considered the panacea for all problems.

Typically, SMEs opt for readily available off-the shelf systems and services that need to be inexpensive and easy to install, maintain, and use. Proprietary systems also are used frequently, and SMEs are compelled to do so by, for example, a major business partner (with all associated problems). The non-use of many standards-based services by SMEs is due largely to the fact that insufficient knowledge and resources are available to employ these systems, which are perceived as being extremely complicated to deal with. In fact, this perception may be considered a major impediment to a more successful uptake of standards-based systems by SMEs. This exemplifies an urgent need for simpler standards.

Figure 5. The naïve view of a standards setting process (Source: Jakobs, 2004)

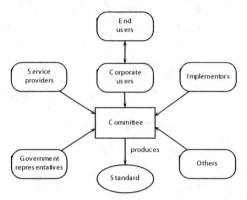

The procedures adopted by the individual standards-setting bodies suggest that the degree of control over and influence on the standards-setting process is about equally distributed among the different stakeholders (see Figure 5).

Unfortunately, this does not quite capture reality. Especially, the assumption of an equal influence of all stakeholders appears to be flawed (Swann, 2000). In fact, it appears that, so far, development of IT standards almost exclusively has been technology-driven. This can be attributed largely to the fact that relevant standardization committees typically have been dominated by vendors and service providers. Accordingly, a more realistic model is called for and will be presented in section 5.

SMEs in Standards Setting: A Small Study

As part of a project co-funded by the European Commission, one of the authors did a small study of selected ITU and ISO working groups in order to learn about some issues relating to SME users in standards setting[12]. In summary, it became clear that both ITU and ISO are indeed dominated by large companies. SME representation (if any, that is) occurs primarily through small consultancy firms, as opposed to actual users. Also, the influence that real SMEs (i.e., excluding consultants) have on the process is said to be very limited.

Respondents' opinions were split about SMEs' influence at the technical level. A sizable minority basically stated that in many cases, influence is related to market power. This holds particularly for the voting level, in which appropriate (and perhaps national) strategies are playing an important role. Obviously, SMEs, if represented at all, stand little chance of competing with the big multinationals.

Things look slightly different at the working level, though (i.e., in working groups in which the actual technical standardization work is being done). The majority of respondents noted that the individual capabilities of the representatives (i.e., technical skills, language proficiency, willingness to take on responsibility, etc.) are the deciding factors.

SME participation would broaden technical expertise of a WG, as they are frequently closer to state-of-the-art technical development than big companies and less bound by internal rules and administrative procedures. Also, they would be welcome as a counterweight to the interests of the big companies. This holds particularly if they represent fora or some other form of umbrella organizations. However, it was also noted that the typical sporadic or infrequent participation of SME representatives might lead to inadequate familiarity with both technical aspects discussed and procedures, thus causing unnecessary delays to the process.

Cost of participation is considered the major obstacle that SMEs will face if they want to become active in standards setting. Suggestions how this could be overcome include increased deployment of electronic media to replace meetings, lower or waived fees for SMEs, and provision of dedicated travel money. In addition, it was suggested that SMEs join forces and co-sponsor representatives.

Electronic Marketplaces: Two Examples

So far, we have looked at the role that SMEs may play in the context of largely proprietary, sector-specific standardization processes that are driven and dominated by large companies. An additional case study about the development of standardized business processes of two electronic marketplaces in the automotive industry will describe if and how SMEs, which are supposed to be the main target audience for the use of such marketplaces, were involved in the development of standardized business processes of those marketplaces.

Each OEM has an extensive network of suppliers. They, in turn, frequently supply more than one OEM. In this situation, bilateral standardization of the complex processes and technology that enable the cooperation both between OEMs and suppliers and between different suppliers is less than effective, as it would leave suppliers with the need to maintain one system per OEM. Still, this is the approach of choice in many cases. This is the reason that sector-specific electronic marketplaces absolutely would make sense.

Introduction

In order to enable increased collaboration and outsourcing, all large OEMs since the 1980s have launched a number of strategic programs to ensure networking across their entire value chain, including electronic collaboration in the form of EDI systems and electronic catalogue projects. The implementations of IOS such as EDI have been linked strongly with the need to move away from competitive supply chain relationships and toward closer collaborative relationships. EDI implementations thus were seen to support the changes toward higher outsourcing and collaboration in the industry (Webster, 1995). Despite its advantages, EDI systems adoption was limited to large companies (OEMs and tier-1 suppliers), with small suppliers lagging behind. One of the reasons was the significant investment associated with EDI deployment, which impeded the ability of smaller suppliers to participate in the EDI game and reap the benefits.

The expectations of the OEMs were built around a vision to standardize intra- and interorganizational processes in an effort not only to reduce costs but also to increase the efficiency of information exchange on a global basis by taking advantage of leading-edge technologies. To support this vision toward global collaboration, OEMs in the late 1990s began to deploy Internet-based portals in order to integrate applications and give real-time data access to their suppliers.

Example One: Covisint

In 1999, the Internet hub Covisint[13] (**C**onnectivity, **Vi**sibility, **Int**egration) was founded by a number of large OEMs such as DaimlerChrysler, Ford, and General Motors, and software companies such as Oracle and Commerce One. The aim of Covisint was to connect the automotive industry to a global exchange marketplace with the offer of one single point of entry to all connected applications and functionalities. It thus aimed to represent a de-facto industry standard for the entire automotive industry. First of all, Covisint offered different e-services; for example e-auction or e-collaboration tools. Second, the e-service offer aimed to improve the interconnection between and integration of OEMs and suppliers through standardized portal technology. This technology provided uniform personalized access from any location and any device between networked organizations. The functionality and infrastructure that characterizes such open architecture allowed the integration of diverse interaction channels. To a large extent, the supplier community is the same for all OEMs. Concretely, the same suppliers were using the same OEM-own applications that always needed different log-ins and passwords. Therefore, the big picture behind Covisint was the idea of one single point of entry for suppliers of every company size in order to facilitate and enable integration and collaboration. The vision behind Covisint was to enable the connection of the entire automotive industry to a single, global exchange marketplace with one single point of entry, standardized business processes, and standard applications. Covisint thus aimed to represent a de-facto industry standard and open integration framework for business process integration.

The development process was characterized by an iterative approach. Before Covisint started to develop and implement the standardized portal technology, one of the OEM founders already had started to develop a portal registration process, one of the core processes in a supplier portal (based on the best practice in the industry: the development of standards has benefited from the development of portals by other organizations before). Since all the founders were very interested in taking the most benefit out of Covisint on a short-term basis, they were highly motivated to develop standard processes that later could be implemented in their own organizations.

In a first instance, standards development was related to best practices in the industry and had been worked out by a limited number of specialists from the OEMs that were involved in Covisint. In a later stage, this small-group approach to standard development has been replaced by a consortium of the Covisint stakeholders and the software companies that delivered pieces of software to complete the offer of the Internet hub. The consortium approach was more similar with the typical approach to standard development following specific procedures and having different working groups that met regularly. Additionally, industry experts of associations were invited to presentations and workshops to contribute to the standards development. In a second phase, in order to increase legitimacy among suppliers, they were included in the process. However, participation in the consortium was closely controlled, and the working procedures were less rather than more transparent and open. Only well-known, mostly tier-1 suppliers, who already had participated in other pilot projects, were asked about their input in the form of commentary feedback to already developed processes. The restrictions in participation and the lack of transparency and openness regarding the work within the consortium could be explained by the desire of the OEMs to achieve the initial goal of a standardized industry solution.

Due to the fast-to-market strategy of Covisint, the standards were developed in parallel with systems development and implementation. The emphasis of the standardization itself was on speed and on finding compromise solutions that fitted all parties rather than on long-term quality solutions. The development phase of the standardized portal was very complex with regard to the existing complexity of already existing IT infrastructure and the difficulty to integrate all different systems and applications in an overall company architecture. The overall inconsistent strategy of the OEMs with respect to the implementation of the e-collaboration tools, particularly online bidding, significantly affected the suppliers' negative perceptions of portals in general. Whereas some of the OEMs preferred the standardized industry solution managed by an electronic marketplace, others, such as the VWGroup, voted for the in-house option, which meant not to draw on a third party service.

According to a representative of a tier-1 supplier, the supplier community was "deeply concerned and felt threatened" by the sheer market power concentration. One result of these concerns was SupplyOn, founded by a number of large tier-1 suppliers. It became one of the major competitors of Covisint in the field.

Example Two: SupplyOn

Whereas Covisint was envisaged by its founders to streamline the business processes of all participants and to enable them to collaborate seamlessly across organizations' borders, this was not necessarily the perception of the suppliers. There were two reasons for this.

First, the suppliers were excluded from the early development process, with only a few of the largest and most powerful tier-1 suppliers being asked to become involved during a later stage of the development phase. However, even at this stage, the suppliers' involvement was limited mainly to providing feedback over the OEMs' decisions rather than actively participating in negotiations. The decisional power remained almost entirely with the OEMs. As a result, by and large, suppliers' requirements were neither part of the Covisint vision nor included in the development of the standardized technology. Therefore, despite the acclaimed aim of Covisint to address the costs and risks reduction pressures across the entire industry, the development stage included the requirements and visions of only a limited number of OEMs.

Second, suppliers already struggled with the administration of a number of such standardized portals, and the suppliers who were approached at an early stage showed mixed feelings regarding the OEMs' approach to volume bundling and pricing.

The development of Covisint was the trigger for the tier-1 supplier community to set up SupplyOn to counterbalance the OEMs' obvious power consolidation and the Goliath gigantic-like marketplace. In April 2000, the tier-1 suppliers Robert Bosch GmbH, Continental AG, INA Werk Schaeffler oHG, SAP AG, and ZF Friedrichshafen AG signed a letter of intent and kicked off a new e-marketplace business—SupplyOn.

The basic vision behind SupplyOn was the same as for Covisint; namely, to join forces, to bundle know-how, and in a collaborative effort to set up industrywide standards (e.g., for logistic processes). However, whereas the initial objective of SupplyOn was the same as the Covisint approach to the development of standardized business processes, in the end, it diverged from the original vision. In contrast with Covisint, which followed the U.S. management model, the founders of SupplyOn made explicitly clear from the beginning that they denied the American way of doing business, opting in contrast for an approach based on smaller but concrete step-by-step efforts and results rather than big visions that, they argued, were often impossible to implement. SupplyOn thus was positioning itself in direct competition with Covisint, representing the suppliers' approach to the development of a standardized industrywide portal.

However, even though SupplyOn was the brainchild of suppliers, one should take into consideration that large tier-1 suppliers initiated a competing standard, pretending that they would better understand the business requirements of the supplier world. But, as in the case of Covisint, SMEs were not very involved in the SupplyOn development process, either. SME participation was reduced to feedback, as well.

Summary

Today, most would agree that both electronic markets, Covisint and SupplyOn, by and large failed or, at least, struggled to set up a de-facto industry standard for business processes for a number of major reasons with an organizational, economical, and technical nature[14]. Certainly, SMEs played a weighty role in the whole e-game; they simply did not participate and even tried to escape the new electronic (and supposedly better) world offered by the OEMs.

Organizationally, SMEs did not have a great say in the development processes of the e-marketplaces. This holds despite the fact that the original idea of electronic marketplaces in general, and sector-specific marketplaces such as Covisint and SupplyOn, in particular, was to integrate all suppliers, particularly SMEs. Covisint did not fulfill the expectations of the industry; most members of the supplier community were disappointed with the way Covisint was set up. In particular, tier-1 suppliers feared the dominance of Covisint (and the resulting power of the participating OEMs) and, consequently, formed their own marketplace—SupplyOn. In the case of Covisint, the relation between the founding OEMs and Covisint was difficult to handle for the OEMs (in terms of roles and responsibilities) and difficult to understand for SME suppliers. An SME supplier had a business relationship with its OEM, which was manifested in a written contract. With Covisint, this relation was getting more complex in two ways: first, the use of Covisint required the supplier to become a member of Covisint. Although initially the participating OEMs paid the membership fee for their suppliers, a lack of enthusiasm clearly was shown by the supplier community, because it (rightly) feared additional cost of participation in a later phase. Second, some of the OEMs forced their suppliers to sign an additional document called an e-marketplace contract in order to avoid warranty claims of suppliers in the case of the nonavailability of Covisint.

Another important organizational issue was to harmonize the business processes of the different consortium partners. The requirements of the participating companies were very difficult to understand for third parties. This led, for example, to difficulties in the development of the portal registration processes. For SME suppliers that were working on an international basis, it turned out to be difficult to register with Covisint due to an inadequate registration processes (despite the promise that Internet technologies would help to simplify business and make it faster).

As a result, this quick-to-market approach led to incomplete solutions (at a technical level) that were difficult to integrate into already existing IT infrastructures and were expensive to realize. Here, as well, SME suppliers mistrusted the OEMs, fearing larger investments for their back-end integration.

Economically, the inability of Covisint to manage the business and the technology development and standardization as well as the inability of its founders to attract the potential users to buy into the Covisint vision led to the formation of two competitive standardized solutions in the industry, with the majority of SME suppliers favoring SupplyOn. Neither the founding OEMs nor Covisint was able to explain clearly the distribution of benefits of working with Covisint. Suppliers did not see a win-win situation. Thus, when severe technical problems and intractable project management issues arose later during the implementation of Covisint, suppliers withdrew their support for Covisint altogether.

Another reason for the lack of participation could be the fact that both e-marketplaces were sector-specific, and, from a certain tier level, most SMEs did business not only with the automotive sector but also with other industries.

In conclusion, the development of standardized electronic marketplaces was much more complex in organizational, technical, and economic terms than was expected by the founders of both Covisint and SupplyOn. In the case of Covisint, OEMs had significant difficulties adapting their internal processes to the marketplace. Moreover, the integration of the portal's different components into an overall standardized architecture was extremely difficult. Additionally, because of the organizational and technological difficulties integrating the often divergent OEMs' business requirements within a standardized approach, the benefits of adhering to the standardized processes associated with using the portal were not directly evident to potential users and led to the formation of SupplyOn.

Discussion

Today, according to the study, active participation in ICT and e-business standards-setting is limited largely to large, multinational companies. In particular, SMEs hardly stand a chance to make their voice adequately heard. Since standardization and policymaking are mutually dependent, this is an extremely unsatisfactory situation. Ultimately, it means that the influence of globally acting multinationals on European policy is out of proportion with, for example, the number of jobs they provide in Europe. In a way, SMEs are part of a modern-day Third Estate with respect to their capability to influence standardization and, thus, ultimately, policymaking. This holds despite the fact that there are more than 20 million SMEs in the EU.

Figure 6. Relations between stakeholders in standardization (Source: Jakobs, 2000)

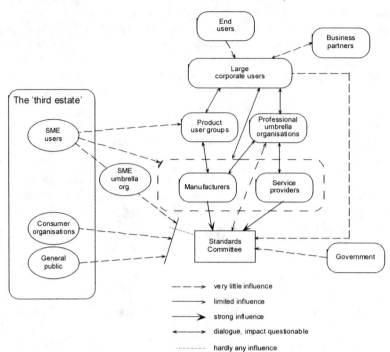

Standardization processes should provide a platform in which opportunities for technologies, requirements of various types of companies from all sectors, consumer preferences, and other societal needs (e.g., protection of the environment) are mediated efficiently. Standards that are useful for all relevant stakeholders should be the outcome of these processes.

Unfortunately, it appears so far that development of IT standards almost exclusively has been technology-driven with standards produced that solely reflect providers' and implementers' priorities such as manageability rather than usability. Most other stakeholders, including the general public, consumer organizations, and, most notably here, SME users, constitute what one might call the Third Estate of IT standards setting (see Figure 6).

The figure shows that the members of the Third Estate (specifically, SMEs) are separated largely from the key players, with SME umbrella organizations perhaps located somewhere in between. Although they represent the vast majority of standard users, these groups have extremely little say in the standards-setting process. This holds, despite the fact that organizations such as ANEC, the European Association for the Co-ordination of Consumer Representation in Standardization, and NORMAPME, the European Office of Crafts, Trades and SMEs for Standardization, are participating actively in selected standard working groups on behalf of their constituencies.

Four reasons for the current, less-than-adequate representation of (individual) SMEs in ICT standards setting may be identified: inadequate technical expertise[15], very limited interest, lack of funding, and dependency from vendors. The former two are interrelated. A minimum of technical expertise and sophistication is required in order to make meaningful contributions to standards setting. Thus, limited expertise contributes significantly to the considerable lack of SMEs' interests in active participation in standards setting that may be observed today. Moreover, it is very unlikely that such active participation will to offer any short-term return on investment. Thus, getting involved in standardization is simply not economically feasible for many SMEs.

Inadequate technical expertise, lack of funding, and, particularly, dependency from vendors could be overcome if SMEs with similar interests and/or in similar situations joined forces. For example, it is easily conceivable that a group of tier-1 or tier-2 suppliers in the automotive industry would join forces in order to fund a standards specialist to represent them in the relevant working groups. In addition to a better representation at the technical level, the combined economical power also should lead to a more adequate representation at the strategic decision level.

Moreover, user and SME representatives may have to prove their credibility (i.e., demonstrate that they are actually representing a constituency broader than just one single company) (e.g., the SME community as such, as opposed to just their respective employers). This was never demanded from technical people representing large vendors, manufacturers, or service providers; it may be expected that the representative of an SME umbrella organization would not face this problem, either.

It frequently has been observed that individuals may drive and direct the activities of an entire standards working group, at least at the technical level (Egyedi, Jakobs & Monteiro, 2003; Jakobs, Procter, & Williams, 2000). Being represented by such an individual would not only solve (or at least reduce) the credibility problem but also would allow a group of SMES (or an umbrella organization) to punch well above its weight.

The Covisint study shows that standardization efforts are triggered by a complex array of nontechnical and technical considerations. The case illustrates that ICT standardization is not only about bridging the gap between the technologies and business processes of different companies but also about bridging complex social processes.

As suggested by the SST perspective, this vision of industrywide collaboration has been used actively by OEMs in order to mobilize resources internally and to attract suppliers into buying into Covisint. However, a number of factors has shaped the OEMs' and suppliers' choices during the development and implementation of the standardized technology, which eventually has led to a very different outcome than what initially was envisaged by the founding OEMs.

Each of the founding OEMs has an extensive network of suppliers. They, in turn, frequently supply more than one OEM. In this situation, bilateral standardization of the complex processes and technology that enable collaboration both between OEMs and their suppliers and between the different suppliers, is less than effective, as it would leave suppliers with the need to maintain one system for each OEM. Moreover, market pressures were forcing OEMs to reduce costs, increase the efficiencies in the industry, and enhance collaboration with their suppliers. Therefore, the idea to join forces in order to provide a single point of entry and set an industry standard seemed advantageous for both groups. Furthermore, when the Covisint idea emerged in late 1999, the use of leading-edge Internet technology to reorganize internal and external business processes to support collaboration across the entire supply chain was on every company's agenda. Consequently, the foundation of Covisint was a natural step in order to increase the effectiveness of the industry through a collaborative effort of the largest industry players. Indeed, such collaboration was required in order to share the risks and costs among a number of players.

The three founders showed their commitment to the Covisint vision through an initial investment of about $500 million. However, due to the distribution of power that historically characterized the relations between OEMs and suppliers, the latter were apprehensive of Covisint. They saw it as just than another exercise to intensify OEMs' power pressure. Some suppliers also feared that Covisint would require significant additional resources and investments from their side, whereas the benefits would materialize mostly at the OEMs' side.

However, on the OEM side, significant resources involving not only additional budget but also extra human resources were required in order to address the pending integration issues. The need for these additional resources led to negotiations concerning their allocation across different Bus (Business Units) within the OEMs. As a result of these negotiations, some application owners (the BUs within the participating OEMs) abandoned the idea of adopting standardized business processes and started blaming Covisint for not providing mature, workable solutions. It even was claimed that suppliers already working with the applications did not see any of the benefits. Consequently, far from reaching stabilization and closure, the choices made by the OEMs further deepened the disagreement regarding the approach to an industrywide standardized portal, which was deserted not only by suppliers but also by some of the BUs within the founding OEMs.

The previous discussion seems to indicate that SME suppliers were not particularly satisfied with the standardized solution developed by their large customers. Yet, it would appear that SMEs do not necessarily fare any better in today's open standards-setting processes.

Conclusion

Regarding the role of SMEs in open standards setting, "standardization is a prerequisite for a broad deployment and use of ICT, and will trigger and enable new business" (PWC, 2004, p. 7) (see also Blind et al. [1999] and Swann [2000] for similar accounts). With the creation of new businesses high on the agenda in Europe, it would be extremely unhelpful if SMEs, which, after all, form the employment and growth engine of the EU, were excluded from shaping this infrastructure upon which they rely very much.

However, there is no one-size-fits-all solution in order to give SMEs a greater say in actively participating in standardization development. One possible approach would be to provide funding for suitable SME umbrella organizations (we are not even starting to think about the potentially resulting or, at least, claimed distortion of competition). It then would be their task to identify those standards committees whose work is of particular relevance to SMEs and to represent their constituency's interests there. Yet, in this case, two problem areas need to be addressed.

First, SME users are not a homogeneous group. Accordingly, something needs to be done about the problem of diverse and context-specific user requirements (Jakobs, Procter &

Williams, 1998). In particular, there is a need for a mechanism to align these requirements. This ideally should happen prior to the actual standardization process. Dedicated SME user groups might be an option worth considering, despite the problems that have to be associated with this approach (Jakobs, 2000).

Along similar lines, sector-specific standards may be a way to raise the interest of SMEs to actively participate in standards setting, as such standards might be closer to their specific business interests. This approach, however, carries the risk of introducing incompatibilities among different sectors.

Here, the sectoral organizations, such as the Verband deutscher Automobilindustrie (VDA) at the German level or the Organization for Data Exchange by Tele Transmission (ODETTE) at the European level, actively could take part in informing and influencing their members (mainly SMEs). In the past, they struggled to reach a common position regarding the development and implementation of Internet-based technologies and their standards and the related consequences for suppliers. Such organizations reach a large number of suppliers of all sizes and, therefore, have the chance not only to inform but also to educate SME suppliers. Moreover, provision of additional information (through Web sites or brochures) could help to keep suppliers informed about developments of standards in their areas. Regional associations also might consider redefining their roles and trying to actively represent the interests of their members in European organizations.

This, of course, would imply the need for a mechanism to guarantee intersector interoperability. Another related option would be to deploy the national standards bodies to a greater extent as SME representatives in the far more important international arena. Lower travel budgets and the prospect of communicating in their native languages might be an incentive for more SMEs to participate in standards setting and to let the national bodies represent them in the international/global arena. This might also resolve at least partly the problem of requirements alignment.

The task of developing and implementing standardized business processes in order to collaborate more effectively across the full supply chain is more challenging than ever. Supplier portals are one of the options to collaborate more closely and to harmonize cross-company business processes. Apart from the technical issues surrounding the development of standardized business processes across the entire industry (i.e., the complexity of technology, integration issues, and security concerns), a range of organizational, social, and economic factors has influenced the OEMs' and the suppliers' choices and actions, which eventually have led to the undesired outcome of failing to accomplish the initial vision of industrywide collaboration supported by common industrywide standards.

However, given the failure of the large portals, the industry at least should consider turning to committee-based standards in the future instead. Such standards could be developed under the responsibility of a standards-setting body based on consensus and due process and with all stakeholders having the chance to participate and to contribute their ideas and needs.

References

Adolphs, B. (1996). *Stabile und effiziente geschäftsbeziehungen—Eine betrachtung von vertikalen koordinationsstrukturen in der deutschen automobilindustrie* [unpublished doctoral dissertation]. University of Cologne, Germany.

Blind, K., et al. (1999). *Economic benefits of standardization* (in German). Berlin: Beuth Publishers.

Cargill, C. F. (1995). A five segment model for standardization. In B. Kahil & J. Abbate (Eds.), *Standards policy for information infrastructure* (pp. 79-99). Cambridge: MIT Press.

Cunningham, C., & Tynan, C. (1993). Electronic trading, inter-organizational systems and the nature of buyer and seller relations: The need for a network perspective. *International Journal of Information Management, 13*, 3–28.

Dankbaar, B., & van Tulder, R. (1992). The influence of users in standardization: The case of MAP. In M. Dierkes, & U. Hoffmann (Eds.), *New technologies at the outset—Social forces in the shaping of technological innovations* (pp. 327-349). Frankfurt; New York: Campus/Westview.

Egyedi, T., Jakobs, K., & Monteiro, E. (2003). *Helping SDOs to reach users* (Report for EC DG ENT, Contract No. 20010674). Retrieved January 16, 2006, from http://www-i4.informatik.rwth-aachen.de/~jakobs/grant/Final_Report.pdf

European Commission. (2004). *Innovate for a competitive Europe: A new action plan for innovation.* Retrieved January 16, 2006, from http://europa.eu.int/comm/enterprise/innovation/consultation/docs/innovate.pdf

Gerst, M., & Bunduchi, R. (2004). The adoption of standardised technology in the automotive industry. In P. Cunningham, & M. Cunningham (Eds.), *E-adoption and the knowledge economy: Issues, applications, case studies* (pp. 287–294). Amsterdam, The Netherlands: IOS Press.

Graham, I., Spinardi, G., Williams, R., & Webster, J. (1995). The dynamics of EDI standard development. *Technology Analysis & Strategic Management, 7*(1), 3–20.

ISSS. (Eds.). (2004). *ICT standards consortia survey* (9th ed.). Retrieved January 16, 2006, from http://www.cenorm.be/cenorm/businessdomains/businessdomains/isss/consortia/survey+table+of+content.asp

Jakobs, K. (2000). *User participation in standardisation processes—impact, problems and benefits.* Braunschweig, Wiesbaden, Germany: Vieweg Publishers.

Jakobs, K. (2003). Information technology standards, standards setting and standards research: Mapping the universe. In *Proceedings of the Stanhope Center's Roundtable on Systematic Barriers to the Inclusion of a Public Interest Voice in the Design of Information and Communications Technologies,* Cotswolds, UK (pp. 118-123).

Jakobs, K. (2004). *E-business & ICT) standardisation and SME users—Mutually exclusive?* In *Proceedings of the Multi-Conference on Business Information Systems, Track 'E-Business—Standardisierung und Integration,* Göttingen, Germany.

Jakobs, K., Procter, R., & Williams, R. (1998). Infrastructural technologies to enable electronic commerce. In *Proceedings of the 3rd International Conference on the Management of Networked Enterprises*, Montreal.

Jakobs, K., Procter, R., & Williams, R. (2000). The making of standards. *IEEE Communications Magazine, 39*(4).

Koch, O., & Gerst, M. (2003). E-collaboration-initiative bei DaimlerChrysler. In R. Bogaschewsky (Ed.), *Integrated supply management—Einkauf und beschaffung: Effizienz steigern, kosten senken* (pp. 207–234). Cologne: Deutscher Wirtschaftsdienst.

Kumar, K., & van Dissel, H.G. (1996). Sustainable collaboration: Managing conflict and cooperation in interorganisational systems. *MIS Quarterly, 20*(3), 279–300.

Lamming, R. (1993). *Beyond partnership, strategies for innovation and lean supply*. Upper Saddle River, NJ: Prentice Hall, International.

McKinsey. (2003). Studie HAWK 2015—Wissensbasierte veränderung der automobilen wertschöpfungskette. *VDA 30 Materialien zur Automobilindustrie, 30*. Franfurt: Verband der Authomobilindustrie.

Monse, K., & Reimers, K. (1995). The development of electronic data interchange networks from an institutional perspective. In R. Williams (Ed.), *The social shaping of interorganizational IT systems and electronic data interchange* (pp. 109–127). Luxembourg: European Commission.

PWC. (2004). *Rethinking the European ICT agenda: Ten ICT-breakthroughs for reaching Lisbon goals*. Retrieved January 16, 2006, from http://www.eskills2004.org/files/Rethinking%20the%20European%20ICT%20agenda_def.pdf.

Swann, P.G.M. (2000). *The economics of standardization* (Final Report for DTI). Retrieved January 16, 2006, from http://www.dti.gov.uk/strd/economic%20benefits%20of%20standardisation%20-%20EN.pdf

Thompson, G. (1954). Intercompany technical standardization in the early American automobile industry. *Journal of Economic History, 14*(1), 1–20.

Webster, J. (1995). Networks of collaboration or conflict? The development of EDI. In R. Williams (Ed.), *The social shaping of interorganizational IT systems and electronic data interchange* (pp. 17–41). Luxembourg: European Commission.

Williams, R., Graham, I., & Spinardi, G. (1995). The social shaping of EDI. In R. Williams (Ed.), *The social shaping of interorganizational IT systems and electronic data interchange* (pp. 1-16). Luxembourg: European Commission.

Endnotes

[1]   Original Equipment Manufacturers

[2]   Small and medium-sized enterprises

[3]   The European Committee for Standardization/The European Committee for Electrotechnical Standardization

⁴   The International Organization for Standardization/The International Electrotechnical Commission

⁵   The International Telegraph and Telephone Consultative Committee, later ITU-T (see the following)

⁶   The European Computer Manufacturers Association

⁷   The European Telecommunications Standards Institute

⁸   The Telecommunications Industry Association

⁹   The World Wide Web Consortium

¹⁰   The Organization for the Advancement of Structured Information Standards

¹¹   General Motors' Manufacturing Automation Protocol (MAP) and Boeing's Transport and Office Protocol (TOP) are particularly instructive cases in point. At that time, specifically GM had to spend millions of dollars annually to interconnect incompatible IT systems at their plant floors. Thus, the idea behind MAP and TOP was to define precisely the individual protocols and optional protocol features of the then popular OSI protocol stack (Open Systems Interconnection) to be implemented in plant floors and office environments, respectively. This was at least due to the fact that only very large companies (like the two initiators) participated in the initiative. In particular, no SMEs were involved, despite the fact that they represented the majority of suppliers. As a consequence, their needs and requirements largely were ignored. Yet, SMEs were not able to implement this highly complex technology, and the initiative eventually failed dramatically (Dankbaar & van Tulder, 1992).

¹²   The full report may be found at http://www-i4.informatik.rwth-aachen.de/~jakobs/grant/Final_Report.pdf

¹³   In 2004, Covisint was bought by Compuware, which still offers some e-marketplace functionalities, including the portal functionality.

¹⁴   In general, most of the electronic marketplaces, whether or not they were sector-specific, were not successful in the sense of making money out of the e-marketplace business model; for example, Connextrade (Swiss e-marketplace for commodities) and Answork (French e-marketplace for commodity buying of banks) did not fare very well, either.

¹⁵   With the possible exception of specialist vendor (Jakobs, 2004).

Chapter XIV

Conclusion

Ann Hodgkinson, University of Wollongong, Australia

Robert MacGregor, University of Wollongong, Australia

This book contains applied studies of clusters across a range of industries, operating in a number of countries and written by analysts from a variety of disciplines – economics, marketing, management and information systems. The first aspect that strikes the reader is the commonality of approach across these disciplines, drawing on a standard knowledge base of concepts, analytical frameworks and methodologies. Cluster analysis at both the theoretical and applied levels is truly inter-disciplinary and lacks the ideological barriers often found in other areas of business studies, which prevent analysts from different disciplines working together on common problems. This finding is positive for the future development of this area of study and indicates that our understanding of clusters will continue to develop rapidly in both conceptual and applied terms.

In applied studies, there is a particular interest in the questions of what type of intervention can / should be used to promote clusters and how it can be most effectively implemented. The argument that clusters contribute to industrial and regional development is well established at the conceptual level and has been demonstrated in a number of well known cases, such as Silicon Valley in the U.S.A., Toyota City in Japan, and the industrial districts in north-eastern Italy. Efendioglu provides another example of the biotechnology sector in California in this book. The current question, addressed by several chapters in this book, is whether these success stories can be duplicated elsewhere, and is so, how.

Our authors look at interventions in terms of government programs, government – business partnerships, private sector association programs, and big-business initiatives. Overall, they conclude that clusters appear to arise in response to special economic environments, and have developed spontaneously through natural, organic economic forces. The authors in this volume conclude that is extremely difficult to artificially recreate such conditions to induce the formation of clusters as a tool for regional development. This is demonstrated by the case studies presented by Efendioglu for Taiwan, McRae-Williams for Australia, Perry for New Zealand, and Rosson and McLarney for Canada.

Conceptually, it is argued that clusters provide a useful development tool for smaller econo-mies. However, the case studies presented in this book question their relevance for small, open economies such as Australia, New Zealand and Canada. The concept of clusters devel-oped in large, industrialised countries with specific cultural pre-conditions which facilitated cooperation (Italian industrial districts) and in industries where rapid technological change necessitated cooperation (biotechnology, information technologies). Such countries also had the advantage of a large domestic market in which new products could be developed in conjunction with customers and quick sales achieved before commencing international exports. Smaller economies do not have these preconditions and there are only a limited number of partners available for joint production or specialist supply. They suffer from the problem of 'organisational thinness' as demonstrated by Rosson and McLarney and Perry, which makes it difficult to establish the client-supplier linkages identified as essential to achieving the business relationship model of clusters. They also need to export to gain economies of scale, which immediately exposes them to the full strength of international competition before having the time to develop their product, customer relationships, joint production and trust within a domestic market first. In smaller, open economies competition tends to dominate cooperation, limiting the natural development of clusters.

A number of authors discussed the appropriate nature of intervention to assist cluster forma-tion. Effective intervention is not about reducing business costs via 'cheap' loans or provi-sion of subsidized buildings and land, even though businesses often initially expected this. It is not even essentially about the provision of technological or export support programs. Effective intervention is more about encouraging a supportive environment and building trust among local firms to overcome their natural tendency towards local competition. The role of government or other support agencies is to act as an 'honest broker' where competi-tors can meet, communicate and demonstrate their capacities safely. Then opportunities for joint activities - production, marketing, sharing of labour, etc. – can be recognised and acted upon. Trust takes time to develop and cluster promotion programs do not show quick results. The importance of trust as a component in cluster development programs is clearly demonstrated in the project developed for the Sultanahmet region of Istanbul in Turkey. It was also highlighted in the paper by Merrilees, Miller and Herington. As trust developed, inter-firm cooperation increased, resulting in strong improvements in revenue and employment.

The importance of regional innovation networks was another common theme in these stud-ies, particularly those in high technology sectors. These are represented by three studies of the biotechnology sector included in this book. Cluster relationships were generally considered less relevant to the function of generating new products, but more concerned with the process of encouraging entrepreneurship and commercialisation of that research. The paper by Tiegland, Hallencreutz and Lundquist provides an example of establishing a new institution to encourage closer links between business and researchers in an attempt to encourage more commercialisation of innovations developed in that region within its own boundaries. This demonstrates that the innovation issue can still be a problem even in well established regions such as Uppsala in Sweden. That study illustrates the problem of rigidities that can arise in mature regions as discussed in Falcone (chapter three), and provides one means of rejuvenating such districts.

Rosson and McLarney, on the other hand, address the problems of trying to establish a new cluster in the biotechnology industry in a peripheral region. They also identified a poor commercialisation culture as a barrier in Halifax, Canada and suggested developing an industry – research Centre as a solution. The Uppsala BIO Institute provides an example they could consider. Efendioglu provides a study of the successful biotechnology cluster in San Francisco, California. This study emphasises the role of the University of San Francisco's international business planning competition, which attracts innovators into the region to help sustain that region, as well as a natural entrepreneurial culture, which also generates start-up firms. This has ensured that that cluster, despite being in existence since 1979, has remained in its growth phase. All these studies emphasise the importance of research institutions and of establishing effective business – research relationships to cluster development in high technology sectors.

Some insights into methodological issues can also be obtained from a review of the chapters in this book. The widespread use of case studies is clearly demonstrated. As clusters are now a well established area of research, it might be expected that analytical studies would move into more rigorous statistical investigations based on broad databases. Yet only one chapter, that by MacGregor and Vrazalic based on a sample of over 300 Swedish SMEs, ventures into this methodology in a sustained manner. The other chapters provide an explanation of why case studies are still dominant.

Firstly, it can be explained by definitional issues as discussed by McRae-Williams. Clusters do not normally contain one simple industry sector as defined by statistical authorities. Their very nature involves synergies and interactions between firms from a variety of different sectors through joint production and in supply relationships, as well as complementarities in research between organisations in different sectors, which is the keystone of innovation. Further many clustered sectors, such as tourism, biotechnology, information technologies, are not readily classified into standard industry codes. Thus large secondary databases, which provide the resource for most econometric analyses cannot readily be utilized in cluster analyses.

MacGregor and Vrazalic demonstrate that important issues in cluster research can be analysed using common statistical techniques, in this case whether firms in clusters / alliances behave differently to those that are not. However, it also demonstrates that to undertake this type of analysis, the researchers have to undertake original data collection involving surveys of relevant firms. This is time consuming and expensive. Thus statistical analyses are often restricted to instances when such databases, generated for other purposes, fall into the hands of cluster analysts. In such cases, the data may not be collected on the definitions or coded in the way most appropriate to apply to cluster analysis questions.

Thirdly, of course, many of the questions asked by cluster analysts are inherently qualitative, particularly those around the important issue of 'trust', and are not readily analysed in quantitative terms. Nevertheless, it may be time for cluster analysts to venture beyond specific case studies and attempt to establish some of their elemental propositions on a more rigorous basis. One way in which this is occurring is by using a panel approach, where base line data is collected at the beginning of the cluster process and then repeated after a period of time, often five years. If these data collections are undertaken rigorously, the observed changes can be traced to elements in that cluster.

As argued earlier, there is common acceptance across disciplines of the definition of clusters as being a group of firms that are both located in close geographical proximity to each other, and which have some forms of interaction with each other, either as customer – suppliers, undertaking joint activities (production, marketing, research), exchange information either formally in established institutions or tacitly through informal personal relationships, and / or share a common resource pool, including labour. However, not all studies examined relationships purely within this definition of clusters. Some used the more nebulous term of 'groups', which simply required firms in a sector to be co-located. Groups of firms in one or similar sectors are frequently found located in the same region, but may not have any active inter-relationships. They do, however, form the basis on which it is believed clusters can be developed, using government sponsored intervention programs to facilitate relationships among these firms or by providing encouragement through financial incentives as discussed by Perry for New Zealand. Industrial districts are an earlier term derived from the work of Alfred Marshall in England and Piore and Sabel in Italy. They are a forerunner of clusters but are more limited in that they emphasise mainly business relationships among constituent firms. The cluster concept places more explicit focus on psychological and cultural factors, always inherent in the Italian industrial district concept, and on applications to higher technology rather than traditional manufacturing industries. Thus research, innovation and technology transfer become more important in cluster analysis, evolving into the latter concept of an innovative or creative milieu. The final terms used in these studies are networks and strategic alliances, which are most common in the information systems studies. This is not coincidence. These terms are well established in the business literature on collaboration. However, unlike groups, industrial districts, clusters and innovative milieu, they are not innately spatial. Networks and strategic alliances involve productive relationships between firms but do not require these firms to be co-located. Often these relationships are international in scope. The development of long distance inter-firm collaborations was facilitated by developments in information and communication technologies. Thus the range of terms used in cluster analysis reflects an evolution of the concept over time.

Information technology strategies—e-commerce, e-business, c-commerce as discussed in this book—challenge the specific geographical component essential to the economic and managerial analyses of clusters. Co-location is no longer necessary to establish relationships between firms, although trust is still essential for successful collaborations, virtual or personal. Whereas other disciplines make clear distinctions between clusters and other forms of collaboration such as groups or strategic alliances, arguing that clusters provide the most substantial and enduring economic development potential, IT studies return to the earlier concepts of networks and alliances. They argue that electronic communication systems allow the development of relationships with suppliers, customers and partners that provide the same business and efficiency benefits as geographically-constrained clusters but allow these to occur in an unconstrained a-spatial or international context. It is argued here that IT strategies have not to date been heavily adopted by small businesses. As they become more common, it raises the question of whether they may cause the end to clusters as an economic development tool.

The second factor that is contributing to the decline of clusters is the growing significance of international competition as product and service markets inextricably become global. With markets throughout the world rapidly opening to foreign imports due to reduced tariffs and other forms of trade protection and the movement into market economics by previously centrally controlled countries, few firms no matter how small, are now not exposed to some level of external competition, if only through the internet. Conversely, this process is opening up new export market opportunities to firms throughout the world. International competition is having a profound effect on the industrial districts of Italy as discussed in Falcone (chapter 3). Previously stable, dense supply-chain relationships are breaking down in the face of cheaper imports and as leading firms relocate many of their activities to low wage foreign regions. High technology clusters have been better able to survive under this pressure. Cluster analysts have to confront the impact of this realignment of world production systems with the technology-intensive, design intensive and corporate activities remaining in the industrialized world while production moves into cheaper labour regions. Cluster-like relationships may still continue to exist among firms, but at an international level facilitated by information technology. Further, the imperative of needing to be internationally competitive in terms of cost, quality, design and customer service may be making it extremely difficult to establish new clusters outside the industrialised countries. Firms may no longer have the time to establish local inter-firm and personal relationships, the essence of cluster advantages, before confronting the pressures of international competition. These items form the next agenda for cluster analysts both in theoretical and applied studies.

The question of how clusters establish, grow and survive in competitive environments has particularly been the focus of marketing analysts. They universally look to the concept of 'branding' as a means of differentiating clusters in different regions and those operating in particular sectors. Branding is not just image projection. It requires firms in a cluster to analyse their strengths and identify what particular unique attributes that they can offer members. Further, it requires members to accept a common framework of values, which forms the basis of developing trust among themselves, leading to the density of relationships that generate the advantages which being a member of a cluster generates. Once this branding process is established, the cluster organisation can then undertake the activities needed to position its member firms in the global market and to ensure its continuing growth and regeneration within this new global market environment.

Finally, the pre-eminence of the work of Michael Porter in applied cluster analysis must be acknowledged. Reading these chapters, his name appears repeatedly in the literature reviews, regardless of the discipline of the author. His contribution occurs at the conceptual level, with the Porter 'diamond' and supply-chain analysis taking over from input-output analysis as the essence of the industrial complex approach to analysing regional industrial development. The economic antecedents of this model have now been almost completely overshadowed outside that discipline itself. Secondly, his contribution has been paramount at the applied level. It has been the inspiration for numerous government and other programs aimed at encouraging clusters as the major means of regional development. The prevalence of this ideology is now so great that it is very difficult to argue, as several authors in this book do, that outside the established industrial regions, existence of groupings of firms in a sector in a region will not necessarily mean a cluster can be developed as the basis of regional development. Perhaps this book will help in encouraging a more critical evaluation of the value of clusters as a regional development policy. It highlights both the practical difficulties of this approach and the need to rethink the position of clusters as they are increasingly exposed to international competition.

Glossary

Agglomeration Economies

Savings or benefits firms realize by clustering together (S&dS). Frequently associated with the collective use of the infrastructure of transportation, communications facilities and other services (JGS).

Bartlett's Test for Sphericity

Sums the determinate of the matrix from which the inter-correlation matrix is derived. This is converted to a chi-square and tested for significance.

Biotechnology

The industrial application of living organisms and/or biological techniques developed through basic research. Biotechnology products include pharmaceutical compounds and research materials.

Broad Cluster Definition

Broad cluster definition relates only to traded clusters. Broad cluster definition defines industries not unique to the cluster. These industries may fall into and overlap with other traded clusters. For example, electronic computers, computer storage devices, and computer peripheral equipment fit the broad cluster definition of the communications equipment cluster. But, these industries fit the narrow cluster definition of the information technology cluster only.

Business Incubator

Is an economic development organization designed to accelerate the growth and success of entrepreneurial companies through an array of business support resources and services that could include physical space, capital, coaching, common services, and networking connections. A business incubator's main goal is to produce successful firms that will leave the program financially viable and freestanding.

Business Intelligence

Business intelligence (BI) is a broad category of application programs and technologies for gathering, storing, analyzing, and providing access to data to help enterprise users make better business decisions. BI applications include the activities of decision support, query and reporting, online analytical processing (OLAP), statistical analysis, forecasting, and data mining.

Business Retention Strategies (BRS)

BRS are systematic efforts designed to keep local companies content at their present locations within the city area. Strategies include helping companies cope with changing economic conditions, addressing new markets and even assisting with internal company problems. Business start-up support: Business support includes the full range of services available to people starting in business for the first time. Initiatives include: training, business advisory support, business networking and mentoring and financial assistance (grants, loans, interest rate subsidies are traditional methods; a more innovative approach to financial support is to try and attract as much private sector investment as possible, rather than public sector).

C-Commerce

A business strategy that motivates value-chain partners with a common business interest to generate value through sharing information at all phases of the business cycle (from product development to distribution).

Cluster

A cluster is a geographically proximate group of interconnected companies and associate institutions in a particular field, including product producers, service providers, universities, trade associations.

Competitive Advantage

The benefit for consumers and/or customers which competitors may find difficult or uneconomic to replicate. Perhaps one of the most important aspects of a business plan. How will the product or service gain market share, recognizing that it is not good enough to be only as good as the competition, it will have to be better. However, in commodity-based investments like agriculture, competitiveness may be viewed more from an internal point-of-view than external. Claims of competitive advantage should be fully reviewed and challenged.

Contingency Planning

The development of a management plan that uses alternative strategies to ensure project success if specified risk events occur. Examines one uncertainty at a time as a base case and develops a response to that uncertainty. Can also be the sum of all such plans that deal with many different uncertainties. If defined as the meta-plan, certain events might trigger a particular branch or subset of the contingency plan to be executed.

Convergence Strategies

A hedge fund strategy that involves a portfolio manager believing that a market factor (eg equity volatility) is too high or too low and will revert to more normal levels. The manager buys the underpriced asset and sells the corresponding overpriced asset.

Cumulative % of Variance

If the cumulative % of variance of three factors is 72.987%, for 10 variables, this means that 72.987% of the common variance shared by those 10 variables can be accounted by the three factors.

Demographics

Common characteristics used for population segmentation. Typical demographic data points include age, gender, postal code, and income.

Disintermediation

The process of bypassing functions between the original supplier and the customer. These functions are usually in marketing and distribution, where digital content can be delivered electronically, or where customers can find information themselves.

Disruptive technology

Refers to a technology, which when introduced, either radically transforms markets, creates wholly new markets, or destroys existing markets for other technologies. More on disruptive technology

E-Business

An overarching term for service, sales, and collaborative business conducted over the Internet, either business-to-consumer or business-to business. Some define e-commerce as a monetary transaction segment of e-business, by in most cases, the terms are synonymous.

E-Commerce

An emerging concept that describes the process of buying, selling or exchanging services and information via computer networks.

Efficiency

The ratio of the output to the input of any system. Economic efficiency is a general term for the value assigned to a situation by some measure designed to capture the amount of waste or "friction" or other undesirable and undesirable economic features present.

Eigenvalue

The eigenvalue of a factor explains the amount of variance of that factor, compared with a single variable. For example an eigenvalue of 4.234, indicates that the variance of that factor is 4.234 times as much as a single variable.

Entrepreneur

Innovator. One who recognizes opportunities and organizes resources to take advantage of the opportunity. One who assumes the financial risk of the initiation, operation, and management of a given business or undertaking. Individual who starts a new business. Venture capital is often used to finance the startup costs in return for an equity share. Once the business is established, an entrepreneur may choose to raise additional capital by selling equity shares to the public through an initial public offering.

Entrepreneurship

Entrepreneurship is "the process of looking at things in such a way that possible solutions to problems and perceived needs may evolve in venturing." Ethics standards and dealings based on morals and values. Feasibility. Is an idea feasible? Can the idea be made to work? Many people would like to travel into space but it will be a long time before a tourist industry based on space travel is feasible.

Evolutionary Economics

These are observed to have grown out of the institutionalist school. There is an underlying vision of dynamics which is evolutionary, in the biological sense, in character. The evolutionary concept is a counter-position to that of static equilibria. The question of incorporating evolutionary dynamics into economics was raised at the beginning of institutionalism by Veblen and even earlier by Marshall. Evolutionary economics is a relatively new economic methodology that is modeled on biology. It stresses complex interdependencies, competition, growth, and resource constraints.

Factor Analysis

Given a set of variables, what are the underlying dimensions (factors) that account for the patterns of colinearity among the variables?

Feasibility

The mechanism for balancing business constraints with technology constraints to produce a cost-effective solution. The extent to which a study or project may be done practically and successfully. The extent to which resources allow an evaluation to be conducted.

Foreign Direct Investment

Investment made by a foreign individual or company in productive capacity of another country ñ for example, the purchase or construction of a factory. FDI is defined as a firm based in one country (the 'home country') owning 10 percent or more of the stock of a company located in a foreign country (the 'host country') -- this amount of stock is generally enough to give the home country firm significant control rights over the host country firm. Most FDI is in wholly-owned or nearly wholly-owned subsidiaries. Other non-equity forms of FDI include: subcontracting, management contracts, franchising, and licensing and product sharing.

Governance

The act of affecting government and monitoring (through policy) the long-term strategy and direction of an organization. In general, governance comprises the traditions, institutions and processes that determine how power is exercised, how citizens are given a voice, and how decisions are made on issues of public concern. See the Institute on Governance. Also see the Canadian Centre for Philanthropy.

Hard Infrastructure

Hard infrastructure includes all the tangible physical assets that contribute to the economy of a city. For example, transport infrastructure (roads, railways, ports, and airports), industrial and commercial buildings, water, waste disposal, energy, telecommunications etc.

Horizontal Integration

Merging of two or more firms at the same level of production in some formal, legal relationship. In hospital networks, this may refer to the grouping of several hospitals, the grouping of outpatient clinics with the hospital or a geographic network of various health care services. Integrated systems seek to integrate both vertically with some organizations and horizontally with others.

Human capital

People and their ability to be economically productive. Education, training, and health care can help increase human capital. See also capital and physical capital. May be considered a metaphor for the transition in organizational value creation from physical assets to the capabilities of employees - knowledge, skills, and relationships for example. Closely related to terms such as "intellectual capital" and "intangible assets." Recent estimates suggest that as much as 75 percent of an organization's value is attributable to human capital.

ICT Information and Communication Technology

The catch-all phrase used to describe a range of technologies for gathering, storing, retrieving, processing, analysing and transmitting information. Advances in ICT have progressively reduced the costs of managing information, enabling individuals and organizations to undertake information-related tasks much more efficiently, and to introduce innovations in products, processes and organizational structures.

Industrialized Country

A country with a market economy comprising a significant portion of world production and trade markets.

Information Transfer

Synonymous with data transfer. Information is a broader term than data. Information includes: voice, graphics, and other types of signals.

Innovation Systems

The network of public- and private-sector institutions that initiate or import, modify, and diffuse new technology in a country .In current OECD discussions, the term encompasses ways in which a country organizes its systems of education, scientific research, and technological diffusion, and—in conjunction with macroeconomic and competition policies—their combined impact on the rate of innovation.

Institutional Economics

This approach to economics focuses on the notion that the power of social organizations needs to be emphasized as well as the nature of the market. In economics, the institutional economics school goes beyond the usual economic focus on markets, to look more closely at human-made institutions. Institutional economics was once the dominant school of economics in the United States, including such famous but diverse economists as Thorstein Veblen, Wesley Mitchell, and John R. Commons.

Intellectual Capital

E.g., the commercial value of trademarks, licenses, brand names, formulations, and patents. It is the same as the knowledge asset of an organization. Knowledge assets help achieve business goals. This capital is the set of intangible assets that includes the internal knowledge of employees have of information processes, external and internal experts, products, customers and competitors. Intellectual capital includes internal proprietary reports, libraries, patents, copyrights, and licenses that record the company history and help it plan for tomorrow.

Kaiser-Meyer-Olkin Measure of Sampling Adequacy

If two variables share a common factor with other variables, their partial correlation will be small and the KMO will be closer to 1 than to 0. The closer to 1 the KMO is, the more reliable factor analysis will be.

Key Performance Indicators (KPIs)

Key performance indicators are quantifiable measurements, agreed to beforehand, that reflect the critical success factors of an organization.

Local Cluster

Local clusters are made up of local industries. Local industries provide goods and services almost exclusively for the area in which they are located, which explains why they must spread all across the country. Indeed, local industries show employment in every region, regardless of the natural or competitive advantages of a particular location. As a result, their regional employment should be roughly proportional to regional population, so that the most highly populated states like California, New York, Texas, and Florida will figure as the top local employment states.

Local Industrial Systems

Where the system is geographically based focusing on the interdependence of the innovation process within clusters of firms.

Market

A market is a mechanism which allows people to trade, normally governed by the theory of supply and demand, so allocating resources through a price mechanism and bid and ask matching so that those willing to pay a price for something meet those willing to sell for it.

Market Conditions

Refers to the strength of the market or a market segment, like the interest in computer or airline stocks. Market conditions are good in a bull market. They are bad in a bear market.

Market Positioning

The adoption of a specific market stance, either leader, challenger, follower, flanker or adopter, vis-à-vis competition. In marketing, positioning is the technique by which marketers try to create an image or identity for a product, brand, or organization. It is the 'place' a product occupies in a given market as perceived by the target market. Positioning is something that is done in the minds of the target market. A product's position is how potential buyers see the product.

Market Research

A study of consumer groups and business competition used to define a projected market. The process of gathering, analyzing and interpreting information about a market; about a product or service to be offered for sale in that market; and about the past, present and potential customers for the product or service.

Market Segmentation

Division of the market or population into subgroups with similar motivations. Widely used bases for segmenting include geographic differences, personality differences, demographic differences, use of product differences, and psychographic differences.

Marketing Mix

The blend of product, place, promotion, and pricing strategies designed to produce satisfying exchanges with a target market. A marketing mix is the combination of product offerings used to reach a target market for the organization. The marketing mix comprises the product (what the actual offering comprises), price (the value exchanged for that offering), promotion (the means of communicating that offering to the target audience, promotional mix) and distribution (also known as place, the means of having the product offering available to the target audience). The marketing mix is also known as the four Ps.

Narrow Cluster Definition

Narrow cluster definition relates only to traded clusters. Narrow cluster definition defines industries that are unique only to the cluster. For example, telephone and telegraph apparatus, radio and TV communications equipment are unique to only to the communications equipment cluster. Every U.S. industry is uniquely allocated in a cluster.

National Systems of Innovation

National systems of innovation: in innovation theory, an umbrella term for the interactions and linkages between those carrying out research in an economy—for example, universities—and the other parts of the economic system.

OEM

Original equipment manufacturer. The original manufacturer of a hardware component or sub-component.

More recently, OEM is used to refer to the company that acquires a product or component and reuses or incorporates it into a new product with its own brand name.

Outsourcing

The concept of taking internal company functions and paying an outside firm to handle them. Outsourcing is done to save money, improve quality, or free company resources for other activities. Outsourcing was first done in the data-processing industry and has spread to areas, including telemessaging and call centers. Outsourcing is the wave of the future.

Portal

Usually used as a marketing term to describe a Web site that is or is intended to be the first place people see when using the Web. Typically a "portal site" has a catalog of web sites, a search engine, or both. A portal site may also offer email and other service to entice people to use that site as their main "point of entry" (hence "portal") to the Web.

Private Sector

The private sector of a nation's economy consists of those entities which are not controlled by the state—i.e., a variety of entities such as private firms and companies, corporations, private banks, non-governmental organizations, etc.

Product Life Cycle

A marketing theory in which products or brands follow a sequence of stages including introduction, growth, maturity, and sales decline.

Product Mix

The percentage of a particular product (such as televisions, stereos, etc.) of the stores' total inventory or compared to the total units on rent. The number of individual products produced or sold by an organization. The mix is defined by the industry and manufacturing environment, and management strategies that position the company as a specialty, niche or broad-based supplier of goods and services. Instances where the product mix varies widely from period to period often requires more investment in facilities and inventory, and may result in lower levels of customer service.

Product Positioning

A product's position represents how it is perceived relative to the competition on the determinant attributes desired by each segment. Developing a product and associated marketing mix that: (a) is 'placed' as close as possible in the minds of target customers to their ideal in terms of important features and attributes; and (b) clearly differentiates it from the competition.

Public Sector

Comprises the sub-sectors of general government (mainly central, state and local government units together with social security funds imposed and controlled by those units) as well as public corporations, i.e., corporations that are subject to control by government units (usually defined by the government owning the majority of shares).

Quality Control

The operational techniques and the activities used to fulfil and verify requirements of quality.

Regional Innovation Systems

Is developed. These systems now consist of the knowledge bases of all industries located in a particular region, the institutions available to support their technological innovations and the institutional context of laws, regulations, political cultures and acknowledged 'rules of the game' operating in that region.

Scree Plot

A plot of eigenvalues.

Seamless

Complex technology that is transparent to the user. (Many Internet-based interactive technologies are not considered seamless as they require a high degree of user-intervention and knowledge: installing software, connecting the modem, downloading plug-ins, etc.).

Sectoral Innovation Systems

Based on the idea that different industries operate under different technological regimes based on a specific industry knowledge base.

Seed Financing

Money for applied R&D given before normal VCs recognize a project as viable. Funds to take an idea from conception to the pre-competitive stage of building a prototype.

Soft Infrastructure

Soft infrastructure relates to the less tangible aspects of LED such as education and training provision, quality of life infrastructure such as park, leisure and library services, housing, business support, business networking and financing services, etc.

Spin Off

A divestiture by a corporation of a division or subsidiary by issuing to stockholders shares in a new company set up to continue the operations of the division or subsidiary. The new company formed by such a divestiture.

Stakeholder

An individual or group with an interest in the success of an organization in delivering intended results and maintaining the viability of the organization's products and services. Stakeholders influence programs, products, and services. Specific people or groups who have a stake in the outcome of the project. Normally stakeholders are from within the company, and could include internal clients, management, employees, administrators, etc. A project may also have external stakeholders, including suppliers, investors, community groups and government organizations.

Strategic Alliance

A strategic alliance is a partnership between two or more companies to pursue a set of agreed upon goals while remaining independent organizations. Strategic alliances come in all shapes and sizes, and include a wide range of cooperation, from contractual to equity forms.

Strategic Planning

Long-term plans based on the organizations overall business objectives. Strategic plans are typically multiple years and reach out 5 or 10 years (or more) using scenarios or other planning methods that identifies assumptions, risks, and environmental factors.

Supply Chains

The products and processes that are essential to the production of a good or service. For example, to produce frozen fish, the supply chain inputs will extend from fish catching, handling, processing, and freezing to packaging, storing and distribution. These are all elements of a supply chain. Integrated LED strategies will try and capture as much as possible of the higher value end of the value chain in their area. In this case fish processing, packaging, storing and distribution will be adding value and therefore be seen at the higher end of the value chain. An industry cluster is a grouping of related industries and institutions in an area or region. The industries are inter-linked and connected in many different ways. Some industries in the cluster will be suppliers to others; some will be buyers from others; some will share labor or resources. The important thing about a cluster is that the industries within the cluster are economically linked, they both collaborate and compete and are, to some degree, dependant upon each other; and ideally, they take advantage of synergies.

Tacit Knowledge

The knowledge that is in people's heads, their experience. Is knowledge that people carry in their minds and is, therefore, difficult to access. Often, people are not aware of the knowledge they possess or how it can be valuable to others. Tacit knowledge is considered more valuable because it provides context for people, places, ideas, and experiences. Effective transfer of tacit knowledge generally requires extensive personal contact and trust. Based on Polyani's work (as cited in Nonaka, 1994; Davenport and Prusak, 2000), tacit knowledge is personal, rooted in action, with commitment and involvement in a specific context. It consists of paradigms, viewpoints, beliefs, and concrete know-how, such as crafts and skills.

Technological Change

How much technological change will be additionally induced by climate policies is a crucial, but not well quantified, factor in assessing the costs of long-term mitigation of greenhouse gas emissions. A change in a production function that alters the relationship between inputs and outputs. Normally it is understood to be an improvement in technology, or technological progress, and it is of interest in international economics for its implications for trade and economic welfare.

Trade Liberalization

The reduction of tariffs and trade barriers to permit more foreign competition and foreign investment in the economy.

Traded Cluster

Traded clusters are made up of traded industries. Traded industries sell products and services across economic areas, so they are concentrated in the specific regions where they choose to locate production, due to the competitive advantages afforded by these locations. Employment levels in traded industries thus vary greatly by region, and have no clear link to regional population levels.

Transnational Corporations

Are corporations that operate in more than one country. Usually, headquarters are in one or more nations and production or services are in other nations. TNCs have come to dominate the global economy and some large TNCs are richer and more powerful than many national government. Also referred to as "multinational corporations."

Value Chain

The sequential set of primary and support activities that an enterprise performs to turn inputs into value-added outputs for its external customers. An IT value chain is that subset of enterprise activities that pertain to IT operations, both to add value directly for external customers and to add indirect value by supporting other enterprise operations.

Venture Capital

Money used to support new or unusual undertakings; equity, risk or speculative investment capital. This funding is provided to new or existing firms which exhibit potential for above-average growth.

Vertical Integration

Economic term that is often used to describe a trend in the agriculture industry. When an agriculture corporation is vertically integrated, it is involved in more than one phase of meat production. Many of these big businesses have their own feedlots, slaughterhouses, meatpacking plants, and distributors, so they have complete control over the lives and deaths of the animals they raise.

About the Authors

Robert MacGregor is an associate professor in the School of Information Technology and Computer Science at the University of Wollongong, Australia. His research interest is in e-commerce adoption and use in small and medium enterprises, and over the years, he has published extensively in this area. MacGregor is a former head of information systems at the University of Wollongong and was the founder and editor of the *Australasian Journal of Information Systems*. In 2004, he received the New South Wales Prime Ministers Award for Excellence in Business Community Partnerships.

Ann Hodgkinson is an associate professor and head of the School of Economics and Information Systems at the University of Wollongong, NSW, Australia. She has a longstanding research interest in regional development, particularly on aspects related to organizational change within a regional context. Her work is predominantly empirical and includes studies of innovation in regional firms. She has undertaken several surveys that focused on how regional firms respond to changes in the macroeconomic environment, including responses to changes in industrial relations, and global competitive market conditions. She also advises local government on issues related to local economic conditions.

* * *

Melih Bulu received his PhD with the dissertation *Profiling Micro Clusters: Identification of Value-adding Production and Service Chains by Using Graph Theoretical Approach* from Bogazici University, Istanbul. He worked various parts of the private sector both as a professional and an entrepreneur. Currently, he is general coordinator of URAK (International Competitiveness Research Institute), an NGO established for strengthening Turkish economic competitiveness. In addition, he teaches strategy-related courses at the university. His main interest areas are cluster theory, local development, and social network theory. He has various publications and conference proceedings in national and international environments.

Janice Burn is foundation professor in the School of MIS at Edith Cowan University, Australia. She has extensive experience in the UK, Hong Kong, and Canada. Burn is a prolific academic writer with more than 200 refereed publications in journals and international conferences and is on the editorial board of numerous information systems journals. She was a member of the Australian Research Council from 2000 to 2003 and an advisor to the Australian Government on IT and National Research Priorities in 2002. Her research interests relate to information systems strategy and benefits evaluation in virtual organizations with a particular emphasis on social, political, and cultural challenges in an e-business and e-government environment. She holds five ARC grants and is the chief investigator in an ARC research project that is looking at collaborative commerce for SMEs in the West Australian context and that reflects an interest in virtual organizations, collaboration, and clustering.

Alev M. Efendioglu is a professor of management at the School of Business and Management, University of San Francisco. He has extensive consulting experience and is the author of two books, chapters in five other books (*Design and Management of Effective Distance Learning Programs*; *Encyclopedia of E-Commerce*; *E-Government and Mobile Commerce*; *Encyclopedia of Online Learning*; *Digital Economy: Impacts, Influences and Challenges*; and *Chinese Economic Transition and Its Impact on Marketing Strategy*), and articles in numerous professional publications, including *Business Horizons*, *Journal of American Academy of Business*, *Journal of Asia-Pacific Business*, *Journal of Small Business Strategy*, *Interacting with Computers*, and *China International Review*. You can find more detailed information at http://www.usfca.edu/alev/alev.htm.

Hakki Eraslan was born in Elazig and is living in Istanbul. He has an MSc (1995) from Coventry University. He was supported as a researcher by Higher Educational Council (YOK) and became a member of the International Competitiveness Research Institution (URAK), Turkey. He is now coordinator of academic research of URAK. He published various papers regarding competitiveness and did research projects addressing cluster and regional sectoral developments including textile, leather, tourism, automobile, and marble sectors.

Paola Falcone (PhD, Marketing, University of Rome, La Sapienza) is a professor of marketing and communication in the post-graduate Master.Cor of the University of Rome "La Sapienza", Italy, and managerial trainer in marketing and communication for firms and public institutions. Her research interests include marketing strategy, service marketing, external communication, and branding for both firms and not for profit organizations. A part of her research activity has been dedicated to small organization networks and districts. She is director of the Research and Training Division of the CRC.

Martina Gerst holds a degree as Diplom-Kauffrau from the University of Saarbruecken, Germany, and the Grand École Institut Commerciale de Nancy, France. After starting her career with the central purchasing department of Siemens, Germany, she joined the KPMG procurement practice in Paris, where she worked in the area of procurement and supply, followed by engagements such as content director for Commerce One and consultant for the Global Procurement & Supply department of DaimlerChrysler. Currently, Gerst is a research fellow at The University of Edinburgh's Research Centre for Social Science, UK. In parallel, she is writing her doctoral thesis studying the development of supplier portals in the automotive industry. Current research interests include the development and adoption of RFID technologies and, more generally, Internet-based technologies and their outcomes on interorganizational relationships and business processes.

Daniel Hallencreutz is founder and CEO of Intersecta AB, an Uppsala-based research consulting firm (www.intersecta.se), Sweden. He is also an associated researcher at the Centre for Research on Innovation and Industrial Dynamics (CIND) at Uppsala University in Uppsala, Sweden (www.cind.uu.se). Dr. Hallencreutz has a PhD in economic geography from the Department of Social and Economic Geography at Uppsala University. His research interests lie in regional development and industrial competitiveness and growth.

Carmel Herington, PhD, is a lecturer at Griffith University, Gold Coast, Australia. Her research interests include relationship marketing in service organizations with a particular focus on the impact and interaction among relationship networks and their impact on organizational success. She previously has been published in the *Journal of Qualitative Market Research.*

Kai Jakobs has been with Aachen University's (RWTH) Computer Science Department, Germany, since 1985. His current research interests include various aspects of IT standards and standardization processes. In addition, he has been working on a number of projects on various aspects of information networks. Jakobs is (co-)author/editor of a textbook on data communication and, more recently, seven books on standards and standardization processes in IT. He is also editor-in-chief of the *International Journal on IT Standards & Standardization Research* and has been on the program committees of numerous conferences. He has served as an external expert for various European R&D programs on both technical and socioeconomic issues and holds a PhD in computer science from the University of Edinburgh.

Per Lundequist has a Ph.D. in Economic Geography from the Department of Social and Economic Geography at Uppsala University in Uppsala, Sweden. His research focuses particularly on industrial restructuring, cluster dynamics, and public program and performance measurement. Dr. Lundequist is a Partner and Senior Consultant at Intersecta AB (www.

intersecta.se) and an Associated Researcher at the Centre for Research on Innovation and Industrial Dynamics (CIND) at Uppsala University (www.cind.uu.se).

Carolan McLarney is an associate professor in the School of Business Administration at Dalhousie University, Canada. She teaches the undergraduate and graduate international business and strategic management courses as well as in the MBA (financial services) program. McLarney's research interests include the interface between small businesses and international business strategy, and the use of strategic alliances.

Pamela McRae-Williams is a lecturer in business and research associated with the Centre for Regional Innovation and Competitiveness, University of Ballarat, Australia. Her recently competed doctoral research focused on regional wine and tourism clusters and their complementarity; this research has set the agenda for further research into regional sustainability and resource allocation. Her background stems from environmental management and results in her multidisciplinary approach to research.

Bill Merrilees is Professor of Marketing at Griffith University, Gold Coast, Australia. He has a PhD from the University of Toronto, Canada. His research is especially in strategy, retailing, and e-retailing. Professor Merrilees has jointly published three books: *Retailing Management, Strategic Marketing Management*, and *E-Retailing*. He has published numerous journal articles in international journals including *Journal of Advertising Research*; *European Journal of Marketing*; *Long Range Planning*; *Journal of Business Research*; *Journal of Business Strategies*; *Journal of Relationship Marketing*; *International Marketing Review*; *Journal of Product & Brand Management*; *International Journal of Retail & Distribution Management*; *Corporate Reputation Review*; *International Review of Retail, Distribution & Consumer Research*; *Marketing Intelligence & Planning*; and *The International Review of Retail, Distribution & Consumer Research*.

Dale Miller, PhD, lectures in the Department of Marketing at the Griffith Business School, Griffith University (Gold Coast), Queensland, Australia. Her research focus areas are marketing and retail branding, strategy and innovation, marketing channels, community and business networks, and supply chain management. Her research work has been published in international journals including *Journal of Business Research*; *Long Range Planning*; *International Journal of Retail & Distribution Management*; *Journal of Retailing and Consumer Services*; *Service Industries*; *Journal and Jahrbuch Fur Wirtschaftsgeschichte (German Economic History Yearbook)*; and *Tourism Analysis*. She has also co-authored several books and book chapters.

Aslihan Nasir is currently an assistant professor at the Department of Management Information Systems, Bogazici University, Turkey. She holds a bachelor's degree in economics and a master's degree and PhD in business administration. She is the author of several articles published in prestigious international journals such as *Journal of Consumer Satisfaction, Dissatisfaction and Complaining Behavior*; and the *Journal of American Academy of Business*. She also has had articles published in reputable international conference proceedings such as IMDA (International Management Development Association), GBATA (Global Business and Technology Association), and EuroChrie.

Martin Perry teaches in the Department of Management and Enterprise Development at the Wellington campus of Massey University, New Zealand. Prior to returning to New Zealand in 2001, he was an associate professor in the Department of Geography, National University of Singapore. His most recent book is *Business Clusters: An International Perspective* (Routledge, 2005).

Philip Rosson is acting dean of the Faculty of Management and Killam chair of technology, innovation and marketing at Dalhousie University, Canada. His research interests include the impact of the Internet on marketing, corporate visual identity management, international marketing, and industrial cluster development. Rosson is a past co-editor of the *Canadian Journal of Administrative Sciences* and an editorial board member for the *Journal of Business Research*.

Michelle Rowe is a PhD candidate in the School of MIS at Edith Cowan University, Australia. She is part of the ARC research project team and is looking at collaboration of SMEs using IT (collaborative commerce). The relationship between clustering and collaborative commerce for SMEs is significant in this research. Prior to this candidacy, Michelle was a lecturer in management both in Sydney and Queensland. Rowe is interested in assisting SMEs in the adoption and implementation of e-commerce and c-commerce.

Robin Teigland is an assistant professor at the Center for Strategy and Competitiveness at the Stockholm School of Economics (SSE) in Stockholm, Sweden, and an associated researcher at the Centre for Research on Innovation and Industrial Dynamics (CIND) at Uppsala University in Uppsala, Sweden (www.cind.uu.se). Her research interests revolve around the creation and diffusion of knowledge through formal and informal business networks such as cluster initiatives, communities of practice, networks of practice, and electronic communities. Prior to her doctoral studies at SSE, she worked as a consultant for McKinsey & Company. Additionally, she holds a BA in economics with distinction from Stanford University, an MBA from The Wharton School, and an MA in international studies from the University of Pennsylvania. More information on Teigland can be found on her department Web page at www.hhs.se/csc/teigland.htm or on her personal homepage at www.knowledgenetworking.org.

Lejla Vrazalic is a senior lecturer in information systems at the University of Wollongong, Australia. She was awarded the University Medal in 1999. Her research interests are in human computer interaction and e-commerce adoption in small business. In 2004, she received the Vice Chancellor's Award for Outstanding Contribution to Teaching and Learning at the University of Wollongong and the New South Wales Prime Minister's Award for Excellence in Business Community Partnerships.

Index